THE THEATRE OF BRIAN FRIEL

Christopher Murray is professor emeritus in the School of English, Drama and Film at University College Dublin where he lectured as associate professor until 2006, having co-founded the postgraduate Drama Centre in 1990. He was editor of *Irish University Review* for ten years, and at present is chairman of the management board. He was a founder-member of the Irish Theatre Archive and is former chair of the International Association for the Study of Irish Literatures. He joined the board of directors at the Gaiety School of Acting, Dublin, in 1996 and was elected chairman in 2011 in succession to Joe Dowling.

His other publications include *Twentieth-Century Irish Drama: Mirror up to Nation* (1997), *Sean O'Casey: Writer at Work* (2004), and (ed.) William Philips, *St Stephen's Green, or The Generous Lovers* [1700] (1980), *Selected Plays of Lennox Robinson* (1981), *Selected Plays of George Shiels* (2008), and (edited) *Brian Friel: Essays, Diaries Interviews: 1964–1999* (1999), *Samuel Beckett: 100 Years* (2006) and *'Alive in Time': The Enduring Drama of Tom Murphy* (2010).

In the same series from Bloomsbury Methuen Drama:

THE PLAYS OF SAMUEL BECKETT
by Katherine Weiss

THE THEATRE OF DAVID GREIG
by Clare Wallace

THE THEATRE OF MARTIN CRIMP: SECOND EDITION
by Aleks Sierz

THE THEATRE AND FILMS OF MARTIN MCDONAGH
by Patrick Lonergan

THE THEATRE OF SEAN O'CASEY
by James Moran

THE THEATRE OF TENNESSEE WILLIAMS
by Brenda Murphy

THE THEATRE OF TIMBERLAKE WERTENBAKER
by Sophie Bush

THE THEATRE OF HAROLD PINTER
by Mark Taylor-Batty

Forthcoming titles in the same series:

BRITISH THEATRE AND PERFORMANCE 1900–1950
by Rebecca D'Monte

MODERN ASIAN THEATRE AND PERFORMANCE 1900–2000
by Kevin J. Wetmore, Siyuan Liu and Erin B. Mee

THE THEATRE OF BRIAN FRIEL

TRADITION AND MODERNITY

Christopher Murray

Series Editors: Patrick Lonergan and Erin Hurley

B L O O M S B U R Y
LONDON • NEW DELHI • NEW YORK • SYDNEY

Bloomsbury Methuen Drama
An imprint of Bloomsbury Publishing Plc

50 Bedford Square
London
WC1B 3DP
UK

1385 Broadway
New York
NY 10018
USA

www.bloomsbury.com

Bloomsbury is a registered trademark of Bloomsbury Publishing Plc

First published 2014

British Library Cataloguing-in-Publication Data
A catalogue record for this book is available from the British Library.

ISBN: HB: 978-1-4081-5734-3
PB: 978-1-4081-5449-6
ePub: 978-1-4081-5450-2
ePDF: 978-1-4081-5451-9

Library of Congress Cataloging-in-Publication Data
Murray, Christopher.
The theatre of Brian Friel: tradition and modernity/Christopher Murray.
pages cm. – (Critical companions)
Includes bibliographical references and index.
ISBN 978-1-4081-5734-3 (HB) – ISBN 978-1-4081-5449-6 (pbk.) – ISBN 978-1-4081-5450-2 (e-book) 1. Friel, Brian–Criticism and interpretation. 2. Friel, Brian–Themes, motives. 3. Dialectic in literature. 4. Ireland–In literature. I. Title. II. Title: Theater of Brian Friel.
PR6056.R5Z836 2014
822'.914–dc23
2013036201

Typeset by Deanta Global Publishing Services, Chennai, India
Printed and bound in India

For Kathleen

'The very pulse of the machine'

CONTENTS

ACKNOWLEDGEMENTS

In the first place, I wish to thank Brian Friel for his kind permission to quote from his papers lodged in the National Library of Ireland and from all of his published works.

Acknowledgement is hereby made to Friel's publishers, Faber and Faber, London, for permission to reprint from Brian Friel, *Essays, Diaries, Interviews 1964–1999* and *Plays: One* and *Plays: Two*, *The Home Place* and *Performances*, and to the Catholic University of America Press for the quotations from *Plays 1*. Credit for permissions also go to Leah Schmidt and The Agency (London) Ltd., and to Faber and Faber, Inc., an affiliate of Farrar, Straus and Giroux, LLC, for licensing World Wide rights (excluding Ireland) to *The Loves of Cass McGuire, Crystal and Fox, Lovers, Volunteers, Communication Cord, Give Me Your Answer, Do!, The Home Place, Performances, A Month in the Country, Three Sisters, Hedda Gabler* and *The Yalta Game.* To Peter Fallon and Gallery Press, Loughcrew, Co. Meath, holder of the Irish rights to these plays and to *Selected Stories*, I also acknowledge kind permission to quote. I credit Gallery Press also with permission to quote from Thomas Kilroy, *The O'Neill* and *Pirandellos (Two Plays).* I credit Faber and Faber, London, and Farrar, Straus & Giroux for kind permission to quote from Seamus Heaney's *Preoccupations* and *Stepping Stones*, edited by Dennis O'Driscoll, as well as from Tom Stoppard, *The Real Thing*, David Hare, *Asking Around* and John Osborne, *Look Back in Anger*. Acknowledgement goes to the Penguin Group (USA) for permission to quote from *Molly Sweeney* and *Give Me Your Answer, Do!* I credit here also Michigan University Press, Ann Arbor, for the quotations from *Brian Friel in Conversation,* ed. Paul Delaney. Permission is gratefully acknowledged to Howard Jacobson and Bloomsbury for quotations from *Whatever It Is, I Don't Like It.* For other epigraphs to chapters, acknowledgement is hereby given to Faber and Faber, Fourth Estate, Picador, Penguin, Routledge, Gallery Press,

Grove Atlantic and the Shaw Estate. Every effort has been made to contact owners of copyrighted material and credit is hereby extended to any I may, for whatever reason, have failed to reach.

Acknowledgement is also due to the editor of *Irish University Review* for permission to reprint the article by Shaun Richards, 'Placed Identities for Placeless Times: Brian Friel and Post-Colonial Criticism', to Ríonach uí Ógáin and Coiscéim for the article by Csilla Bertha, 'Art as a *lieu de mémoire* in Brian Friel's *The Home Place*', revised for the present book, and to *Modern Drama* and the University of Toronto Press for the article by the late David Krause, 'The Failed Words of Brian Friel'. The cover photograph, of *Translations*, directed by Adrian Dunbar at the Millennium Dome, Derry, 2013, is by kind permission of Bobbie Hanvey.

In conversation and/or correspondence, I am indebted in particular to Tom Kilroy, Ulf Dantanus, Patrick Mason, Seamus Deane, Tony Roche, Joe Dowling, Éamonn Jordan, Joe Mulholland, Richard Pine, Ann Saddlemyer, Donald Morse, Csilla Bertha, Mária Kurdi, Patrick Burke, Diarmaid Ferriter, Michael Colgan, Lyndsey Turner and Christa Mrowka-Velten. As always, I am indebted to the National Library of Ireland and the James Joyce Library, UCD.

I wish also to thank my editors, Mark Dudgeon at Bloomsbury Methuen Drama and Patrick Lonergan, series editor, for their support and encouragement. To my typist Brian Prunty, my sincere thanks. Any errors have to be mine.

To my family, particularly Paul, Felicity and Chris, my thanks for much-appreciated interest. Thanks go to author Kevin Brophy for stimulating literary discussions. I acknowledge, above all, the unswerving support of my wife and best friend Kathleen, to whom this book is dedicated.

COMPLETE LIST OF PLAYS BY BRIAN FRIEL

Unpublished Stage Plays

A/The Doubtful Paradise (originally titled *The Francophile*)
The Blind Mice

Radio Plays

A Sort of Freedom
To This Hard House

Published Stage Plays (in order of staging)

The Enemy Within
Philadelphia, Here I Come!
The Loves of Cass McGuire
Lovers
Crystal and Fox
The Mundy Scheme
The Gentle Island
The Freedom of the City
Volunteers
Living Quarters
Aristocrats
Faith Healer
Translations
American Welcome [one-act]
Three Sisters (after Chekhov)
The Communication Cord
Fathers and Sons (after Turgenev's novel)
Making History
Dancing at Lughnasa
A Month in the Country (after Turgenev)
The London Vertigo (after Charles Macklin)
Wonderful Tennessee
Molly Sweeney
Give Me Your Answer, Do!
Uncle Vanya (after Chekhov)
The Yalta Game (from Chekhov's 'Lady with Lapdog')
The Bear (after Chekhov)
Afterplay
Performances
The Home Place
Hedda Gabler (after Ibsen)

CHAPTER 1
SITUATING FRIEL

Our secret desires fester inside us, to be what we are not! So! We perform! Performance! [. . .] Do you know what that's like? To be able to change? To have an endless appetite to perform?

– Thomas Kilroy, *Henry* (*after* HENRY IV),
in *Pirandellos: Two Plays* (Gallery Press, 2007)[1]

Putting down the Markers

It is commonplace to remark that with the premiere of *Philadelphia, Here I Come!* at the Dublin Theatre Festival in 1964, Brian Friel (born in 1929) made his grand entrance into world theatre. Huge international success was to follow. Friel is the author of twenty-four published plays (plus three apprentice pieces, unpublished), together with eight published adaptations or versions (beginning with *Three Sisters* in 1981). If success alone supplied the narrative, the history of Friel's career *would* be commonplace: failure tests the lasting reputation of the best writers. But over what is usually termed a lifetime in the theatre the successes, measured as much by critical appraisal in books on Friel (15 monographs, plus 2 forthcoming), collections of articles on Friel (at least 6), books with chapters on Friel (at least 12) and monograph articles (in the hundreds), as by frequencies of production and performance on the international professional stage, have stood out so consistently that Friel's name is assured in all the histories of twentieth-century drama. So much is already well known about this achievement that it must be questioned if much more remains to be said.

Nevertheless, a great writer who has proved his mettle over the years and whose work holds the stage commandingly is usually so many-sided as to justify a fresh commentary, a new angle of vision.

Further, it is my belief that, in recent years, the focus in Friel Studies has been predominantly political and that this emphasis now threatens to overwhelm the commentary. To the contrary, it has always seemed to me that Friel is a Proteus figure, who, like the sea god, is constantly changing his shape in an effort to escape categorisation, being identified with any one theatre, any one style or set of beliefs. No sooner has Friel been lauded on Broadway as the comforting bearer of the Irish tradition than he takes off in another direction to assert his independence. A deceptively cosy *Philadelphia* is followed by a powerfully experimental *Loves of Cass McGuire*, a heart-warming *Dancing at Lughnasa* by a surprising spiritual lesson such as *Wonderful Tennessee*. No sooner has a critic decided on the road map than Friel is off over the hills working on some counter-statement. A play like *The Freedom of the City* is followed by a *Gentle Island*, a *Translations* by a *Communication Cord* which you pull at your peril. My inclination is to see Friel as chameleon-like. He confounds definition. The short-story writer (*The Saucer of Larks*, 1962, *The Gold in the Sea*, 1966) is father to the playwright: each narrative stands alone, finds its own shape and maintains its own secret. Although there are stories he mined again for plays, such as 'The Foundry House' for *Aristocrats* (1979) and 'The Highwayman and the Saint' for the second part of *Lovers* (1967), Friel has always insisted that the playwright's technique is 'the very opposite of the short-story writer's' because of the audience and its 'collective mind'.[2] Just as he moved on from short stories to stage plays, so Friel moves on from one play to another.[3]

Interpretation of the work is possible only in partial, contextual terms. 'If the mask fits, wear it, I say,' Friel makes a character say in his version of *A Month in the Country* (1992), and the witticism speaks to his own stance: like T. S. Eliot before him, he is the invisible poet.[4] Likewise, Friel believes that nowadays the playwright 'cannot appear to exhibit the same outrageous daring that the painter shows': he is necessarily more 'devious' in his revolutionary purpose.[5] If the playwright is 'of his time', however, truly clued in and in some sort of symbolic relationship to the art and culture of his time, as Oscar Wilde saw himself,[6] then the difference with the painter vanishes because then the playwright's 'flux' will be, in Friel's words, 'as integral but better camouflaged, his groping as earnest, his searching as sincere'.[7] These terms provide the justification for interpretation at a deeper level than Friel's nonchalance seems to authorise. But there can be no last word, no definitive answer to the complexity of Friel's oeuvre. Instead, Friel's eclecticism continues to offer opportunities for new provisional attempts to approach the texts as texts and the productions as attempts constantly to renew meanings.

At this stage of Friel Studies, the approach I adopt is to view the plays with a few convictions firmly in mind. The first is that Friel is a committed artist of the theatre; he wishes a play to be successful but he is not disturbed if it fails on stage when he is convinced it answers to his artistic intentions. Friel resembles Beckett in that respect. Failure is but another kind of success. He has from the outset measured himself against the best. It follows that he is best interpreted in that context. Accordingly, my reading of a Friel play is both text-based and holistic in the sense of interpretation of content and form as unified achievement. So far so old-fashioned. But allied to this analysis, I offer a comparative, contextualising method on the basis that 'No poet, no artist of any art, has his complete meaning alone.'[8] I frequently frame a Friel play with one by another author. Even Shakespeare does not escape, for what Anglophone dramatist does not carry echoes from the great tradition? I have always thought that the shadow of *Hamlet* falls across *Philadelphia, Here I Come!* and that *Faith Healer* owes a lot to *Macbeth*. But sometimes the textual friendship is closer to home: *Philadelphia* is aware of a now nearly forgotten Irish play to be discussed in the next chapter, while *Molly Sweeney* and several other Friel plays are indebted to Synge and the Abbey tradition. I would insist that this critical method is only a strategy to facilitate interpretation of a writerly writer. He is extremely well read. Friel's awareness of Eliot, for example, is noteworthy and extends from Eliot's major essays, such as 'Tradition and the Individual Talent', through the poems, especially *Four Quartets*, and the plays, *Murder in the Cathedral* and *The Cocktail Party* in particular. The intertextuality Eliot himself made part of the modernist discourse runs deep in Friel's writing.

The core of Friel's artistic strategy lies in a lifelong commitment to style. He is a very good writer because he takes care to be one;

one does not become a favoured author at the *New Yorker* unless one is committed to the discipline of style. It has not been noticed that at St Patrick's College, Maynooth, which Friel attended from 1946 to 1949, there was in the English Department a lecturer (professor from 1948) who took the matter of style or 'Elocution' seriously. Friel would have received a good grounding from Neil Kevin (1903–53), an avid admirer of Walter Pater, whose *Appreciations, with an Essay on Style* (1889) he put on the syllabus as soon as he took the chair.[9] Kevin had written his M.A. thesis on Matthew Arnold. As late as 2012, Friel could still recall his book *No Applause in Church* (1947), recommended reading, one assumes, for the small class taking English for B.A.[10] Other alumni have had much to say concerning Kevin's interest in literary style. A contemporary of Friel remarked: 'I believe Pater's *Appreciations* was his [Kevin's] favourite book. He seemed to spend half the lectures of one year mulling over it'; adding, 'If I learned anything at all about style I learned it then.'[11] Kevin's successor to the chair of English at Maynooth in 1954, Peter Connolly, a year ahead of Friel as student, put it another way: 'for theory, he [Kevin] had a weakness for Pater and Victorian aesthetes.'[12] Early in his career, Kevin published a series of articles on 'English in Ireland'. In one of these he stressed the need to develop 'a style of writing, remarkable for its exactitude and delicacy': two qualities Friel certainly exhibits in his prose. Kevin also emphasised nonchalance, another Frielian attribute, 'the power of concealing effort' or 'the art of gaining our effort by understatement'.[13] The better writers (and speakers) put 'reticence' before 'impressiveness'. The worst fault a spiritual writer's style could manifest is 'a straining after the infinite' in expression. Here the giveaway word, 'the word which includes defeat', would be 'ineffable'.[14] Readers of Friel will recall Frank's use of the word in *Wonderful Tennessee* (1993) in an attempt to describe 'what is beyond language. The inexpressible.'[15] In that play, it takes a dancing dolphin to teach a would-be author (Frank) his lesson on style as jointly a moral and linguistic discipline.

The commitment to style was lifelong for Friel. At the start of his career he wrote a weekly column for the *Irish Press*. George O'Brien sees the sixty pieces as sitting 'uneasily' beside Friel's early 'artistic attainments' and 'an unusual departure from them'.[16] Not so. They are part of Friel's artistic DNA. O'Brien calls them 'trial pieces'; the columns show Friel inventing himself *through* style. Now that he was a full-time writer, having resigned his position as a schoolteacher in Derry in 1960, he needed extra money; knowing himself to be an artist, he at the same time could only write a weekly humorous column if it offered a challenge. What if – and this is mere speculation – one Saturday morning, having scanned the humorous column by John D. Sheridan (1903–80) in the *Irish Independent* on his way to the book reviews, Friel asked himself 'why not' try a similar piece in the more politically favourable *Irish Press*?[17] Why not test the Wildean proposition[18] in mock earnest that 'In matters of grave importance, style, not sincerity, is the vital thing'? Perhaps it all depended on what is meant by 'vital'.

John D. Sheridan's vitality lay in his productivity. No fewer than ten books were published from his weekly columns. They had lively titles such as *I Can't Help Laughing* (1944), *Funnily Enough* (1956) and *Joking Apart* (1964). One of them was titled *Half in Earnest* (1948) but mostly Sheridan stuck to self-effacing, simple absurdity. Friel's first column, 'Meet Brian Friel', in April 1962, had the general heading 'The Lighter Side of Life', as if in blatant competition to Sheridan. It was almost insolently autobiographical – he even gave details of his bank account – as if Friel were intent on subverting expectations by overdoing the facts. The 'Lighter Side' was dropped as heading, but the column was never in fact serious. It described the trivial mishaps and embarrassments of a Chaplinesque but middle-class anti-hero. The humour is deadpan. Only one piece (23 March 1963) gestures towards Wilde: 'The Importance of Being *Frank*', a piece referring to *The Francophile*, his preferred title for the 1960 play *A Doubtful Paradise*.

Negotiating Wilde's dichotomy between style and sincerity, Friel's mentor Neil Kevin remarked: 'A lively, though not insidious, form of insincerity is a flair for exaggeration.'[19] This nicely describes the style of the *Irish Press* columns. They are, as O'Brien says, both 'performative' and 'the projection of a persona'.[20] They are playfully insincere, a feature of Irish storytelling, nowadays more a feature of the stand-up comedian. Sincere people, wrote Kevin, 'have a bark that is the equal of their bite, but they are distinguished by neither. Their way has no drama in it, so that they remain unadvertised.' Yet these are the 'really valuable ones among our acquaintances' because, 'motivated by an absolute sincerity, their style, like all good style, is inconspicuous and restrained: it does nothing for effect, it shrinks from show, it bides its time for ever.'[21] This is Brian Friel encapsulated. The short stories are sincere. The plays may be said to fuse the press columns and the stories, combining 'insincerity' in the performative sense and style in the sense of pursuit of the right words to meet the dramatic occasion. In a programme note for a revival of *Molly Sweeney* at the Dublin Gate in 2011, Friel chose to write about language: 'The tools that are available to the playwright to tell his story are few enough – words, action, silence' but 'words are at the core of it all'. Yet language in drama is not mere words, because the playwright's words are 'scored' for 'public utterance' so that an audience hears his public and private voices, a 'duet' that 'makes the experience of theatre unique'.[22] Friel knew how to make ordinary language sing while at the same time shaping ordinary speech with precision and rhythm. Here I differ sharply from David Krause, who, in his challenging article, 'The Failed Words of Brian Friel', included in Chapter 10, argues that Friel's style lacks the poetic force of Synge and O'Casey.

Denis Donoghue defines style as 'the dancing of speech' concerned with 'ways of being free, or enjoying the exhilaration of feeling free'.[23] Such a gloss allows us to make a connection between Friel's commitment to style and the tension between tradition and modernity which I propose as the dominant theme of his plays. Unlike Beckett or Pinter, for example, Friel combines sophistication of style with a good deal of traditionalism. There is a conservatism in high tension with radicalism, a localism in lockstep with cosmopolitanism. The plays are mainly set in rural Ireland, in the invented location of Ballybeg. But, as the poet Patrick Kavanagh (1904–67) emphasised, 'it requires a great deal of courage to be parochial' and thereby avoid provincialism or bourgeois conformity.[24] Friel has always displayed this type of courage while avoiding obscurantism.

Throughout his career Friel has remained living in Ulster, first within Northern Ireland and from the late 1960s in northern Donegal (being declared 'Donegal Person of the Year' in 2011[25]). During the Troubles he experienced double alienation, ideologically through his minority status in the North (which he saw as 'a schizophrenic community'[26]) and politically from the South which he was inclined to view with a mixture of amusement, affection and disdain. Scott Boltwood has explored the implications of this alienation for a reading of the plays in *Brian Friel, Ireland, and the North* (2007). The topic goes to the heart of a dilemma which Friel has repeatedly confronted. Yet the mercuriality of his imagination – striving to be free in a deterministic world – probably renders him too elusive for the category of the 'subalternity' Boltwood employs. As Anthony Roche has emphasised, as to North and South, 'Brian Friel never writes about one jurisdiction without some oblique relation to the other.'[27] While remaining steadfastly a Northerner, moreover, Friel has managed to embrace both the Abbey tradition and the aesthetics of the more cosmopolitan Dublin Gate Theatre. In his long career he has oscillated between these two opposite signifiers. Significantly, however, he was to declare in 1978 when the Gate celebrated its fiftieth anniversary: 'I am not aware that I have any theatrical pedigree; but if I had to produce documentation I would be pleased to claim – to paraphrase Turgenev's comment on Gogol – that I came out from under the Edwards-Mac Liammóir overcoat.'[28] These founders were, it should be borne in mind, *English* actors who settled in Dublin in 1928. In that context, in finding equality between the binaries Abbey and Gate, Friel demonstrated his autonomy. It gave him the independence to adopt the Anglo-Irish Tyrone Guthrie as his mentor in Minneapolis in 1963 and to broaden his outlook on theatre to an extraordinary degree.[29]

There are aspects to this tradition versus modernity dialectic which are artistic, postcolonial and European. On the artistic side, content and form in Friel's plays are crucially involved. With the arrival of modernism at the beginning of the twentieth century, the organic synchronisation of form and content became deeply problematic. Even while writing his early plays of Irish life, Friel moved away from the Abbey tradition and looked more towards Chekhov and other experimenters such as Pirandello, O'Neill and Tennessee Williams. By the mid-1960s, for Friel, 'the days of the well-made play are gone, the play with a beginning, a middle, and an end' wherein some major *problem* is addressed and resolved 'according to the Queensbury Rules of Drama' still being observed on Broadway and the West End. The reason for this shift was clear to Friel: 'because we know that life is about as remote from a presentation-problem-resolution cycle as it can be'.[30] Instead of this traditional paradigm, Friel had begun to write experimentally with *Philadelphia* (as will be shown in Chapter 2) and even more so with *The Loves of Cass McGuire* (the subject of Chapter 3). From this point onwards Friel's dramatic form is highly conscious of the need to avoid conventional 'Abbey' realism.

Consequently, it can be said that Friel was steadily negotiating his way through and around the crisis in modern drama identified by Peter Szondi and others. Szondi, whose *Theory of the Modern Drama* was published in German in 1956 but not translated into English until 1987, was an associate of the Frankfurt School. Following Lukács on the novel, he saw epic as the form to which narrative in drama was returning in order to concern itself with 'the process of disintegration and fragmentation of established cultural formations'.[31] Szondi rather startlingly saw the epic as 'the depiction of the entire world in a pre-subjectivist period whose wholeness was never questioned and which was unaware of *the split between the ego and the world*' in modern times.[32] I italicise the phrase in order to make contact here with Beckett's developing aesthetic in the 1930s, to which Friel is closer. For Beckett, this breakdown between subject and object amounted to 'rupture of the lines of communication'. The writer aware of this new event can only 'state the space that intervenes between him and the world of objects' as, according to Beckett, T. S. Eliot had done in *The Waste Land* or Jack Yeats in his paintings.[33] Both Beckett and Friel are playwrights for whom 'lack of communication' is a major philosophical theme, clearly seen not only in *Philadelphia* but also in the development towards the monologue form in *Faith Healer* (see Chapter 5). Friel's plays make Szondi's theory of the drama obsolete. Intuitively, Friel understood the crisis in modern drama from the outset. *Philadelphia* is all crisis.

The tradition-modernity dialectic also has for Friel a postcolonial dimension. Shaun Richards's article (in Chapter 10) clarifies in masterly fashion what this means. It may still also be useful to attend to Edward

Said's essay 'Yeats and Decolonization', written for Field Day, in which Said argued that much of the resistance against imperialism in nineteenth-century Ireland – as elsewhere – 'was conducted in the name of nationalism': a problematic matter as it led to 'a sort of dependence between the two sides of the contest', and 'instead of liberation after decolonization one simply gets the old colonial structures replicated in new national terms'.[34] This analysis has been accepted by many late-twentieth-century commentators on Friel and Irish Studies, sometimes without sufficient sensitivity to the complexities of the Northern politico-cultural situation. Said himself did not understand these complexities. His legacy is to the formation of postcolonial theory, not to the understanding of Irish drama. The debate has now moved on towards the view that Friel's later plays developed 'a critique of postmodernism which has a very direct postcolonial inflection'.[35] Yet it remains a major scruple with Friel to ensure the priority of a play's *aesthetic* unity: an open-ended form precludes a content that is declaratory. Ulf Dantanus's unease over the introduction into the debate of a new grid of 'a globalised postcolonial theoretical model' being imposed as a 'critical paradigm' for Irish Studies is thus well founded.[36] Nevertheless, a globalised interpretation of Friel's drama seems to be gaining strength, as indicated by the studies of Lionel Pilkington, Patrick Lonergan and Victor Merriman.[37] Accordingly, the topic of the relationship of Friel's drama to postcolonial theory needs constantly to be updated.

Plan of the Book

As one emphasis is on what David Grant calls 'the stagecraft of Friel' or the creative artist in the theatre, so two major and related preoccupations persist.[38] The first is with Friel's skill in imbricating individual consciousness in drama with social significance, what Friel calls 'flux' or national mood. 'This has got to be done, for me anyway, at a local, parochial level, and hopefully this will have meaning for other people in other countries.'[39] The other preoccupation is with Friel's commitment from 1963 on to developing metadrama, an aesthetic based upon the performative self in the modern world. If so many of the plays are memory plays it is the case, as Éamonn Jordan has shown regarding *Dancing at Lughnasa*, that 'Memory shares the values of meta-theatricality' and play.[40] It is obvious that at times one or other consideration, history or play, predominates in Friel's oeuvre, and at other times both together. There are phases in his work but no direct straight lines. 'A play offers you a shape and a form to accommodate your anxieties and disturbances in that period of life you happen to be passing through. But you outgrow that and you change and grope for a new shape and a new articulation of it.'[41] My purpose is to select for analysis plays representative of both these preoccupations beginning with *Philadelphia, Here I Come!* and ending with *Performances*. In between these bookends, Chapter 3 on *The Loves and Cass McGuire* and *Crystal and Fox* deliberately attends to two non-canonical plays of the 1960s in order to demonstrate, with some mention of Pirandello, the genesis of Friel's aesthetic and his commitment to experiment in form. That chapter is crucial; otherwise, moving on immediately to the material of Chapter 4, *The Freedom of the City* and *Volunteers*, only reinforces the mistaken impression that Friel is essentially a political playwright and that the early work is hardly more than preparation for a career in that area. As Chapter 4 argues, these two political plays emphasise that Friel's political feelings struggle with the exigencies of art to the point where his tragic sense takes over. Chapter 5, on *Living Quarters* and *Faith Healer*, is probably the key one in that argument. One either believes *Faith Healer* to be Friel's best play or not, depending on one's aesthetics of drama. To me it is his greatest work because it is at once his most intense, most beautifully shaped and most theatrically mesmerising. To others, *Faith Healer* must bow to the different values flagged by *Translations*, the subject in Chapter 6 of the history play as Friel modernised that genre. There is a trajectory from *The Enemy Within* to *The Home Place*, as Friel counteracts a determinist notion of history with an enduring sense of, to coin a phrase, the divided self. Chapter 7 deals with gender issues in and Chekhov's influence on *Aristocrats*, *Dancing at Lughnasa* and *Molly Sweeney*: a tall order, whereby politics engage with art to engrave Friel's hallmark, the indeterminate ending pregnant with future possibilities. Chapter 8 explores Friel's rare response to contemporary society, in *Wonderful Tennessee* and *Give Me Your Answer, Do!*, in comparison with Hugh Leonard's *Summer* (1974). All but finally, Chapter 9 merges with a general conclusion to reassert the importance of *Performances* in Friel's oeuvre, its 2013 revival during Derry's City of Culture confirming Friel's finesse in harmoniously fusing feeling and form, art and argument, tradition and modernity, metaphor and performance.

Three critical essays are included in Chapter 10, in accordance with editorial design for the series. The late David Krause's 'The Failed Words of Brian Friel' is included as a combative and refreshing questioning of Friel's style. Shaun Richards's piece on Friel and postcolonial criticism is a characteristically sinewy investigation of a topic at the core of Friel's reception. Csilla Bertha's essay on memory, art and history in relation to *The Home Place* takes up the postcolonial theme but expertly focuses also on Friel and music and spiritual dilemmas in Friel's work. All three articles, rich in critical thought and reference, will inspire alternative ways of reading Friel's plays today.

CHAPTER 2
COMING OF AGE: *PHILADELPHIA, HERE I COME!*

The alien home may have gems of gold;
Shadows may never have gloomed it;
But the heart will sigh for the absent land,
Where the lovelight first illumed it.

– John Locke (1847–89), The Exile's Return

Introduction

When, in July 2012, *Philadelphia, Here I Come!* enjoyed a new production at the Donmar Warehouse in London, the run was a sell-out. The reviews were so positive that one has to rejoice in this acknowledgement of an Irish play grown into a classic since its premiere in 1964. Four of the London reviews gave the play a five-star rating; before any review at all appeared, the Donmar was promoting *Philadelphia* as 'the play that established Brian Friel as one of the greatest theatrical voices of the English language'. Perhaps Tim Walker in the *Sunday Telegraph* spoke for all when he proclaimed: 'This production mainlines into the soul.' Thus, forty-five years after *Philadelphia* had its London premiere at the Lyric, when 'the first-night reviews were almost unanimous in welcoming it',[1] Friel's breakthrough play triumphantly showed its continuing power to move, amuse and illuminate. It has remained, to borrow a phrase from Shaw, 'as fresh as paint',[2] the main criterion for the definition of dramatic art. Or, as the director of the 2012 Donmar production Lyndsey Turner has commented, *Philadelphia* is still 'a brilliant, bold, brave, clever piece of writing' that 'doesn't remotely feel like a period piece'.[3]

It was with *Philadelphia* Friel discovered, with that kind of leap in creativity which transforms the craftsman into an artist, the joy and liberation of 'play'. Up to that point, although he had published a volume of short stories, he had done nothing in the line of drama to suggest he was anything special. He was a writer in search of the means of unifying his narrative skill with the vital power of holding an audience. It was a happy discovery, which was to lead him further into the subtler mode of stretching his audiences to stay with a play even where – in accordance with the theatre's economy and the urgencies of dramatic satisfaction – he would seek to bring them into darker, more complex and far more challenging territory. There is a link between *Philadelphia* and *Faith Healer* but before Friel himself could forge it he had to go through the journey which paradoxically took him fifteen years and yet was but a short step in space. Both works are attempts to explore the theatre of the inner self in conflict with different kinds of determinism; both reveal the indeterminacy in which performativity subsists; both launch the audience into an intimate sharing in a modern dilemma of being and non-being. And all of this is, to use Beckett's phrase, 'just play'.[4] This chapter, then, attempts to clarify how *Philadelphia* situates itself as the threshold through which Friel advanced as modern dramatist.

Friel opened his career as a dramatist in Belfast, Northern Ireland, with two radio plays. Both *A Sort of Freedom* (1958) and *To This Hard House* (1958) were produced by the BBC, or Northern Ireland Home Service, as it was then called. Each was a realistic sixty-minute family drama in the style then popular, dealing with economic and social issues. In various ways they seem indebted to Arthur Miller's early plays, *All My Sons* (1947) and *Death of Salesman* (1949), and as apprentice work they probably try too hard to be both dramatic and up to date.[5] Friel's first stage play *A Doubtful Paradise* (1960) – Friel's preferred title *The Francophile* was rejected – is in much the same vein. It was staged by the well-respected Ulster Group Theatre in Belfast. Although the Group enthusiastically tackled the modern classical repertory, 'the inner impulse and indeed the outer and public claim was for the Ulster play'[6] as written by Shiels, St John Ervine and Tomelty. For almost forty years, various attempts had been made to establish Irish drama on the Belfast stage in rivalry with the Abbey Theatre in Dublin. But there was always the question of autonomy, of Northerners finding their own voice and style. This aim did not, however, amount to the development of a *political* theatre in the North. Hotly contentious matters were, for the most part, avoided until John Boyd's *The Flats* (Lyric, 1971) held an unwavering mirror up to the current outbreak of the Troubles. The Ulster Group Theatre, in the meantime, was emphatically conservative.[7] Its frailty was to be seen in the Group's failure to allow Sam Thompson's anti-sectarian *Over the Bridge* (1960), set in the Belfast shipyards, to be staged as written. The resulting controversy, in May 1959, exposed a serious weakness in the Group's programme.[8] Where did Friel stand? Having given his first play to the Group, he never gave another. The reviewer of *A Doubtful Paradise* for *The Belfast Telegraph* (28 August 1960) commented: 'The author, an Ulsterman, [. . .] is trying to say things about us [*sic*] which are not political, not kitchen comedy and yet which are funny and sad at the same time.' Anthony Roche sees it today as one more 'Ulster Comedy' of its time.[9]

Friel turned away from Belfast and looked south after his first mild encouragement. He had to find his feet, begin to find his identity and his real subject matter. A new play by the Group, John Murphy's *The Country Boy*, staged 7 April 1959, may have given him the lead. A first play by a southern writer, it was an immediate and phenomenal success not only in Belfast but also in Dublin's Abbey, where it opened in a new production one month later directed by Ria Mooney. Director as well as play would have lessons for Friel. Mooney would direct Friel's first play at the Abbey, *The Enemy Within*, in August 1962.[10] *The Country Boy* would contribute to the shaping of Friel's *Philadelphia.*

Another factor is that the director Tyrone Guthrie, who had made his name at the Old Vic, was a good supporter of the Group venture and occasionally directed for them. Guthrie was extravagantly Anglo-Irish, in some ways a reverse image of Friel himself. An admirer of Friel's short stories, Guthrie befriended him. It was to 'his' theatre in Minneapolis Friel would travel in 1963 for a strange internship, a position as 'observer' at rehearsals. He would later describe Guthrie as his 'foster-father'.[11] In practical terms, as he put it himself in

Self-Portrait (1972), in Minneapolis Friel 'learned a great deal about the iron discipline of theatre, and I discovered a dedication and a nobility and a selflessness that one associates with a theoretical priesthood.'[12] For a man who had abandoned training for the actual priesthood in Maynooth, this is a significant metaphor, Joycean in its implications. It was only upon his return to Ireland after his spell at Guthrie's large feet that Friel for the first time understood his real vocation and was enabled to write *Philadelphia* in a burst of inspiration.

Philadelphia and Emigration

That old trope 'going into exile' was part of the Irish literary tradition since the time of George Moore, George Fitzmaurice, Joyce, of course, and after Joyce, Liam O'Flaherty and O'Casey. (On this topic, Beckett was outside the loop.) It was, and even today remains, a highly emotive theme. It was not until the 1940s and 1950s, however, that emigration in the sociological sense began to be dramatised as a serious national problem. Cultural and political historians today – J. J. Lee, Tom Garvin, Claire Wills, Diarmaid Ferriter, among others – can look back at emigration in mid-century Ireland as a malaise comparable to the Great Famine for its terrible implications and consequences. For the playwrights of the time, M. J. Molloy, John B. Keane and Tom Murphy in particular, it was a scandal and a source of moral outrage. Molloy, now largely forgotten, was an Abbey playwright whose work articulated the misery of the impoverished rural people of the West fated to leave family and community for the building sites and factories of England's major cities from which they had no likelihood of ever returning. Only the better educated could think, like Friel's Gar O'Donnell, of America. Most were destined, as Friel depicts them at the opening of *The Gentle Island* (1971), for a life of drudgery, manual labour and alienation. Molloy's *Old Road* (1943) pioneered the tragic note taken up by his successors, but his *The Wood of the Whispering* (1953) was more effective in showing the desperation and even madness induced by the depopulation in the countryside associated with chronic emigration.[13] Even though *Philadelphia* was to be premiered at the Gate and not at the Abbey, Friel was about to embrace the Abbey tradition on his own terms. Instead of decrying traditional calamity, he would sidestep the economic factor driving the emigration theme.[14] His Gar O'Donnell is neither unemployed nor impoverished, but a man with a year's university education – although wasted – and heir to a small family business which he is not prepared to fight for. Accordingly, the nonconformist Friel began as an outsider and remained so. He was not engaging in this raw debate on the evils of emigration, as sustained also in Keane's *Many Young Men of Twenty* (1961) and in other plays of the era.[15] Friel was not one to be in any sense bogged down, now that he had liberated himself from his early work.

When he wrote *Philadelphia* following a number of worthy problem plays, Friel made 'a quantum leap'.[16] He now focused on new material, a new subject: youth frustrated rather than angry, youth confused and unable to reconcile desire and reality. Only Tom Murphy was interested in similar material. But Murphy deals in his work more with lost souls struggling for something to believe in when disillusion enveloped Ireland in the economic conditions of the late 1950s and the death of Pope John XXIII resulted in Ireland's rejection of a liberal agenda within the Second Vatican Council. For Murphy, the subject of emigration was bound up with the legacy of the Great Famine and was symptomatic of a moral inertia: 'Never the freedom to decide and make the choice for ourselves.'[17] Friel, however, imagines a protagonist who *does* have the freedom (and luxury) to decide. Thus, Gar O'Donnell is conflicted less from circumstantial than from ontological causes. This was entirely new territory in 1960s' Ireland: loss of faith in faith itself.

Besides Tom Murphy, there is the other Murphy to be considered here. John Murphy (1924–98), born in County Mayo, wrote only one successful play, *The Country Boy* (1959), a big hit at the Abbey playing at the Queen's in Dublin. The *Irish Press*, the nationalist daily for which Friel was to write in 1962, said the play had 'a deep ring of authenticity about it' and although Murphy had not 'erected any dazzling beacon to guide his fellows', he had at least 'lit a small candle in a dark place' (12 May 1959). The *Irish Times* of the same date declared it was 'quite a time since the Abbey has had so promising a debut'. The much-maligned Ernest Blythe[18] saw *The Country Boy* as 'quite out of the ordinary' and 'one of the most notable first plays to come to the Abbey Theatre for a considerable time'. Its author had emigrated to the United States and had returned, thereby showing himself capable of seeing 'both sides of two pictures'.[19] The play deals with the return home (on vacation) after fifteen years in the United States of Eddie Maher and his New York wife Julia, a walking stereotype, 'fat, forty and loud'.[20] Eddie, the star role, was played by Ray McAnally, soon to play Friel's Columba in *The Enemy Within*, and thereafter the lead in *Living Quarters* (1977) and *Translations* (1980), as well as in such films as *My Left Foot* and *The Mission*. Back home on the farm, Eddie finds that his younger brother Curly, aged twenty-five, is about to make the same mistake he did. He wants liberty. Because his father, Tom Maher, is constantly bullying him and resisting his adult status on the farm, Curly is determined to leave for New York like his brother, regarded as heroic for reinventing his life abroad. The play reveals how mistaken Curly is. Eddie is now a failure and an alcoholic, his marriage to Julia a disaster; he has really returned home broke and in desperation. He also has a deep sense of regret over losing his true love by emigrating and suffers a major shock when news is brought during a long night of drunken reminiscence that she has died in childbirth. In the best scene of the play, Eddie lashes out at all the pretence surrounding his return and convinces Curly of the folly of following in his footsteps. The outburst clears the air. Curly sees that emigrating would deprive him of his true love; and Tom Maher reacts positively to Curly's insistence on his rights. (There is a conventional Irish mother in the play, acted by Eileen Crowe, a figure Friel took good care to omit from *Philadelphia* as a live presence.)

Abbey manager Blythe's conventional aesthetic insisted that plays should have 'a constructive influence' socially.[21] This idea explains why Blythe disliked the production which *The Country Boy* followed in the 1959 repertory season: the Irish premiere of O'Neill's masterpiece *Long Day's Journey into Night*, the point of which he could not see. He was proud that *The Country Boy* had seventy performances that season, excellent by Abbey standards.[22] He would not have been surprised that the amateur dramatic movement took *The Country Boy* to its heart the following year, when it won the national trophy at the all-Ireland Festival in Athlone. None of this could really impress Friel. Although he enjoyed *The Country Boy* on stage, he could not understand its success.[23] Knowing that his own play went against the grain, he ensured that *Philadelphia* was undertaken by the modernist Gate Theatre. He nevertheless absorbed some useful hints (or inspiration) from John Murphy's play while going in a new direction. As a writer, Friel's is ever an assimilative Autolycus, the self-confessed 'snapper-up of unconsidered trifles'.[24] *The Country Boy*, with its father-son conflict, its plaintive threnody for lost love, its use of one of Moore's *Melodies*, 'The Last Rose of Summer', sung by Curly's girlfriend during Eddie's drunken scene and evoking painful memories, must have been like popular music to Friel's ears to be transmuted into pure Mendelssohn. In Friel's play, emigration is what T. S. Eliot called an 'objective correlative': not quite a pretext but a context, a framework or a means of filtering feelings into an impersonalised form.[25]

The root of feeling in Friel's drama is always personal but transformed by imaginative pressure. A key instance is the memory which haunts Gar O'Donnell, of the day in boyhood when he felt intensely his father's love. When he tries to describe the memory and its source, he can barely control his yearning to have his father recall it too in equal measure and restorative power. When this childhood experience of Wordsworthian radiance is denied by Old Screwballs, all is turned to dust in Gar's soul and he despairs. He does not stay to listen to his father's painful efforts to patch up his son's faulty recollection; for Gar, this failure on S. B.'s part signals the end of any possibility of renewal. At this moment of tragic recognition, Gar comes of age. The play, however, is not quite over at this point. Although it is the small hours of the morning, Gar meets Madge, his substitute mother, in the kitchen ('Turning into a night club, this place') for the last time.[26] She protects her private disappointment. Their brief exchange ironically replicates the two preceding scenes. Anxiety dominates all three characters at the change taking place. Madge is right: at heart the two men are 'as like as two peas'. Each has his fixed memory of the other, although it is falsified. To Friel, it does not matter that in the area of memory 'the fact is a fiction': each has his own individual, solipsistic and partly imagined version of the truth.[27] We live by such truths, for they signify our very identity. Emigration makes no difference to such memories, unless it magnifies them for validation, as Gar's last speech suggests when he mentally records Madge's exit for future recollection. Thus, the play is less about emigration than about the isolated self which subsists on memories.

Guthrie, Ritual, Subversion

Tyrone Guthrie saw immediately the originality of *Philadelphia*, although he was not free at the time to direct it. 'Meaning is implicit "between the lines" of [Friel's] text,' he said on BBC radio, 'in silences, in what people are thinking and doing far more than in what they are saying; in the music as much as in the meaning of a phrase.'[28] Friel's indebtedness to Guthrie is well known; he has acknowledged it generously on countless occasions. Every major commentator on Friel's career as playwright, from Desmond Maxwell (1973) to Anthony Roche (2011) and Maria Szasz (2013), has described the significance of Friel's four- or five-month visit (accounts differ over the duration) to Minneapolis in the spring/summer of 1963, where he sat in on Guthrie's rehearsals of *Hamlet* and *Three Sisters*[29] and had his eyes opened to the possibilities of theatre beyond his meagre experience up to that time. The immediate result was the writing of *Philadelphia, Here I Come!* upon his return to Ireland. It has been suggested that Friel began *Philadelphia* while still in Minneapolis but all the evidence points to an explosion of creativity after he reached home and got the last of his *Irish Press* articles into publication on 10 August 1963.[30] Elsewhere, on radio in 1965, Friel said what he learnt from Guthrie had less to do with 'curtain-lines and entrances and exits' than with 'the whole meaning of theatre, this strange ritual of make-believe'.[31] It is this reference to ritual I want to pick up on here.

Guthrie made a thing of ritual, declaring that 'theatre relates itself to God by means of ritual. It does so more consciously than any other activity, except prayer, because, like organized prayer, it is the direct descendant of primitive religious ceremonies.'[32] Friel himself spoke in a similar idiom: 'Ritual is part of all drama,' indeed it is its 'essence'.

Drama, he emphasised, using capitals, 'is a RITE, and always [*sic*] religious in the purest sense'.[33] It is a curious exaggeration. Clearly, not *all* drama is ritualistic or religious in character. What is true historically is that drama, both tragedy and comedy, has its roots in rituals related to the god Dionysus and in medieval times to Jesus Christ. But from the Renaissance onwards, drama of whatever genre developed more and more towards realism. In a sense, what Guthrie had in mind in an age when naturalism had become the modern classicism was similar to what W. B. Yeats had in mind earlier: 'The theatre began in ritual, and it cannot come to its greatness again without recalling words to their ancient sovereignty.'[34] There was a lot of support for such an alternative theatre in the first half of the twentieth century. Although Sophocles' *Oedipus the King* remained for him a paradigm of ritualistic drama, Guthrie was mainly a Shakespearean director, and the tragedies, particularly *Hamlet*, most received his attention at the Old Vic. He pioneered the modernised theatre-in-the-round and in a sense Friel strayed into something truly momentous when the Guthrie Theatre was formally opened on 7 May 1963 during his sojourn. What he saw in the *Hamlet* rehearsals must have been stunning to Friel. Yet for Friel's own style of drama, which is in the main grounded in realism, Guthrie's gospel held only limited possibilities. Friel preferred to explore the negative effects of outworn ritual, as in Yeats's later, scornful and minimalist plays.[35]

It is therefore more fruitful to regard Friel's use of ritual as subversive. *Philadelphia* is a play without a plot, where Gar's last night at home takes on the nature of a vigil or even an 'Irish wake' only to the degree that such a framework works to expose the sterility and spiritual emptiness of Ballybeg. Gar is driven to keep busy, fill the time on his last evening, more to distract himself from painful thoughts and memories than to take part meaningfully in any 'ritual' or ceremonious action with a religious theme. Everyday rituals such as supper with his father (but not Madge) are mercilessly used to show S. B. O'Donnell in a bad light: silent except for the most banal, meaningless phrases, and satirised for his immovable adherence to habit ('Sure you know I never take a second cup' (p. 50) when Gar suggests more tea). The point of view is nearly always that of Gar himself, the central consciousness, giving the play its unity (as in expressionism) and appeal (as in comedy): empathy is thus engaged on behalf of the young. In traditional comedy, fathers are universally at odds with their sons. S. B. O'Donnell is not unique in *Philadelphia*: Ned's father is also cursed as a 'stupid bastard', 'such a bloody stupid bastard of an aul fella!' (p. 75). Katie's father, Senator Doogan, is a more refined patriarch: if Gar is an ironised version of Hamlet, then Katie is his Ophelia ('frailty, thy name is woman!') and Senator Doogan an ironised, superior version of Polonius. To the audience, however, Gar is not blameless in his attitude towards his father but habitually '*assumes in speech and gesture a surly, taciturn gruffness*' when speaking to him (p. 34). The word 'assumes' implies a mask. The rituals of domestic intercourse are bearable only in this guise, allowing Gar's unconscious to ridicule his father at such times and thereby dehumanise him, or to provide him with the role of a female model on the catwalk, a ludicrously inappropriate ritual for presiding over the tea table. To be sure, as Old Screwballs, Gar's father is robotic. As such, he is rendered a source of laughter, 'something mechanical encrusted on the living'.[36] But Gar's cruelty is also a factor.

The major ritual in *Philadelphia* is the nightly recitation of the rosary, as dramatised in Episode 3. For a long time, up to the Second Vatican Council in the 1960s, the Catholic Church applied pressure to have the rosary part of the social and religious life of the family. The convention was given special emphasis in the Marian Year of 1954 when an Irish-American priest Fr Patrick Peyton (1909–92) toured Ireland, holding large rallies with the slogans, 'The family that prays together, stays together' and 'A world at prayer is a world at peace.' Known as 'the rosary priest', he had won fame on American radio and even had a theatre programme on radio.[37] Fr Peyton's international crusade was quite successful as pious evangelism, an anti-communist weapon in the age of the Cold War. But Friel exposes how meaningless the rosary ritual can be when a member of a family such as Gar, too intelligent to remain concentrated on the repetitious formula to be kept up for five 'decades' of the sacred 'mysteries' (Joyful, Sorrowful or Glorious) in the life, death and resurrection of Jesus Christ. Far from meditating on the religious images evoked by each 'decade', Gar allows his mind to drift into fantasy, even into erotic dreams which ludicrously undermine the purpose of the ritual. The travesty is theatrically effective as comedy but it also constructs a satire of the crusade.

Friel continues the mockery when the parish priest arrives, as he does nightly, to meet Madge's routine remark that he invariably misses out on one ritual while ensuring that he arrives for another: the taking of tea at a game of draughts. 'She says I wait till the rosary's over and the kettle's on,' a refrain he repeats several times, allowing S. B.'s response, 'She's a sharp one, Madge' (p. 84), also repeated on cue, mechanically, ritualistically, emptily. The laugh is turned against them through Private Gar's comments. The game of draughts that ensues is likewise mocked as an evasion of Gar's problems; the irresponsibility of the priest for his failure to 'translate' all the 'loneliness, this groping, this dreadful bloody buffoonery into Christian terms that will make life bearable for us all' (p. 88) is clearly underlined. While this extraordinary scene goes on, Public Gar is absent, immured in his bunker, his refuge from reality. This means that Private's angry speech directed at Canon O'Byrne remains virtual: it does not give rise to any debate. Friel's use of ritual, therefore, while ironic, has no *dramatic* agency. It is for the audience silently to interact with: they are included in Private's final phrase 'bearable for *us all*'. Friel assists by terminating the game of draughts with a Jacobean-style use of hidden meaning, when the Canon is winning but urges against despair: 'You're not too late yet [. . .]. No, I wouldn't say die yet' (p. 90). At this point, Private is no longer on stage. He has voiced what cannot be said by Public to his two fathers, natural and spiritual, in pathos, humour and anger. He has even called for 'pity' on father and son, and 'on every goddam bloody man jack of us' (p. 89), again including the audience. We are reminded that a more authentic ritual is then and there invisibly taking place in the theatre. At bottom, Private declares, the problem is silence: the refusal rather than the inability to communicate.

Visitations and the Divided Self

Philadelphia is a vigil play, a series of variations on the waiting game. Canon O'Byrne's is the last of five visitations in the course of Gar's final evening at home. Each is revelatory, to Gar himself and of Gar to the audience. It is an effective technique. Unlike *Waiting for Godot*, for example, where the two visits by Pozzo and Lucky are surreal intrusions, serving mainly as exhibitions of futility in power relations, the five visits in *Philadelphia* are arranged to highlight the divided self. Three of the visits occur in Episode Two where the play reaches its emotional crescendo, with one each in Episode One and Three. Only one is a flashback, a memory scene: the visit from *Philadelphia* in Episode Two of Gar's Aunt Lizzie, her husband and male friend. The other visits, by Master Boyle, the 'boys', Katie Doogan and Canon O'Byrne, all serve to maintain unity of place and time in a classically constructed play where meaning is deeply questioned. The arrangement is not arbitrary: Master Boyle, the first, and Canon O'Byrne, the last, visitors, complement each other. Although at odds with the priest as school manager, Boyle feels 'a peculiar attachment for him' (p. 53). He enters, however, not just to bid farewell to Gar but also to 'borrow' money. Like Aunt Lizzie's visit which follows it, Boyle's visit reveals Gar's yearning for the mother he never knew: the split in his psyche is never more apparent than in scenes where intimacy itself is almost unendurable. The visit by Katie which concludes Episode Two with huge emotional effect is related to Boyle's visit in that Gar borrows Boyle's language to punish Katie for the suffering she has caused him. He berates Ballybeg – 'a bloody quagmire, a backwater, a dead-end!' in which everybody goes mad 'sooner or later' (p. 79). Katie's presence before him causes such inner turmoil that Private is driven to the longest passage from Edmund Burke's *Reflections on the Revolution in France* (1790) in the whole play. Always a mantra for Gar's self-control, its use here seems to identify Katie with the 'delightful vision' of Marie Antoinette, whereas at other times the latter stands for Gar's mother. Nothing Katie says now in the placatory mode will calm Gar; his fury is fully unleashed in a contorted scornful mixture of braggadocio and hate. In his passion, like Hamlet with Ophelia in the 'nunnery' scene, Gar's desire to hurt barely conceals his love: 'You're stuck here! [. . . .] And you'll die here! But I'm not stuck! I'm free! Free as the bloody wind! [. . . .] Answerable to nobody. [. . .] Impermanence – anonymity – that's what I'm looking for; a vast restless place that doesn't give a damn about the past' (p. 79).

He stops short of quoting Master Boyle further: 'Be one hundred per cent American' (p. 53), itself a quotation from *A Streetcar Named Desire* (1947) laden with irony for Gar, whose identity is more brittle than that of Stanley Kowalski and whose future in Philadelphia will magnify the split already visible in his personality. He will have to become that dubious hybrid, an Irish-American, no more than fifty per cent either way like Patrick Palinakis (p. 59).

The visit by the 'boys' is in an entirely different style, mood and category. If one stays with the *Hamlet* framework, it is a Rosencrantz and Guildenstern scene with the hero: Gar takes the visit as in the beaten way of friendship but discovers it is a set-up. The boys were sent for. Gar discovers this only after the most boisterous have left for metal more attractive: the ultra-innocent Joe, infantile to a degree which makes Gar sympathetic (for infantilism awaits himself in *Philadelphia*), confesses Madge's involvement. The realisation of betrayal drives Gar Private into a tirade, 'They're louts, ignorant bloody louts and you've always known it!' (p. 77), which spills over onto Katie. Friel's theatrical art is skilfully revealed in the scene with the boys, a little play-within-the-play for which his stage direction prepares. Before the friends enter, they are heard off, their laughter '*exaggerated*' before they burst in, when '*their bluster is not altogether convincing. There is something false about it*' (p. 69). Clearly, the acting must deliver this duplicity well enough to fool Gar himself and to leave him with very mixed feelings when the truth dawns. Performativity is greatly to the fore here, as it is at other times when Gar is alone and playacting.[38]

All of these scenes provide cumulative shocks to Gar. But they also reveal how much the passive observer he is. Even before he sees through the boys' staged visit, he ponders on the discrepancy between the tall tales they tell to boost low self-esteem and the reality of experience. Friel's device of having two actors to represent the ego and unconscious works superbly in such scenes, drawing upon both the traditional Elizabethan convention of soliloquy and the modernist experiments of playwrights such as O'Neill (in *Strange Interlude* (1928)). It allows Gar the status of outsider without further complications. Existentially, Gar finds the world as hostile and as morally diseased as a character in Eliot, Camus or Sartre. In his desire to honour Guthrie's insistence on the priority of entertaining an audience, however, Friel, showing great detachment, ensured that the comic side is not forgotten. It is instructive also to recall Miller's original title for *Death of a Salesman* (1949), one of the four plays staged in Minneapolis in the season of Friel's sojourn, namely *The Inside of his Head.*[39] It applies as aptly to Friel's *Philadelphia*, described by Lyndsey Turner, director of the 2012 Donmar production, as 'a psychological drama which finds a theatrical form for the voices in our heads'.[40] Miller used a mixed form of realism and expressionism, the latter to represent the dream scenes summoned through Willy Loman's memory. In Friel's play, however, the dream nature of Gar's two memory scenes, the courting of Katie Doogan and the visit by Aunt Lizzie, is not expressionistic. When the bedroom light goes up after the scene where Lizzie throws her arms around Gar to his confusion, Gar Public and Private are re-installed and '*The kitchen is empty*' (p. 66): visibly so to indicate the *unreality* of the disembodied scene just witnessed.

As in *Death of a Salesman*, Friel's play uses three distinct spaces: kitchen, bedroom and an apron as a neutral area. Jo Mielziner's stage design for *Salesman* was partly symbolic[41]; Hilton Edwards's direction of Friel's premiere called for a more traditional, less symbolic style. The actor who played S. B. O'Donnell in the premiere of *Philadelphia* called Edwards 'a director of the old school [. . . .] He heard the play in terms of classical music, and he saw it in terms of the pictorial composition of the great painters.'[42] With Friel's play, he combined tradition and modernity. He was the next best thing to Guthrie around.

Conclusion: What is the Architecture?

It may be said that *Philadelphia, Here I Come!* is less about Irish emigration than about universal loneliness. Written within the Irish tradition, it reached out to Broadway and beyond. Its indebtedness to John Murphy's *The Country Boy* was perhaps at once incidental and felicitous. Juxtaposition of the two texts lights up Friel's as the work of a master of understatement and of character analysis. As I have suggested, *Hamlet* and *Death of a Salesman*, two of the four plays in rehearsal during Friel's stay in Minneapolis, also provided significant inspiration for the young playwright. I remain convinced, however, that *Philadelphia* sprang from feelings deep within Friel himself. Loneliness was something he deeply understood from his Maynooth experience. Personal loneliness may have provided the main spur for *Philadelphia*: as exile, he was through misadventure a considerable time on his own, first in New York, subsequently in Minneapolis, before being joined by his family. The release from that period of estrangement could well have pitched the writer into the joy and high spirits which, for all its modernist traces, is fundamentally a hopeful play. One must not forget the final scene, in which Gar expresses joy at the birth of Madge's niece. It is one of those details that can easily pass without notice: like the ominous death of the baby in the final scene of *Translations*. At the end of *Philadelphia*, however, the arrival of a new baby, to be named Brigid, is a happy sign in the face of the anxiety signified by Gar's abandoning his ageing father. In the Irish calendar, St Brigid, one of the three patron saints of Ireland, is also a pagan goddess associated with the arrival and the rites of spring: a divided self, in fact. Gar, having healed himself abroad, can perhaps return, like his inventor, joyous and whole, unlike Cass McGuire (see Chapter 3). Adam Phillips has written 'in praise of the unlived life', the possible other existence we might have if we chose or dared: 'There is no more fundamental picture of the human subject than as a creature trying to get out of something.'[43] Frustrated on more than one level, Gar needs to get away from Ballybeg. But his fantasy life of America is such that even he, when 'eejiting about' (p. 32), does not take the place seriously: it is there to be parodied. Gar half-knows that in the city of Philadelphia he will need once again to escape. Philadelphia is an illusion. He will be right back where he started from; the play's theme song will have it so.

When he first enters in *Dancing at Lughnasa*, Father Jack, a returned exile, is quite confused about the home place: he cannot even find the word 'layout' in his memory and thinks it is 'architecture'.[44] In John Murphy's text of *The Country Boy* the opening stage direction describes the setting, a farmhouse kitchen, as 'of the type that has now almost completely replaced the thatched cottage' in 1950s' Ireland with modernisation (p. 1). In the key scene of that play, where the drunken Eddie relives his past in this kitchen, he mentally recreates the *old* house, its furniture and trappings, while standing in the existing space remembering his true love Katie, and John Murphy stumbled on an image he was unable to exploit to the full. But Friel was. In Friel's *Philadelphia* he can be said to superimpose a new architecture on what went before. This marks his breakthrough. It is a question of dramatic form. Writing elsewhere on *Translations*, I have referred to this skill as a use of palimpsest.[45] Friel can take Murphy's play and erect his own structure on its old foundations, sensing the metaphorical implications of the process and how it can facilitate the use of double time on stage. As *Philadelphia* closes, in diminuendo fashion, Friel meshes a range of feelings within a framework which evokes loss and sorrow rather than the expected reconciliation and resolution. 'Like a man to double business bound,' Gar stands in pause where he shall first begin.[46]

A quick curtain leaves Gar's dilemma with the audience. Is this any way to end a play? It is perhaps to build a new architecture there and then on the stage, abstract, transparent, capable of enclosing the past while facing the future with proportionate dread, so revising what went before as to create a new, interrogative space in the imagination. The relevance is not only for the young hero's coming of age in a world destabilised and devoid of certainties, but also equally for 'us all' and for the playwright's career.

CHAPTER 3

FORMATION OF AN AESTHETIC: *THE LOVES OF CASS MCGUIRE* AND *CRYSTAL AND FOX*

Wherefore, sweetheart? What's your metaphor?

– Shakespeare, *Twelfth Night*, 1.3.70

Introduction

As the 1960s advanced, Friel wished to assert his intention to be seen internationally as an experimental playwright. He had two main strengths to develop, a gift for storytelling and a capacity to convert style into formal inventiveness. This chapter exhibits his courage in developing these skills at the expense of easy popularity. *The Loves of Cass McGuire* is about the fate of a returned exile. In that regard, it looks at the individual in modern society from the opposite perspective of *Philadelphia, Here I Come!* There the focus is on a young man, discounted and starved of love but nevertheless at the beginning of his life, going into exile with property at his back and security waiting in Philadelphia. The shape of Gar's fuller life has yet to be created. By contrast, Cass McGuire is a seventy-year-old woman journeying in the other direction. Indeed, in writing the play Friel at one point toyed with making a forty-five-year-old Gar the 'Yank' he had in mind.[1] Cass has made her life, such as it was, in New York's Lower East Side and after her partner dies, she decides to return 'home' to Ireland to live, as she thinks, with her younger brother and his family. Her return is tragic, in that a huge shock awaits her and her life is to be robbed of meaning. *You Can't Go Home Again* was the title of the American novel by Thomas Wolfe, whose hero George Webber supplies Friel's theme: 'He never had the sense of home so much as when he felt that he was going there. It was only when he got there that his homelessness began.'[2] As Thomas Kilroy has said, *Cass McGuire* was a 'response'[3] to the extraordinary success enjoyed by *Philadelphia, Here I Come!* after it reached Broadway on 15 February 1965, where it ran for nine months before touring for a further six. In New York, the perceived theme of *Philadelphia* was nostalgia, as the actor who played S. B. O'Donnell noted.[4] Friel shrank a little from the American audience's sentimental response, and for his next play he determined to show the opposite situation as equally true to the human condition. Just as later on *The Communication Cord* (1982) was written to counteract the over-nationalistic response to *Translations* (1980), so too was *Cass McGuire* an 'antidote'[5] to *Philadelphia*, although by no means a farce. The initial point to be made is that Friel refuses to be defined by public taste. Further, *Crystal and Fox* remains a powerful reminder that following *Cass* Friel continued to defy expectations by extending further into metadrama.

Concerning returned emigrants, an Irish sociologist tells us that the majority experience 'problems with readjusting' attributed to the 'false or unrealistic expectations' they had about life in Ireland. In a survey taken covering the 1970s, eighty-five per cent of returned emigrants 'felt that they had been changed by the experience of emigration'.[6] Returned emigrants did not typically have the equipment to see wherein exactly they had been changed. Two decades later, returned emigrants recognised that living abroad gave them the opportunity 'to reflexively "reinvent the self"' (p. 180). These people already had 'high levels of cultural capital' before emigrating, which allowed development of goals and a life plan. On return, such people were 'highly self-aware' and ready for 'the process of reinvention' leading to 'the reconfiguration of the self, based on newly acquired skills and experiences' (p. 181). Significantly, little of this 'reinvention' applies to Cass, whose cultural capital is close to nil. Her lot in the play is tragically to 'reinvent the self'; what happens to her is less typical than metaphoric.

Philadelphia, *Cass McGuire, Lovers* (1967) and *Crystal and Fox* are all 'inspections of the diversities of love, undertaken in the way that a sculptor views his work from different angles'.[7] Within the text of Friel's second play in this series, the protagonist quarrels with its title: '*The Loves of Cass McGuire* – like I was Mata Hari or something.'[8] The title is ironic. Cass had but two loves in her long life: her childhood sweetheart Connie Crowley whom she left behind and remembers (as often with offstage characters in Friel) with genuine, disturbing affection; and the disreputable Swede, Jeff Olsen, who owned the seedy New York restaurant Cass worked in for fifty-two years, 'one block away from Skid Row', among 'deadbeats, drags [transvestites], washouts, living the past!' (p. 17). Jeff, it would appear, was the love of her life, a relationship impossible for her family back home to understand, much less condone. Therefore, it is ignored; it is not to be regarded as fact. Cass will have to reinvent. In Friel's description of the set there is a back wall 'of glass and French windows' opening on to a 'formal garden' in which 'a Cupid statue (illuminated) is frozen in an absurd and impossible contortion' (p. 7). Here is the key to Friel's theme. Cupid, son of Venus, is emblematic of romantic and sexual love; but the statue is a grotesque representation. This icon in the background, spotlit for attention, informs the audience that what they will see of love on stage is merely a contortion. Mother's paralysis symbolises this failure; Cass's brother Harry, his wife Alice and son Dominic represent social callousness.

Cass's tragedy arises through delusion. The real reason she returns from New York is that her lover Jeff Olsen is dead. The shock makes her realise she has nobody who cares for her. She decides to go 'home' and this is her tragic error. At first, her reception by her brother Harry and his wife Alice is welcoming. She is instructed to look on herself as a member of Harry's family: 'this is your home now, Cass' (p. 33). A welcome party is to be arranged for her – one of those affairs in Friel, like the Mass Father Jack is to say in *Dancing at Lughnasa* which, long promised, never happens. Its absence is a sign in itself; in both cases the reason is the transformation of both Cass and Jack. Once Cass recognises the futility of her lifelong sacrifice in sending money home which was never needed and which she herself might have used, she is shattered by the news and her vulgar, Dionysian side comes out and renders her unlivable with. She is packed off to a retirement home, ironically named Eden House. Her own actions thus shape, but do not cause, her downfall.

Whereas the situation in Eden House is a long way from that of Kesey's novel *One Flew Over The Cuckoo's Nest* (1962), it nevertheless comparably critiques modern society and its cruelties. A better comparison however is to be made with Brian Moore's *The Lonely Passion of Judith Hearne* (1955), a Belfast novel of loneliness, alcoholism, religious crisis and mental breakdown. It was a novel Friel admired to the point of writing the screenplay for a posited Hollywood film (to be directed by John Huston), but when Friel 'refused to change his (even more) downbeat ending, his version was scrapped'.[9] The film, with screenplay by Peter Nelson, was made in 1987 with Maggie Smith in the title role replacing the original casting of Katharine Hepburn. In the novel, the ageing Judith Hearne, spinster, ends up in a nursing home facing a bleak future. The final words of her inner dialogue relate to how, with the aid of the photograph of a mother-aunt and on oleograph of the Sacred Heart, 'a new place becomes home'.[10] It is safe to say Friel began here when he conceived *The Loves of Cass McGuire*, which would explore the ambiguities of 'home' on many levels.

Viewed as tragedy, *Cass McGuire* depicts Cass as at one level victim to the siren song of Trilbe and Ingram, fellow inmates of Eden House, and at another level as Cass succumbing to her destruction in reaction to recognition of her circumstances. As Anthony Roche puts it, 'The fantasy life of Eden House represented by Trilbe and Ingram's dream narratives steadily and progressively *usurp on Cass's independence*, until it is finally extinguished.'[11] It is easy to see these two as harmless pretenders, dreamers of what might have been. They exploit the romantic poetry of Yeats and the even more romantic opera music of Wagner to create a strange, even hallucinogenic argument. They urge letting go of reality and embracing fantasy. They offer a way of reinventing the self by suggesting a new narrative both comforting and consolatory. But it is a doctrine based on a lie, a distortion of what gives basis to personality and therefore dangerous, a softened version of fashionable 1960s' escapism resulting in the destruction of 'individuation' or 'self-realisation'.[12] Friel's use of fantasy in this play cannot be seen positively. Although it is true that in *Philadelphia*

Gar also willingly embraces fantasy, yet unlike Cass, he is not broken mentally. He may be schizoid in the way in which Beckett's Murphy[13] self-consciously exhibits the Cartesian split between mind (private) and body (public) but he is not schizophrenic. Indeed, Gar's use of fantasy provides a means of *maintaining* sanity. In the dialogue between Public and Private Gar, there is no confusion over what is real and what is fabricated: Gar is not delusional. Gar's playfulness and performativity define his ability to scrutinise his own experiences with one clear eye on their absurdity. Cass McGuire, however, is offered fantasy by others like a drug which she eventually accepts. The winged chair into which she finally sits for this acceptance represents a deadly form of surrender into delusion. The pathos is in the delusion. Looking around at her new surroundings, now accepted as permanent, Cass approves: 'Home at last. Gee, but it's a good thing to be home' (p. 63), echoing the tragic irony of Brian Moore's ending of *Judith Hearne*.

The Loves of Cass McGuire and Metatheatre

Friel worked extremely hard on the text of *Cass McGuire*. Crucially, he had Pirandello's example in mind from the outset: 'I was then praying to Pirandello.'[14] Luigi Pirandello (1867–1936), who won the Nobel Prize for Literature in 1934, was one of the most influential playwrights of the twentieth century. By focusing on self-conscious theatricality, he broke down the fourth wall between stage and audience in a series of tragicomic plays probing the fate of modern humanity with humour and philosophic depth, making theatre itself a renewed psychological metaphor. Here was a new model for Friel. Arguing with himself in his notes over the direction *Cass McGuire* was taking, Friel commented:

> The writer creates these characters, but once they are written – as in [Pirandello's] SIX CHARACTERS – they have a life of their own, so that there are times when the author, by putting certain dialogue into their mouths, <u>forces</u> them to say things that they wouldn't say of their own volition.

> They could achieve a measure of liberty and self-expression, then, if they were to divert from the script occasionally; if it were established at the very beginning that there is a free and a written man.[15]

In *Six Characters in Search of an Author* (1922), a rehearsal is loudly interrupted by the sudden appearance of six figures demanding that their own, more 'real' story be substituted by director and actors for the artificial text they are languidly going through. And so the form becomes a vehicle for modern tragedy, where determinism is an iron law which Friel both accepts and, in line with existentialism, seeks to redefine.

Friel thought of a 'Pirandello opening' for *Cass McGuire* in which Cass squabbles with the cast in rehearsal and calls for the author to decide where the play is to begin. The author comes on stage and tells the actors they may include or exclude what they wish from his text but 'they'll always be themselves in character'.[16] Although he did not retain this opening, the idea remained in Friel's mind and he went on to make Cass's mental state relate to her awareness of the audience and her quarrel with brother Harry over where exactly her story should begin – in short, who should control the narrative. The concept was topical in critical circles in the 1960s, evidenced by Lionel Abel's *Metadrama* (1963) and Anne Righter's *Shakespeare and the Idea of the Play* (1962). Such studies make it clear that what Pirandello did for modern drama in *Six Characters* was not new but was rooted in medieval drama. Righter coined the term 'the play metaphor' to indicate the double-layered nature of medieval drama in its nudging the audience towards an understanding of drama as representing life at one remove and the stage as signifying the world.[17] Obviously, Shakespeare expanded this 'play metaphor' well beyond medieval parameters. *Hamlet* exhibits a deep ontological scepticism whereby life and dream seem inextricable. Modernism merely rediscovered Shakespeare's theatrical vehicle. No doubt, Friel's Gar in *Philadelphia* found himself surrounded by the avant-garde novelty seen in Beckett's *Godot*. But in spite of the Guthrie-influenced theatricalism of *Philadelphia* (with Gar cast as a Hamlet figure), Friel is conservative in that piece: Gar never overtly acknowledges the audience. He broke new ground in *Cass*, even if the play proved a 'débacle' on Broadway in 1966,[18] as its Dublin success subsequently showed.

The reception of Irish drama in New York was itself at fault. With the success of *Philadelphia*, Friel's Broadway reputation was being forged in narrower terms than he was willing to approve. Many reviewers happily saw the play as reinforcing Irish traditional stereotypes, invoking O'Casey for instance.[19] Almost an insult. In a 1970 interview Friel openly declared: 'I'm not an O'Casey fan. [. . .] O'Casey is so intensely Dublin that I can admire him from a distance, but I'm never moved by him.'[20] Comparisons in this area are odious.[21] Friel wanted to be seen in New York as a *new* Irish author and not one more broth of a boy: he was still searching for his own voice. He had to show he could do better than be perceived as peddling 'the latest installment of a popular product from the Emerald Isle'.[22] *Cass*, then, was unacceptable as an Irish play on Broadway. It was, perhaps, too full of what Friel termed 'obligatory deviousness'.[23]

For example, *Cass* opens with a quiet domestic scene which Cass violently disrupts by her entrance: 'What the hell goes on here?' Everyone on stage 'freezes' and Cass addresses the audience directly in monologue fashion. '*They are her friends, her intimates*' (p. 12). When we read on, we discover that Cass's 'entrance' into the narrative is deferred until early in Act 2, where, as a returned sister, she is as 'normal' as can be. The play requires to be read sideways, realism and metatheatre being interspersed for most of the play in kaleidoscope fashion. The key moment occurs in Act 3 when Cass can no longer see the audience before her: therefore, she is lost, cut off from those who validate her performance and, thus deprived, her identity begins drastically to dissolve. If the time sequence of *Cass McGuire* is not grasped, then her vulgarity – which in its grosser manifestations is a reflex response to humiliation – must appear merely offensive. The demands of the play may be too well camouflaged for its own good. The irony here is that *Philadelphia*, while decidedly not a stock Irish play, was received as such on Broadway. John P. Harrington has argued that with its success, 'New York capitulated to a simplistic and reductive notion of Irish drama, and consequently of Ireland, that still [in 1997] prevails.'[24] *Cass* stands as stark proof of that argument.

In Dublin in 1967, however, a totally different play was seen, as would also happen with *Faith Healer* in 1980 (see Chapter 5). This is not because Friel rewrote the text (he would not) but because *Cass* found a home on the newly opened, rebuilt Abbey stage. There the leading director Tomás Mac Anna instantly understood that *Cass* is a metaphor about acting and the alienated self. He cast Siobhán McKenna (a much-admired Pegeen Mike in Synge's *Playboy of the Western World* on stage and screen) as the aged Cass. Ruth Gordon was wrong for the part on Broadway because Cass is partly phoney – when she projects herself as offensive – and has an identity split between the Bowery and small-town Ireland. Whereas in Elizabethan comedy a boy can play a woman who disguises herself as a man, in Irish theatre Cass is a role where a star Irish actress plays an outrageously rough American who is pulled back into her home-based Irish identity and thence into fantasy. McKenna was good at this fluidity. In the film *Daughter of Darkness* (1949), she played a schizophrenic angel-demon figure. In a 1970 radio version of Yeats's *Words Upon the Window-pane* (1930), she played the medium at a séance who slips from plain, heavy-breathing facilitator to the childish contact Lulu, to Swift's love Vanessa, and finally to Swift himself in gravel-voiced fury. In later years McKenna similarly created Tom Murphy's Mommo in *Bailegangaire* (1985), her final role. In all of these, as in her Juno and Mrs Burgess, she played *against* her own natural elegance and beauty. In *Cass*, her appearance at age forty-five belied the vulgarity in the ruined figure aged seventy. To a considerable degree, such was the esteem in which McKenna was held in Ireland that she could as easily represent the nation *qua* Cathleen Ní Houlihan as Maud Gonne had done in Yeats's heyday. 'For people of my generation,' Friel declared in his graveside oration for McKenna in 1986, 'she personified an idea of Ireland.'[25] Accordingly, when she played Cass McGuire at the Abbey she sold out the show because to a lot of people she *was* Mother Ireland. An Irish audience could accept Cass (a possible prototype for Beckett's Mouth in *Not I*) as empathetic. Friel told director Mac Anna that 'at last he had seen the play as he had written it'.[26]

Friel works musically. *In Music and the Irish Literary Imagination*, Harry White argues that in contrast to other Irish playwrights who use songs and music in their texts, Friel orchestrates a text by creating a structure in itself musical. His plays are 'operas of the Irish mind'.[27] It is an Irish thing. It was the English aesthete Walter Pater who declared in *The Renaissance* (1873) that 'all art constantly aspires to the condition of music' but it was Synge who wrote: 'Every life is a symphony, and the translation of this life into music, and from music back to literature or sculpture or painting is the real effort of the artist.'[28] Shaw, a music critic before he turned dramatist, confessed: 'Opera taught me to shape my plays into recitatives, arias, duets, trios, ensemble finales and bravura pieces.'[29] Virtually all Irish playwrights after Shaw keep music in mind, Tom Murphy and Billy Roche being two contemporaries who rival Friel in this respect. In Friel's oeuvre, however, his use of music is probably more stylistic and more organic than any of his confreres. In this context, it is entirely appropriate that he should have written a play about the composer Leoš Janáček, calling in *Performances* (2003) for a quartet of musicians to appear on stage (see Chapter 9). For *Cass McGuire* the ambition was no less radical in invoking Richard Wagner. Friel said in 1970: 'Wagner is my favourite.'[30] In his prefatory note to *Cass* he refers to the 'three rhapsodies', one in each act of the play, as 'part of the formal pattern or ritual of the action; and the musical term, rhapsody, seemed to me to be the most accurate description of them'. In each rhapsody, Trilbe, Ingram and Cass, in turn, take 'the shabby and unpromising threads of his [or her] past life and weaves it [*sic*] into a hymn of joy, a gay and rapturous and exaggerated celebration of a beauty that might have been'. The rhapsodies were to be recited against the background of music from Wagner's *Tristan and Isolde* because, Friel insists, it 'has parallels of sorts in Cass McGuire's story' (pp. 7–8). The parallels, Patrick Burke reminds us, include Cass and Jeff Olsen as Tristan and Isolde, Connie (who does not appear in the play) as Morolt and Pat Quinn as the evil Melot.[31] At the same time, Friel wants Cass to be 'soloist' in the play heard as 'concerto'. The contradiction here need not bother us.[32] It is up to the director to find the right balance. Indeed, in his prefatory note Friel concedes that the Wagner music

(*Liebestod*) towards the end of the play can be dropped, but insisted upon 'counterpoint' as crucial to the clash of styles in the play.

The 'parallels' with *Tristan and Isolde* Friel speaks of are ironic in the modernist style. There can hardly be an actual parallel between the seventy-year-old alcoholic Cass and the young and beautiful Isolde. If set beside the archetypal Isolde (who was Irish),[33] Cass puts us in mind of the grotesque statue of Cupid emphasised in the opening note on the set. Yet the young Cass has her young Tristan in Connie, for whom the one-legged Jeff stands as an absurd counterpart: the real and ideal constantly collide in this play. Wagner's love-philtre becomes a bottle of whiskey. But just as Wagner's love potion 'performs the office of Fate' as in Greek tragedy,[34] whiskey and the fantastic Trilbe and Ingram become fatal agents in *Cass*. The outcome is all the grimmer for resembling parody. Here again Friel would have been well served by Siobhán McKenna, adept at transformations such as from Yeats's Old Woman to the young girl with the walk of a queen at the end of *Cathleen Ní Houlihan*. This parallels the relationship between Cass and Isolde. The latter must be visible in the former.[35]

Memory

From *Philadelphia* on, in a Friel play memory is as significant as in any of Beckett's. But in Friel memory is usually related to music. The memory sequences in *Cass* can be distinguished from Pirandello and metatheatre. They are scenes rather than mere monologues, closer to Miller's use of the flashback in *Death of a Salesman* noted in Chapter 2.[36] Cass does not indulge in memory as Gar does. As she says, 'I don't go in for the fond memory racket!' (p. 17). Her phrase is crucial; and she reverses it when she sings Thomas Moore's 'Oft in the Stilly Night', where 'Fond memories' conjure up old realities (p. 34). Up to this point, memories are far from 'fond'; when one forces itself on Cass she represses it fiercely. Because she, as it were, 'owns' the play, Cass succeeds in so arranging the scenes as to make sense of her drunken abandonment in Eden House. But in time (literally), she loses this power of control and with it her ability to keep memory at bay.

The question to be raised again at this point is: when Cass begins to listen to Trilbe and Ingram and accept that the reshaping of the past can provide a comforting version of the 'truth', is this a victory or a loss? Is this what living in postcolonial Ireland entails?

The narratives Trilbe, Ingram and under their tuition Cass create as sustaining are manifestly inventions. The word the Wagnerian pair use is 'dreams', borrowing it from Yeats's short lyric (eight lines in all), 'He Wishes for the Cloths of Heaven', where it is thrice repeated. In Yeats, the lover declares rhetorically that if he possessed the heavens' embroidered cloths he would honour her in dashing style by laying them at her feet, but because he is poor (and an artist) he has only his dreams. Yeats's intricate change of tenses is used by Cass's tempters to weave a spell, to entice her into a realm of the mind where dreams are validated and transcend such facts as poverty and worldly standards of achievement. Dreams become the basis of Cass's redemption of her wretched history. Does this mean that 'fond' memories are untrue? In *Philadelphia*, Gar is sustained by the memory of an idyllic moment spent as a boy with his father. When S. B. fails to validate the memory, Gar Private cries out to his alter ego: 'So now you know: it never happened!' (*Plays 1*, p. 95). In 'Self-Portrait' (1972), Friel himself argues that such a 'memory' is nevertheless valid. He provides an instance from his own childhood where what he remembers is denied by the facts. Then he moves on to claim existence for the *supposed* fact because 'for some reason this vivid memory is there in the storehouse of the mind'. Further, the mind had 'shuffled the pieces of verifiable truth and composed a truth of its own'.[37] Here is the root of Friel's concept of memory. It derives in part from Augustine's *Confessions*: 'It is I myself that I remember, I the mind.'[38] The joy we remember, says Augustine, relates to the good life, and 'a happy life is a rejoicing in *the truth*'.[39] For Augustine, this truth is God; for Friel, it is rather a realisation of the transcendental self. Augustine allowed that the mind can create a false memory of an event by combining two things we have sensed. The mind gathers together various images stored in the memory 'to compose *fabricated sights* by taking all sorts of things recorded from here and there and as it were sewing them together'.[40]

In an early piece of journalism 'Memories and Vagaries', Friel questioned the validity of autobiography. For him, nothing cohered in memory, as it seemed to do for writers of autobiography. 'No, there is nothing for it but *invention* and when it comes to *concocting*, I am as good as the next.'[41] Although written in a humorous context, the words I have italicised refer to the creative process, the art itself. Therefore, the dramatist Friel creates characters who, in turn, 'invent' or 'concoct' their histories via memories. Cass *re*-invents and by that means she herself becomes a projection of the creative artist. Memory is transformed into a sustaining and consoling truth. But memory is not, as for Augustine, or for the modern philosopher Paul Ricoeur, 'a specific search for truth'.[42] To Friel, it is exclusively an artistic resource. His aesthetic is erected on a dismissal of any moral issue arising here. Friel remembers school, when he '*took refuge from all external reality*, in a stubborn silence that made a fair *bid at disguising* my mediocrity'.[43] Cass, too, finally takes a similar kind of refuge and assumes a similar disguise. In this way, Cass discovers the tragic sense in its duality in the world. All those in Eden House are dreamers, although only the elect know it and find it 'good'. Eden House is a state of being rather than a place. It is a metaphor for those broken ones who aspire to becoming whole again while their new selves remain rooted in falsified memory. Such is their Fate. The external world stands framed in Cass's memory as a fallen world, cruel, distorted and hellish.

Dream versus Reality

'The past did have meaning,' decides the narrator of a Friel short story, 'It was neither reality nor dreams.'[44] Elmer Andrews uses this last phrase as subtitle of his study *The Art of Brian Friel* (1995). *Cass McGuire* builds towards this irresolution, a twilight zone which could be called a postmodern Celtic Twilight. Whatever about his personal beliefs and his philosophy of history, Yeats was an enabling force for Irish writers. He gave them licence to accept that in the quarrel between dream and reality there did not need ethically to be a winner. You could have your idealist cake and eat it too. Shadow and substance could coexist in epistemological equipoise within the Irish mind.[45] This is the direction in which Friel developed his aesthetic. In that context, a problem is something to be solved but 'a mystery is something to be witnessed and attested'.[46]

But when he was writing *Cass McGuire* Friel was acutely aware that inescapably the play was a critique of the decline in spirituality: 'The New Irish have made substantial progress on the material plane. [. . .] What occurs to me, though, is that there has been a corresponding diminution in feeling, perception & sensitivity. [. . .] One can't achieve the social position – and here lies the tragedy – and then return to the early life of the spiritual.'[47] What seems like progress is actually regression. The appearance is mistaken for the reality. In the play itself, Friel does not, of course, preach. He takes great care to bury the social critique in the characters (especially Harry and Alice) and the action (the dumping of Cass into the so-called rest home). But in his notes, Friel also frets over the conflict between 'dream' and 'reality', less a moral than a metaphysical problem: 'We live among strangers who never suspect the truth. And which – dream or actuality – is the truth [?].'[48] Friel ponders the question as if he did not know the answer. Among the themes for *Cass* he lists 'the reality of dreams – (because of the impossibility of love)'. Therefore, dreams represent a substitute. Life, he decides, is both 'dreams' and 'reality' and he sees the people in Eden House as having discovered *The Secret* (a temporary title for the play) 'that dreams are the only reality; and their dreams are entirely of their own making'. The inference is that the act of choosing a dream-life in preference to Freud's 'reality principle' is laudatory because it provides shape and form in place of intolerable chaos. Friel is questioning, as Patrick Burke has said, whether life is 'ultimately unlivable'.[49]

In a programme note for the 1967 Abbey production, Friel placed *Cass* firmly within a 'dream' which had sustained her in 'exile' in New York: 'the dream of coming back to her relations'. In the play she returns, Friel said, 'to inherit her dream'. As if rehabilitating *Cass* after the failure of the play on Broadway, Friel now described her 'tremendous courage and tenacity and generosity of spirit'. There was also her 'happy survival at a different level of experience' following her being beaten down 'by outrageous fortune' (the brief allusion to

Hamlet is startling). He denies in the programme note that Cass's final state should be thought of antithetically 'in terms of "dream" and "reality"'. In contrast to the philosopher's task, the writer's is not to define reality or 'propound a relationship between subjective and objective existence' but 'to analyse the truth of an individual'.[50] And the playwright's task, presumably, is to place on stage an efficient and moving representation of conflicted humanity. Insofar as Cass's end is tragic a cathartic resolution seems in order. Cass McGuire is one of the wretched of the earth, but pity rather than terror marks her end. Bearing in mind the 'grotesque' reference in the opening of the play (p. 7), one intuits that Friel intended that his audience would respond uncomfortably to Cass's final situation; that would be part of his aesthetic. The result would be an apportioning of blame to family or society or the gods (if any). But Friel's programme note actually *endorsed* Cass's final choice of her own truth even if it is off the map, 'has no counterpart in the world of verifiable fact', like Friel's own notion of memory. He cannot solve his problem dramatically. The power of Wagner's 'song of death' is tapped into but finally cut off, leaving an aporia at the end of *Cass McGuire*. I doubt if the play can be satisfactorily played thus today. For what does it mean to say Cass is 'happy' in her hallucinatory state? Realism keeps breaking in. We have to wait for the end of *Molly Sweeney* (1996) for Friel to set this problem right.

Crystal and Fox and the Representation of Love

Crystal and Fox marks another attempt to inspect the human figure 'among the ruins' of romantic love. Like *Cass*, it highlights the theme by foregrounding the art of theatre. Both plays prefigure the theatricalism of *Living Quarters* and *Faith Healer* (see Chapter 5). *Crystal and Fox* is a play about a travelling theatre company, in a manner of speaking it represents the very essence of theatre itself. Thespis, credited with founding the profession in ancient Greece, travelled the countryside in a cart which was probably much the same in Friel's early days, even if the cart was motorised. Strolling players – as Shakespeare knew them in Elizabethan England and introduced into *Hamlet* – were always to be revered and feared in equal measure.[51] The English police who enter *Crystal and Fox* looking for Fox's son refer to the players as 'Bloody gypsies. Same all over.'[52] In Ireland, dozens of companies, known as 'fit-ups',[53] continued to tour the countryside until the 1960s, with many very successful actors and their families involved, the D'Altons, Carrickfords, O'Rourkes and others, including the family of Cyril Cusack, who played Friel's Fox Melarkey. The most famous was probably Anew McMaster's fit-up, which flourished in the 1950s and in which Harold Pinter learnt his trade.[54] Friel's play focused on the last days of such a fit-up.

Of its very nature, *Crystal and Fox*, named for the wife-and-husband owners of the travelling company The Fox Melarkey Show, is metatheatre at its most basic. A play-within-the-play is to be expected. In fact, the play itself opens 'during a brief interval before the final episode of their drama, *The Doctor's Story*' (p. 11), and we meet the cast and the manager Fox backstage. The atmosphere of an ongoing performance is immediately created. For example, urging on his troupe to return to a restless audience, Fox cries: 'They're a noisy pack of bailiffs so belt it out a bit more. Plenty of guts' (p. 12). The play-within-the-play, although something of a send-up of the film *A Nun's Story* (1959), is less a parody than a travesty made wretched by the poor casting forced on it by Fox Melarkey himself, who, it emerges, is gradually sabotaging his own business. The real question must be: why would a man sabotage his own livelihood? 'It is his only family. He is nothing without it.'[55]

At first, Friel thought his theme was 'community'. He was looking at the troupe as metaphor for society, where individuals subordinated selfish aims in the service of the ensemble. But then it became apparent that it was not, in itself, enough: 'the story of the decline of a touring company who have seen better days' was too anodyne.[56] Friel was then confessedly in complete confusion over the direction of the play. Why was the company 'disintegrating'? By 4 December 1967, he had pushed himself to a reply: 'They are disintegrating because Fox loves them so much, he kills them.' Reformulated, this becomes: 'Why does Fox destroy his own show? Because he loves it; because it is his life.'

Now Friel had his theme. The focus lay in the psychology of a complex character who, for reasons not apparent to himself, much less to his wife Crystal, his son Gabriel and the rest of the company, is bent on betrayal. Pursuing this line of thought, Friel sees Fox as simultaneously impelled towards self-destruction and having 'extravagant dreams' *for* the company, 'loving and killing' at the same time. This leads him to cite a crucial line from Wilde's *The Ballad of Reading Gaol*: 'Yet each man kills the thing he loves.' The question remained, 'why?' As in *Cass McGuire*, distorted love would drive a tragicomedy.

Following Beckett, recent dramatists such as Alan Ayckbourn and Michael Frayn have shown that tragedy is best communicated nowadays through comedy.[57] Friel worked in a similar spirit. Here again he combined the traditional Abbey comedy such as Lennox Robinson's ever-popular *Drama at Inish* (1933) with modernist metadrama to create tragicomedy.[58] Using comedy, he knew he could be 'deadly serious all the time'.[59] So it is with the ridiculous melodrama Fox's company stages, set in a hospital in darkest Africa, which gets more absurd as the competent actors are forced out of the company and Fox improvises with unsuitable substitutes. It is hilarious, but we wonder what is going on. In wrecking his business piecemeal Fox displays some form of breakdown. To say he is evil is to rush to judgement; yet what Fox cumulatively does to his own people can only ultimately be called evil. Everything he does is somehow connected to his relationship with his wife Crystal, the love of his life. In a note he made to himself while struggling with the play, Friel said that Fox 'has passed beyond human relationships – except Crystal's. And his error is in the belief in the quality & durability of his/her mutual loyalty & love.'[60] To speak of 'error' in this context is to speak of the tragic *hamartia*. But Friel insisted that 'the tragedy must be kept at arm's length – even at the very end when nothing is left'.[61] But the tragedy must still be felt. Richard Pine's admiration for Fox's courage in dismantling 'the hierarchy and affiliations of his family' seems misplaced.[62] Such 'courage' reads more like hubris.

Friel so structures the play that the onus falls mainly on Fox. He makes Crystal subordinate, although she takes pride of place in the title. Like Grace in *Faith Healer* (1979), she lacks autonomy: the woman is merely an object within the private world of the thinking male. Crystal will remonstrate with Fox – 'what's got into you?' (p. 21) – when she sees how he is sabotaging the company. She is present when the enraged El Cid openly calls Fox 'twisted as a bloody corkscrew!' (p. 20) and she fails to see the truth of the accusation. She is destined to stand by while Fox pulls their life together down around them in ruins. Their son Gabriel's sudden return after five years' exile provides another example of Fox's total isolation. This returning 'prodigal son' (p. 37), unlike the returning Owen in *Translations* (1980), is a catalyst. Gabriel is on the run from the police for a violent crime committed in Manchester. To Crystal's horror, the police, 'acting on information received', take him away to prison. Fox later tells her he was the informer. Was this the truth? It seems not. But why would Fox blacken himself in the eyes of his beloved wife? This is the mystery Friel picks at in the play, the mystery of evil, although, in effect, Fox does not seem to know why he does what he does. Terry Eagleton calls evil 'obscene enjoyment', the 'sneering cackle of those who believe that they have seen through everything, yet who perversely rejoice in the gimcrack, kitschy nature of it all.'[63] This is the language of melodrama – a 'sneering cackle' is good where villains are being identified on stage, the site of the 'gimcrack' and the 'kitschy'. And so, the definition may fit.

One thinks of Iago in *Othello*, but he is not running a travelling theatre. In Friel's *Crystal and Fox*, evil takes the form of the acting out of Fox's impossible dream of turning back time and rediscovering Eden. It transpires that Fox, in middle-age crisis, is so bored and tired with his career that all he wants is to get back to a golden time when he and Crystal were young, carefree and in love. It is a mad scenario but only an exaggeration of the tragedy people can create from the frustration and panic arising from fear of death. It is clear Fox loves Crystal with a romantic yearning based on their first meeting and early fulfilled life together. But he has come to a recognition of the futility of what he is doing: 'Weary of all this . . . this making-do, of conning people that know they're being conned' (p. 40). In an echo of Edmond Tyrone's mystical speech[64] in *Long Day's Journey into Night* (1956), Fox recalls a moment of truth: 'Once, maybe twice in your life, the fog lifts, and you get a glimpse, an intuition; and suddenly you know that this can't be all there is to it – there has to be something better than this' (p. 54). O'Neill's play was revived at the Abbey in 1967, the year before *Crystal and Fox* premiered. Friel was to draw on *Long Day's Journey*, that classic study of the older actor in crisis, again in *Faith Healer*. Its tragic power lends clarity to the more difficult situation Fox finds himself in at the end of *Crystal and Fox.*

As the play moves towards its strange and powerful ending Fox is about to sell off his theatre company, while he and Crystal are back where they were as young lovers, on the road together. Fox has a golden memory of his and Crystal's early life together, a moment by the sea, 'Just the two of us' (p. 61). This is what he was after: a return home to that ideal time. But the epiphany fails, as it must. As in *Cass McGuire*, one cannot go home again. In Friel's work 'exile' is a permanent psychic state. Crystal keeps thinking of their son Gabriel and of his certain imprisonment in Manchester. Her attention can no longer be uniquely focused on Fox. In a drunken state, she dares to question him about the wreckage he made of the theatre company and in passing reveals she has already guessed Fox poisoned Pedro's performing dog. Somehow Fox is shocked at her knowing this and still loving him. '*As if he were in a dream*' (p. 70), he lies and tells her he also betrayed their son to the English police for money (which the audience knows is untrue). This is Fox's last and maddest act of self-destruction. Appalled, Crystal leaves him on the open road, with the tatters of their theatrical regalia around them, her last words being to call Fox 'Evil' and unknowable (p. 73).

Left alone, the defeated Fox soliloquises that 'love alone isn't enough now, my Crystal, it's not, my love, not enough at all, not nearly enough': perhaps the key line in the whole play. As he turns the rickety wheel of fortune Fox sings a version of a nursery rhyme, 'A hunting we will go,' adapting it to the absent Crystal seen as the hunter of the fox: 'You'll catch no fox and put him in a box' (p. 74). Adopting a '*Fairground voice*' he then barks out his invitation to play the game of chance, seen as a metaphor of life itself, 'because the whole thing's fixed, my love, fixed-fixed-fixed [. . .] but who am I to cloud your bright eyes or kill your belief that love is all' (p. 74). Determinism rules all. These are the closing lines of the play, heard only by the audience. Fox is left alone to hitch-hike on a road to nowhere. Dream and reality cannot be reconciled.

As in *Cass McGuire*, Friel is hard on his audience. He wanted to confront them with despair without providing release or catharsis. Referring to the fictional audience attending the travelling show, *The Doctor's Story*, Fox had exhorted his unfortunate players: 'Belt it out. And plenty of tears. All the hoors [whores] want is a happy ending' (p. 14). Friel denies his real audience such luxury. In his working notes, he put to himself what the 'message' (a 1960s term) was to be, and it is bleak: 'Man is absolutely alone. There is no Crystal, never was; no audience, never was. The drama & the jokes were attempts to fill the void; but nobody, not Fox, was ever fooled by this.'[65] Friel was resolute in his determination to stick it to his audience. Time has shown that this is not a wise move. Neither *Cass* nor *Crystal and Fox* has worn well. Neither is staged much nowadays. But both show how serious Friel was in developing an aesthetic of modern tragedy. They provide an important extension of his 1967 essay 'The Theatre of Hope and Despair' by serving to clarify Friel's idea of a theatre. Without them we cannot fully appreciate the more assured achievements of the later plays or of the Friel canon in general.

CHAPTER 4

SPEAKING OUT: *THE FREEDOM OF THE CITY* AND *VOLUNTEERS*

Art enacts the history of the culture that makes it.

– Howard Jacobson, 'Dying Like a Gentleman', *Whatever It Is, I Don't Like It* (London: Bloomsbury, 2012)[1]

Introduction

In the later 1960s, as we have seen in the preceding chapter, Friel showed much interest in metatheatre. This self-consciousness, the mark of a writer not content to remain a success but determined over a lifetime project to refine his work as art, persisted into the 1970s with fascinating results. *Lovers* (1967) was a commercial success on Broadway, in stark contrast to *The Loves of Cass McGuire*. *Lovers* stands as guide to what Friel was now devoted. It contains two one-acts, unrelated except by ironic juxtaposition. One, with two teenage lovers, is entitled *Winners* although they die; the other is called *Losers* because it studies middle-aged lovers who survive into pointlessness. In each it is the design, the special structure, which leaps out as introduction to *The Freedom of the City*. For *Losers* (the first in order of playing), the stage is divided into three equal areas representing an upstairs bedroom, a kitchen/living-room and a backyard in a terraced house. The design resembles that for *Philadelphia* and Miller's *Death of a Salesman*, promising fluidity of action and a use of space which dramatises consciousness. *Losers* offers Brechtian alienation without a hint of political analysis. It has its own dramatic merits but it is *Winners* which paves the way for Friel's political theatre.

In dedicating the published text of *Lovers* to Tyrone Guthrie, Friel immediately declared his vote for the 'bare stage' Guthrie championed. Between the two Commentators presiding over *Winners*, Friel calls for a raised platform to represent '*the hill that overlooks the town of Ballymore*' (p. 5). The platform is pentagonal, accessible by '*four or five shallow steps all round*', and bare except for two high-backed chairs for the Commentators. Thus, Friel wanted spatially to highlight the two protagonists, who are separated from the town and on view on an altar of sacrifice. The Commentators, called MAN and WOMAN in the text, in their late fifties and dressed formally in '*good dark clothes*', appear on a lower level, cut off from the young lovers, aged seventeen. The setting defines *their* alienation. The Commentators are the very opposite of Brechtian narrators: their bourgeois nature precludes them from knowing anything but banalities about the dead youngsters. This division between private and public will reappear in *Freedom*, the setting reflecting the division in similar style. The effect of the juxtaposition of Commentators and lovers, then, is to create irony in the modernist style. The gap between them must be filled by audience awareness.

Brecht, who established irony on the modern stage in 1928 with the success of *The Threepenny Opera*, used the phrase 'complex seeing' for his technique of getting audiences to think twice and called it 'the epic style'.[2] Brecht's Alienation-effect implies breaking the illusion so that *time* is allowed for an audience to reassess what is being viewed.[3] Even though Friel's pursuit of 'complex seeing' is not political in *Winners*, the scenes showing the vulnerability of the lovers certainly deepen the ironic response. The time difference between the public world of Commentators at an inquest and the private world of the lovers engenders irony as we realise that the teenagers are actually, in 'real' time, dead.

The Freedom of the City is a play dictated by real events, those that occurred on Bloody Sunday, 30 January 1972, in Derry city, 'the worst massacre of British citizens by British troops since Peterloo in 1819'.[4] Friel himself was present on this day. It was, he said later, 'really a shattering experience that the British army, this disciplined instrument, would go in as they did that time and shoot thirteen people'.[5] Equally distressing was the subsequent *Widgery Report* published on 18 April 1972 exonerating the army. To Friel as to so many people at the time, this *Report* by the Lord Chief Justice was as 'shattering' as the killings themselves. 'We still have some kind of belief that the law is above reproach. We still believe that the academy is above reproach in some way, don't we?'[6] The rhetorical question characteristically hangs in the air.

For the artist, the problem with such experiences is how to transmute them into significant form. It has boldly been said that *The Freedom of the City* 'marks the beginning of Friel's maturity as a major modern dramatist'.[7] Equally it has been said that it is one-sided and polemical: 'an entertaining piece of unconvincing propaganda'.[8] In New York in 1974, the critic Clive Barnes dismissed it as anti-British, while Irish reviewers, although sympathetic to the perceived attack on British injustice, failed to appreciate Friel's use of Brechtian technique. Because of this sharp division of viewpoint, *The Freedom of the City* 'can be extolled for its virtues or condemned for its faults all depending on your political or religious persuasion'.[9] The debate goes on. As so much time has passed since the play's premiere at the Abbey Theatre on 20 February 1973, followed by a fresh production at the Royal Court (directed by Albert Finney) one week later, the actual historical events on which *The Freedom of the City* may be said to be based have come into clearer focus and dissolved certain long-lasting grievances. The *Widgery Report* has been discredited: The Saville Inquiry has, in its comprehensive report in 2010, vindicated the claims of nationalists in exonerating all fourteen victims on the civil rights march on Bloody Sunday of 'any wrong-doing'.[10] David Cameron fully apologised in Parliament on 15 June 2010 for the terrible injustice, adding: 'Bloody Sunday was a tragedy for the bereaved and the wounded, and a catastrophe for the people of Northern Ireland.'[11] All of these developments have made space for Friel's play to be discussed less as a docudrama than as an extraordinary piece of modern tragic theatre.

For Friel, the argument over whether or to what extent *The Freedom of the City* was in its conception an 'engaged' play like Yeats's *Cathleen Ní Houlihan* was not the worrying factor; of course, it is just as engaged. Why write it otherwise? What concerned him afterwards was that it may have been too blunt, too careless of the need to subordinate appropriately the demands of the public to those of the private or artistic conscience.[12] Friel would have favoured Eliot's impersonal theory of creativity: 'the more perfect the artist, the more completely separate in him will be the man who suffers and the mind which creates' and the more 'perfectly' will the mind 'digest and transmute' the material and the 'passions' arising.[13] In an interview in 1973 just before the Abbey premiere of *The Freedom of the City*, he echoed Eliot: 'It's the old problem of the distinction between the mind that suffers and the man who creates. The trouble [. . .] is that people are going to find something immediate in it, some kind of reportage,' which he denied.[14] If anything, *The Freedom of the City* exhibits signs of over-control.

The Play and the Play-within-the-Play

Although Friel was already thinking in 1970 of a play about poverty in Northern Ireland and the civil rights movement founded in 1968, he made no progress at that time. He returned to the topic after Bloody Sunday and the publication of the *Widgery Report*.[15] It was the actual text he set out to subvert. The wording of the *Report* is drawn upon repeatedly in the stage tribunal which sits in judgement on the three fictional characters at the heart of *The Freedom of the City* who are shot as 'terrorists'. In outlining his interpretation of the terms of reference, Lord Widgery insisted that the Inquiry was 'essentially a fact-finding exercise' and that its task was 'to try and form an objective view of the events' of Bloody Sunday without making 'moral judgements'. These actual phrases recur in Friel's text as the nameless Judge outlines his procedures.[16] Similarly, at the end of the play, three out of the four conclusions Friel's Judge offers stem from the *Report*, although appearing more outrageous because the points are summarised and edited somewhat in the style of 'translation' Friel was later to provide Owen with in *Translations*. Thus, Widgery's opening sentences of the

'Summary' are added to as indicated in the words in square brackets below:

> There would have been no deaths in Londonderry on 30 January if those who organised the illegal march had not thereby created a highly dangerous situation [and had the speakers on the platform not incited the mob to such a fever] in which a clash between demonstrators and the security forces was almost inevitable. (*Report*, p. 97)

This is point one of four conclusions made by Friel's Judge.[17] Further exoneration of the soldiers follows from Widgery: 'There is no reason to suppose that the soldiers would have opened fire if they had not been fired upon first.' (*Report*, p. 99) This barefaced statement is given verbatim by Friel's Judge (point three). Friel's second point takes the sentence which follows the one just cited, neatly inserting a note of irony into the official defence of a soldiery 'aggressive' and 'quick in decision' from training, although some soldiers showed 'more restraint than others':

> 2. There is no evidence to support the accusation that the security forces acted without restraint or that their arrest force behaved punitively. (*Plays 1*, p. 168)

This is a mischievous 'translation'.[18] Friel's fourth point goes further. The *Report* says: 'None of the deceased or wounded is proved to have been shot whilst handling a firearm or bomb' (p. 99). Friel makes the Judge say the opposite: 'I must accept the evidence of eye-witnesses and various technical experts that the three deceased were armed when they emerged from the Guildhall, and that two of them at least [. . .] used their arms' (*Plays 1*, p. 168). The audience, like the reader of the play text, knows for a 'fact' that this is simply not true. Here lies the kernel of Friel's play.

In writing a play which obliquely, although powerfully, offered a critique of the calamity which was Bloody Sunday, Friel attempted to create distance by changing the time, the place and the circumstances in which his representative characters lose their lives. It seems clear that moving the date of the events back two years to 1970 (and giving a new date, 10 February) was pointless; nobody now sees *The Freedom of the City* as referring to any event other than Bloody Sunday and the ensuing Tribunal of Inquiry (21 February–14 March 1972). Setting the action in the Guildhall in Derry, however, was a masterstroke. In actuality, no trouble took place in Guildhall Square, much less in the Guildhall itself, on Bloody Sunday. The civil rights march from the Creggan estate was originally planned to have its destination in Guildhall Square where speakers, including Bernadette Devlin, MP, would address the crowd but the security forces blocked access and the march was re-routed to Free Derry Corner in the Bogside area. Here, Devlin tried to calm the panicking attendance when the initial pressure came from the army with the cry, 'Stand your ground. [. . .] We outnumber the army fifteen to one.'[19] Friel makes use of this moment. He has a nameless Woman address a meeting offstage in Guildhall Square, and when it is interrupted by the noise of 'approaching tanks', she shouts: 'Stand your ground! [. . .] This is your city!' (*Plays 1*, p. 111). Likewise, at the play's opening, Friel makes use of the iconic image of Fr Edward Daly waving a handkerchief as he tended the bodies of the three central characters.[20] The TV Commentator, named as Liam O'Kelly, clearly parodies Kevin O'Kelly, a Radio Telefís Éireann (RTÉ) reporter who delivered the actual commentary on the funerals of the thirteen men killed. While shifting the time and place, Friel still incorporates figures from the day and its aftermath. This technique provides a paradigm of the way Friel structured the play. One never can be certain when he is inventing.

The stage design could be called geometric. Overhanging and framing the action on stage are the 'battlements', an image of Derry's walls, historically associated with the victory of the Williamite loyalists in 1689. On any stage, speaking from on high confers a godlike status. On the Greek stage, the *deus-ex-machina* came and went from the roof of the scene building, striking awe, presumably, into the audience. On Shakespeare's stage, a speech from the balcony was likewise godlike, for example, Prospero enters '*above, invisible*' in Act 3, Scene 3, of

The Tempest to observe the behaviour of his enemies, on whom he plans revenge. In Friel's *The Freedom of the City*, the Judge speaks regally from on high and so, too, does the Priest, that other nameless authority figure whose bias becomes comically clear as the play progresses. The main area of the stage is given over to the Mayor's Parlour within the Guildhall. Although realistically furnished as a council chamber, the Guildhall setting is clearly symbolic. The Parlour is the inner sanctum of power. This main space has both a different location and time scheme than the Inquiry which frames it. The Inquiry took place in Coleraine, some thirty miles east of Derry city, and its hearings began three weeks after Bloody Sunday. The time scheme within the Mayor's Parlour is 'real time', carefully noted by those on stage: not much over one hour. But the geometric shape Friel imposes on the narrative, where scenes alternate between present and past (sometimes the Inquiry is 'now', then successively the Mayor's Parlour) is managed within a space where concentric circles emanate from the fixed, realistic area. The Sociologist, the Television Commentator and the Balladeer, these 'commentators' who try to mediate the meaning of what the audience sees, all use the apron because at one remove from what actually occurs in the central space. This is the centre of a web. One of the three marchers who share this space, the astute Skinner, sings the nursery rhyme, 'Will you come into my parlour, said the spider to the fly' (p. 138), clearly implying awareness that they are in a trap. Friel's initial title for the play was *The Mayor's Parlour*. To use Anthony Roche's term, the 'politics of space' follow from such imagery.[21] It is literally impossible to have two time schemes, past and present, coexist spatially; it is likewise contradictory to ask that two places thirty miles apart can be seen within a single framework. Yet theatre can achieve such absurdities. The individual imagination can conceive them and the collective imagination can accept them, as Samuel Johnson forcefully argued in his day: 'The truth is that the spectators are always in their senses and know, from the first act to the last, that the stage is only a stage.'[22] It is all down to theatrical convention.

Yet the general question of illusion/delusion remains. In a section on Brecht in *The Empty Space*, Peter Brook raises it again: 'When Brecht stated there was something in the theatre called illusion, the implication was that there was something else that was not illusion. So illusion became opposed to reality [to establish which is which].'[23] Brook himself is clearly not against illusion, and he does not believe Brecht was either, only 'the heavy-handed Illusion that does not begin to convince us'. What is needed is the illusion 'that is composed by the flash of quick and changing impressions' which 'keeps the dart of imagination at play'. That is it exactly. Further, this series of 'impressions' can be 'equally a series of alienations: each rupture is a subtle provocation and a call to thought'.[24] Thus was *The Freedom of the City* written for the stage.

The heart of the matter, as in *Winners*, is embodied in the separation of the three named, main characters from the world outside the Mayor's Parlour. We know they are to die; correction, we know they are dead. How can we hold in mind this blatant contradiction as we come in and out of their scenes? Stephen Watt puts a different question: 'What remains uncertain, however, is how and why their shootings occurred.'[25] I do not believe audiences are left in any doubt on that point following the opening scene. Every member of the audience is a witness and could, if pressed, give an unambiguous answer to the question of 'how', just like a narrator in a Brechtian 'Street Scene'. The indeterminacy lies more in the 'why'. Again, a political answer seems readily available once we attend to the opening remarks of the Judge and bear them in mind for the rest of the play. He speaks of limiting the Inquiry to 'that period of time when these people *came together, seized* possession of a civic building, and openly *defied* the security forces' (*Plays 1*, p. 109, emphases added). Each of the three verbs here is belied by what is to be seen once the three characters ('these people') enter and play out the scenes in the Mayor's Parlour. Further, the Judge declares that the 'facts' he hopes to 'garner' during the Tribunal may indicate one of two things. Here, we may expect him to offer straightforward alternatives, guilt and innocence, although he has also just said that the Tribunal 'is in no sense a court of justice'. What he *does* say is ominous: that the garnered facts 'may indicate that the deceased were callous terrorists who had planned to seize the Guildhall weeks before the events of February 10th', *or* 'the facts may indicate that the misguided scheme occurred to them on that very day while they listened to revolutionary speeches' (pp. 109–10). Either way, the deceased are *a priori* 'terrorists' who acted deliberately. 'After such knowledge, what forgiveness?'[26] The three 'people' were shot because they were deemed to be terrorists. As Richard Pine puts it, Friel 'counterpoints the tribunal's "objective" approach with the "subjective" text required in order to make "sense" out of the whole event and its hinterland of hope and despair'.[27] But this is achieved through the illusory use of time and space.

In various ways, those on the periphery of the three main characters alienate the audience by their myth-making (the Balladeer), their hypocrisy (the Priest), their lip-smacking unctuousness (RTÉ Commentator) and their analysts (the sociologist, the pathologist and the forensic scientist). To excess, Friel demonstrates, with a certain amount of glee, how useless most commentary is, how beside the point if not downright absurd. In addition, the sociologist Dodds seems like a walking parody of academic discourse. Parachuted into the action, he never once refers to Derry and seems to know nothing of the deaths of the main characters. It has been said (Pine, McGrath) that Friel draws on Oscar Lewis's *La Vida* (1966) for the discourse on the culture of poverty. So be it. But the Derry hinterland is not and never was commensurate with Puerto Rico, as Friel well knew in writing his play. Dodds's discourse is thus thoroughly alienating and theatrically serves as such.

The main characters, Michael, Lily and Skinner, enter the Mayor's Parlour as refugees from the CS gas shot by the British army to break up the civil rights march. Their entry upon what Skinner – always the first to assess a situation – calls 'the holy of holies itself!' (p. 116) is therefore adventitious. Once inside and recovering from the CS gas, all three begin to relax. Then commences a play-within-the-play sealed off from the world outside. It is important to note that none of the three mentions shooting, other than of water cannon, rubber bullets and CS gas. Therefore, the sense of horror which overwhelmed the eyewitnesses on Bloody Sunday is simply not present. Friel assumes the audience's familiarity with 'reality'. Instead, an atmosphere of carnival begins to be established as Skinner, the playboy of the trio, responds in delight to the accident of their delivery into opportunities for making free with the forbidden facilities. As master of ceremonies, Skinner lavishly supplies drink and cigars.

Skinner is perhaps Friel's best portrait of the outsider, an existential figure of the time, 'a man who has awakened to chaos'.[28] He is the playwright's voice, to a considerable extent. Lily calls him a 'clown' (p. 151), and he lives up to that description in his subversive antics and performance (the dressing-up, the telephone conversations, the fake council meeting he chairs). He is glib; he is flippant; but he is more medieval trickster than harmless fool. He is of the school of Augusto Boal. Michael calls him 'a trouble-maker', would not be surprised if he was 'a revolutionary', and ultimately identifies him among 'the hooligans' (pp. 132, 138). The latter term says more of Michael than of Skinner, because it is the official word used in the *Widgery Report* for Bogside protesters, or what Éamonn McCann called 'marching fodder', and is thus contaminated.[29] Skinner can see through Michael's high-minded idealism ('Shite') and can appreciate the genuineness of Lily's real motive for marching. He '*switches to flippancy*' (p. 155) whenever he finds himself being too serious about the political situation, but he knows, too, how to make a real 'gesture' within an unreal situation (p. 163). His sense of play is thus a double-edged sword, although a 'ceremonial' one (p. 161). Lily is a better foil – no pun intended – for Skinner than Michael, because she understands carnival and accepts its 'lavish and luxurious goings-on' (Guthrie's phrase for good theatre)[30] and goes along 'just for the hell of it' (p. 144), although the phrase be ironic. Virtually Lily's last line before exiting to her death is: 'Lord, I enjoyed that. The crack was good' (p. 166). Skinner brings out the best in her, which he acknowledges with the kiss that drops all facetiousness to establish a son-mother bond between them before they face the 'real' world again and find it deadly.

Freedom of the City as Theatre of Commitment

When he submitted *The Freedom of the City* to Tomás Mac Anna at the Abbey Friel knew what he was doing. Mac Anna had turned *The Loves of Cass McGuire* into a success a few years earlier. Now with a far more political play he was the best Irish director for the job. Long an admirer of Brecht, he had staged *The Life of Galileo* at the Queen's in 1956, 'regarded by many as a break-through in lighting, production and acting'.[31] In 1967 Mac Anna designed a successful quasi-Brechtian production of *The Borstal Boy*, adapted from Behan's memoir. It was to reach Broadway in 1970, where it won both a Tony award for best foreign play and the New York Drama Critics' Circle Award for best play 1970–71.[32] In 1971 Mac Anna co-devised a satirical sketch based on Brecht's 1920s' style of revue.[33] *A State of Chassis* angered Northerners when it premiered in the Peacock on 16 September 1970. Perhaps the caricature of Bernadette Devlin was a *gestus* too far: Éamonn McCann, very much present, assaulted stage and players, crying foul, and had to be physically removed from the theatre, but not before he had informed the audience that 'the people here are total hypocrites'.[34] In the years ahead Friel too would come around to some such view, although never so rudely expressed.

In the event, Mac Anna's production of *The Freedom of the City* – which I saw – was well judged; its political point of view was honestly sustained; its Brechtian ironies were well embodied in performances, interpretation and staging. The set by Alan Barlow was far more in line with Friel's text than the 1999 revival directed by Conall Morrison (which used some ten minutes of film dealing with the 1972 civil rights march and its disruption).[35] Dublin reviewers of the 1973 premiere failed to understand or appreciate the Brechtian irony and so found the play itself less than satisfactory. But the discerning, such as the committed theatre-goer and academic John Devitt, could accept what Friel was doing: '[I]t was responding to a specific occasion. Bloody Sunday was devastating, it was really difficult. [. . .] It was a bad, bad business. But the play addressed that, and did it in a very interesting kind of way.'[36] That way was Brecht's way.

Friel was aware that the context in which *The Freedom of the City* was premiered was as political as it could be. After Bloody Sunday, the Irish Republican Army (IRA) campaign of violence in the North and in Britain escalated into increasingly horrific intensity. Any serious writer was bound to consider his/her artistic responsibility. A few years earlier, Friel had pondered the fashion for docudrama and the trend for exposing social and political corruption. It was not a *movement*, he declared. Those diverse dramatists – Rolf Hochhuth, Peter Weiss, et al. – did not constitute a movement, 'which implies a period of stability and uniformity'. Instead, 'their only unity is dissension. Their only uniformity is their *commitment* to revolt and rejection.'[37] At that stage of his career, however, Friel would likely have been politically on the opposite side, although well aware of the debate. In America in 1967, where Friel delivered his lecture on 'The Theatre of Hope and Despair', Eric Bentley, translator of Brecht's plays into English and drama critic for the *New Republic*, also raised the subject. Worried about the trendiness of 'commitment' among writers and its too-easy identification with 'alienation', Bentley preferred to draw them together: '*after* being Alienated, and *because* one is Alienated, one the more easily Commits oneself'.[38] Bentley's point was that the popular sense of 'commitment' exposes its obviousness: 'You could have a viable play against J. Edgar Hoover, but not one in favour of him' (p. 198). However, Rolf Hochhuth's controversial play *The Deputy* (1964), condemning Pope Pius XII for his non-intervention in the Nazi's extermination of the Jews, was biased in a necessary way, 'because the roots of the Hochhuth play are in a sense of outrage pre-existing in the playwright and other people'. The drama is in the outrage. The term Bentley wishes to employ as distinguishing Theatre of Commitment is 'polemical', and this offers the best definition of Friel's play. The aim in *Freedom of the City*, as in *The Deputy*, is 'to recreate the author's sense of outrage' by deliberately avoiding well-rounded characterisation and using instead 'enactors of the outrageous on the one hand, and, on the other hand, victims of outrage and rebels against outrage' (p. 224). As with Brecht, whom Bentley associates here with Hochhuth (being German and having Erwin Piscator for director), Friel too has in *The Freedom of the City* contributed to genuine (rather than merely fashionable) Theatre of Commitment. Events had converted him. One can see why Ulick O'Connor entitled his fiery pamphlet *Brian Friel: Crisis and Commitment* (1989).

But is this question as simple as Bentley implies? The aim of Drama of Commitment, he says, is 'to get people to commit themselves' (p. 226). To what, ideally? *The Freedom of the City* situated itself awkwardly before Dublin, London and New York audiences in 1973–4 as a play stating the unthinkable: that the British army cynically and brutally gunned down civilians on a protest march *and* that the Lord Chief Justice saw no wrong in this, finding the victims culpable. It is blatantly not a case of Brechtian rationalisation: 'Things are thus, need they be so?' Things *were* thus, incredibly, but they were 'bound' to continue so if 'normality' was to continue. Whoever is in charge, whoever is ultimately responsible (not present on stage) is, like Pius XII, given what Bentley calls 'an acquiescence that is really *carte blanche*' (p. 218). So, public protest of some form is called for. This was the age of the Vietnam War and of the civil rights movement; it was the age also of the Living Theatre and audience involvement. It was out of Northern Ireland's civil rights movement that Fiel's play was born. But the response it called for was emphatically not more street marches.

At about the same time as Bentley, Theodor Adorno wrote his essay 'Commitment'. Here Adorno quarrelled with Benjamin's endorsement of Brecht and argued for a new way of viewing political drama. In short, Adorno rejected Brecht's way in order to champion Beckett's art as dealing with a 'highly concrete historical reality'.[39] Does this make Friel a follower of Adorno?[40] In general, Bentley's understanding of 'commitment' is more useful for an interpretation of Friel's play as a whole simply because Bentley was a man of the theatre and Adorno was not. Bentley tells us that 'what Brecht wishes to do is not flatly either to please people or to instruct them [the classical binaries]. It is something closer to waking them up.' The later Brecht included a drama with 'a negative emotional content', showing impatience and anger, as in 'the movement toward defiance and resistance' found in *Mother Courage*.[41] Friel, too, was defiant and searching among the ruins for that assertion of nobility in human endurance which signals the justification of art. He too could hit a humanistic note in concert with a political. This dialectic is literally central to the play-within-the-play. At play's end, the institutional political apparatus has outrageously vindicated army violence.

Friel's Judge delivers his provocative summation from on high (the 'battlements') while the three accused stand 'as before' downstage, '*staring out, their hands above their heads*', unflinching even after the sound of gunfire which annihilates them. The 'as before' refers not to the play's opening, when the three bodies were 'grotesquely' prone downstage (p. 107), but to the opening of Act 2, the moment *after* they were shot. At that point, in defiance both of realism and of literary decorum, Friel invested each of his three victims with a rhetoric out of character. This is the real, as opposed to the ironic, 'freedom' bestowed on them in the play by Skinner; Friel boldly steps in in order to do it. It is his gesture. Equally, at the end, as they stare out into the audience, where the sound of applause will echo that of the guns, realism is defied in the name of human dignity. The three should be on the floor. There are few things in the modern theatre more moving than this final image of defiance, which anticipates the end of Beckett's *Catastrophe* (1982). Thus is the text of the Widgery Inquiry wholly discredited by Friel's own text and the sheer power of theatre.

Volunteers

Friel himself seemed stunned into silence by *The Freedom of the City*, as if figuratively he stood in spirit alongside his three fictional victims, staring out into the abyss. It took a few years before he could address his audience again. *Volunteers* is a bitter, uncompromising play filled with gallows humour and outspoken politics. It has had an unhappy life in the theatre. Submitted to the Abbey, it failed to gain Mac Anna as director; the premiere in March 1975 was directed by Robert Gillespie, who was unable to make the play meaningful. It was received 'with almost universal put-downs by the critics of the national newspapers'.[42] Damage was done. Attendances fell off and the Royal Court decided not to do a London production. Seamus Heaney's review in the *Times Literary Supplement* – to be discussed below – was an important but unavailing defence. This marked a low ebb in Friel's fortunes. The situation was that until he had the theatre company he required, in Field Day, politics was not a theme a Southern Irish audience wanted from him, however experimental the dramatic form might be.

Language, Image, Theme

The text of *Volunteers* is subtle and nuanced, every line and stage direction written with remarkable precision. F. C. McGrath describes it as 'a play intimately concerned with the functions of language and narrative'.[43] Anthony Roche, while bowing somewhat to the precedence of David Storey's *The Contractor* (1969) as Friel's posited model, sees it as more concerned with setting and 'work structure' than with language.[44] Richard Pine sees *Volunteers* as pursuing 'a relentless but remorseful discourse by providing a bridge, for the critic at least, between *The Freedom of the City* and *Faith Healer*'.[45] I think thorough a better epithet than relentless to apply to Friel's work. Neither am I much impressed by *The Contractor*. I should prefer to invoke Pinter's *No Man's Land*, premiered in the same year as *Volunteers*, because each is about a landscape of power and betrayal. Both writers sought for, or accepted, the image inspiration offered as the germ of a new play. Pinter would imagine a couple of characters in a room, perhaps, and query what their meeting signified. Like Friel, 'he remained haunted by characters of no fixed spiritual abode'.[46] Only, Friel's *donné* usually led to larger vistas.

An image came to Friel at his desk in September 1973: 'Conor, his wife, his crying children frozen in a group against the Foe/Peelers. And then – the group still frozen – Conor steps outside it'[47]: an existentialist moment. It came to nothing. If one opens the text of *Volunteers* (published 1979), one will find not a single direct link back to this image. Instead, an image of excavation presented itself, an archaeological dig, which proved luckier. Excavation implied history, tradition; what fuelled the embryonic play was anger. Friel was angry with the Republic for its failure even to debate the future of the North, much less shape it. He needed to 'disparage' the complacent Irish society in the South. Even for some politicians, as Diarmaid Ferriter reports, 'carnage in Northern Ireland seemed to offer an opportunity for pious and patently false assertions about the tolerance of the Republic.'[48] There was duplicity at all levels of public discourse on the North. When asked in 1972 by the British ambassador how seriously reunification of Ireland mattered to the Irish people, the Taoiseach of the day, Jack Lynch, replied, in effect, that they could not care less.[49] A few years earlier, Friel could look upon such hypocrisy with satirical humour: *The Mundy Scheme* (1969) was benign, although thorough, in its exposure of political opportunism in the Republic.[50] But *The Mundy Scheme* was a farce, a form unthinkable for Friel in the wake of Bloody Sunday. He would have to find a way, a form, of unifying his satirical impulse with his tragic sense if he were – like Ibsen in *An Enemy of the People* (1882) – to create a vengeful play exposing contemporary corruption.

Friel's solution was to combine tradition/history with modernity/globalisation in a single setting, a single critique. Instead of the unitary, absurd conceit underpinning *The Mundy Scheme* (the West of Ireland transformed into a vast cemetery), Friel now fused two disparate metaphors: archaeological excavation and political internment. The mix provides his 'no man's land'. In the text of *Volunteers*, the primary metaphor is the one visualised in the set, representing a large archaeological dig in the heart of modern Dublin where a multi-storey hotel is planned for erection on a Viking site. The clash of values implied is obvious. It was a contemporary reference to an ongoing and revealing controversy over the building of a new Dublin Corporation office block on the Viking site at Wood Quay. The debate over the spoliation involved was slow to grow into national significance, but Friel had early put his finger on a highly significant issue which, like that of the North, was largely a matter of indifference to denizens of the Republic. It is nothing less than uncanny that in 1974 Friel identified the metaphoric power of this conflict between heritage and progress. The protests and mass marches to save Wood Quay did not get under way until 1977; the legal battle was lost in 1981 and the office block was built despite the fact that in 1979 'a whole townscape was uncovered, and not just of one period but of as many as a dozen successive levels within the tenth- to eleventh-century period' of Dublin's history.[51] Now a 'microcosm of the medieval town' was laid bare.[52] This is the stuff of Frielian theatre: history, layers and levels, microcosms. The historian Angret Simms has emphasised the cultural loss: 'The "spaces" that our cities fill become "places" if they are transformed by meaning. We assign meaning to a place if we identify with it, for example our home.'[53] *Space*, of course, is a particularly theatrical term. Making use of it, Friel's play becomes a struggle to find meaning within stage conventions for the current state of Irish identity.

The second metaphor is in placing five IRA 'volunteers' on prison release within the space. There is incongruity here. The term 'volunteer' has a long history, beginning with the defence regiments in Ireland against a possible invasion from France during the American Revolution.[54] With the founding of the Ulster Volunteer Force in January 1913, a far different concept was established, a colonialist rejection of Home Rule. With the establishment, in turn, of the Irish Volunteers in Dublin in November 1913 in defiance of the Northern Unionist Covenant, new battle lines were drawn.[55] Pearse was to lead the Volunteers into the 1916 Rising. Thereafter, a 'volunteer' had a particular meaning in the South, namely, nationalist. With the founding of the Irish Free State in 1922, the legitimate army was called *Óglaigh na h-Éireann*, Gaelic for Irish Volunteers, and the dissident IRA, or Irregulars, attempted to hijack both names from then on. With the recruitment to IRA ranks following Bloody Sunday, the term 'volunteer' returned to prominence, connoting a shadowy or 'provisional' alternative to the Republic's legitimate army. Friel plays ironically with such shadows.

In Friel's play his five volunteers are ambivalent figures. They are imprisoned republicans who have opted for excavation work against orders; they are rebels within a rebel organisation, prisoners twice over. At the end of Act 1, we learn that a kangaroo court in the prison has passed death sentence on them for their 'defection' and 'crime of treason'.[56] The concentric circles which in *The Freedom of the City* extended from the three victims in the Mayor's Parlour (*qua* web) to show a tragic failure of communications here become the wheels-within-wheels of a society layered like an excavation site.

There is a hierarchy within this site and its extension to the world offstage. On stage, there is the site manager George, who is monarch of all he surveys. He is cautious in the way he treats the men but he is literally above them like a guard in Foucault's Panopticon: his little office is reached by a stairway. George patronises the volunteers, except for Keeney, whom he regards as 'a real danger man' (p. 63). George, a foreman who fancies himself as an archaeologist, has, on the final day of the dig, finished restoring a glazed jug from fragments found by the brain-damaged Smiler, a volunteer. The key moment in the play is when Butt, George's pet, brought to see the precious jug as symbol of an order to which he has been tempted to succumb, smashes it in a final, fruitless gesture of revolt. One can say that the action in *Volunteers* consists of the breaking – Kleist-like – of a jug.

The outside world is represented by three figures and a nameless 'they'. Mr Wilson is the prison official who daily escorts the volunteers from and back to prison. He might have stepped straight out of Behan's *The Quare Fellow* (1954), a petty official blind to anything above routine duty and self-interest who is mocked for his social pretensions. Des is a young archaeologist who visits the site twice on this day. Like the priest in *The Freedom of the City*, he abruptly changes his attitude between his first and second appearances. Des sides with the volunteers, who call him 'Dessie the Red', when the secret is kept from them that the dig is over. His rhetoric is rabble-rousing. He plays on their being 'men of passionate conviction' and urges action: whatever 'stance' they take he will approve and 'be fully and whole-heartedly behind you'. He is just '*that bit too histrionic*' (p. 39). Des in an example of Southern political blarney. When he enters again later in the day he is of a different mind, having been won over by his boss to carry on the important work as his deputy. Keeney and his sidekick Pyne make game of this converted revolutionary and flush out the real Des, who responds: 'Over the past few months [. . .] I thought I had come to understand you people and maybe even have a measure of sympathy with you. But by God I think now that hanging's too good for you' (p. 56).

The third figure, the archaeologist Dr King, who is Des's boss, is a kind of Godot figure who never appears on stage. Author of nothing but coffee-table books, he is now satisfied he has material for one more. He is literally of no account, a fact which casts a pall of cynicism over the whole academic exercise of the dig. The nameless other group offstage are the Gardaí, or certain brutal sections of them referred to as 'they'. Their fascism is noted. The brain-damaged Smiler who fell into their hands when he tried to lead an anti-internment march from Donegal was beaten 'for twelve consecutive hours – you know, just as a warning' (p. 46). He escapes from the excavation site, causing as much concern as Rosie's disappearance in *Dancing at Lughnasa* and making the same point, that human concern is imperative in family and community. If 'they' catch him outside, Smiler will be killed 'this time' (p. 48).

To a bourgeois audience, such a scenario is no doubt outrageous. But Friel is Brechtian to the extent that he makes the abject the subject and works to create understanding of a wider reality. The advance over *The Freedom of the City* in this regard lies in the fate awaiting these prisoners at the hands of their *own* people. What they participate in, therefore, while participating voluntarily in public works, is a dance of death. As in the earlier play, there is a master of ceremonies to conduct a grim carnival. Keeney is Skinner reborn as an intellectual and leader. (The role was played in Dublin by Donal Donnelly, the original Gar in *Philadelphia*.) Keeney has no need of a sociologist like Professor Dodds to contextualise his abnegation; he subsumes Dodds's role himself. But he is also the supreme clown, 'always playing' (p. 16). His partner Pyne makes a good double act: between them they create routines as good as any Brechtian cabaret and verge also on Beckettian gallows humour. If Keeney himself is well up to the role of Hamm, he also aspires to Hamlet, taking his cue from the Danish skeleton discovered. Twice, Keeney asks playfully, 'Was Hamlet really mad?' (pp. 21, 26), and in the scene where he makes a mock-ritual of burying the skeleton again, whom he names Leif, he pretends he know him well (*qua* Yorrick) and describes the last time he saw him. Such passages are quite similar to the fantasies launched by Private Gar in *Philadelphia, Here I Come!* with the same purpose of subverting the banality of everyday existence: 'The last time I saw him – the first week of last May as a matter of fact – [. . .] it was a Tuesday, I remember, a warm, breathless day,' Lief was unwell (p. 66). This is Beckettian mock-narrative.[57] There is more. The failing Lief struggles to articulate: 'I must know – I *must* know – was Hamlet really mad?' before he expired (p. 66). There is a political point behind this mock-identification of Keeney, Lief and Hamlet which is, something is rotten in the state of Ireland. On stage the spatial metaphor carries the point forward: the men have isolated the remains of a tiny Viking house no bigger than 'a prison cell' (p. 33). 'Denmark's a prison', Hamlet believed (2.2.249). In a sense, the offstage prison is Ireland; the offstage Ireland is a stage where history and modernity are in conflict.

In *Volunteers*, the *Hamlet* references so reverberate as to bring to mind the graveyard scene in Shakespeare's play while providing an echo of the central metaphor in *The Mundy Scheme*. Keeney, who confesses to 'an antic imagination' (p. 57), self-consciously sees himself as alienated to the point where an antic disposition (or mask) is his only safety valve in 'just trying to keep sane' (p. 28). Like Hamlet, he knows the power of words, but he also knows both their ambiguity: volunteers are 'the criminal element' in Irish society and beyond (p. 44). Irony is the leitmotif. The stage is Kafka territory also: 'Imaginatively, though – regardless of our being spies and informers in reality – we are all so many inmates of the Gulags, each our own lonely warrior of individualism standing up against authority and those who do its dirty work.'[58] Keeney's stories are all parables of identity-formation. They offer structures for a new history. But being fiction they point up the unreality of the prisoners' situation. Among his fantasies over Leif's history, Keeney speculates that he was 'a casualty of language', a reference to Jameson's *The Prison-House of Language* (1972); he adds, including the audience, 'which of us here isn't?' (p. 26).

Theatrically, one of the finest moments in *Volunteers* is Smiler's return and glad acceptance by all except Keeney, who stands aloof, seething, while the others fuss over Smiler, draping him in an old sack for warmth, '*like a ritualistic robe, and ecclesiastical cope*' (p. 59). The image is of the suffering Christ. The passivity of the figure and the emotive response of his fellows anger Keeney, who insists in Nietzschean fashion that Smiler is an 'imbecile' (p. 60). Keeney's anger, in turn, alienates the compassion in this drama of commitment in 1970s' Ireland. We are to see *all* the volunteers as imbeciles, holy fools, victims in a meaningless ritual. It is a complex moment, wrong-footing the audience. While it is true that Friel, like Seamus Heaney in *North* (1975), 'seeks in the myth of Viking Ireland a clearer vision of contemporary Irish politics',[59] it is clarity through a glass darkly. Brechtian complex seeing yields in Friel to complex feeling dramatising public confusion. But the anger remains dominant.

Expecting a play 'about' the rights and wrongs of internment without trial as they took *The Freedom of the City* to be a play 'about' the wrongs of Bloody Sunday, Dublin reviewers of *Volunteers* were puzzled to the point of collective condemnation. *Irish Times* drama critic Seamus Kelly challenged 'what is your point, Mr Friel?' (6 March). Gus Smith proclaimed in the *Sunday Independent*: 'Friel must dig deeper' (9 March). At least, Smith saw the archaeological dimension of *Volunteers* as social metaphor. Seamus Heaney's review for the *TLS* on 23 March ('Digging Deeper')[60] took Smith's review as his target in seeking to correct this gross failure in public interpretation. We now know that at this time Heaney had just completed *North*, exploring correspondences between Viking life in Dublin and the violence in Northern Ireland, to be published in July 1975. There was a 'symbiotic link' between Friel's play and Heaney's poetry.[61]

In October 1974, Friel sent the manuscript of *Volunteers* to Heaney, who had no idea Friel was working in this adjacent field.[62] Heaney commented later that after he had read the play he put together all 'the bog poems and Viking Dublin poems that were to hand', some already published, and found he had a book ready for Faber, that is, *North*.[63] The symbiosis Heaney speaks about relates to a dual gaze on history. Both writers were responding in equal measure to the carnage and chaos that overwhelmed the North in the 1970s and was to enter the South in July 1976 with the murder of the British ambassador, Christopher Ewart-Biggs.

Heaney's defence of *Volunteers* was published while the play was still limping along at the Abbey. Heaney is at pains to say that Friel is a poet in the theatre. This point is made while Heaney displays an intertextuality common in Friel's plays: the two writers share a common modernist-humanist aesthetic. When Heaney says, 'The play is not a quarrel with others but a vehicle for Friel's quarrel with himself,' the hidden quotation is from Yeats's *Mythologies* (1959): 'We make out of the quarrel with others, rhetoric, but of the quarrel with ourselves, poetry.'[64] In a brief review, Heaney manages to cite Wilfred Owen, Siegfried Sassoon, Shakespeare (*Hamlet*), Shelley ('The Masque of Anarchy'), Wordsworth ('Lines Written in Early Spring', 1798), Yeats ('Lapis Lazuli' and 'Nineteen Hundred and Nineteen'),[65]

James Simmons's *The Honest Ulsterman* and even Bertolt Brecht. The latter is particularly apt, as Heaney argues that *Volunteers* represents a new form for Friel, 'a kind that involves *an alienation effect* but eschews didactic address [. . .] a form that allows his gifts a freer expression'.[66] He explains this as a Brechtian style of irony meant to transform audience attitudes through estrangement. As I have shown above, this style begins with *Lovers* and is developed in *The Freedom of the City*. It wasn't invented for *Volunteers*.

Heaney's intervention in the debate made nothing happen. *Volunteers* disappeared from the Abbey repertory. But something else was achieved. It became clearer to Heaney how close in some ways his own enterprise as lyric poet was to Friel's more dangerous assault on Irish sensibilities. As time went on, he and Friel grew close friends. Friel dedicated the text of *Volunteers* to Heaney when it was published (by Faber) in 1979; Heaney dedicated *Station Island* to Friel when it was published (by Faber) in 1984. By that time the Field Day Theatre Company had been founded in Derry, its first production having as its venue the very Guildhall which is the setting for *The Freedom of the City*. Heaney was invited onto the board. In time, he wrote *The Cure at Troy* (1990) for Field Day. Out of all the blood and tears, a new theatrical venture was to rise, and in good time hope and history was to rhyme.

Finally, it should be said that it was not until after the Belfast Agreement of 1998 that *Volunteers* and *The Freedom of the City* began to be appreciated. Mick Gordon's production of *Volunteers* at London's Gate Theatre won very good reviews – 'Digging into the madness of a cause' was the *Financial Times*'s headline (2 November 1998), while the *Times* (26 October), 'Unearthed Gem', just about summed up the general response.[67] *Freedom of the City* was revived at the Abbey in 1999 for the festival celebrating Friel's seventieth birthday, when, according to Patrick Burke, director Conall Morrison 'could have done more to distinguish the play's two dominant modes, the "warm" naturalistic from the "cool" Brechtian'.[68] Such distinctions could at last be examined dispassionately. The case can now be made for these two plays as significant examples of the modern Theatre of Commitment.

CHAPTER 5

UNCERTAINTY, MEMORY, TRAGEDY: *LIVING QUARTERS* AND *FAITH HEALER*

Time passes. Memory fades, memory adjusts, memory conforms to what we think we remember.

– Joan Didion, *Blue Nights* (London: Fourth Estate, 2011)[1]

Introduction

In 1974, just after the staging of *The Freedom of the City* but the year before the premiere of *Volunteers*, Seamus Deane published a short essay, 'The Writer and the Troubles'.[2] As a Northerner himself and a poet, Deane well understood the pressures, inner and outer, then facing the Northern writer. He saw Friel's dilemma. He understood the conflict between the compulsion to respond to public suffering and the inhibition which commands fidelity to the priorities of art. *Freedom of the City* he wrongly saw as only partially successful: 'It gives up on realistic speech in the end in order to ensure we do not miss the morality of the plot.'[3] Deane wanted more 'reality', while Friel wanted less. The collapse of order signified by Bloody Sunday left Deane without hope: 'This is the honeymoon/Of the cockroach, the small/Spiderless eternity of the fly.'[4] He could see only two possibilities for Friel as writer now, two 'exits' from 'the emotional cul-de-sac of his people': one tragic, the other political. Tragedy would focus on a violent solution, 'in which the forces of neurosis or society (much the same) destroy the human'. A focus on politics would require an audience 'to recognise and feel the appropriate anger for such a [tragic] waste'.[5] What Deane overlooked is that these alternatives can be combined, as tragicomedy allows. *Volunteers*, while political, and exposing the 'neurosis' Deane speaks of, is also a kind of national tragicomedy. Where Deane's analysis is most useful, however, is in forecasting the trajectory of Friel's future career as an Irish playwright. Friel would oscillate between commenting and empathy in constructing a form of art adequate to private mood and public occasion, aiming always to represent duality in the form of hybridity. When it came to the Field Day years, however, Friel was bound to find difficulty sometimes in accommodating to the expectations of the intellectuals.

After the trauma of *Volunteers*, too bitter a pill for Dublin audiences to swallow, Friel turned away from the overtly political and embraced the theme of uncertainty. The link is there as *Volunteers* draws to a close. An altercation breaks out between Keeney and Butt, the strongest of the political prisoners. To his quiet assent, betokening Irish resignation, Keeney reacts violently to Butt's mild acceptance of the identification with the skeleton of Lief. 'Maybe. Yes. But for Christ's sake not with the assurance of your yes!', Keeney rages, as he himself is 'sure of nothing now'.[6] On that note of uncertainty, in mind and in outcome, the play ends. The prisoners exit to an unknown fate. This uncertainty is inherent in Friel's dramaturgy from *Philadelphia* onwards: closure is not on offer. To live morally is to abide in 'necessary uncertainty'.[7] If the theme is Frielian it is also a feature of the postmodern temper, seen not just in Pinter and Stoppard but also in Michael Frayn's *Copenhagen* (1998).[8] Friel, charting his own way through these seas, was actually ahead of his time. He wished to combine uncertainty and memory with the problem of writing tragedy in modern times.

Living Quarters and the Representation of Suicide

Living Quarters, written for the Abbey Theatre, provided a fresh start: a modernised adaptation of Euripides' *Hippolytus*, that is, the Phaedra story. A strange subject for Friel, it may be thought. It was one not entirely foreign to the Irish tradition, however. T. C. Murray had drawn on the myth for his most assured play for the Abbey, *Autumn Fire*, in 1924, by coincidence the year Eugene O'Neill's *Desire under the Elms* premiered in New York. Although Murray is now largely forgotten,[9] in the early decades of the twentieth century he was well regarded, and during the Abbey's first tour of America in 1911 O'Neill saw and greatly admired and was influenced by his work.[10] *Desire* had its Irish premiere at the Gate in 1944, directed by Hilton Edwards; the Abbey staged it in 1976, a year before *Living Quarters*. O'Neill's tragic vision was indebted to Greek drama, and Friel in his turn to O'Neill. As Michael Lloyd has pointed out, 'The power of *Living Quarters* derives above all from the [. . .] radical suggestion that everything is fated, even those choices which seem to be most free.'[11] Pure O'Neill.

Living Quarters is set at an army barracks in modern Donegal. The central figure, Frank Butler, is an Irish soldier just returned from overseas duties with the United Nations. The play, contemporary, topical and using realistic speech, seeks to combine Euripides and Pirandello in one more piece of sophisticated metatheatre. Friel turns his back on Brecht now. His preoccupation once again is with the technique of plays such as *Six Characters* and *Right You Are! (If You Think So)* dating from 1922. In Pirandello, each character has a personal, subjective understanding of how things happened; for Friel, the mind shuffles the 'pieces of verifiable truth' in memory or experience and composes 'a truth of its own'.[12] Yet, as in Pirandello's plays, the focus in Friel is mainly on the loneliness of the individual 'trapped in his or her fate'.[13] But if in the reading *Living Quarters* primarily recalls *Six Characters in Search of an Author*, Friel's characters can be seen in search of a director, whom they invent and invest with supreme authority.

Under this figure, Sir, the characters convene in Commandant Butler's living quarters to re-enact the fatal day when he took his own life. They are looking for expiation, a chance to change things. But they are governed by the script or 'ledger' held by Sir from which there can be no departure. Although the characters, Frank Butler himself, his second wife Anna and his four children, plus the army chaplain Tom McCarthy, can argue over the details of what happened, they cannot alter the course of events, which are, in a sense, history. The script is not open to revision, only rehearsal (and interpretation). Thus *Living Quarters* is fundamentally a memory play within a deterministic framework. The characters are not to be thought of as literally present.

Scattered all over the world since Frank's death, they reconvene *in spirit*. Once convened in a collective mind within the imagined domestic space, the extended family members begin to combine realistic conversations with 'scenes' reconstructing the day they all remember differently. The play is therefore a 'rehearsal' play like Jean Anouilh's St Joan play *The Lark* (1933); it also draws upon Thornton Wilder's *Our Town* (1938). So, under the guise of quiet realism, we have Friel presenting a play where the storyline relates to Euripides while the form draws upon modern experimentalism.

There can be no doubt this time as the *Irish Times* had voiced over *Volunteers*, what the 'point' of *Living Quarters* is. It is the breaking point of a man faced with the revelation that his second wife has been unfaithful with his son. That is, roughly speaking, the story originally told of the Theseus-Phaedra-Hippolytus triangle, except for the major changes Friel introduces: (1) He moves the focus from Phaedra to Theseus, making her something of an enigma. (2) He makes his Hippolytus actually seduce his Phaedra. Accordingly, it is possible to see two plays superimposed here in a form of palimpsest. The schema of the classical play yields to a modern one in which the husband (and not the wife) takes his own life. The question to be answered is why.

In *Celtic Revivals*, Seamus Deane describes the 'double stage' characteristically employed by Friel. The vital or, indeed, fatal story lies secret as a play-within-the-play.[14] It may, however, be more useful to regard this 'story' in terms of stage space. In the preceding chapters, we have seen how alienation is made visible on stage by the separation of space (Gar's private bedroom *vs.* the socialised kitchen or neutral apron; the mayor's parlour *vs.* the outside world hostile to those within). In modern drama this is a device stemming from the crafty Ibsen. The eclectic Friel makes good use of this dichotomy.[15] In *Living Quarters* (dedicated to Deane), the stage space is divided between the living room and garden of a detached house facing the audience: the garden lies in front, like an apron area, 'right across the front of the stage'.[16] Exterior scenes are deemed to be in the present, with interior scenes recreating the tragic story from the past. The division should alert us to the convention that at times we are hearing quasi-improvised conversation and at other times text stamped authoritatively by Sir.

The second play going on alongside the Phaedra story concerns the conflict between what *really* happened in the Butler family and what exists still as *possibility*, the reinvention of what might have been.[17] There is also the use of double time to be considered. The characters as actors exist in time present as they recreate the fatal day 'some years ago' (p. 177); at times, like ghosts in a Yeats play, they try in vain to intervene, while at other times they sit and chat like the actors they are, as if in a greenroom. Theatrically, the characters are prisoners of time as well as of space.

Friel's early notes for *Living Quarters* make it clear that he was thinking in terms of classical tragedy. He saw his hero as analogous to Agamemnon and mentions *hubris* as a feature of characterisation and *catharsis*. He was even considering a Chorus before deciding on Sir.[18] Then he abandoned the strictly classical paradigm, although silently bearing it in mind for the domestic drama he set about 'after' *Hippolytus*. Euripides had framed a story of illicit sexual passion within a battle of the gods. This religious dimension endured through later versions of the myth, most notably in Racine's *Phèdre* (1676). The issue is always how Aphrodite, goddess of love, impels the feelings of Phaedra towards her son-in-law Hippolytus, in open conflict with her counterpart Artemis, goddess of chastity, to whom the young man is devoted. When he rebuffs the overtures of Phaedra, Aphrodite sees to it that Hippolytus is punished by drawing his father Theseus into the situation. The outraged husband calls upon the gods for vengeance against his son. This comes in the form of a mighty wave, in effect a tsunami but expressive of the power of the 'hidden god', the monster from the sea representing sinful passion, which destroys Hippolytus on a hunt, after Phaedra has killed herself for shame. In the end, it is Theseus who is left to ponder the unaccountability of the gods: the uncertainty principle *avant la lettre*, because nothing actually happened between Phaedra and Hippolytus. It was all in the mind. As Beckett argued, Racine's modernity began here.[19]

Friel made huge alterations to this scenario historically visible in the copious versions in English down to Sarah Kane's *Phaedra's Love* (1996). For Kane, as for modern audiences, the madness of love needs no supernatural agency and is no less dangerous for lack of it. But Friel attempts something more unexpected. His Phaedra figure, Anna, while described by Friel as 'mature, intelligent, [and] passionate' (p. 175), is marginalised in the after-story structure of the play. She is mainly seen as Frank Butler's trophy, a love object destined to mirror Frank's ego. She has no subjectivity. She is cast as a bimbo, a '*femme fatale*' as Richard Pine dubs her.[20] She is an enigma, like Laura in the Hollywood film noir. Indeed at play's end when she quizzes Sir to disclose what his ledger reveals of her future he has nothing but blank pages to show. Like many of the women in Friel's plays, her selfhood is effectively subdued by the overpowering force of the man in her life. From what we hear of Frank's first wife (who died six years before), she too was crushed. In Ibsenist fashion, Frank speaks only of joylessness and duty in their relationship during her final illness. Anna, he tells his estranged daughter, restored 'joy' to him; if he *is* a 'hero', he says, it is because of Anna (p. 197). That this is delusion the play ultimately reveals. Anna has no positive feelings for Frank. Her role is subversive.

The father-son relationship is at the heart of the Phaedra story. The Hippolytus figure in *Living Quarters* is Ben, a major departure from the archetype. Ben is anything but heroic; if he is a devotee of the divine Anna, chastity is not his driving motive. Friel describes him as twenty-four years of age, 'hesitant, nervous, with a volatile face' (p. 175): not the stuff of tragedy. Ben is a modern son unable to come to terms with a powerful father. He is Gar O'Donnell over again, without a fraction of Gar's balance or effervescence; like Gar, Ben also has a dead mother whose loss is crucial to his schizoid state. A difficult son-father relationship – Ben is terrified of Frank – is compounded by a passionate love of his mother. His sister Miriam, a hearty model of fecundity and good sense, dismisses Ben as 'a spoiled mother's boy' (p. 187). On his first entrance Ben mistakes his other adult sister Helen – glamorous and sensitive in contrast to Miriam – for his dead mother. It is a moment of uncertainty and confusion over what *seems* and what *is*: 'for a second my heart expanded with an immense remembered love for her, and then at once shrank in terror of her' (p. 205). The characterisation is close to that of Casimir in *Aristocrats* (1979). The frailty in each case derives from a dominant father figure; yet Ben is the more seriously troubled and dangerous son. His hatred is sufficient to impel Ben to sleep with Anna; his equal subordination to a mother he both idolised and feared has disabled him from any genuine relationship with Anna, who cares little for him in any case. Ben is a broken figure, a university dropout, a drifter: a lost soul. But there is ambivalence. Although Ben in effect kills his father, he also bears great love for him and – like Gar – has a tender memory of a moment of closeness between them (p. 228) which Frank dismisses as damningly as S. B. in *Philadelphia*. Later, Ben rebukes Sir for not allowing that 'moment' because it would have been a declaration of love. 'And even though it wouldn't have been the truth, it wouldn't have been a lie either' (p. 245). Ben's guilt cannot occlude his father's failure to love. Friel reworks old material on more than one level.

Friel's main focus in this reshaped Phaedra story is clearly on the Theseus figure, Commandant Frank Butler, who is in charge of a small army barracks in County Donegal, where he feels unfulfilled. A family man in his early fifties, Frank is ambitious for the promotion that would release him to Dublin from provincial inertia. The day on which the play is set marks the occasion when the Commandant is being officially honoured for his recent military exploits. It is also the day when Anna openly tells him of her 'affair' (the chosen word). This revelation in the presence of his family drives Frank Butler to shoot himself. Wanting to unsettle his audience, Friel changes the plot of the original play. He wanted to subvert *Hippolytus* by omitting all mention, much less agency, of God or the gods. Father Tom, who is Frank's 'confidant' and who apparently knew nothing of the love 'affair', is, like all priests in Friel's plays, irresponsible and incapable. Friel's Theseus figure lacks any real power of redress; his shame brings Frank only frustration. Having no option to call on supernatural agency, he must internalise his hurt, not play the man of honour like Ajax in Sophocles' play[21] but in the modern style shoot himself at home, in private, in disgrace.

Suicide has been a growing concern in Irish society in recent decades. At the time Friel wrote *Living Quarters*, however, it was still a taboo subject concerning which traditional Catholicism ensured suppression from public record. Friel makes of self-destruction an attempt to create value in a context where the 'sin' attached is obliterated. If Frank's action appears absurd, this is the very point, following after Camus.[22] Al Alvarez points out in *The Savage God* (1990) that motives for suicide are always equivocal: 'A man may destroy himself not because he wants to die but because there is a single aspect of himself which he cannot tolerate.'[23] Alvarez argues that 'suicide is a closed world with its own irresistible logic' (p. 143). But Frank Butler's motive in *Living Quarters* is a form of rebellion, as in Camus' *The Rebel*, a text Friel cites in his essay 'The Theatre of Hope and Despair'.[24] The seemingly compulsive repetition of the act foregrounds its tragic meaning. We have the suicide as rebel. A rebel is defined by Camus as 'A man who says no, but whose refusal does not imply a renunciation.' That ambivalence ('the rebel slave says yes and no simultaneously'), like Frank's formal objection before death, 'affirms the existence of a borderline'.[25] The latter raises a political idea as a way of apprehending *Living Quarters*. Frank Butler is a Donegal man, close to the border with Northern Ireland. Partition shaped his schizoid identity. He longs to get out, forsake the local for the metropolitan life; he despises the simple people who have honoured him (as national hero) with a floridly written testimonial. Frank then finds himself humiliated by his wife's disclosure and 'confronts an order of things which oppresses him with the insistence on a kind of right *not* to be oppressed beyond the limit that he can tolerate'.[26] As his protest fails, Frank's resistance becomes implacable. His sense of self-worth is on the line. As with Camus' rebel, 'it becomes for him the supreme good'. It is only through rebellion that Frank becomes fully aware of his core self.

To see *Living Quarters* in this light is to re-read the text and find every character blind and deaf to the crucial issue at stake. They must revisit the terrible day of Frank's self-destruction just because they have no conception of its meaning. Most of the play is in the comic vein: all are having fun, enjoying the occasion, while bracing themselves for the big bang at the end. But the audience cannot attend with such unawareness. Friel's Pirandellian techniques make it difficult for the audience *not* to empathise unequivocally with the Butler children and to see Frank as ogre, an egotistical snob. But as Camus implies, because Frank can only demand respect for himself 'in so far as he identifies himself with a natural community',[27] it is for the reader/audience to see what is really at stake. It is justice. As in *The Freedom of the City*, but here much less explicitly, there has to be 'identification of one's destiny with that of others and a choice of sides'.[28] The rebellion, Camus argues, 'reveals the part of man which must always be defended'.[29] Even if it is a fool who rebels, it is a matter of solidarity for us to respond adequately: 'I rebel – therefore *we* exist.'[30] The camouflage of which Friel writes as a necessity to the modern dramatist is donned as emergency equipment for *Living Quarters*.[31] Frank is a false hero.

Ray McAnally (1926–89) played Frank Butler in the 1977 Abbey premiere of *Living Quarters*. He had played Columba, the leading role, in Friel's *The Enemy Within* (1962) and would play Hugh in the Field Day premiere of *Translations* (1980). Friel called McAnally 'one of the major Irish actors [. . .] one of the last survivors of a great period of Abbey actors.'[32] He was such a strong Macbeth at the Abbey in 1971 (Hugh Hunt directing) that he caused the Macduff to fall off the stage during rehearsal of the final combat: a new Macduff had hastily to be found. When I questioned him once regarding his cameo role of Hatch in Bond's *The Sea* at the Peacock (1979) and praised the 'business' he introduced, he said, 'I radiate meaning.' I believe he did, on film as well as on stage. In *Living Quarters* he replayed Macbeth. But once again he had no Macduff strong enough to make a fight of it, so that egocentrism bore it away. Did he radiate meaning as Frank Butler? To me, at a preview on 23 March 1977, he did not. So completely did he merge his personality into the domineering figure of Butler that I came away convinced that *Living Quarters* was no more than a mishmash of Pirandello and early Chekhov (*Ivanov* for preference). Now I see it as far more assured, the first Irish existential tragedy.[33]

Joe Dowling, who directed the premiere of *Living Quarters*, has nothing to say about either it or McAnally in *The Achievement of Brian Friel* (1992). But he does make the point that Friel is 'an actor's writer' rather than a director's, 'where the director sees himself as co-creator of the dramatic piece'.[34] McAnally was his own director, one might say; therefore in playing a character who stands up to the director-as-mandarin, Sir, and coming off second best and subsequently shooting himself in protest, McAnally this time radiated the wrong meaning. What the play gropes uncertainly for is the opposite of what

McAnally as actor habitually communicated by his own through-line. Frank Butler, like that other Frank in *Faith Healer*, is anti-hero rather than hero; his death is meaningless unless it conveys the seeds of new awareness in the audience.

Faith Healer as Avant-Garde Tragedy

There is some debate over whether *Faith Healer* is Friel's greatest play; there is no question whatever of its standing as a masterpiece. The idea of a 'faith healer' or itinerant magician is universal. He is in most cultures a shaman figure, a saint or blind prophet, perhaps even a *file* or bard. The most famous faith healer was Jesus Christ: to believe in him was the prerequisite to being either cured or saved. Brian Friel's play taps into all of these areas from the shamanic tradition to the question of uncertainty underlying the seemingly magical skills of Jesus. There remain two other features of the figure which Friel introduces: the theatrical and the artificial. Every prophet is regarded in his own country as suspect (as Tiresias to the intellectual Oedipus). So, there is always the question of deception suspended over the head of a 'faith healer'. Doubt surrounds him by definition. In that regard he is a piece of theatre, a figure whose very ambiguity is inextricable from his performance strengths. Here, the faith healer is to be associated with the subversive 'trickster' figure in society, imitated by Augusto Boal for his street theatre in the 1970s.[35] The trickster, like the Fool in Tudor society, has always been a licensed danger figure, one who required careful control. Or else like the witch figure he/she might pull the wool over people's eyes to the point of leading them to damnation.[36] The playwrights of the Elizabethan age pointed up the close relationship between the magician-healer and the star actor (Faustus, Subtle the Alchemist, Prospero). In modern film we have a variation on the faith healer in Ingmar Bergman's *The Magician* (1959), described as 'a symbolic self-portrait by one of the cinema's great directors'.[37] Here is a possible, unacknowledged source for Friel's *Faith Healer*. In the film, the magician Dr Vogler, who tours with a travelling troupe of players, has his revenge on an aggressive sceptic but then finds himself 'trapped within his own mystery',[38] proving that 'the artist is both privileged and damned'.[39] Friel's play could be said to start here, with the union of actor and miracle worker.

The Play

'If we begin with certainties', wrote Francis Bacon in *The Advancement of Learning* (1623), 'we will end in doubt, but if we begin with doubts and bear them patiently, we may end in certainty.' This very Renaissance fascination with doubt[40] also has a shape to its formulation which can apply, as the sentiments plainly do, to *Faith Healer*. The structure of the play is daring in its originality. The arc it describes is that of the tragic fall from assurance, through pathos (suffering), into release and, if Yeats is to be believed, 'joy'.[41]

But the story of *hubris* and its nemesis (in the form of Frank Hardy's anti-self, the 'cripple' McGarvey,) is told in four monologues rather than enacted dramatically. Friel goes clean against classical principles, as articulated by Aristotle in the *Poetics*, who famously pronounced: 'Tragedy [. . .] then is a representation of an action which is serious, complete, and of a certain magnitude [. . .] in the mode of dramatic enactment, *not narrative*, and through the arousal of pity and fear effecting the *katharsis* [purgation] of such emotions.'[42] To Aristotle, and to traditionalists in this field of aesthetics, the most important feature of tragedy is plot or 'plot-structure' (*mythos*), which is driven by character in action. The plot-structure in this definition 'is the first principle and, so to speak, the soul of tragedy' (*Poetics*, p. 38). But Friel's play, apart from the physical movements of the actors in their roles, is all narrative, and yet is all soul. There is no plot-structure as such. Accordingly, when *Faith Healer* was first staged, at the Longacre Theatre on Broadway, there were many who faulted it as simply undramatic. Actually, it was entirely original, defying conventions even beyond Beckett, who always insisted, for example, that his radio play *All That Fall* (1957) could *not* be staged. Friel's monologue style upset 'most reviewers, who found themselves consistently perplexed, fatigued and even angry at the play's format', as Maria Szasz, fully covering the topic, explains in *Brian Friel and America*.[43] Friel himself, in recollection, saw the rehearsal period as 'a very difficult time' because of the casting of Grace and Teddy. The lead was capably played by film-actor James Mason, 'on top of his craft'; his wife, Clarissa Kaye, for whose sake Mason agreed to play Frank Hardy, was entirely at sea as Grace and broke down in rehearsal, unfit for the role and unable to understand José Quintero's direction. Mason insisted that she go on; Ed Flanders, who had his own problems rehearsing Teddy, eventually refused to play with Kaye and was replaced 'at the last minute' by Donal Donnelly, who had played Gar O'Donnell in the original *Philadelphia*. As Friel saw it, when *Faith Healer* opened in New York on 7 February 1979, the main problem was Clarissa Kaye, who had by this time withdrawn into herself. She 'sleepwalked through her performance every night. She was living a kind of exile.' So, the production was a failure, running for only twenty performances. 'A very difficult time,' Friel concludes.[44] But he gained from the experience nevertheless. Walter Kerr's review in the *New York Sunday Times* stoutly defended the play, arguing that the true artist creates the taste by which he/she is understood: 'The play's progress and outcome must be pieced together, mosaic-style, by an audience willing to do – or mesmerized into doing – the necessary work.'[45] (So, too, the reader.) Beginning with a triumphant Irish premiere the following year, *Faith Healer* has won countless audiences worldwide to share Kerr's enthusiasm. Friel has been vindicated: *Faith Healer* is nowadays regarded as a classic. It may be added that another gain from the terrible experience of the Broadway flop was that Friel may have found in Clarissa Kaye's collapse the germ of *Molly Sweeney*, also forced by dominating males into 'living a kind of exile' (see Chapter 7).

In form, then, *Faith Healer* is subversive of the conventional tragic genre. It is postmodernist rather than modernist. It has even been cogently argued that it is 'postdramatic'.[46] There are but three characters in the text, each isolated in time and space, with no interaction whatsoever. But the many voices within the narratives of the three monologuists create a Dickensian world populated with characters given virtual 'walk-on' roles. We do well in reading *Faith Healer* to note these voices quoted in Bakhtinian (dialogic) fashion within the monologues. Discourse creates the fisherman named Campbell in Kinlochbervie and his deaf mother; Frank's father; Grace's mother and her nerves; the London figures who people Teddy's monologue, the policeman, the dog trainer named Mary Brigid and the 'city gent' who confronts Teddy in outrage over the purloining of the poster put out with the garbage. Although *Faith Healer* is a minimalist work, it mobilises a mythos which imposes itself convincingly just as the greatest drama does. 'The essential is to get upon the stage this precise statement of life which is at the same time a point of view, a world [. . .] which the author's mind has subjected to a complete process of simplification.'[47] Eliot anticipated today's debate concerning Mikhail Bakhtin and 'voices', arguing that the third voice, after the lyric and the direct poetic address, was the dramatic monologue. In poetic drama, 'all three voices are audible'.[48] Although Eliot's battle to create a new poetic drama is well lost, his legacy remains.[49] Bakhtin wrote specifically about heteroglossia in relation to the novel; he appears deaf to the voices within modern drama. But Marvin Carlson has shown how the term dialogism – 'producing the expression of multiple perspectives through contrasting voices' – *can* be applied to modern drama. In referring to Chekhov's 'glancing and oblique discourse', Carlson paves the way for an interpretation of Friel's work. Friel was writing his version of *Three Sisters* around the same time as *Volunteers* and *Faith Healer*. Carlson argues that indeterminacy and a text 'much more clearly open-ended' characterise the Chekhovian style of dialogue.[50] It is fair to say, then, that Friel's experiment in *Faith Healer* is a significant development of the resources of 'the third voice' beyond Chekhov. Teddy's monologue, in the vein of a stand-up comedian, easily shows Friel's skill in heteroglossia.

What emerges in *Faith Healer* is that two of the three monologuists are dead. Frank and Grace thus speak from beyond the grave. They resemble the characters in *Living Quarters* in that they appear before us with their urgent memories as embodied spirits from time-space and yet are actors in the theatre-space. In *Living Quarters* the 'hero' dies to *assert* his sense of self; in *Faith Healer* the protagonist gives himself up to death with two conflicting reasons, altruistic and escapist (to still the 'maddening questions' in his mind).[51] This contrast extends also to the fate of the two women, Anna in *Living Quarters* and Grace in *Faith Healer*. Grace takes her own life when her husband is destroyed by others; Anna is the *femme fatale* causing her husband's death. Although Grace and Anna have different ends (Grace accepting the Phaedra option), the two plays interrelate with a single theme: the failure to love or respond to love in a fully human way.

Occupation and Identity

Faith Healer is named for Frank Hardy. There is no definite article in the title. It is meant as attributive. If there were an article, we should think, 'Oh, Frank Hardy *the* Faith Healer': the description would pin down his identity. As it stands, the title suggests that this is a play about *a* faith healer: the occupation, whatever preconceptions we bring to the two words in juxtaposition, is given emphasis. Foregrounded thus, it can be separated from the man associated with it. At a crucial moment of *Othello* (3.3.364), the protagonist declares in anguish, 'Othello's occupation's gone.' Does he mean what Iago means when he talks about 'reputation'? To Cassio, to lose one's reputation is to lose 'the immortal part' of himself, his soul; to Iago, reputation 'is an idle and most false imposition'. But if occupation depends on reputation, then identity itself is brittle. Both Othello and Frank Hardy are undone by this fact.

In the opening monologue of *Faith Healer*, Frank draws attention to the banner which accompanies his occupation. It reads, 'The Fantastic Frank Hardy/Faith Healer/One Night Only' (p. 331). 'The Fantastic' is a bit of meaningless showbiz engineered by Teddy, yet the banner conveys on Frank a specific identity through the addition of those two words. Frank is now not just any faith healer but one advertised as extraordinary. Further, each of the three monologuists pauses over the term 'faith healer'. Frank is tentative: 'A craft without an apprenticeship, a ministry without responsibility, a vocation without a ministry.' (p. 333) His definition sways between the spiritual and the secular-political: vocation/craft/apprenticeship and ministry/responsibility, with a pun on the government post 'Minister with responsibility' and a deliberate collision between 'vocation' and 'ministry' in the clerical sense. Friel himself once thought he had a vocation to the priesthood and then, discovering he did not, left the seminary at Maynooth with a BA in search of a ministry as a primary-school teacher. Friel's real calling was to be an artist: he resembles Joyce in this respect. Writing can indeed be a kind of unofficial priesthood. Thus, Frank's guarded self-description of his 'occupation' relates closely to the playwright's.

In her monologue, Grace surprises herself with the answer she recalls giving the doctor she attends in London (almost a year after Frank's death) when he asked, 'And what was your late husband's *occupation*, Mrs Hardy?' (p. 346, emphasis added). 'He was an artist,' she replied, adding, 'Wasn't that curious? Because the thought had never occurred to me before.' But now, because the doctor wrote it down she knew it was 'true'. A little later she reflects: 'Faith healer – faith healing – I never understood it, never. [. . .] I couldn't even begin to apprehend it – this gift, this craft, this talent, *this art, this magic* – whatever it was he possessed, *that defined him*, that was, I suppose, *essentially him*' (p. 349, emphases added). Teddy, however, believes that Frank was 'Never more than a mediocre artist. At best.' (p. 357) To be sure, Teddy's standards are drawn from performing dogs. Yet in some awe, he describes the curing of ten people in one night in a Welsh Methodist church. This was beyond pretence. 'It was like as if not only had he taken away whatever it was was wrong with them, but like he had given them some great content in themselves as well.' (p. 359) Strangely, Grace does not mention this night, perhaps the pinnacle of Frank's career. It is as if she does not remember it. She remembers better the other times, when Frank's power failed him and he flew into rages largely visited upon her, the perceived cause. Frank himself refers to this major cure in Part Four as 'one of those rare nights [. . .] when I could have moved mountains.' Faith, of course, is said to move mountains (Mt. 17.20). Frank saw himself as Christ that night, asking 'where are the [other] nine?' (Lk. 17.17), when only one of the ten returns to thank him (p. 371). Of all the contradictory and contested memories recalled in the four monologues making up the play, this is the only one backed up by evidence: in the form of a newspaper report, which Frank keeps by him until near the end. Therefore, it happened. Amid other uncertainties, this at least is certain.

Frank coped with his demons through reliance on whiskey: the healer as *poète maudit*. With Frank self-doubt is a severe neurosis, virtually pathological. He is habitually racked with uncertainty over the nature of his 'power' and the question of its endurance: 'Was it all chance? – or skill – or illusion – or delusion?' (p. 333). Was he in control of it or it of him? Was his gift a matter of instilling 'faith' in someone else or a call to that person to have faith in him? 'Could my healing be effected without faith? But faith is what? – in me? – in the possibility? – faith in faith?' These and other tormenting questions were, he says, what 'rotted' his life (p. 334). All he really knew was that when he *was* able to heal, the personal satisfaction was overwhelming: the questions were silenced and he had a temporary sense of becoming 'whole in myself, and perfect in myself, and in a manner of speaking, an aristocrat,[52] if the term doesn't offend you' (p. 333). It is a strange version of job satisfaction, the artist's joy at getting a poem or a scene or a character right. Grace insists that for Frank the people he healed were his 'fictions' (p. 345). After his death, she found she needed him to sustain her 'in that existence' as another fiction (p. 353). She literally could not. But for Frank the joy of creativity was not enough. The uncertainty was unbearable: the unbearable heaviness of being.

Teddy, as extravert, has no real access to Frank's anguish. He is always 'just outside the circle' (p. 352), an observer, detached but excluded from the privacy that defined Frank's being, his artistry. Teddy's role is to minister to Frank and Grace, to be their servant: he represents the audience as a chorus might, capable of commenting on the protagonist's failings but out of his depth in understanding what drives and destroys him. Yet Teddy has the common touch as every chorus has. While he admits that Frank was 'a bastard in many ways' (p. 363), Teddy has the compassion to grant that 'being the kind of man he was [. . .] maybe he had to have his own way of facing things' (p. 365): like Father Jack in *Lughnasa*, another doubtful shaman. Teddy stays with Frank selflessly; Frank inspires that selflessness, although Teddy is also in love with Grace. Teddy is no more than 'dedicated acolyte to the holy man' (p. 345), helpless to intervene in the tragedy. That may be one reason why audiences always take him to their hearts.

It was Ian McDiarmid and not Ralph Fiennes who got the Tony award on Broadway in 2006. Teddy, as Thomas Kilroy has well said, is 'the spirit of Theatre itself'.[53]

Metaphor and Catastrophe

Friel said to Fintan O'Toole that *Faith Healer* is 'some kind of a metaphor for the art, the craft of writing [. . . .] How honourable and how dishonourable it can be.' This concession was meant to emphasise 'the element of the charlatan' in 'all creative work'.[54] Like Beckett, Friel believes that 'to be an artist is to fail, as no other dare fail, that failure is his world and the shrink[ing] from it desertion'.[55] The artist is thus an extreme example of the natural tragic circumstance, 'original sin [. . .] the sin of having been born.'[56] Frank Hardy is a born failure dying to rehabilitate himself. Ultimately, as both Grace and Teddy testify, his talent to heal becomes less and less controllable; it was never a matter of will but of inspiration. When he describes his feelings of being 'whole in myself, and perfect in myself' whenever he *was* successful as healer, Frank recalls another failure, Macbeth. Problematic as a hero, Macbeth nevertheless has a dream of the absolute, a state of utter security which is chimerical. Like Frank, he laments his loss of such assurance: 'Then comes my fit again: I had else been *perfect,/Whole* as the marble, founded as the rock' (3.4.21-22, emphases added). But 'else' was never to be. Macbeth goes on as before, 'bound in' to terrible 'doubts and fears', until the catastrophe, when 'equivocation' and uncertainty are at last undone. Frank Hardy too is impelled onwards in search of non-existent fulfilment and 'integration' (p. 372). Although Macbeth is a destroyer where Frank Hardy is a healer, each has a destiny to confront. This is why Frank describes himself as an 'aristocrat'; this is his autism speaking. He understands to his discomfort that he is different and has a superior role in the world, even if Grace's father dismissed him as a 'mountebank' (p. 348) and his occupation as mere 'chicanery' (p. 371). There is equivocation in his life also. If life for Macbeth the king is being 'a poor player/That struts and frets his hour upon the stage' (5.5.24-5), for Frank Hardy it is an endless string of one-night performances. 'Cawdor' appears in his mantra of Scottish place names; *Faith Healer* is nothing if not Celtic. One thinks of Orson Welles's film of *Macbeth* (1948).

A catastrophe implies a massive and surprising turn of events leading on to a violent end. *Faith Healer* is unusual in that the protagonist shapes and describes his own catastrophe. Part Four brings back Frank as a monologuist. The place name 'Kinlochbervie' is repeated obsessively in each of the three opening lines, and again a little later: it was a site of great trauma. Frank begins here, in Scotland, where the turning point lies. All three speakers describe Kinlochbervie in discrepant terms. In Part One, Frank omits any mention of a baby; in Part Two, Grace says Kinlochbervie was where her only child was stillborn, and Frank buried it there. In Part Three, Teddy affirms the stillbirth but blames Frank for running away at the time, ignoring the birth and leaving it to Teddy to tend to Grace. In Part Four, Frank again offhandedly praises the beauty of the place, which he locates exactly as the other two speakers do, but says they were 'holidaying' there (p. 370); once again he omits any mention of a birth. Indeed, he firmly denies there was such: 'I would have liked to have had a child. But she [Grace] was barren. And anyhow the life we led wouldn't have been suitable' (p. 372). Outvoted two to one by the other witnesses, Frank must be lying. How often he is lying all through his two monologues is hard to estimate, but both Grace and Teddy more than once contradict his details, including those surrounding the death of his father and the major cure in Llanblethian. But none is so momentous as this of the baby. It is the source of the catastrophe. It is as important as the baby in *Oedipus the King* and as symbolic as the dead baby at the end of *Translations*.

Like Fox Mellarkey in *Crystal and Fox*, Frank Hardy is a dangerous figure. If R. D. Laing is right that '*The unconscious is what we do not communicate, to ourselves or to one another*,' then Frank's guilt over his conduct when his baby was born is the crux of his deterioration.[57] Because they never interrelate as dialogue, all monologues articulate the unconscious, paradoxically allowing unspoken thoughts. But they also suppress. (See O'Neill's *Strange Interlude* (1928).) 'Our civilization represses not only "the instincts" [as Freud had declared], not only sexuality, but any form of transcendence.'[58] To repeat, Frank is adept at blotting out the 'other', a source of resentment for Grace who is literally at his mercy, acutely aware that she had not only sustained him but had also 'debauched' herself for him in so doing (p. 344). Is Frank being literal or metaphorical when he confesses to 'blatant unfaithfulness' to Grace? (p. 335) We cannot say. He is the archetypal unreliable narrator. Although Grace says he denied her a stable identity, gave her different names and birthplaces, even at times denying they were ever married, we cannot be certain of all that. But it seems highly significant that when Frank starts off Part Four intoning 'Kinlochbervie' in every line of his incantation he is repeating Grace's lines at the end of Part Two. She speaks after Frank's death; he speaks some months before hers. Is she echoing him or he her? After all, he is the man with a mantra, and he only begins to emphasise Kinlochbervie *now*, close to his end. He refers to it and quickly passes on to seemingly pointless reminiscences, as if evading the subject to get back to narrating the Ballybeg experience and his violent end. If Kinlochbervie is what truly obsesses him, then his own end must be seen as a form of expiation for what happened *there*.

All three characters agree in many details about the trip from Stranraer to Larne and across Northern Ireland by van to 'lodgings' in a 'lounge bar' in County Donegal in the Republic. As in *Living Quarters*, this setting is liminal, border country. 'There was no sense of home-coming,' Frank Hardy says in Part One (p. 338). Was he returning from exile in hope or in despair? With a plan or just on the run? It is rather as Eliot has it: '[T]he end of all our exploring/ Will be to arrive where we started/And know the place for the first time.'[59] In their monologues, Frank's acolytes emphasise the sense of ease he emanated in Donegal. But everything changed when a stranger in the pub challenged Frank to heal a damaged finger. In his second account, Frank says 'that boy Donal *threatened me* with his damned, twisted finger' (p. 372, emphasis added). Grace sees it differently: 'Frank suddenly leaned across to one of the wedding guests, a young man called Donal, and said, "I can cure that finger of yours"' (p. 352). Teddy saw nothing. Teddy is carried off drunk to bed before anything happens. Exit witness. As to Donal's finger, it is more in character that Frank took the initiative than that he was challenged. It was an act of hubris and it was to this unwanted bravado Grace responded, realising 'instinctively' that he was in the vein to 'measure himself against the cripple in the wheelchair' (p. 352).

This action was unwonted because Frank was a consultant, one *to* whom people came, whether in hope or merely to have their despair confirmed. But on this night he was reckless, not himself, as the saying goes, but one, perhaps, 'Driven by daemonic, chthonic/Powers'.[60] Having healed Donal's finger, Frank was ready for a 'Dionysian night' (p. 340) when by definition a sacrificial victim will be 'torn to pieces' but will rise again.[61] Like Frank Butler in *Living Quarters*, his mind is in the frame of the suicide: determined to see through what he has started. He will not be deterred, neither by Grace nor by the landlord who issues a timely warning. Frank chooses his fate because he knows 'with cold certainty' that he will fail to cure the man in the wheelchair. He wills the catastrophe to appease his accumulated guilt. In doing so he certainly frees himself from the 'atrophying terror' (p. 376) his 'occupation' had brought him, but his grand gesture totally ignores Grace's fate (bound up with his) and Teddy's alcoholic future. In the final monologue, he quotes Grace from the past: 'If you leave me, Frank, I'll kill myself'; he realised then he would 'have to be with her until the very end' (p. 374), but reneges on that intuition.

Ritual, The Actor and the Audience

Faith Healer is Friel's most arcane play. 'One of the measures of a great work of the imagination,' Nicholas Grene has written, 'is not just its openness to several different interpretations, but the unexplained residuum that it leaves after any and every interpretation.'[62] There is always another way of looking at a blackbird. *Faith Healer* is in the broadest sense a mystery play. If it puts the artist under scrutiny, it is not by arraignment as in Edward Bond's *Bingo* (1973). Friel keeps Frank Hardy's secret. A problem is something to be solved, Denis Donoghue remarks, but 'a mystery is something to be witnessed and attested'[63] because, he says, 'what remains hidden is the presence of the work' (p. 32). The 'presence' is the secret meaning waiting to be interpreted. According to Frank Kermode, the four gospels in the bible provide 'instances of certain problems common to the interpretation of all texts, such as the elusiveness of secret senses'.[64] In that context, *Faith Healer*, with its four monologues, is analogous to the four gospels in secreting within the form (different versions of the life and death of a tragic hero) some overwhelming truth. But we are all free to read between the lines, because 'without interpretation there would be no mystery'.[65]

In the theatre, the actors – as well as the director – precede the critic in interpretation. Although *Faith Healer* first failed on Broadway, Friel thought James Mason 'magnificent' as Frank Hardy. What he did on stage was 'superb acting and I enjoyed working with him'.[66] The reviewers, as seen already, praised all three actors and damned the play.[67] Joe Dowling's direction of the Irish premiere at the Abbey the following year was a triumph because cast and director were able to communicate the many-faceted brilliance of the text. Dowling has a particular empathy with Friel's plays and insists that 'It is the minutiae of the work which provide its most important exploration.'[68] In short, the text is in its way sacred, a notion which has to be theatrically rather than literally understood. Dowling holds that Friel is 'always clear in both meaning and form'.[69] The risk taken with *Faith Healer* at the Abbey was great, as the acting style was at that time still reliant on ensemble playing. Donal McCann (Frank), Kate Flynn (Grace) and John Kavanagh (Teddy) were asked to act against the naturalistic grain. For McCann, whom Friel wanted as Frank,[70] the role proved stellar. He brought out the histrionic qualities in Frank Hardy, who always speaks of his occupation as 'performance'. Frank *is* theatrical, a bit of a dandy, a professional liar. He is *aware* that his being is theatrical and that the world he inhabits is itself a theatre. In the Donegal lounge bar, when he cures the crooked finger, he says to Grace, 'That's just the curtain-raiser' (p. 352). Earlier, querying his own role-playing, he enquires of himself, 'You're beginning to masquerade, aren't you?' (p. 334), and speaks ironically of his Donegal behaviour as 'pretending to subscribe to the charade' (p. 341). He knows all about masks. McCann felt entirely at home with such imagery; offstage he had barely a word to say for himself, but onstage he was riveting. After his untimely death,

Sebastian Barry described him as 'a man of unalterable greatness'.[71] In John Huston's film of Joyce's *The Dead* (1987), McCann would draw on his *Faith Healer*, especially in the final monologue, so perfect a fit had it become over the years.[72] He said of his Frank Hardy: 'I found myself on a level of being so confident and I was being comforted by the thing I was doing in an extraordinary way.'[73] There is something priestly, hieratic, in the role. Joe Dowling sees the perfect fit between actor and role deriving from McCann's 'combined intelligence, sensitivity, *spirituality*, excessive behaviour and the awareness that talent cannot be trusted, that the performance doesn't always happen on demand'.[74] Indeed, McCann saw the theatre as, for him, 'a most revealing, spiritual place'.[75]

Consequently, *Faith Healer,* a play about 'occupation', may be read as a spiritual play. There is a moment in O'Neill's *Long Day's Journey into Night* (which Friel also drew on for *Crystal and Fox*) which supports this interpretation. The ex-Shakespearean actor James Tyrone ruefully remembers the night when Edwin Booth praised his Othello: 'I made the manager put down his exact words in writing. I kept it in my wallet for years. I used to read it every once in a while until finally it made me feel so bad I didn't want to face it anymore.'[76] At the opening of the Fourth monologue, Frank Hardy produces a newspaper clipping, '*very tattered, very faded*' (p. 370), recording his finest 'performance', when he cured ten people. He does not know why he has kept this cutting and, in a sudden switch of mood to narrative, declares: 'And that night in that pub in Ballybeg I crumpled it up (*He does this now*) and threw it away.' (p. 371) The record of his miracle galls Frank Hardy as much as his fame galls James Tyrone. Tyrone mourns the loss of the *testimony*, however, while Hardy throws it away in contempt. Both realise in their separate moments that they have thrown their lives away too. The right actor, McCann, Ralph Richardson, David Suchet, can bring out the tragic reverberations of such a moment within the theatre.

The path to Frank Hardy's final step into the heart of darkness is by way of ritual. Yeats remarked: 'I always feel my work is not drama but the ritual of a lost faith.'[77] The notion is embedded in much contemporary Irish drama. In his opening monologue, Frank Hardy describes the venues for his faith healing as old church buildings and the like adorned by 'relicts of abandoned rituals' (p. 332). The inference in his description is that only the theatre itself can now supply the want left by the general abandonment of churches. One thinks of Philip Larkin's poem about a visit to a deserted church and the meditation it inspired on the bleak future of such obsolete places.[78] Perhaps only the theatre can nowadays assuage such hunger with its reinvented myths and rituals.

As Frank makes his way in his second monologue to his narrative of the ritual killing, he is both participant and memorialist. At first, his speech is stream of consciousness, digressing from the lie about Grace's sterility back to the newspaper clipping. He should like to have had a son, for 'What is a piece of paper?' He moves into a dark place mentally, Macbeth territory, brooding on what he can no longer 'look to have': all now is 'Nothing, nothing, nothing', even Grace's 'absolute loyalty' (pp. 371–2). When McCann articulated the word 'loyalty' here, he split up the three syllables and spat them out as if he could not bear the burden of such attachment, or the 'devotion' her wraith-like mother told him she needed. A memory of his father likewise looms up. Earlier he could not cope with the challenge his grieving father posed over bringing mother back to life: 'Jesus, I thought, O my Jesus, what am I going to do?' (p. 338) Now the dead father haunts like a vanquished Banquo. The ritual becomes a vigil as time is syncopated in narrative. '*He walks up stage.* (*Pause.*) I must have walked that floor [in the hotel lounge] for a couple of hours' (p. 374). We are back in the present, which is also the past in Friel's isochronous world; the actor walks while recording the pacing, as he awaits the arrival of his nemesis. As he tells it, Frank both is and was alone: the synthesis marks the convergence of the twain (in that other Hardy's sense). The others are abed; the landlord makes himself scarce, predicting disaster. We are suddenly *out* of time, past and present being fused in illusory theatre time. Space, too, begins to dissolve before our eyes to become real in the imagination.

When the wedding guests arrive Frank is called outside. '*He puts on the hat and overcoat and buttons it slowly*' (p. 374). He is still upstage, where he describes the two yards behind the lounge, the second of which was to be his Golgotha. 'And I knew it at once.' (p. 375). It is a space as in a painting, which Frank throngs with realistic detail. He is his own Messenger in a Greek tragedy, describing a death. Frank has a transcendent 'intimation' of solitude, as if he, McGarvey and his friends 'had ceased to be physical and existed only in spirit, only in the need we had for each other' (p. 376). This joint need can refer to actor and audience in tandem. And now occurs the main *action* as such in *Faith Healer*, the manifestation of its through-line, in the sequence of movements Frank initiates when he (literally) '*takes off his hat as if he were entering a church and holds it at his chest*'. He is '*both awed and elated*' (p. 376), a cue for the actor, as Frank moves slowly downstage, to the edge beyond which the unseen McGarvey awaits him, off, in the auditorium. The narrative voice resumes. Frank 'offered' himself to the group, the word reminiscent of the 'surrender' of the princess he would heal in Teddy's fantasy (p. 372). But now it is he who *surrenders*, like Jesus Christ, to his destiny. In offering himself to his executioners, Frank has a 'genuine sense of homecoming', an ironic *anagnorisis* or moment of recognition. In stepping towards the audience and into a theatrical blackout, Frank Hardy establishes communion with the audience as healer, and vice versa in the two-way traffic of the stage. In contrast to the end of *Living Quarters*, this Frank's death fructifies in the lives of others. So it was, on that glorious night at the Abbey premiere on 28 August 1980, when the audience sat stunned for a whole minute, it seemed, while registering the catharsis, pleasurable release after terrible, shared uncertainty.

CHAPTER 6

A KIND OF TRILOGY: *MAKING HISTORY, TRANSLATIONS* AND *THE HOME PLACE*

I shall cheerfully bear the reproach of having descended below the dignity of history.

– Macaulay, *History of England*, Vol. 1, Chapter 1 (1849)

Introduction

In some ways, *The Enemy Within*, Friel's first play at the Abbey in 1962, stands as prolegomenon to what I call Friel's 'trilogy'. It is not, in fact, a trilogy, but arranging the above three plays in historical rather than in order of composition serves to foreground ideas of history and evolution which otherwise tend to remain undelineated. A deliberate reordering can reveal patterns and themes within an integrated structure of feeling. *The Communication Cord* (1982), a farce deliberately written to offset the misguided reception of *Translations* as crypto-propaganda, will also be deployed as an indicator of Friel's determination to maintain the lines and perspective of his historical vision.

The Enemy Within is important as a play which encodes many of Friel's lasting preoccupations. It is the key to the subsequent history plays. *The Enemy Within* concerns the sixth-century Columba or Colmcille from Derry, in what is now Northern Ireland. He is one of the three major saints of the Irish church alongside Patrick and Brigid. But he was also a warrior, a scholar and a prince of Clann Uí Néill, the royal house of Ulster: to which Hugh O'Neill of *Making History* also belonged and was consecrated head. Columba was officially exiled from Ireland and in terrible distress undertook the monastic life on Iona in Scotland, from where he founded the important mission to Christianise England.[1] From the modern perspective, there is irony in this role, reversing the colonisation of Ireland. But perhaps the major feature of Columba's character Friel emphasises is his yearning for home, never to be fulfilled. As a translation of one of Columba's own verses puts it, 'I ever long for the land of Ireland/where I had power,/An exile now in midst of strangers,/sad and tearful.'[2] It might be the voice of his descendant Hugh O'Neill as he ends his days exiled in Rome, a victim of history and the counter-Reformation. In Friel's play, the themes of place and vocation are bound up with nostalgia (in its proper sense of 'home-sickness') and these were to be major themes in the history plays which were to follow. The 'enemy within' is whatever conflicts with these concerns, be it conscience, desire for freedom or family allegiance, as in *Making History*, *Translations* and *The Home Place*. Friel himself compared his Columba to James Joyce for courageously 'turning his back on Ireland and on his family' in order to pursue his art.[3] Integrity was the core value; the individual, liberal conscience its ultimate instrument.

Friel's history plays find their dramatic context between the Irish and the modernist traditions. On the one hand, there is the nineteenth-century narrative of loss, dramatised in many a melodrama applauded at the Dublin Queen's Theatre in the decades before 1916. However, there is the rebirth of the history play as modern allegory, fathered by Shaw in *St Joan* (1920) and taken up by Brecht, Arthur Miller and many others down to the 1960s. Robert Bolt's *A Man For All Seasons* (1960) could be contrasted with Friel's endeavour. In his St Thomas More, Bolt portrayed 'a man with an adamantine sense of his own self. He knew where he began and left off.'[4] His was 'a vivid Sartre-like picture of the existential helplessness of modern man'.[5] Friel's emphasis is different. Once again, it is the uncertainty, the self-division in the hero, that he portrays, and failure is the inevitable outcome. His historical figures are never for *all* seasons but only for those that illuminate national identity at moments of great cultural crisis.

Making History

Making History, being a postmodern text, is totally different in form from the other two under survey here. Yet, while engaging with the career of Hugh O'Neill (*c.* 1550–1616), it may be read partly as an allegory of Irish-English affairs in the atmosphere of the 1980s in Northern Ireland. *Making History* was a Field Day production, Field Day having been established in 1980 by Friel and the actor Stephen Rea to create a debate about Northern politics and to illuminate way(s) through which culture could hope to intervene and move the conversation towards reconciliation.[6] It can be claimed that this happened, that the cultural climate for discussions of disarmament, decommissioning and eventually the fruition of the Belfast Agreement in 1998 was in no small measure conditioned by Field Day and Brian Friel.

As hero, O'Neill's vocation was never in doubt; his credentials were impeccable. The 2009 *Dictionary of Irish Biography* describes the historical Hugh O'Neill as 'one of the most adept politicians in Irish history', 'as able in negotiations as in battle' and 'possessed of a charisma which captivated the men and women who came in contact with him'.[7] Ironically, this description, apt for Columba, does not get us far in understanding Friel's representation of O'Neill. Yet there is one passage in the *DIB*'s sober assessment of O'Neill's career which lends support to Friel's whole approach. Having described the famous moment when the Earl of Essex, defeated by O'Neill, went back to Queen Elizabeth to 'browbeat' her into accepting O'Neill's plan for peace, the account briefly refers to Essex's arrest (he was sent to the Tower for his pains and executed). Then this phrase follows: 'When he heard this news, O'Neill broke off *the peace process*, though unbeknown to him Robert Cecil, Essex's rival, was still interested in concluding a peace on account of war-weariness in England' (p. 269). The phrase I have emphasised was a buzz one in the 1990s when the IRA/Sinn Féin movement was dallying with negotiations for ways to end the war raging ever since Bloody Sunday. This kind of anachronistic phrasing was the very tactic Friel had in mind in writing his play. He was less interested in the sixteenth than in the twentieth century, less interested in historical accuracy than in aiming for a play of ideas. As he put it in a programme note in 1988, *Making History* is 'a dramatic fiction that uses some actual and some imagined events in the life of Hugh O'Neill to make a story'. The insistence is that the play, any play, is a fiction. In the programme note, Friel declared: 'Part of me regrets taking these occasional liberties. But then I remind myself that history and fiction are related and *comparable forms of discourse* and that *an historical text is a kind of literary artifact*'[8] (italics added). And again: 'You don't go to *Macbeth* for history.'[9] *Making History*, then, is a kind of fulcrum between *The Enemy Within* and *Translations*. It is less a slice of history than a lively piece of literary theory in dramatic form, a Field Day pamphlet of a different kind, intended to release some fireworks and throw dust in the eyes of his critics. It is, in essence, playful. Yet it is also, inevitably, a tragedy.

Friel could have found a model in Thomas Kilroy's *The O'Neill*, staged at the Peacock, annex of the Abbey Theatre, on 30 May 1969. The date is significant because it falls *before* the 'troubles' erupted in Belfast in August of that year. Its two acts swivel around the Battle of the Yellow Ford on 14 August 1598. Kilroy's play is set 'in Ireland and London, before, during and after O'Neill's victory'.[10] At the Yellow Ford, in County Armagh, in what is now Northern Ireland, 'O'Neill had achieved the greatest victory ever achieved by Irish arms against the English.'[11] This is the very achievement Friel omits from *Making History*. Kilroy, too, presents O'Neill as a modern man. In an argument with Mabel Bagenal, his wife, Kilroy's O'Neill says: 'If I'm splintered it's because my people have eyes only for their own bits of property. Good God, I'm struggling with generations of small-minded men. And I'm the only one who sees this, the only one. [. . .] Maybe I was born in the wrong place and at the wrong time' (pp. 34–5). To the Gaelic poet, O'Neill declares he wishes to be 'a modern man [. . .] questioning myself at all times' (p. 29). Here were strong hints for Friel, whose play leapfrogs neatly from Kilroy's onto a different plane. In between, available to both writers as source, stands Seán O'Faoláin's powerful study *The Great O'Neill* (1942, republished 1970). To Kilroy, this text gave the facts and the romantic concept of a figure, like himself, 'born with a Protestant mind in a Catholic body', virtually an Anglo-Irishman.[12] O'Faoláin has a brilliant reading of O'Neill's character which finds its way into both Kilroy's and Friel's characterisations: the replacement of the old 'Patriot myth' of each new hero rising against the old tyrant with the alternative, sixteenth-century myth of the *old* hero against a new tyrant, a feudal knight against king/queen. From Queen Elizabeth's point of view, O'Neill's ambition mirrored her own struggle for absolute power. She saw him as part of the whole system of which she was head: O'Neill, in turn, understood this but his followers, stuck in the old myth, did not.

What emerges from O'Faoláin's thesis are two major emphases which Friel eagerly adopted. One refers to the annalists and their role in perpetuating the old myth as an inspirational tool, whereby the failure of the hero can be accepted as just cause for a new, recurring revolution (rather like the hopeless Bonny Prince Charlie myth in seventeenth-century Scottish history). Friel's Lombard enters the picture here. Peter Lombard (c. 1554–1625) was an historical figure, a theologian and archbishop of Armagh in exile in Rome. He and O'Neill did not meet until the latter arrived in Rome as an exile in 1608, when Lombard had been O'Neill's agent in Rome for many years, bolstering O'Neill's plans to lead – with the help of Catholic Spain – the counter-reformation on Irish soil. Lombard was still working on his *Commentarius* on this topic, revising and altering the thrust of what was in manuscript by 1600; publication did not take place until 1632, when both men were dead. Far from being preoccupied with O'Neill's biography, the *Commentarius* was zealous propaganda for the counter-reformation. In its closing section, however, Lombard's text argued that a victory for O'Neill would bring 'great benefits to the catholic religion'.[13] But O'Faoláin saw Lombard's book as Friel was to see it, as 'the creation of the patriotic myth about Tyrone' [O'Neill].[14] Those like Lombard who made a 'pious patriot' of O'Neill, O'Faoláin claimed, 'have denied him the intellectual judgement to which his stature entitled him' (p. 277).

In *Making History*, Friel makes 'play' with this argument. (He understood the nature of hagiography from his research on Columba for his *Enemy Within*.) He has O'Neill apprehensive from the outset. Lombard, who is present at O'Neill's fortress in Dungannon, County Tyrone, is ambivalent over the purpose of his 'history'. He dodges the question whether what he writes will be the 'truth': 'Maybe when the time comes my first responsibility will be to tell the best possible narrative. Isn't that what history is, a kind of story-telling?'[15] His bottom line is: 'History has to be made – before it's remade' (p. 258). Here, he is making a pun echoed by Friel's title for the play itself. 'Making' history is on the one hand action, public achievement, creating change; however, 'making history' is scribal, the recording *and* interpretation of events. One is objective, the other subjective. But which is which? How can we, Yeats philosophically asked, 'know the dancer from the dance?', especially now in the age of Hayden White and the new historiography.[16] When all is over, when O'Neill is exiled and impotent in Rome, he accuses Lombard of 'going to embalm me – in – in a florid lie' (p. 329). The discussion is vital to O'Neill because his identity depends upon the full truth being told about him. Otherwise, he is in bad faith. Lombard insists that 'narrative' is all he will offer. O'Faoláin said Lombard did not understand O'Neill, neither his arrogance and ambition nor that O'Neill was 'realizing in himself all the tragedy of his country's defeat'.[17] In Friel's ending, Lombard outrageously expects O'Neill to sacrifice the full truth about himself, to facilitate the construction of 'a national hero' (p. 335) for future use. Needing the 'myth', Lombard insists on the stakes: 'we are talking about a colonized people on the brink of extinction' (p. 334). Addressed to an audience in 1988 or soon after, this assertion is positively Shavian (compare *St Joan*, and Shaw's preface).

The other area where Friel most emphatically plays with O'Faoláin's biography of O'Neill and thereby with history is over Mabel Bagenal. Historically, she was the daughter of O'Neill's enemy Sir Nicholas Bagenal, who, in 1591, had succeeded his more famous father Henry as marshal of the army in Ireland and was killed at the Battle of the Yellow Ford. O'Neill had eloped with Mabel in 1590 as a political stroke to gain advantage. Friel makes it a love match, a crossing of the sectarian divide, what Jimmy Jack in *Translations* calls 'exogamy' or marrying outside the tribe. 'And you don't cross those borders casually – both sides get very angry.'[18] Whereas in *Translations*, Yolland pays the price, in *Making History* Mabel has the courage of her commitment, forsakes family, religious and political allegiance for Hugh O'Neill and dies having his child. She appears in three scenes only but these are the vital ones. Indeed, the scene where Mabel's sister visits her is the most original and most significant scene in *Making History*. The sister, Mary, is solidly Anglo-Irish and voices the coloniser's point of view. What the audience needs to be aware of is what the future holds: the plantation of Ulster after O'Neill is defeated and unaccountably exiles himself in Rome. The plantation, whereby lands owned by the O'Neill sept for centuries, and by the other great Gaelic chiefs, were handed over to royal favourite and adventurers, was an intense, ongoing scheme of colonising Ireland. O'Neill had successfully interrupted the plantation of Munster through his victory at the Battle of the Yellow Ford and subsequent ending of Essex's campaign, but in the longer time frame his failure at Kinsale (1601), which O'Neill's Spanish supporters had occupied but the English successfully besieged, left him exposed to eventual humiliation. In the play, Mabel is the figure who highlights what this means in the cultural as well as in the political sense.

Mary sees O'Neill's people as 'doomed': 'Their way of life is doomed [. . .] because civility is God's way [. . .] and because superstition must yield before reason' (p. 279). This is the coloniser's classic argument. The poet Edmund Spenser (1552–99), having spent almost twenty years in Ireland as a significant official in Elizabeth's administration and as 'planter' in Munster with a large estate, was the first to argue as Mary argues for the civilising reform of the barbaric natives. Spenser and the burning of his house by the native Irish 'in the troubles' (telling phrase) are mentioned in the play (p. 316). Also, Spenser's imagery of 'planting' and harsh pruning exposes the violent means through which order must be introduced if 'reforms' are to take place: 'Even by the sword for all those evils must first be cut away with a strong hand before any good can be planted, like as the corrupt branches.'[19] Mary sees O'Neill as 'barbarian' and blames her sister for letting herself (and country) down in giving herself to him and his 'savage people' who 'refuse to cultivate the land'. Those who so refuse, and pursue pastoral farming (cattle) instead of tillage, 'have no right to that Ireland' (pp. 278–9). To Mary, O'Neill is a traitor. Thus she and Mabel stand on either side of a sectarian divide which endured even as the play was being staged, as Seamus Deane testified in his Field Day pamphlet,

Civilians and Barbarians (1983). When the sisters say 'we' and 'they', they mean opposite things.

When O'Neill interrupts this conversation a more tense debate begins. O'Neill lays on irony in order to get under Mary's skin when she uses words like 'loyalty' and 'rebels'. He mockingly apologises for his friend Maguire: 'Trapped in the old Gaelic paradigms [a deliberate anachronism] of thought.' He is aware of the stereotyping on both sides. 'It's so familiar – and so tedious' (p. 282). The audience too is meant to recognise the two discourses. O'Neill then becomes more serious, leaving aside the easy stereotyping: 'we both know that the conflict [*sic*, again, a contemporary word] isn't between caricatured national types but between two deeply opposed civilizations, isn't it? We're really talking about a life-and-death conflict, aren't we? Only one will survive' (p. 283). It is O'Neill's dilemma but at the same time, in late-twentieth-century Northern Ireland also the dilemma of a whole population, still at the mercy of 'the slow, sure tide of history' (p. 283).

The (literal) seeds Mary leaves with Mabel to grow a herb garden provide the dominant imagery in this debate. O'Neill plays word games with the names and accompanying instructions, signifier and signified, for example, 'coriander seed: "Watch this seed carefully as it ripens suddenly and will fall without warning." Sounds like [the rebel] Maguire, doesn't it? – Coriander Maguire.' Or borage, '"inclined to induce excessive courage, even recklessness." That's O'Donnell [O'Neill's closest ally], isn't it? Borage O'Donnell' (p. 286). In contrast, Mary has just warned Mabel against hybridity: 'Don't plant the fennel near the dill or the two will cross-fertilize. [. . .] You'll end up with a seed that's neither one thing or the other' (p. 275). Civilians and barbarians don't mix. That has been the enduring tragedy of the North, which has always also included a casualty of language, a failure in communication. As allegory, this scene goes back to the garden scene in Shakespeare's history play about power and order, *King Richard II* (Act 3, Scene 4), but the idea of order is now ironised and made strange.

Friel reinvents the historical Mabel (who ran away from the marriage) and makes her the central figure in O'Neill's tragic situation. The real Mabel died in 1595, before O'Neill's star reached its apogee in the victory at the Yellow Ford; Friel moves her death to coincide with the nadir of O'Neill's hopes after the debacle of Kinsale in 1601. In the meantime she is 'loyal': that ambiguous word which the ultra-Gaelic chieftain O'Donnell applies to her at that point (p. 309): 'She's a very loyal wee girl.' It is not that she has 'gone over', in the crudest sense. She is inspired by Hugh and he, in turn, by her. It is a strange, new love story in the midst of political turmoil. After Lombard brings news from Spain and a Papal Bull from Rome which now defines O'Neill's project as 'a holy crusade', Mabel tries to help Hugh to see beyond the implications. In jingoistic style, Lombard plays the nationalist card: 'we are no longer a casual grouping of tribes but a nation state united under the Papal colours' (p. 291). It is a tipping point for O'Neill, as his memory of his English foster-father Sidney's warning indicates. He can no longer play both sides but must claim his identity as liberator. But Mabel disagrees. 'This isn't your way,' she tells him (p. 296). She can read him better than he can himself. She warns that what Lombard envisages is but pie in the sky: 'At best you are an impromptu alliance of squabbling tribesmen' (p. 297). She knows it is *not* a religious war. She is revealed as a woman Shaw might have created, a rock of sense, analytic, gifted with words, superior to the male in fundamental understanding. 'This is a war that England must win because her very survival is at stake' (p. 298).

Once again, the sentiment is aimed straight at an audience at the end of the Thatcher era. It refers to Northern Ireland in the decade of the hunger strikes, but it also refers to the larger struggle for order and authority in the whole United Kingdom and its imperial dominions (which included the Falklands). Apologetically, Mabel backtracks: 'I'm sure I don't really understand the overall thing' (p. 299). At this juncture O'Neill is deaf to her warning, although she slips into her prophetic comments the name of the new Lord Deputy, Mountjoy, who was to be O'Neill's 'nemesis'[20] and the main architect of the colonisation of the North. In self-defence, O'Neill can only deliver a party political speech concerning his aim to 'open these people' to 'the strange new ways of Europe' and change, while also 'trying to keep them in touch with the life they knew before they were overrun' (p. 299). Modernity in lockstep with tradition, in short. Her response is brief and to the point, 'So have your war' (p. 300). And he does. And loses. Robert Cecil, secretary to Elizabeth, had already dismissed O'Neill's nationalist programme as 'Utopia',[21] with a nod towards Thomas More.

Thus, Lombard's continuing emphasis on 'an emerging nation state' (p. 330) is merely poignant. O'Neill's defeat at Kinsale was to relegate such an ambition to the realms of myth, the stuff of recurring dreams of breaking the 'link' with England. The opening of Act 2 of *Making History* indicates how terrible was the aftermath of Kinsale: 'a complete collapse', the countryside in 'chaos', everywhere 'slaughter, famine, disease' (p. 305). But as Hugh O'Donnell points out, who is chief is unimportant because according to Gaelic/Celtic belief, the land itself, being female, 'is the goddess that every ruler in turn is married to. We come and go but she stays the same' (p. 308). As soon as news comes of Mabel's death in childbirth, we realise she, too, was the goddess of her adopted land. (Here, Friel is inventing.) Even O'Donnell can see now that 'Mabel was right' (p. 315). In the next and final scene set in Rome years later where the exiled O'Neill, in total contrast to his counterpart Columba at the end of *The Enemy Within*, finds no inner peace or satisfaction, Mabel's ghostly presence dominates. This too is entirely Friel's invention and serves to validate an anti-heroic, gendered idea of history, less revisionist than new-historicist (à la Stephen Greenblatt). If the dominating force of *The Enemy Within* is God, making that play God-centred, the dominating, although historically peripheral figure in *Making History* is Mabel, making that play woman-centred.

Yet that final scene is, theatrically, dominated by a text. Lombard's unfinished history lies on his desk where his chronic guest, the drunken O'Neill, discovers it on this specific night, at the end of his tether.[22] He has become 'a pitiable, bitter bastard' (p. 325), no longer the stuff of heroes. But he will fight his last battle, he declares, over Mabel's place in the history written by Lombard. This is the secondary meaning of the 'making' of history (as text) resumed from the start of the play. Like Sir's text in *Living Quarters*, it will be fixed, definitive. But in advance of such finality – which he questions – O'Neill quarrels with the 'making' of his story and its status as truth. The gap between experience, or event, and record, or report, is filled by Lombard's rhetoric: in a word by *style*. Friel, though a master of style himself, is always suspicious of its power. The inventiveness of his lively characters can make a falsehood seem true. This is what the artist does. This is what Lombard also does; the only weapon he has left for his propaganda is style. O'Neill is mistaken when he says, 'There is no way you can make unpalatable facts palatable' (p. 333). History plus rhetoric can do this with ease, transforming subjectivity into apparent objectivity. As Lombard says, all people want is a 'story' (p. 334), an echo of Fox's mockery of a happy ending in *Crystal and Fox*. Lombard will not concede the gap that exists between reality and myth.

As Lombard reads aloud the opening of his selective, biased history, O'Neill himself recites the shameful text of surrender he had signed in 1603 not knowing Queen Elizabeth was dead. Both are false documents. The two voices counterpoint each other ironically, exposing O'Neill's failure to be true to Mabel's inspiration. He can only beg her forgiveness as the lights go down. A broken man, like Christopher Gore at the end of *The Home Place*, O'Neill is locked into a history to which Mabel alone, the Other, had the key. The audience, however, is left with an alternative text for the imagination to explore, and the question of *how* Mabel's notion of 'the overall thing' might become reality today.

Translations

Translations is an Irish history play but helps to clarify this 'overall thing', so far as Friel's idea of history is discernible. Although it is a play that ends in stasis like *Making History*, its 'retrospection will be all to the future'.[23] With his characteristic use of double time, Friel continues to make a history play so reinterpret the past as to interrogate the future – which in the theatre is ever shifting. I would suggest that *Translations*, carrying forward the theatrical double focus of *Making History* – in spite of the order of composition – is energised by a Darwinian view. Although O'Neill's case enshrined him as founder of the Catholic nationalist cause in Ireland, initiating centuries of similar flawed attempts to defeat the coloniser, nevertheless, freedom was to evolve from all this failure. *Translations* is not concerned with armed rebellion but it finally gestures towards it as the inevitable route. The 'overall thing', then, looks to the horizon of expectation where lie the supposed markers for national independence and ultimate unity. The problem with this interpretation, however, is Hugh.

To a considerable extent, it appears that Hugh is Friel's spokesman in the play: learned, witty, liberal. He is also accommodating. Is his final attitude to accepting 'inevitabilities' and moving on, the one we are to accept as the 'message' of the play? But to anticipate slightly here: we do well to regard Hugh as confused, as confronting the audience finally with hesitancy in delivering a translation of Virgil's origin of Rome's greatness out of the fall of Carthage as if two cultures could never subsist together. We have to query Hugh's role, as Shaun Richards brilliantly does in his article in Chapter 10 in relation to the postcolonial debate raised by *Translations*. Hugh will be discussed further under 'Fathers and Sons' below.

Language and Authenticity

Although Friel famously stated that *Translations* 'has to do with language and only language',[24] it has also been claimed that it is 'both a parable about, and a diagnosis of, the conditions of the post-partition [i.e. in 1922] Catholic community in Northern Ireland'.[25] That is to say, *Translations* is both a play about language *and* a political play. It is both, because it is an *Irish* history play. In Ireland, language itself is inescapably political. But is *Translations* a history play in the same sense as *Making Histo*ry? No. It is neither self-conscious in representation nor concerned with 'a hero and the story of a hero'.[26] It is concerned with a representative community, native-speaking and traditionalist, which is suddenly and aggressively exposed to the modern world. The kind of question such a play invites an audience to consider today relates to bilingual societies everywhere, and to multicultural urban communities in the Anglophone world where migrants form a large proportion of the population, or where indigenous peoples find themselves ostracised from their native landscape. The play studies Irish history and culture but its implications are universal.

Translations is a situation play. It is set on the cusp of massive social and cultural change. It is not a piece of propaganda. It creates a world of ordinary people in a rural setting in what within the text is an uneasy time of transition and anxiety. The 'sweet smell' from the potato drills presages famine in the minds of a community for whom subsistence is always precarious.[27] As the camera, so to speak, moves in on the chosen setting, we see that it is a '*disused barn or hay-shed or byre*' (p. 383) used as a schoolhouse by an old scholar who with his son, a young scholar, lives in a loft over the schoolroom. It is a hedge-school and therefore, as Helen Lojek has said, unstable.[28] There is no family as such, no mother, not even a Madge as in *Philadelphia*. All is fragmented, lamed, muted. Except for one exterior scene (the love scene outside an unseen house where a dance takes place), this location remains the space in which Friel creates his early nineteenth-century world. With no hint of antiquarianism or of a cultural museum – much less of anything kitsch – this is a workplace. Yet a school can become a microcosm of society.

Embarrassed by what he felt as wrong-headed, misplaced approval of an essentialist, over-nationalist reception of *Translations* on its first production in 1980, Friel hastened to provide his own corrective in *The Communication Cord* (1982), set in modern times. Without insisting that the sequel is necessary reading before attempting to interpret *Translations*, one can at least claim that the precaution is salutary. The parody mocks contemporary Irish pretensions of *pietas*, love of supposed past values, primitivism, poverty or the nostalgia masking corrupt self-deception. A glance at the opening stage direction of *The Communication Cord* is sufficient here to indicate the cliché-ridden response to *Translations* which imperils that text even yet: '*The action takes place in a "traditional" Irish cottage.* [. . .] *Every detail of the kitchen and its furnishings is accurate of its time (from 1900 to 1930). But one quickly senses something false about the place. It is too pat, too "authentic". It is in fact a restored house, a reproduction, an artefact of today making obeisance to a home of yesterday.*'[29] Alongside 'traditional' (used twice in the full-stage description), the word 'authentic' leaps out here. *The Communication Cord* exists to mock the *in*authentic, the worship of a bogus originary tradition. 'Authenticity' offers the 'way in' to interpreting *Translations*. It relates to a fierce impatience Friel felt with theatre and society in the Republic, where blandness and complacency reigned in the 1970s. Much of this anger comes through in *Volunteers* (see Chapter 4), but it is most nakedly expressed in the essay 'Plays Peasant and Unpeasant' (1972), where he identifies a 'deep schizophrenia' in Dublin, 'the coexistence of Chase Manhattan money with bomb-throwing chauvinism'.[30] Victory could go to neither side because neither can preserve its 'purity'.[31] For 'purity' read 'authenticity'. Friel adopted the term Lionel Trilling[32] had recently opposed to 'sincerity' to include a whole way of life, a moral outlook, a traditional [Irish] stance in the face of bad faith. By identifying 'style' with English in *Translations*, through the sleight-of-hand of using one language for two, Friel was able ironically to equate it with authenticity.

While in *Making History* the peasantry is absent and history is made by aristocratic figures who are both English earls and Irish chieftains, in *Translations* history is made on the backs of the people: it is the offstage figures like the Donnelly twins who have agency. The best the others can do is, like Doalty, to make a gesture indicating a 'presence' (p. 391). In that way, the play itself asserts a presence to the minds of a modern audience, exerting pressure to re-evaluate autonomy. In *Culture and Imperialism* (1993), Edward Said praises *Translations* as an example of 'the culture of resistance' and its 'search for authenticity, for a more congenial national origin than that provided by colonial history'.[33] Ideologically, however, Said's postcolonial argument contributed less to Friel's history play than George Steiner's *After Babel: Aspects of Language and Translation* (1975), as Helen Lojek has best demonstrated,[34] even though Said may aid interpretation.

Field Day and the Abbey Model

A month before finishing *Translations* on 5 November 1979, Friel heard from the actor Stephen Rea proposing the idea which was to develop into the Field Day Theatre Company. Friel offered him

Translations for their first production.[35] The two men were agreed that a new venture in Irish theatre was called for. It had to be authentically Northern. To that end, the casting had to be exclusively Northern, the directors likewise, when such were needed in August 1981 to allow for 'charitable status' to be obtained for the company. The carefully selected members were all male and from Northern Ireland: Seamus Deane, David Hammond, Seamus Heaney and Tom Paulin, all writers except Hammond (a musician and folk singer). It was not until 1988 that a southerner was added: the playwright Thomas Kilroy, although he had been consulted as a friend by both Deane and Friel almost from the foundation of Field Day. While otherwise exclusively Northern, a balance was from the outset deliberately made between Protestants (Hammond, Paulin, Rea) and Catholics (Friel, Deane and, later, Kilroy). Gender balance was never on the Field Day agenda.

Both Friel and Rea were adamant that the model for the new idea of a theatre should not be the Abbey. To Rea, the Abbey was 'just a dead space'[36] with no interest in the play of ideas. Friel's impatience is less understandable as the Abbey had recently premiered *The Freedom of the City* and *Living Quarters* and was poised to premiere *Aristocrats* and *Faith Healer*. He had begun to identify the Abbey as politically collusive with what he despised in the Republic. He persuaded himself that Derry should be the epicentre of Field Day and that Field Day should provide an alternative to the Abbey. It would stage plays for a new, non-metropolitan audience and it would tour to small-town venues, community halls and the like, north and south. At the time, the Irish Theatre Company (1974–82) in the Republic was the only comparison, but it lacked a comparable ideology. The Lyric in Belfast, while then nationalist in *ethos*, was with the Abbey firmly ruled out as model. The Druid in Galway seems to have been overlooked. Ironically, Field Day most resembled the *ur*-Abbey, the Irish Literary Theatre (ILT) founded in 1897 by Yeats, Lady Gregory and Edward Martyn with no touring remit but with quite similar ideas. The ILT's declaration was for new Irish plays 'written with a high ambition' to 'build up a Celtic and Irish school of dramatic literature', experimental but focused exclusively on 'the deeper thoughts and emotions of Ireland'. Above all, 'We will show that Ireland is not the home of buffoonery and of easy sentiment, as it has been represented, but the home of an ancient idealism.'[37] Friel, too, declared: 'We hope to do plays of excellence and to do them excellently,'[38] which seems a fair translation. And later, Friel defined the general aim of Field Day very much in Yeats's terms as 'to forge a cultural identity for Ireland free of the influence of both London and the nationalist mythologies of the Republic'.[39]

Synge, who appeared on the scene in 1902, was for Yeats exactly the writer the ILT was looking for, passionate, rooted, pure artist and 'truly a National writer as Burns was when he wrote finely'.[40] Friel responded in much the same way: Synge 'successfully solved' the problem Friel was himself profoundly interested in, making words in the English language 'distinctive and unique to us'.[41] Synge alone had done this: 'apart from Synge, all our dramatists have pitched their voices for English acceptance and recognition'.[42] So, Synge was adopted as a model of authenticity. The rest follows. Although the politics were different, Field Day set out, in effect, to renew the revolution Yeats and Synge had initiated. Further, although Field Day founded their theatre specifically on a Northern basis, it intended to be inclusive in its political agenda (and its all-Ireland touring remit). Seamus Heaney put the point succinctly: 'We believed we could create a space in which we would try to redefine what being Irish meant in the context of what had happened in the north.'[43] Accordingly, like the premiere of *Cathleen Ní Houlihan* in Dublin in 1902, when the audience sang 'A Nation Once Again',[44] the first night of *Translations* in Derry in 1980 was a triumph. Staged at the very Guildhall which provided the setting for *The Freedom of the City* at the Abbey in 1973, it somehow made history and theatre to change places. As Chris Morash reports, 'it was possible for the unionist Lord Mayor of Derry to lead a standing ovation on the opening night'.[45] It was as with the praise of the 1902 pioneers: 'They made a live thing, a true expression of the life of Ireland, out of what had been a literary experiment.'[46]

Themes and Meaning

The dominant themes in *Translations* are obvious; the problem is to interpret them. Through the controlling images of map-making and place-names on the one hand, and the spectre of an English-dominated school system on the other, language and politics are skilfully interwoven: to what end remains to be seen. The mapping is of territory, which must be distinguished from both 'land' and 'soil' in the Irish political memory.[47] The territory makes up the state and is national; land is material and relates to Ireland as an economy; the soil is an emotive term, relating to Ireland as a cultural reality. As *Translations* represents it, the Ordnance Survey is not a harmless, objective or purely scientific enterprise. The soldiers in dazzling red enter upon a schoolhouse. However polite the entrance, it creates crisis. The exterior presence of the soldiers has already caused more than curiosity to the community. Doalty feels impelled to interfere mischievously in their surveying. While this is mere play on Doalty's part, it signifies feelings of intrusion which, although not so strong as Skinner's driving a ceremonial sword through an oil painting in *The Freedom of the City*, are nevertheless indicative. Manus as teacher can interpret Doalty's action: a 'gesture' to indicate 'a presence' (p. 391). Neither Gaelic nor English, the gestural language is the universal response of the offended when space is invaded. By the end of Act 1, largely because of Owen's dishonest translation of his superior's account of the aims of the Ordnance Survey, Manus will declare in outrage downstage (and hence privately) to Owen: 'it's a bloody military operation' (p. 408). Because such is the perception, that is the reality for the representative community in the classroom. This initial resentment is certain to find *public* utterance in due course. Symmetrically, Friel has a second intrusion of soldiers in Act 3; then the mask is off and threats of violence against the people are made. No amount of softening of the play's interpretation can hide this bedrock. The territorial argument is central to what *Translations* is about. By the play's end, Doalty's voice will sound out loud and clear: 'I've damned little to defend but [Lancey]'ll not put me out without a fight' (p. 441). That is how Doalty had seen the Ordnance Survey from the start. Someone was trying to evict him from his land.

That said, it is not just a 'paper landscape' that Friel is charting but a psychic one also. Here, the other major trope in the play, translation itself, has to receive equal attention. The extraordinary theatrical conceit of using one language to represent two being spoken on stage carries a political theme over into a spiritual one. Yolland speaks for Friel in *Translations*: 'The private core will always be . . . hermetic, won't it?' (p. 416). The reader or director of the play may go to Steiner for a full argument on the cultural level, beginning with the claim that 'inside or between languages, human communication equals translation'.[48] But we all know that what is lost in translation is not verbal equivalence but something much more elusive and emotional. It happens that 'loss' is the very image Friel wishes to exploit. Loss is poignantly implicit in the ramshackle cultural chaos of Hugh's schoolroom. Bridget's headline emphasises that loss of the classics is, however, regarded as a serious matter: 'It's easier to stamp out learning than to recall it' (p. 393). This is the forbidding argument of another Steiner text with which Friel was familiar, *In Bluebeard's Castle: Some Notes Towards the Redefinition of Culture* (1971). Friel correlates the classics and Gaelic (the latter has been dying for over a hundred years) as part of the tragic pattern of *Translations*. In Inishowen, where the play is set, after 1861 'in the one generation Irish went away like the snow off the ditches'.[49]

But it is through the love story that loss is most powerfully and most dramatically registered. The love at first sight between Máire and Yolland forms the tragic substance of the action. A love scene is not cool in serious theatre today. Irony keeps breaking in. Not since Bernstein's *West Side Story* (1957) has there been such a poignant and passionate scene of young, forbidden love as the scene between Yolland and Máire in *Translations*. Behind *West Side Story* lies *Romeo and Juliet* and here too lies a seed of Friel's powerful scene in Act 2. 'What's in a name?' is the centre of it, a key question in the whole play. How Friel choreographs the love scene is masterly, as often noted. The lovers are first at cross purposes using different languages, as indicated by the chiasmus inherent in the exchange: 'The grass must be wet. My feet are soaking.'/'Your feet must be wet. The grass is soaking' (p. 426).

From that point, the lovers struggle with names to reach intimacy. Here, it is the love scene in *Henry V* that springs to mind, even if the context, a royal courtship, is different. Victorious Henry woos Katharine of France for a political marriage; and yet the struggle is with language, whereby 'thy speaking of my tongue, and I thine, *most truly-falsely*, must needs be granted to be much at once'

(5.2.203-205, emphasis added). Friel's lovers are more romantic, and the 'truly-falsely' element in their exchange is palpably urgent with passionate invention. Frustration goads them prettily on until they hit upon the exchange of Irish place names. The fact is that Shakespeare's Henry knows more French than Yolland knows Irish, and Katharine, while patronised by Shakespeare's phonetic spelling, knows enough English to play language games with him. When Katharine balks at Henry's attempt to kiss her, horror confines her to French and Henry must ask a third party: 'Madam, my interpreter, what says she?' (line 281). The whole point in Friel's scene is that the lovers continue to be interpreters of *each other's* feelings by transcending the limitations of language. And so Yolland can be falsely true: 'Máire, your English is perfect!' (p. 428), which always gets a laugh. The erotic intensity of their exchange increases even though, having reached out and held hands, '*Each now speaks almost to himself/herself*' (p. 429). The audience has the benefit of hearing in English the torrent of words each of them speaks, with interjections not to stop or confessions of trembling. And finally, suddenly, they kiss. Then the scene is interrupted by Sarah, who in shock cries out Manus's name 'almost to herself' and runs off to inform the rival. Well may Friel melodramatically cue, '*Music to crescendo*' (p. 430) to conclude the love scene which beats Shakespeare – not to mention Boucicault – at his own game. Its poignancy finally resides in the impossibility of fruition. Yolland disappears; Máire is left distracted. To one American audience, Yolland's disappearance was senseless, as director Garry Hynes discovered during a production in 2006.[50] But to an Irish audience, especially in the North at the time of the premiere, the inference was crystal clear. For a woman to 'go' with a British soldier was to betray the community. In 'Punishment', Seamus Heaney graphically documents the terrible 'revenge' taken against a woman in such or kindred circumstances.[51] The soldier in such cases stood in danger of ritual execution, his body not to be found. Although the 'disappeared' includes more than soldier-lovers, its wider constituency allows Friel to hit a painful nerve. Yolland's dramatic disappearance signifies the gathering swell of loss which sweeps over the play as its tragic design demands. That suffices.

As with the place names so with the mapping image. Both fuse within Máire's mind in Act 3. Friel links Máire's desolation after Yolland goes missing to a makeshift map of Norfolk showing his home place. The poetic depth of the image of Yolland, mapmaking and writing in wet sand (compare Spenser's Sonnet 75), finds its counterpart as Máire replicates his map on the schoolhouse floor. She sounds the litany of the foreign villages: 'Winfarthing', 'Barton Benish', 'Little Walsingham' (p. 437), a litany beautifully chiming with the incantation of Gaelic place names which became the language of love in the preceding scene. Máire's map is within, inscribed forever in memory and therefore real: 'I have it all in my head now' (p. 437), like Jimmy Jack and his Homer. In a good production, this cartography of feeling is imprinted on the audience's collective mind.

Father and Sons: A Conclusion

The hedge-school setting of *Translations* supplies a synecdoche for a society in crisis. Friel's imagined community is a depleted family ripped apart by the force of history. Yet the framework of a history play is not allowed to diminish the emphasis on close ties, loyalty and love. Colm Tóibín claims that 'mothers get in the way in fiction' and are best substituted by aunts who come and go. Although drama, unlike fiction, has a different time scheme and cannot wait for 'the slow growth of a personality',[52] Friel does appear to keep mothers at bay in his work. Fathers are the formative figures. More space is thereby created for the father-son contest in all its symbolic power. Hugh has fond memories of his Caitlín Dubh whom he briefly forsook to join the 1798 Rising in Connaught, perhaps at Killala where Yeats's *Cathleen Ní Houlihan* is set. How Hugh's Caitlín died is not dwelt upon but in her absence her drunken husband managed to cripple their infant son Manus. Strangely, the relationship between father and son in the play is exemplary. Manus holds no grudge against Hugh, cares for him solicitously and always defers to his authority. When the position of master of the new National School materialises, Manus refuses to compete against his father. But this deference costs him the loyalty of Máire, while the love triangle that Yolland's arrival creates eventually makes Manus's position impossible. He leaves. Perhaps his over-compensation of his father's perceived guilt towards him makes it necessary. Ambivalence over his motive derives from a gap between private and public feeling; if Manus goes 'on the run' his action is a kind of suicide. His loss is immediately marked by Sarah's regression to aphasia. In that regard, Manus's self-exile resembles the futile Flight of the Earls in *Making History* when O'Neill left the fatherland and destroyed himself. Manus's father, the voice of those left to mourn his loss most, represents the plight of a community in turmoil.

Hugh was originally intended as the main character in *Translations* but in the writing Friel gave that role to Owen. Friel effectively divided Hugh into two. Hugh is, indeed, the *raisonneur*, if not a one-man chorus. His knowledge of Steiner and of linguistics, moreover, ironically qualifies him as guide to the fall of a community; his pragmatism leads him to see the 'overall thing' in proto-Darwinist terms. Soon he is endorsing change, survival through adaptation, the acceptance of 'inevitabilities' (pp. 418–19). Not to do so, he decides, choosing the word carefully, means to 'fossilize' (p. 445). Hugh has the ambivalence of a native Gaelic speaker towards the Ordnance Survey project. Friel himself was in two minds about it, his doubt permeating the play. He was thinking of the scholar John O'Donovan (1809–61), 'an important source' for his theme, who caused Friel unease as if a participant in 'a major military operation' and yet deserved credit for giving stability to Donegal place names 'so that for a period of our [*sic*] lives we knew with certainty where we lived'.[53]

Owen has a journey to go before he can arrive at that kind of understanding. He is the real John O'Donovan figure, giving off 'a whiff of unease'[54] in spite of his charm. He is a more subtle character than his brother, whose difference he seeks to disarm: 'in a way we complement each other' (p. 408). When first drafting *Translations*, Friel thought he had Owen's measure as a treacherous, self-serving go-between, a playboy, perhaps like Synge's ('and isn't it by the like of you the sins of the whole world are committed?').[55] When Friel saw that if Stephen Rea were to play Owen he could become the fulcrum instead of Hugh, he rewrote in order to bring out Owen's mercuriality. Rea did play the role and brought to it the ambiguity and charm he had brought to similar 'playboys', Skinner in the London production of *The Freedom of the City* in 1973 and Eamon in the premiere of *Aristocrats* in 1979. Charm is a form of magic which, if exercised for its own sake, can be irresponsible. Owen enjoys performing before his own people, a bit of a villain in the Irish sense of trickster. He deliberately distorts his translation of Captain Lancey's explanation of the Ordnance Survey. As a modernist character, however, he is deceitful only because he views life as performance. (Field Day plays, in which Rea often took the lead, tended towards identity-performance, as Aidan O'Malley has argued.)[56] When Owen lets Yolland and the army believe his name is 'Roland', he sees nothing amiss in this: 'It's the same me, isn't it?' (p. 408). There is a beguiling innocence in Owen which makes it credible Yolland would befriend him. Both are dreamers. But Yolland thinks Ballybeg 'heavenly', and like Shaw's Broadbent in *John Bull's Other Island* (1904), falls head over heels in love with the whole utopian fantasy of a pastoral Ireland.[57] 'Don't be such a bloody romantic,' is Owen's Shavian response (p. 414), but instead of debating utopia puts the question: 'Do you believe in fate?' (p. 415) He gets no answer. Owen eventually repudiates his allegiance to the British Army and the Ordnance Survey, 'my mistake – nothing to do with us' (p. 444). He can say 'us' now in solidarity with his threatened kinfolk. Like Hugh, he too has his tragic *anagnorisis*. But while Hugh believes in inevitabilities, Owen believes in fate, Ireland's fate. Yolland could never have understood what this means, not with *his* family history. In the end, awakening to an old world come again, Owen assumes a rebel role, while Hugh, who senses everything, foresees this son's loss too.

'Our work is fulfilled when we take it into the national consciousness,' Friel said in Yeatsian style in 1989, with Field Day in mind.[58] *Translations* was intended as both an entertainment and a poetic stimulation to debate over the Ireland-England question. It is a history play with a difference. As art, it purposes to find echoes in the human mind; as theatre, it aims through performance to bind an audience together in reflection. Although Kevin Whelan sees *Translations* as 'both a parable about and a diagnosis of the conditions of the post-partition Catholic community in Northern Ireland',[59] it is interesting that sectarianism is never an issue in the play. Friel deliberately ignores the implications of Catholic Emancipation (1829), wanting instead to present a secular community as a model for today. Included, offstage, however, is the death of a newborn baby, father unknown. Why that detail? Maybe we should see *Translations* as less a thesis play than a representation of ebb and flow, life undergoing change, instructive tragedy.

In a downbeat ending, faintly echoing but at the same time critiquing that of O'Casey's *Juno and the Paycock*, Hugh has the last word. He is neither fantasist nor escapist. During the course of the play, Hugh has developed into a pragmatist. He falteringly quotes from Book 1 of Virgil's *Aeneid* in translation, into Irish, heard as English. He falters because he fears the implications of the text, its dying fall predicting the destruction of an ancient culture. Virgil was both prophet and poet. So also is Friel. But history is not destiny; it can be constructed as well as imagined; there is no 'always' to anything. The new Hugh can call it a silly word. The lights go down on Hugh's uncertain recitation and what it may portend when translated into the future for Northern Ireland. In the twenty-first century, the actor playing Hugh will have new things to convey in that final speech,[60] even though the text still emanates instability.

The Home Place

Written six years *after* the Belfast Peace Agreement brought the Northern wars to an end, *The Home Place* comes as something of a surprise. It has been called '*Translations* revisited' but this seems inadequate.[61] In a letter to the present writer, Friel remarked: 'one of the thoughts in the back of my head was to propose to Unionists/ Northern Protestants the idea that a dual accommodation, a dual loyalty was available to them. But maybe that nice liberal concept got lost somewhere in the execution.'[62] Allowing for the irony hovering over the word 'liberal' – a suspect term in the Irish political lexicon[63] – one may accept that *The Home Place* is a coda to *Translations*. In *Stepping Stones* (2008), Seamus Heaney saw *Translations* as interactive: 'What happened on the stage woke something in the collective consciousness' and invited audiences 'to see parallels between the dramatic action and the present moment'. It was a play which 'agitated the spirit' while holding the spectator at bay.[64] While *The Home Place* was premiered (in Dublin) at quite a different moment in 2005, it too marks the intervention in the debate ever-evolving in the North as power-sharing took root, and Ian Paisley and Martin McGuinness learnt to work together in government.

In *Making History*, O'Neill believes that 'the slow, sure tide of history' is in his favour, even though circumstances are against him.[65] Although there is for him no grand narrative, Friel seems to believe in Shakespeare's (i.e. Brutus's) 'tide in the affairs of men,/Which, taken at the flood, leads on to fortune'.[66] Nevertheless, Friel would not have been blind to the irony that Brutus too was a loser: the tide is nothing without the favourable circumstances. For Shakespeare, in the history plays, the 'overall thing' is governed by providence. No such naïve belief is credible today. Indeed, as Friel's O'Neill says: 'the formation of nations and civilizations is a willed act' (*Plays* 2, 300). The debate Friel enters is post-Enlightenment and concerns freedom and identity as much as power. But he would probably agree with Yeats that 'Ireland divided in religion and politics, is as much one *race* as any modern country.'[67] How to make that perception universally acceptable was the continuing challenge.

Set in Donegal in 1878 just as the land wars were being declared, *The Home Place* focuses on the Big House within Anglo-Irish culture. At the intersection between past and present, an unforeseen future hovers. The political battle is to be one of minds and cultures as well as of physical force: the possibility of change is the primary fear or hope. The 'home place' too is in the mind, a zone of contention, a remembered and coveted Eden. It is once again a Fifth Province in a four-province space,[68] but this time from the perspective of the unionist community. The Field Day Theatre Company, itself history by 2005, was in its prime just that: a mobile Fifth Province in search of a home place which might be translated into 'a nation once again'. Was the dream still sustainable in the new century?

The text of *The Home Place* occupies this site of cultural debate. The crucial fact disclosed in the opening scene is that a local Anglo-Irish landlord has been brutally murdered, throwing fear into that community. The central character, Christopher Gore, a peace-loving man in spite of his surname, returns from the funeral terrified at what might occur to himself and his estate. Violence is in the air as if the Donnelly twins from *Translations* had come into their own. In 2005, when violence had been officially repudiated as a means of solving irredentism and intransigence, Friel provided a backward look at the roots of the conflict. To him the matter was not closed. In the play, he evokes an atmosphere of incipient terrorism conjured up on stage before an audience literally bound to feel this as *déjà vu*. Friel is not flogging a dead horse but bringing a contemporary audience, aware of the history, to a renewed realisation of how 'knowledge' on its own is insufficient; how reprise reveals not only the old errors, prejudices and discriminations, but also the tipping points calling for understanding and compassion. Adapting Brecht's maxim at the conclusion of *The Resistible Rise of Arturo Ui*, Friel's play asks 'things were thus: need they *continue* to be so?' *The Home Place* is a warning against complacency.

The presence on stage of a menacing Fenian, Con Doherty, in the opening scene offers an image both melodramatic and iconic. He is '*soft spoken and very controlled*' and melts '*into the thicket when he hears someone coming*'[69]: the traditional, colonised Irishman up to no good. When joined by the hit-man McCloone, the two again '*merge into the thicket*' as soon as their presence is registered at the Lodge (p. 15). These tenants are not just close to the land which, following the doctrines of Fintan Lalor, they plan to repossess; they are part of the very landscape itself. A stereotype can have its own kind of reality, especially on a stage. Moreover, Friel's note on the set describes a 'crescent of trees' which 'encloses the entire house and lawn' so that 'it seems to press in on them' (p. 8). 'For the house of the planter/Is known by the trees', as Clarke's well-known lines atavistically declare.[70] But here that image is rendered theatrical, as in O'Neill's *Desire Under the Elms* (1924). Nature itself, stifled within the Big House, is on the side of the Land Leaguers.

For Christopher Gore the writing is on the wall, just as the white crosses must soon be on the trees for thinning out. It is all very well for David, Gore's only child, to assert that the 'unease' caused by the 'Lifford business' (murder of a local landlord) does not affect the Gores: 'nothing to do with us' (p. 25). David is simply blind to the kerns who hover in the bushes. A different kind of 'sweet smell' is in the air than that dreaded in *Translations*. Friel's audience knows more than those on stage. No fewer than 192 Big Houses owned by the Ascendancy were burned down in the early 1920s,[71] exemplified in, for example, Elizabeth Bowen's novel *The Last September* (1929). Friel can project such horrors further back into his text as historical, giving the play an estranging impact. It is likely that it was the 'culture wars' of the 1990s, over 'whether Ireland was or was not a post-colonial society',[72] which stimulated Friel to inspect this issue by foregrounding an Anglo-Irish landlord as a tragic victim. In 1985, Frank McGuinness had shown in *Observe the Sons of Ulster* how the Unionist tradition could be seen as self-destructive and at the same time, in its blind devotion to empire, worthy of understanding and pity. In a different context, Friel now holds the Gore family up as sympathetic figures.

Two examples of Friel's technique will illustrate the allegory. One concerns the use of music, the other Friel's introduction of cousin Richard Gore. Both show Friel map-making on a different scale from *Translations*. The music which opens the play and holds Margaret O'Donnell (chatelaine and so a 'key' character in the play) rapt is Thomas Moore's lyric 'Oft in the Stilly Night'. Csilla Bertha explores the relevance of this song in Chapter 10. Here, I wish only to indicate its centrality to Friel's own structure of feeling.

As poetry, 'Oft in the Stilly Night', from *National Airs* (1818), looks a lot simpler on the page than when considered as music set by Moore to an Irish air and performed by him in London drawing rooms. The rhythm of the verse is not identical with the rhythm of the printed music.[73] Moore later saw his songs and politics as interconnected: 'how much they are connected, in Ireland, at least, appears too plainly in the tone of sorrow and depression which characterises most of our early Songs'.[74] That is to say, the songs can be allegorical. It is easy enough to fault the poetry, which is prisoner to what Wordsworth in his 1802 preface to *The Lyrical Ballads* called 'poetic diction'. For all that, the imagery works musically at a profound emotional level, bound up with memory, loss and atavism. Friel ensures that 'Oft in the Stilly Night' is political by immersing it in the mood and atmosphere of *The Home Place*. In the opening scene, Margaret, beloved by both the landlord Gore and his son David, '*stands motionless, enraptured*' as the singing wafts its way across the fields from the schoolhouse, in broad daylight (p. 11). It has special meaning for her, a Catholic at the Protestant Big House, because it is being sung by a children's choir at her father's national school. This is a thinly veiled piece of autobiography. Friel's own father, a schoolteacher, likewise set Moore's song for children's choir in which the ten-year-old sang: 'and we won the cup at Omagh Feis [competition] and he was inordinately proud of us – and of himself'. Friel goes on: 'And I imagine that that may have been my earliest intimation of the power of music to move an audience.'[75] This recollection was published six years before *The Home Place*. The school teacher Clement O'Donnell is thus a Moore-like memory of a loved father/teacher. As Harry White has said, the choral song as arranged 'attains the significance of a "real presence" in *The Home Place*', referring to Steiner's *Real Presences* (1989) and the primacy of music among the arts.[76] When O'Donnell enters later on, it is to ask if the Gores heard his choir singing (for their benefit) earlier. They did and did not. Their carelessness over the matter symptomises their general indifference to the names and affairs of their tenants. Undaunted, O'Donnell offers a reprise of the song for the evening time. The offer is politely if unenthusiastically accepted. Before he leaves, O'Donnell, fortified no doubt – to his daughter Margaret's mortification – by whiskey, stays to inform Richard Gore, the landlord's brother, of the significance of Moore, a close friend of 'your Lord Byron' and 'our national poet' (p. 41). Observing Gore's ignorance of Byron, O'Donnell continues ironically.

Moore, 'the voice of our nation', he says, may be over-romantic and given to 'easy sentiment', but 'he has our measure, Mr Richard. He divines us accurately' (p. 42). Reminiscent of Hugh in *Translations*, O'Donnell knows to whom he speaks, the English phrenologist, the measurer of heads himself. The *Observer*'s reviewer caught the point: 'Measure for measure. Who but Friel would pivot a political difference on a pun?'[77] And who else could so effortlessly align a private memory with the central theme of his play? Richard Gore may dismiss him as 'a grotesque' when O'Donnell exits (p. 42), but the play's audience must not respond likewise. Friel's own weight lies behind the schoolmaster's moral voice. In making O'Donnell quote Seamus Deane ('Moore is still, in terms of popular appeal, Ireland's national poet'),[78] Friel associates Field Day with his own statement of 'cultural transformation'.[79] The Field Day people could identify with the Moore who thought of himself as enslaved in Ireland.

Richard Gore the craniologist is a stage villain, but tremendously useful for Friel's purposes. Leigh Hunt commented on a contemporary portrait of Moore: 'His forehead is long and full of character, with "bumps" of wit, large and radiant, enough to transport a phrenologist.'[80] Friel, a close friend of David Hammond, who included the portrait and extract from Hunt in his centenary selection from *Moore's Melodies* (1979), ironically connects Moore and Richard Gore. The Aran connection is subtler still. Richard has been to the Aran Islands during three summers, exactly Synge's programme later on, 1898–1900. But Synge, part-time naturalist and anthropologist, was by this time also poet and embryonic dramatist. It is the *contrast* between Synge and Gore which is significant. Declan Kiberd has defined Synge's attitude in his *Aran Islands* as the opposite of the coloniser's: 'He used the primitive world of Aran much as Lévi-Strauss would employ that of *Tristes Tropiques*: as a basis from which to offer a critique of "progress".'[81] To Richard Gore, who sports a panama hat on entry in *The Home Place* and soon accuses his cousin Christopher of 'going native' (p. 33), the Aran people are 'primeval', a 'vengeful' tribe *because* Irish (p. 31). Richard is a parody of the nineteenth-century craniometrist of the kind Stephen Jay Gould has condemned as supremacists.[82] Richard gives photographs to the Aran people as 'our glass beads' to facilitate his cranial experiments, which are indefensibly racist. There is a clear abuse of science inherent in Richard's purpose to discover an 'ethnic code' revealing 'an enormous vault of genetic information' which would enable scientists to collude with governments malignly: 'we wouldn't control just an empire. We would rule the entire universe' (p. 36). The vista is nightmarish.

By contrast, Synge's vision was utopian. The people he saw in Aran are idealised. 'I felt,' he wrote in his *Walden*-like *Aran Islands* (1907), 'that this little corner on the face of the world, and the people who live in it, have a peace and dignity from which we are shut for ever.'[83] To Synge, the islanders were aristocrats in their own natural way, refined, mannerly and cultured. They knew poetry and song. They knew Moore's *Melodies* in an Irish translation by Archbishop John McHale (1871): one man was able to criticise the translation 'with great severity and acuteness, citing whole poems both in the English and Irish, and then giving versions that he had made himself'.[84] It is not to be doubted where Friel, himself a maker of versions and translations, stands here. The point is rammed home in his play: the likes of Richard Gore, so dismissive and exploitative of the native Irish poor, is a symptom of the terrible malaise of British colonialism. Synge's shadowy presence, in contrast, serves to reinforce the more central meaning of Thomas Moore as key to a radical, revolutionary alternative. While in Aran Synge had 'a dream of music, as if the islands themselves found absolute expression in an orchestral score *as yet unwritten*.'[85] Friel draws attention to this evolutionary possibility. Where the fictional Richard Gore measured the outsides of Irish heads, both Synge and Friel sought a key to the inside, using music as symbolic language for the eliciting of harmonic order from experience.

History as Tragedy

Such, then, is Friel's allegory in *The Home Place*. He is trying to restore a neglected part of the narrative of Irish cultural history. Friel's lacunae are always as interesting as his mythoi. He passes over the militant unionism inherent in the narrative in order to focus on Gore as a figure at the end of a historical line as well as a man at the end of his psychological tether, and leaps instead to modern times, still in 2005 evolving: it was not until May 2007 that devolution (established in 1972) was abolished in the North and government was restored via the unlikely Sinn Féin/DUP alliance. Yet as in the other history plays, the allegory is prophetic: it does not say, 'I told you so' but rather 'this is what could happen; the seeds are here. What do you think?' By 2005, the long wars are over but Friel denies Fukuyama's thesis on 'the end of history'. Attention must be paid to the tragic cost of sclerotic thinking and the weakness of the human spirit. Friel's empathy is with Christopher Gore as a beleaguered representative of a lost cause, whose mettle is tested and who fails catastrophically. The play is as much Gore's personal tragedy as that of the Ascendancy culture, to be briefly addressed here in conclusion.

As *The Home Place* draws to a close Gore, the inefficient landlord sitting on a powder keg, is a broken man still clinging to his dream of the home place in Kent. Friel underlines the painful weakness of such a man, enclosed in a historical prison. Gore is a victim of what George O'Brien calls 'a two-homes syndrome'.[86] His consciousness is schizoid in ways different from the usual Friel protagonist: he is both liberal and myopic. He totally misunderstands those around him, his tenants, his household servants, his son. But neither has he any of John Hewitt's awareness of roots, as when Hewitt cries out on behalf of the colonialist tradition, 'this is our country also, nowhere else;/ and we shall not be outcast on the world'.[87] Although Gore differs with his cousin Richard over standing his ground, his liberalism forces him to back down ignominiously when Con Doherty and Johnny McCloone begin to take over. Richard immediately accuses his cousin of appeasement; Margaret goes further, calling Christopher a coward. In confusion, he collapses, a decent man unfit to cope with history.

The resemblance here to *Uncle Vanya* is startling. In 1998, Friel had created a successful version of Chekhov's play for the Gate Theatre, where *The Home Place* was also to have its premiere. Vanya's collapse, however, derives from a different set of causes than those underlying Gore's, and Sonya is on hand to give him courage and the hope of 'peace' in the final scene.[88] Sonya is more positive than Margaret O'Donnell decides to be. After all, Sonya is daughter to the owner of the Big House in Chekhov's play; Margaret is 'chatelaine' in Gore's Lodge and, significantly, a Catholic dependant and therefore inferior. Margaret's role is ambivalent. She leaves in order to assert her independence: but this is not the theme of the play. To put the matter crudely, Margaret plays the West-Briton for most of the play and in the end goes home to Daddy, leaving the Gores to stew in their Anglo-Irish juice. That she is summoned home by the music wafting again across the fields is, admittedly, closer to what Friel's text insinuates. Thus, Csilla Bertha says Moore's songs 'act as catalysts of change' in the play.[89] The music at the end is again Moore's 'Oft in the Stilly Night', a reprise by Clement's choir as at the opening of the play. Margaret, certainly, is changed by it; things clarify for her and she is ready to leave.

Gore, meantime, is characterised by his isolation, from which there is no exit. His agency is non-existent. Pathos becomes pathological. 'I know you won't betray me, Maggie. I know that': the line breathes insecurity (p. 75). The word *betray* can never be withdrawn. In the Gate premiere in February 2005, Tom Courtenay was literally terrible in his hysteria at this point, totally broken, flailing his arms as if at invisible wolves. But Gore himself is deaf to the music at the end where Margaret is captivated. Here is Friel's image of the tragic rift between communities: a kind of cultural deafness. Ever since *Philadelphia*, where Private Gar interprets the piece by Mendelssohn for the unattending father and Canon Boyle ('what's that noise?'),[90] Friel has insisted that music is not mere background but a potent conveyor of meaning. While Gore gives vent to the unacknowledged pain of the unionist predicament, Friel insists on the permanency and power of art as a mediating force like theatre itself. It is to the human spirit, metonymically, rather than to politics, that Friel looks, in the audience, for agency. Further, it is to the human spirit Friel looks in the trajectory of his history plays; to the agony that must be endured, to the 'enemy within' as well as without that must be confronted and mentally transformed if two nations are happily to share a home place and create 'a viable collective identity'.[91] Christopher Gore is one more exile in Friel's long line of outsiders who, if he cannot change, cannot empathise with the music wafting from the other side of high walls, even peace walls, is surely doomed to build the walls even higher. Thus, *The Home Place*, concluding the trilogy, enacts the catharsis of a nation.

CHAPTER 7
THE CHEKHOV FACTOR AND GENDER ISSUES: *ARISTOCRATS, DANCING AT LUGHNASA* AND *MOLLY SWEENEY*

Ellie *Oh, it* [life] *cant go on for ever. I'm always expecting something. I dont know what it is; but life must come to a point sometime.*

– Bernard Shaw, *Heartbreak House* (1920)[1]

Feminism began by asking for women to have access to the life of the nation-state. Now it wants to make a difference.

– Gerardine Meaney, *Gender, Ireland, and Cultural Change*, (London: Routledge, 2010).[2]

Introduction

Translations is to *Three Sisters* as *Uncle Vanya* is to *The Home Place*, where Chekhov sowed a vital seed. 'The politics of such translations and adaptations has to do with Ireland's colonial experience,'[3] and yet Friel's Chekhov is conservative rather than radical. *Aristocrats* (1979) is the play which most plainly reveals how creatively Friel could assimilate Chekhov's influence. Looking back from that play now, it is possible to detect Chekhovian qualities very early on, in *Philadelphia, Here I Come!* If Friel learnt the technical means of achieving such effects from Tyrone Guthrie's rehearsals of *Three Sisters* in Minneapolis in 1963, the seed fell on fertile ground. The second Field Day production was to be *Three Sisters* in 1981. But the point must be made at the outset that Friel was always his own man, sharing affinities with Chekhov's emotional understatement rather than ever succumbing to his influence.

Later in his career, Friel paid open tribute to Chekhov through a number of lively pieces for the Gate Theatre, *The Yalta Game* (2001), a dramatisation of the short story 'Lady with Lapdog'; followed by *Two Plays After* (2002): a double bill of Chekhov's *The Bear* and Friel's extraordinary *Afterplay*, a two-hander which brings Andrey from *Three Sisters* and Sonya from *Uncle Vanya* together for a middle-aged brief encounter. The title *Two Plays After*, while eliding Chekhov's name, successfully links the two authors in a bond of deep affection. This for Friel was the defining link.[4] In June 2008, he returned to *Three Sisters*, with a revised version of the 1981 text, directed by David Leveaux in an elegant production at the Abbey.[5] By this time Chekhov had definitively become Friel's measure of excellence. In 2013, BBC Radio 4 Extra broadcast a series of plays, stories and documentaries under the title 'Celebrating "the Irish Chekhov": A Brian Friel Season'. The soubriquet was well earned. It can be added that in adapting Turgenev, Friel came to see how, in *A Month in the Country*, Turgenev had anticipated Chekhov by inventing 'a theatre of moods *where the action resides in internal emotion and secret turmoil and not in external events*'.[6] Chekhov, however, brought the new form 'to shimmering perfection'.[7]

The gender issue is another matter. I would not argue that Friel had to go to Chekhov to learn about women in drama. My point is that in making parallels between the two authors the gender issue is one they share without any suggestion of borrowing. Friel's short story, 'A Man's World' (1962), an unrecognised source for *Dancing at Lughnasa,* is an early and ironic indication of Friel's independent feminist sympathies. In theatre, gender has always been a live issue. As female roles were played by men in the classical and Elizabethan-Jacobean theatre, gender was constantly being interrogated within a patriarchal society. It makes a major difference that the actor playing Desdemona who sighs 'O, these men, these men!' was in Shakespeare's day a male (*Othello*, 5.3.60). It means that for dramatists, long before novelists tackled the issue, gender is something to be performed. It is the embodiment of certain visual, vocal, sartorial and ultimately physical characteristics established by custom in social intercourse. The relationship between gender and identity in such a context is flexible, something literally to be played out. So it is in Friel as in Chekhov. This is less a matter of influence than of theatre history.

Friel approaches the gender issue mainly through paternal figures. In *Philadelphia, Here I Come!* the father is mainly seen through the eyes of his son. Madge holds him responsible for driving Gar away. In subsequent plays, the father can assume a godlike, patriarchal presence, vengeful and destructive. Friel's work shows an increasing interest in women within this patriarchal society, even offstage or dead, emphasising their marginality in Irish society. *The Gentle Island* is a special case, dealing with homosexuality in a motherless, homophobic society. But the plight of women is a frequent, if understated, issue in the oeuvre as Friel queries the stereotyping of women's roles in his theatre of revolt. Such is the argument underpinning the rest of this chapter.

Aristocrats

Father in *Aristocrats* is a district judge, a role which lends him unquestionable authority, in domestic as in forensic matters. He resembles a dying king, but one more feared than loved. That he is partly paralysed and bed-bound necessarily holds his power in abeyance, but through the newly installed 'baby alarm', his offstage presence is felt in Acts 1 and 2. His family of four daughters, one son and a son-in-law, is convened for a wedding but, in fact, attends his funeral. He becomes the centre of attention so that the extent of his effect on the family can be fully registered. The one offstage daughter, Anna, creates the reason for his brief and fatal entrance at the end of Act 2 when her voice and violin playing on tape attract him downstairs to his death.

It is well to note the details of Father's appearance, because they represent Friel's malignant picture of inimical patriarchy: '*An emaciated man; eyes distraught; one arm limp; his mouth pulled down at one corner. A grotesque and frightening figure.*'[8] Big Daddy (Williams's *Cat on a Hot Tin Roof* (1955)) he is not, but a 'grotesque' variation. It is ironic that Father's death is caused by his favourite child in a play where the central theme is the destructive effect he himself has had on the family. The use of this death scene strongly contrasts with its prototype in Friel's story, 'Foundry House', the main source for *Aristocrats*. There, the god-like presence of the old man is embedded in the memory of the narrator, Joe Brennan, as 'a large, stern-faced man with a long white beard'.[9] As in the play, the old man (Mr Hogan) reacts in shock not to his daughter's voice but to the music she plays on tape, the 'Gartan Mother's Lullaby', at which he cries out her name and collapses. In the story, we are not told whether Mr Hogan dies. The point there is the narrator's refusal to accept that such a figure could possibly decline from his glowing memory of Mr Hogan's greatness. But then Joe Brennan is no relation, and he is blind to tragic reality. The reader must look to the subtext. In the play, the silliness of the voice on the tape is at odds with reality (Christmas greetings in the heat of summer) and with the varied points of view of those listening (not a factor in the simpler story, where the mother is alive). But the collapse of Father gains more dramatic and theatrical force through the communal audience on stage when general panic ensues. It is significant that the son-in-law Eamon is the one to leap to assist the fallen man. As an outsider, he is rather in the position of Joe Brennan the narrator of 'Foundry House', yet his role is altogether different, as will be seen below.

In *Aristocrats*, the children speak of their dead mother as victimised. Claire, herself the most damaged of the girls, finds she cannot tolerate how the eldest, Judith, has the patience to care for Father: 'Musn't it have been something like that that finally drove mother to despair?' (p. 291). Mother was an actress in a touring company doing Boucicault's melodramas, and possibly out of her milieu as the strict judge's consort. She is spoken of as having 'down periods' (p. 262); her love of song, especially 'Alice Ben Bolt', is remembered, the timid woman who dies. The judge thought the song 'vulgar rubbish' but it seemed to restore to her 'something she had lost, something that had withered in her' (p. 308). Her death at age forty-six or forty-seven was from suspected suicide, so that 'a Christian burial' was allowed – as in *Hamlet* – only at the 'last minute' (p. 309), according to Casimir (an unreliable witness). Thus, when Eamon advises Tom Hoffnung – however cynically – to 'make Mother central' to his narrative (p. 294), we do well to attend if we remember Mabel in *Making History*. Friel's *cherchez la femme* is announced.

The daughters in *Aristocrats* are affected in varying degrees by Father's authority. Anna is the one who got away. As a nun in Zambia, she is completely out of touch, her knowledge of how things are in the family entirely out of date. She is chillingly remote. Her poor musicianship is an insult, but part of her infantilism. She has contrived to create a cocoon around her emotional life through her vocation as a missionary nun. John Henry, her name 'in religion', being male (referring to Cardinal Newman), deprives her of gender; it is her emotional sterility Friel finds sufficiently culpable to make her the cause of Father's death. Claire, who bears the name given the nun in 'Foundry House', is childlike in quite the opposite sense: fragile, sensitive, incapable of independence. She is an artist. In contrast to Sister John Henry, her musicianship is of the first rank. She might have had a career as a pianist had her father not 'thwarted' her (p. 307) when she was awarded a scholarship to study in Paris at age sixteen, dismissing her talent as that of 'an itinerant musician' (p. 259) in line with her mother's. Claire subsequently fell into her mother's 'depression' (p. 268). The audience can evaluate her lost opportunity by hearing her offstage performance of Chopin (in flawless recordings). In the Abbey premiere, the piano was played by Veronica McSwiney.[10] Rather like Chris in *Dancing at Lughnasa*, Claire's health is uncertain; she is on a high just now because of her impending marriage. Her widowed, middle-aged fiancé does not appear but the grotesque nature of the relationship is amply conveyed by the large plastic banana described as adorning his delivery truck. Claire is obviously 'in a mess' and 'so confused' by the match (p. 291), clearly a mistake.

Older sister Alice is an alcoholic, her marriage to Eamon a failure. She does not directly blame Father, who did not approve of Eamon or of his radical politics dismissed as 'vulgar' (p. 272). Damaged like her mother, Alice never came to terms with her own sexual nature. Her comments on seeing her father in illness as greatly 'altered' indicate her emotional abuse: 'he was always such a big strong man with such power' that it shocked her to see him 'so flat under the clothes'. She did not just *touch* his face; she *caught* it between her hands, and held it: 'such a strange sensation' (p. 289). She felt then 'so equal to him' (p. 290). She saw her own crippled status in his but not the link between.

Judith is the strongest of the family and the one on whom the whole play depends. She is the sole carer of Father in his final illness and will brook no assistance. She does what she does out of love, changing soiled pyjamas and feeding him, despite Father's not knowing her. She is Cordelia with a difference. Father has disowned her: 'Judith betrayed the family [. . .] enormous betrayal' (p. 257). In his dementia, he tells her this to her face and she does not flinch from her task. Her betrayal was of Father's rigid ideal of womanhood by leaving Ballybeg Hall to join the resistance in Derry during the Troubles after 1968. There she met a Dutch photographer and had a child by him, now aged seven and in an orphanage. Father never acknowledges this grandson. Judith is thus ready to abandon the house as soon as Father is dead. Being stronger than any of the men in the play, Judith bears some resemblance to Sonya in *Uncle Vanya* but also relates to Shaw's Chekhovian play *Heartbreak House* (1920).[11] Both are plays about class, power and their embodiment in a symbolic Big House. Yet Shaw in his regard for androgyny as the source of renewal of energy (*élan vital*) differs sharply from Friel who sees gender in a more orthodox Catholic light, where the mother figure is passive. Judith's transgressive nature marks her drive towards autonomy. Because the ever-helpful Willie Diver, her factotum, apparently refuses to accept Judith's illegitimate child, there is, so far as she is concerned, no prospect of their marriage. She will strike out on her own, in Shavian fashion. This is never a Chekhovian idea. A woman who attempts autonomy in Chekhov, such as Nina in *The Seagull*, pays the price as a fallen woman. To a certain degree, Friel follows that pattern in *Faith Healer*, where Grace's defiance of her father to follow Frank results in breakdown and suicide. But *Aristocrats* breaks new ground in Friel's *oeuvre* by having Judith disregard convention, abandon Ballybeg Hall and prepare to start a new life elsewhere.

Judith's empowerment supports the others. When Casimir breaks down at the sound of his father's terrifying voice over the baby alarm berating him, Judith is the one to soothe his hysteria, silencing his cry, 'it's not fair – it's not fair' (p. 283). She rocks him like a baby. She can be nurse, mother, daughter and sister. Casimir can cope with his insecurities once he is shown such affection and understanding. He finds the buried croquet lawn through inherent, deep-rooted knowledge, based on imaginative gifts resembling the diviner's in

Friel's short story of that title.[12] It is a feminine trait. Casimir is the Holy Fool type, beloved in all folklore and archetypal literature, such as Erasmus's *In Praise of Folly* (1509). Once on his feet again, Casimir is reborn. In Act 3, he can calmly reflect on his father's inadequacies as a tennis player. He can also address Eamon seriously now, knowing Eamon understands what the house 'has done to all of us' (p. 311). For 'house', this Heartbreak House, read 'Father'. Casimir, then, is not like Gayev in *The Cherry Orchard* (on which Shaw based his comedy), a parasite and a hopeless chatterbox, but a far more spiritual type. Friel makes a point when he allows Casimir to be the father of three boys; he makes another, when at the end, all Casimir wants from the Big House that disabled him is a 'very small' photograph of his mother from the drawing-room mantelpiece, as a 'keepsake' to be cherished (p. 316). Claire, too, has this quality, but as a woman she has less scope for compensation by wild eccentricity. Claire admires Judith for being 'so strong-minded' (p. 291). But it is clear that Judith will not wait around to care for her after the house is disposed of. Claire must find her own way.

And this is Judith's inspiration. Alice is a new woman once she grasps in Act 3 that all is over: the whole weight of the house, its history and her father's disapproval are capable of being lifted. She will get a job in London; she will care for Uncle George over there in a new family spirit. Eamon, too, will have to change. He is a complex figure, a new type in the second half of the twentieth century: working-class, dissident, confused, one of those 'educated out of our emotions' (p. 288). He is Skinner out of *Freedom of the City* given a BA from Queen's. He is Osborne's angry young man, decent yet politicised. But he is also a hopeless romantic, identifying himself with the hedgehog caught in the tennis net, and Judith has to be brutal (and Candida-like) with him. His love for her is immature but no less intense for that. She has to confront him with the harsh reality of her daily household routines: a dreary list delivered in a tone '*tense and deliberate*' (p. 299), not in complaint but in witness of selfless dedication. It silences Eamon on the topic of carnal love. Later, when he lectures her over Tom Hoffnung's intrusiveness, she both defends Hoffnung's role and asserts her prerogative: 'Besides – it's my home' (p. 313).

When Judith puts the question to her siblings, 'what are we going to do?', she voices a dilemma never so directly raised by any of Chekhov's heroes. It is not a question 'aristocrats' put. But it *is* the kind of question Ellie Dunn is likely to put as *Heartbreak House* develops its theme. Ellie says to the aged Captain Shotover: 'But what can I do?' She means she must marry for money. 'They won't let women be captains.'[13] It is a Shavian question, practical, utilitarian and in its way revolutionary. In *Aristocrats*, Eamon, as outsider, trying to browbeat Judith as it becomes clear she intends to close the doors on Ballybeg Hall, merely reduces her to tears. That ends the discussion. But it also draws the family together emotionally so that Judith's new, positive attitude becomes communal. She is not the biblical Judith, then, who slew Holofernes and cut off his head to show her people,[14] but a comparably decisive figure nonetheless. Thus, in *Aristocrats*, the death of a patriarch paves the way for a new dispensation. Alongside Shaw, Friel called for a rethinking in society, a stiffening of the national nerve and a recovery of spirit. It was time to let go of the myth of the Big House and find a 'context', as Alice says, to make 'a new start' (p. 324).

Dancing at Lughnasa

As *Aristocrats* ends, there is a strange stage direction: '*One has the impression that this afternoon – easy, relaxed, relaxing – may go on indefinitely*' (p. 326). The context is quite other: there is a bus to catch, and Willie Diver is apprehensive about its imperative. Friel wishes to end that play on a moment both in and out of time, for it is there, within a Frielian no-man's-land, that he likes to leave his audience caught up in thought.

This, too, is the nature of *Dancing at Lughnasa* as drama. The 'moment' is a whole summer condensed into the two-hour traffic of a modern stage. It is a moment of personal and cultural crisis. Here again, 'Friel's writing runs in parallel worlds.' Seamus Deane is referring to two distinct kinds of play Friel can, with seeming ease, turn to: one historical and the other not. In this latter world, 'the preoccupation is with writing and all the myths of origin, authenticity and strangeness that surround it'.[15] But in *Lughnasa*, I would hold, these two worlds are combined. It is uncanny that Deane should refer to 'writing', the artist's whole concern, as like the conception of a unicorn, both 'fabulous' and 'absurd', when the non-existent is dragged into existence. In *Lughnasa*, Gerry tells Chris he met a cow on the road 'with a single horn coming straight out of the middle of its [*sic*] forehead'.[16] He takes it as a good omen; Chris tells him it was a unicorn. Absurdly, Gerry sees the unicorn as commonplace. 'This was a cow – [. . .] Would I tell you a lie?' (p. 49). Deane does not refer to *Lughnasa* but here it is as if Friel were turning the tables on him with his strange beast of a play. *Lughnasa* is both history (memoir) and myth (or fiction), in which he will go beyond unicorns in search of imagined symbols. 'Would I tell you a lie?' is aimed at the audience as well as at Chris. The challenge in this beyond-Chekhov aesthetic is to see beyond fact and fiction into a third realm.

Friel begins his play about '*those five brave Glenties women*', as the dedication has it, with a monologue from a man. It is *his* story, his memory, the product of his very own 'Foundry House'. He is not Brian Friel, who was not born to a single mother in Glenties. He makes the facts clear in the story 'A Man's World', included in *A Saucer of Larks*. The essential truth in the *mythos* of the play is not exposition by Michael but delivered off-handedly in two instalments into the action like a Brechtian disruption, namely that two of Friel's aunts ended up on the streets of London and died abjectly. This much was true confession, the awful piece of family history Friel had to confront and as artist was urged by fellow playwright Tom Kilroy to dramatise, resulting in 'a very different play to the one that [Kilroy] expected'.[17] The narration of the truth had to be done aslant, as later in *Molly Sweeney*. Michael's main account of aunts Agnes and Rose comes in Act 2 (after a brief reference at the end of Act 1) during a long pause in the dialogue following Rose's return home from the back hills and her triumphant exit. In this monologue, Michael combines the story of Rose and Agnes's wretched end in London with two other tales of Father Jack's decline and Gerry Evans's further history. Then comes the curt direction: '*Maggie, Chris, Kate and Agnes now resume their tasks*' (p. 93). No unicorns on view here. The effect of Michael's narrative is shocking. Its discordancy disrupts the naturalistic representation of the lives of five women. That is how Friel wishes the truth to be framed. It is necessarily unsettling, dramatically and emotionally disruptive.

At the opening of the play, however, Michael's role as male 'author' of these women is strangely endangered. After his first monologue, he remains outside the kitchen while the dialogue between his mother and three of his aunts goes forward. Michael cannot possibly remember it because he was not present. For a few moments, the women are autonomous. A fuss over an inadequate mirror draws attention to self-consciousness and identity. Then after Kate enters from the village Michael is doubly present: as Michael the narrator and as the boy, his junior self, aged seven (Friel's age in 1936, the date when *Lughnasa* is set). The boy is deemed to be on the floor of the kitchen making his kite surrounded by five women while his senior self speaks for him outside this circle. This is how we are meant to imagine the attentive boy all through the play, but in effect his is a movable invisibility. He is sometimes spoken of as hiding outside. That the unfolding story is the work of Michael's memory is thus an illusion carefully established. Just as Michael is in a very limited way Friel's *alter ego*, so is Michael himself only a limited author of the play's memories.[18] The memories comprise Friel's dream play.[19]

A Man's World?

Friel goes two better than Chekhov's *Three Sisters* in placing the Mundy sisters at the centre of *Dancing at Lughnasa*. He has described his own version of *Three Sisters* as 'a kind of act of love'[20] and one may say the same of *Lughnasa*. The way Friel celebrates those five women's lives is mainly through realistic, humdrum routines – bread-making, fetching water from the well, tending the fire, ironing and maintaining a house in which there is no able-bodied man to do the donkey work. There is, strangely, no cow mentioned, so there is no milking to be done; but there are chickens to be fed, as there are universally ('tell me this, Jack', Maggie asks. 'what's the Swahili for "tchook-tchook-tchook?"' p. 96), and even a white rooster that Rose fails to save ('We can hardly expect him to lay for us now', p. 102). The subject of potatoes does not come up, but as no Irish household could subsist without them, someone must have tilled the ground, sowed and dug potatoes enough to feed seven people. There was doubtless hay to be saved also but in the absence of a cow the meadow can become 'the elaborate trompe l'oeil cornfield of Joe Vanek's exquisite set' for the Abbey premiere.[21] There are gaps then in Friel's delineation of a country kitchen. What he is after is not pure realism but images of struggle and survival in circumstances rapidly leading to crisis, unemployment, exile and bereavement. A pastoral setting is therefore, in Michael's memory, deployed in order to throw into relief the life, high spirits and vulnerability of his five aunts. For, as in Chekhov, the cloud of unknowing is always looming over the fate of these specimens of womanhood.

Friel accords individuality to each of the sisters, but also grants them solidarity and community status. Each has her subjectivity, her consciousness of time passing (as in Synge's *The Shadow of the Glen* (1903)), her yearning for love, but all five vary in the intensity of feelings expressed. When Agnes says, 'I'm only thirty-five. I want to dance' (p. 24), she speaks out of her own need but quickly finds an echo from three of her sisters, Kate being invariably one to have second thoughts. A key line in the play is from Chris, repeating the news of the loss of jobs relayed by Vera McLaughlin: 'The poor woman could hardly speak' (p. 81). So it is: the subaltern nature of women at the time decreed such speechlessness. Friel is intent, however, on giving as much voice to the onstage women as realism will allow (nothing approaching Lily's out-of-character summation of her life at the moment of death in *The Freedom of the City*). Simple though she is, Rose does not shilly-shally over her desire for Danny Bradley: 'I love him, Aggie' (p. 14) is spoken straight out, just as she loves Agnes more than chocolate biscuits (p. 24). Kate has adopted a man's role in assuming responsibility for the moral as well as the economic security of the household; her utterances are usually delivered in the masculine mode, corrective, admonitory and dismissive, as the occasion seems to demand. Order is her dream, her goal, and its collapse her supreme dread, as she reveals to Maggie (p. 56), who understands her best (as Agnes does Rose). Kate's discourse is masculine because of the role she has adopted, but it can also be heard as matriarchal, especially when she is referring to 'that Evans creature' (p. 53) or 'nagging' Jack and scolding him for his unacceptable free thinking. Agnes is the only one to contradict Kate, and this is a rare outburst: 'Do you ever listen to yourself, Kate? You are such a damned righteous bitch!' (p. 55). There is more to Agnes than 'clever hands' (p. 94). As Catriona Clutterbuck emphasises, Agnes is a 'visionary – she has a private vision of freedom'.[22] It is Agnes who writes the decisive note, in her 'resolute' handwriting (p. 91), announcing her leaving with Rose for London. Like Judith in *Aristocrats*, she is her own woman.

Maggie's way is quite different. In many ways, she has learnt to accept her domestic lot and be cheerful. She has a good line in absurd riddles. She gets on well with the boy Michael. Her love of popular songs is not unthinking: she can parody and can see the funny side of their distance from her own situation: 'Your frank opinion, cub: am I vagabond material?' (p. 68). But her consciousness is not inner-directed like Agnes's. It takes the mention of offstage Bernie O'Donnell to trigger a memory so profound that it leads on to the solo dance which becomes something of a riot of the sisterhood. Home from London after twenty years, with a Swedish husband and twin daughters, offstage Bernie stands as the epitome of the successful emigrant. In a way, she contrasts with the male emigrant Jack, an Irish failure who has come home to die. Maggie recalls a dancing competition in which she and Bernie participated, when gross injustice was done. Easily the best dancers on the floor, Bernie and partner were adjudged only third; even Maggie and Tim did better, but the prize went to a local couple. 'I mean they must have been blind drunk, those judges, whoever they were' (p. 35). They were almost certainly men. Bernie was 'stunned' by the decision, angered and alienated into emigration. The memory of the injustice still enrages Maggie. The buried life erupts. After a few moments' silence, she responds to the Irish dance band coming over the unreliable radio. With '*a look of defiance, of aggression*' (p. 35), Maggie launches into a '*frantic dervish*' (p. 36) rather than a ladylike compliance to the norms of Irish dancing. Bernie's twenty-year-old grievance is allowed to speak through Maggie's physical parody of what judges might call proper. The others do not follow like sheep. One by one each intuits the anger and frustration already announced by Maggie but expressed in her unique way by each of her sisters. They join but separate again as each focuses on her particular need to express feelings of desire and disappointment. When the radio reception fails, the sisters individually cease in their unsynchronised movements and emerge from the dance '*slightly ashamed*' although still '*slightly defiant*' (p. 37). The defiance articulates identity.

The dance, as written, is a shambles. The amount written on it mainly relates to early *performances* in Dublin, London and New York after it had been choreographed. The sound engineer at the Abbey in 1990 described for Tony Coult the hybrid version of the reel he came up with (not 'The Mason's Apron' in the text) to bring it to four-and-a-half minutes, complicated by director Patrick Mason's desire to give the reel 'a kind of African ethnic vibe [. . .] by doing a lot of bodhrán [Irish drum] over dubs, making it very, very heavy and percussive.'[23] In short, in the recording studio, the music was doctored to suit what the director thought was needed. The choreographer thought the main problem was 'shaping the energies' and technique of 'the girls'.[24] It was an energy transformed into technique that Friel's aunts never possessed. Like the sound designer David Nolan, the choreographer Terry John Bates found himself putting in 'more steps'. He found himself constrained by Friel's stage directions. 'Funny, I've worked with two directors recently [2000] who don't really like the play because, well, it's a "woman's play".'[25] After the success of *Riverdance* (premiered 1994), the dance in *Lughnasa* changed further. It became a 'number', a display of ensemble dance. It is necessary to put all of this technical proficiency to one side if the strange and 'parodic' dimension of the dance as conceived by Friel is to be entered. Or else, find a female director for this woman's play.

Consistent with Friel's tragic vision, *Lughnasa* is centred on the fall of the innocent. The play is not an animated culture museum. Nor is it, as David Krause believed, a play that declares 'dancing conquers all' in the same way as 'love conquers all', in traditional romantic comedy.[26] Rather, it is traditional romantic *tragedy*'s concern with 'the shades of the prison-house' closing around maturing figures.[27] *Lughnasa*, however, is not 'absolute' tragedy, a rare form, says

George Steiner, 'founded rigorously on the postulate that human life is a fatality',[28] as in *Faith Healer*, for example (see Chapter 5). *Lughnasa* is aborted tragedy, its catharsis denied in the end by Michael's aestheticism. As Helen Lojek has pointed out, the 'dangerous freedom' of the dance, in which 'sexual frustration finds an almost frightening release', is in direct contrast to Michael's final memory.[29] At the end of *Lughnasa*, Michael firmly represses his memory of the dancers as transformed into 'shrieking strangers' (p. 8) and so suppresses their tragic condition.

Of the male figures in the play, the offstage priest is represented as malignly effective, the three onstage figures empathetic but ineffectual. The unnamed parish priest makes it his business as manager of the national school where Kate teaches to warn her that she may not be needed in the new academic year. He is attempting to force her to deliver Jack from apostasy to orthodox priestly duties or else expel him as a scandal to the community. As she fails to do either, her job is gone by September. Economically, the household will be impoverished. The priest's decision is a piece of injustice equal to that against Bernie O'Donnell. Like O'Casey before him, Friel shows the influence of the celibate Catholic male clergy on Irish society as negative. But Friel also sidesteps the power of the Irish National Teachers' Organisation (INTO, the primary teachers' union) in order to demonise the parish priest.

Father Jack and Gerry Evans must be seen as counterparts: hence the 'ceremony' of exchange of headgear between them. As outsiders, drifters, dissidents, they mirror each other. Their ineffectuality, at the same time, is tragic, for tragedy invariably sounds the note of what might have been. By becoming chaplain to the British army in World War I, Father Jack put himself outside the pale in Ireland's struggle for independence. Kate, an orthodox nationalist, reminds him of this point (p. 103). The tattered uniform, in which he appears to conduct the hat ceremony, is an image of his ruined career. But if Father Jack's story is a narrative of loss, his 'error' in abandoning the British colonialist code in Uganda for the more satisfying culture of the Ryangan natives is hubristic and received ambiguously by his sisters, especially by Kate. Perhaps the most notable feature of this 'pagan' culture, as concerns a gendered reading of *Lughnasa*, is the central presence of the Great

Earth Goddess, Obi. A female god who sanctions love, dancing and communal celebration replaces in Jack's pantheon both the vindictive god of the Old Testament and the gentle Jesus of the New. As witness to the superiority of the African religion, Jack resembles a Graham Greene character, a 'burnt-out case' and yet one who paradoxically gets to 'the heart of the matter'. To Jack, observances like the wearing of a dog collar by a priest or the saying of daily Mass are irrelevant. For the Ryangans, 'there is no distinction between the religious and the secular' (p. 74), and so they live the good life philosophers have always longed for, where nature and the supernatural are as one. In asking 'What Is a Good Life?', the American philosopher Ronald Dworkin comments: '[I]t is unlikely that we will ever achieve a full integration of our moral, political, and ethical values that feels authentic and right. That is why living responsibly is a continuing project and never a completed task.'[30] Father Jack obviously believed that the Ryangans lived the good life. But the utopia he describes includes a leper colony, a worm in the bud of the prelapsarian rose. These people need medical science, money, expertise, first-world involvement: none of which Jack the romantic mentions. He got on the wrong side of the British colonialist order by rejecting their money. His ideal is accordingly not thought through. It is the dream of a Prospero without any magic books. For all that, it is a good dream, ironised in Friel's style through Jack's shambling scattiness. Under his influence, even Kate comes to sympathise and broaden her narrow moral horizons. She decides Jack is making 'his own distinctive spiritual search' (p. 92), and after his sudden death she mourns him above her sisters. Although a failure, he lived well: 'it is the performance rather than the product value of living that way that counts'.[31] It is left to the audience to determine how radical Jack's views truly are.

Jack sees something in Gerry Evans that others, except for Chris, are blind to. Gerry is a playboy (in Synge's sense), a gigolo (in the world's sense), one of Tennessee Williams's 'fugitive kind'. He is comically indulged in the play – although not by Kate – a man who cannot keep a job or a promise, a pretender to knowledge he does not command ('sparkplugs' to fix a radio?) and a liar of Falstaffian proportions. Even Falstaff lives to be rejected, but not Gerry Evans.

He is a survivor. When he recognises, as his two-timing counterpart Willy Loman never did, that nobody 'wants salesmen that can't sell' (p. 78), he signs up for the Spanish Brigade. Here too, he is irresponsible and farcical. But he sees a purpose in it nevertheless. 'Maybe that's the important thing for a man: a *named* destination – democracy, Ballybeg, heaven. Women's illusions aren't so easily satisfied – they make better drifters' (p. 78). The last phrase is startlingly Wildean, oxymoronic and therefore subversive. It seems to impress Chris, who is buoyed by his going on a mission, overcomes her 'depressions' and actually corrects Kate when she comments that it is a sad day for Ireland 'when we send young men off to Spain to fight for godless Communism'. 'For democracy, Kate,' is Chris's response and raises a smile at Kate's securing her conscience on this point (p. 80). The ethical point in question is whether the Spanish civil war is a good cause and Gerry inserts into the play the quiet insistence that it is: a minority view in Ireland in 1936. Twenty years on, Osborne's Jimmy Porter, who watched his father die after returning from the fight against Franco, measures the present pusillanimity against that former glory: 'people of our generation aren't able to die for good causes any longer. [. . .] There aren't any good, brave causes left.'[32] Of course, Gerry does not die but is sent home after an absurd accident. Yet the comedy does not erase the critique of 1930s' Ireland. Franco is not mentioned in the play, but de Valera is.

It is significant that Michael, as narrator, also favours Gerry. He sees through him but he loves him. He adopts his surname. He protects his memory by keeping the secret of Gerry's prior wife and family in Wales, sharing it only with the audience. Accordingly, Michael identifies with his father, theatricalises him and, in a strange way, sees him as a vagrant exponent of the 'good life' alongside Father Jack. All of this makes the audience complicit in Michael's interpretation. As the final scene shows when the kite is seen full-on, Michael is an artist whose work in its strangeness offsets his sleight-of-hand as a memorialist of sweetness and light. As owner of the play's narrative, Michael remains problematic in his creation of a happy ending and in the suppressed story of his own neglect of the family. That lacuna raises a question mark over his authority and challenges the stability of Friel's text.

The Debate: A Coda

Speaking to Mel Gussow in 1991, Friel said: '[*Lughnasa*] provides me with an acceptable fiction'[33] for his quasi-autobiographical play. He meant 'acceptable' primarily to himself as artist. Although he did not consider it the kind of play likely to change the world, he believed it could 'make some tiny, thumbscrew adjustment on our psyche'.[34] Some critics today are disappointed it did not offer more. Victor Merriman finds, on the contrary, 'an aversion of the gaze from the *realpolitik* involved [. . .] in the daily struggle to live an ordinary life in Independent [*sic*] Ireland.'[35] This is one dimension of the debate, a continuation of the postcolonial critique the play itself mounts on Friel's own terms. On this level, postcolonialist criticism is stymied by the presence in the play of Michael, who refuses to engage in Field Day politics. Patrick Lonergan, disturbed as many critics are by the globalised success of the Abbey's production of *Lughnasa* tending to conceal the rebarbative features of the text, finds that the establishment of *nostalgia* as a predominant theme has led to misinterpretation of its meaning.[36] Éamonn Jordan steers the debate instead towards metatheatre: 'The play is not as much about the preservation of the past and a denial of history's impetus, as a marking of the process of adjustment and realignment within the trauma of ritualized memory.'[37]

But the feminist response is, in the context of this chapter, the most significant contribution. Claudia Harris pioneered the gendered reading of *Lughnasa*, arguing that, 'The Mundy sisters are not simply Friel's artistic representation of women characters on the stage; their repeated performance teaches the gender role *woman*.'[38] This locates the core of the debate. Anna McMullan criticises the failure of the sisters to *sustain* the subversion of 'social and gender conditioning of their world' she sees embodied in their dance.[39] In a review of *The Cambridge Companion to Brian Friel*, Lionel Pilkington went further, complaining that, 'The overall impact of such performances is to reinstate a gendered construction of women as non-rational.'[40] I would suggest there is a general problem here deriving from an interpretation of the big dance scene as 'empowering' in the activist sense. But empowering relates to the group first, then the individual as a selfless part of that group.[41] Friel's emphasis is on the individual first. Each of the sisters dances for herself. Even though they do join hands at one point, they quickly separate to retreat into privacy: the dance is not really Bakhtinian carnival. It is only if the dance becomes a 'number' à la *Riverdance*, or as in the 1999 film of *Lughnasa* (about which Joan Fitzpatrick Dean has written)[42] where it becomes a wheel-of-life homage to Gaia that ideas of solidarity and empowerment arise. Friel's text may *suggest* empowerment but his point lies in its unavailability. In interview with John Lahr, Friel vouched for a 'need for the pagan in life' but only as a means of 'disrupting civility'.[43] Therefore, *The Bacchae* may be a misleading parallel.[44] There is no way these women are going to attack the offstage parish priest or make a move against Danny Bradley, because they are 'caught between a "primitive", Pre-Christian, liberated body, and the permissive, pleasured body of the late twentieth century. They cannot move forward or back but are stuck in a 1936 Ireland', when 'the body was censored, censured and constrained'.[45] The point is now well established that the female body in Friel's oeuvre becomes the site of some form of colonisation. In *Lughnasa* it is the pathos of this condition that is highlighted. We bear in mind that Kate, the central consciousness of the play, weeps all through Michael's final monologue (p. 106). She knows that fine words butter no parsnips. Unlike Evans, Kate did not have to climb a tree to see the future. She has seen it, and it does not work for the Mundy sisters. Unlike the end of *Aristocrats*, then, the end of *Lughnasa* is charged with future loss and separation leading on to a tragic horizon. This is quite different from Chekhov's optimism.

It may be observed, finally, that if *Dancing at Lughnasa* had its origins at a specific moment in Thatcher's England (as Thomas Kilroy testifies),[46] its success took place in Mary Robinson's Ireland, when *mná na h-Éireann* ('the women of Ireland') found their most eloquent and courageous advocate for equality.[47] *Lughnasa*, in moving 'the energies of women from the margin to the centre stage of Irish drama', shared 'the historical moment with the election of Mary Robinson'.[48] But that coincidence can also be misleading. The reception of *Dancing at Lughnasa* must not be confused with its textual coherence. A male figure controls the play and has the last word(s).

Molly Sweeney

There is nothing Chekovian about *Molly Sweeney*. In form it is monologual like *Faith Healer*, written fifteen years earlier. In theme it is to some degree Beckettian, focusing like *Happy Days* on decline and fall into corporal entropy. It is a woman-play of a different kind, however. Beckett's play is wickedly surrealistic, incongruously situating a modern, middle-class woman upright in a burial-mound setting entrapping her body under blazing, infernal sunshine. Friel's terrain is more realistic, his concerns less metaphysical. Beckett's mockery pervades the absurd monologues of Winnie; Friel's empathy towards Molly lends her tragedy a far different tone. And where the men in *Happy Days* – one onstage, one off – are not helpful they do not, as in *Molly Sweeney*, do actual damage. They merely embody the male gaze. We are made to understand that this offstage couple (the Cookers or Showers) are Beckett's butt, representing his scorn for spectators who crossly demand of his work, 'What's it meant to mean?'[49] The audience is alienated. Not so in *Molly Sweeney* where empathy is demanded. Nevertheless, it is of Beckett one thinks when faced with the challenge of interpreting Friel's play because here Friel shares not only with *Happy Days* but also with *Not I* (1973) and *Footfalls* (1976) a deeply felt sense that in the vulnerability of the female body lies the most forceful, theatrical image of human tragedy today.

In that regard, *Molly Sweeney* reads like a case history. With good reason, as it happens, because the idea of a blind person undergoing an operation, finding temporary sight and then complete reversion and terrible decline is based on a case history by Oliver Sacks under the title 'To See and Not See'.[50] As I have written elsewhere on this topic,[51] I wish here only to emphasise that, by altering Sacks's patient from male to female, Friel was claiming the story for transformation. My discussion of the play here, then, relates to its gendered features. If *Dancing at Lughnasa* is aborted tragedy because the women's voices are finally stifled by nephew Michael, who seals up the tragic narrative in artifice, *Molly Sweeney* is the tragedy of a woman who breaks through such artifice to tell her own tragic story.

This play looks back to *The Loves of Cass McGuire* (see Chapter 3) but with an entirely new focus. Cass finds herself in a social drama about a returned exile; Molly embodies a state closer to Cass's *final* condition. They lose their independence in different ways. Indeed, in Friel's work Judith in *Aristocrats* is the only female protagonist who achieves autonomy. For her, the future is something to be created with confidence; tragedy has no hold over her life as the play ends. In contrast, Agnes and Rose in *Lughnasa* achieve only a false liberation in London: they made a worse mistake than Cass McGuire. Economically Molly is in a far better place, but this is not the issue. Although blind, she is a qualified physiotherapist in full-time employment, has her own apartment, includes swimming among her leisure activities and holds more than one diploma in that skill. She also enjoys cycling and dancing, activities which argue both status and poise. All this before she met and married Frank, who may, without hyperbole, be called her destroyer. Dr Rice is merely accessory, although a fatal one, as will appear. Molly's problem was never her blindness, but that she would have been better off alone.

A Farewell to Field Day

After the success of *Dancing at Lughnasa*, there was no going back to the Field Day Theatre Company. Friel resigned from the board in February 1994; when a co-founder resigns from such an artistic enterprise, its death knell is sounded. At the time, fellow director Davy Hammond opined that Friel was 'going on a new artistic journey'.[52] *Molly Sweeney* was written in 1993 and first staged in 1994: not at the Abbey but at the Gate, making two moves in one, away from Field Day and away, just for the moment, from the Abbey. These details serve to define *Molly Sweeney* as special. The fact that Friel directed it himself emphasises this point further. He had never directed before, and here was a play destined to travel to London (the Almeida) and New York (Roundabout Theatre Company). It was a fresh beginning.

The debate concerning *Molly Sweeney* today may be posed as between dialectics and aesthetics. Is the play a feminist critique or what Anthony Roche terms 'a chamber piece'?[53] Anna McMullan claims that *Molly Sweeney* 'directly stages the performance of male authority on the female body'.[54] That 'directly' cannot be right in any event. Claudia Harris also sees Molly as exploited by husband Frank and surgeon Mr Rice, who 'attempt to turn her supposed disadvantage [as a blind person] to their own advantage' whereby Molly 'trusts and ceases to exist'.[55] This interpretation has obvious pertinence, activating the question posed by Simone de Beauvoir early on in the twentieth-century feminist debate: 'Yes, women on the whole *are* today inferior to men; that is their situation affords them fewer possibilities. The question is: should that state of affairs continue?'[56] I do not believe the question, as posed, to be among Friel's most urgent interests. I prefer to consider *Molly Sweeney* primarily as a 'woman play' in Shaw's sense or Beckett's or even Synge's and contextually as a riposte to the feminist critique of the *Field Day Anthology of Irish Writing* published in three volumes on 31 October 1991. This critique was an angry repudiation of the anthology because of its perceived bias towards male authors, male editors and representation of women. Nuala O'Faoláin's attack in the *Irish Times* was devastating. She declared that if such an anthology were published in the United States 'American women would not let it stand. They would demand its withdrawal.'[57] O'Faolain's review ignited the flames of a controversy that burned for some time. Seamus Deane's agreement that Field Day would fund two further volumes to be edited solely by women defused opposition at home. Those volumes appeared in 2002[58] and the feminists were vindicated. In the meantime, the argument ran: 'Field Day has not published pamphlets about women, produced plays by women, or studied nationalism, colonialism and Irish identity as they affect women'; therefore, the 1991 *Anthology* was 'the best illustration of the group's blind spot'.[59] The 'group' certainly included the Theatre Company, of which Friel was co-founder.

With *Molly Sweeney*, Friel in part addressed this 'blind spot'. In identifying Molly's history with Ireland's, Karen M. Moloney sees her as a representative of 'the contemporary Irishwoman, colonized subject of the postcolonial Irish male'.[60] When *Molly Sweeney* reached Broadway, however, and the critics raised the question of the Troubles as part of its meaning, the actress playing Molly (Catherine Byrne) was driven into a panic and had to be reassured by Friel: 'You're playing a woman – just play the woman.'[61] Byrne was his favourite actress at this time; it is said he wrote the part for her.[62] It would appear that in rehearsing *Molly* in Dublin Friel never raised the possibility that the play reflects upon postcolonialism. For him, it was a play about a blind woman fallen among blinder men. Further, Moloney concedes that *Molly Sweeney* is 'a play in which allegory ultimately takes a back seat to human tragedy',[63] an area I shall return to at the end of this chapter.

Blindness and Metaphor

Friel kindly sent me his diary notes on the composition of *Molly* when I was editing *Essays, Diaries, Interviews* (1999), containing references to eye problems he himself suffered at the time he was working on the play. It was this personal experience of ophthalmic surgery which provided the solid basis in feeling and imagination for *Molly*. Although other circumstances impinged, with Friel invariably 'a play offers you a shape and a form to accommodate your anxieties and disturbances in that period of life you happen to be passing through.'[64] Friel's eye operations proved routine and he returned to work.[65] But the theme was born. What if he had always been blind and in midlife were tempted to undergo such an operation: what then? Or what if he were a woman, what difference might that make? Is it a case of '*Molly Sweeney, c'est moi*'? Certainly, like fellow-Northerner Brian Moore in *I Am Mary Dunne* (1968), who begins 'I remember, therefore I am,'[66] Friel accepted the challenge of having a woman narrate her own story. He had done this in *Cass McGuire* but now the challenge was more severe: to choose a woman as protagonist, make her blind and, through her consciousness, filter his own artistic vision of the fragility of human happiness. The dramatic form was to be minimalist, the concentration almost entirely on the human voice, its tones, rhythms and potential for ambiguity. The end was portraiture in sound, a tragic resonance. The woman would be both subject and object.

In *Ways of Seeing* (1972), the art-historian John Berger commented: 'Seeing comes before words. [. . .] The relation between what we see and what we know is never settled.'[67] Berger is concerned mainly with perception, the relationship between seeing and interpretation; he is not concerned with blindness. But as he is considerably interested in the subject-object relationship, he explores also the male-female difference as it affects seeing and being seen. 'To be born a woman has been to be born, *within an allotted and confined space*, into the keeping of men' (p. 46, emphasis added). That is a given. Molly, as a *blind* woman, is doubly 'confined' in space. In a passage which seems to be reaching towards the theory of the 'male gaze', Berger claims a woman must always 'watch herself' and is thus split in two: 'And so she comes to consider the [male] *surveyor* and the [female] *surveyed* within her as the two constituent yet always distinct elements of her identity as a woman.' As a result, a woman turns *herself* into an object, a 'sight' (pp. 46–7, emphases added). Men 'act' and women 'appear' (visually): women show how they would like to be treated, while men treat women on the basis of how they appear to them. Berger's striking comments seem to provide a gendered interpretation of Berkeley's idea as adopted by Beckett (in *Film* but also in the plays), namely *esse est percipi*: to be is to be seen. Berger was a charismatic explorer of art on BBC television: his programmes were found to be sharp-edged and provoking; his book, with illustrations, provides the grounds of his approach. For his part, Friel would have been fully capable of adapting these ideas to the world outside visual art and of rendering them more complex by considering the place on stage of a *blind* woman coping within its confines.

The origin of 'theatre' is the Greek word *theatrum*, meaning 'seeing-place'. It was where spectators came to behold a figure like Oedipus put his eyes out as a metaphor of tragic recognition. Friel usually gives due place to visual design in his plays, even allowing *Lughnasa* to be visually highlighted in production. But he has always been conscious that in the history of theatre – the Greeks, the Elizabethans – the scenery as such and spectacle in particular were firmly subordinated to the writer's skill in evoking a setting in the mind. A bare stage served the Greeks and Shakespeare alike. When Shakespeare wanted

Gloucester in *King Lear* to appear to jump off Dover cliff, he made the whole episode become an act of faith through the power of theatre. Gloucester's blindness becomes a metaphor for audience perception. For *Molly Sweeney*, Friel asks for no *mise-en-scène*. He allocates a separate stage area to each of the three characters, Molly, Frank and Mr Rice, who remain on stage throughout. When the lights go up, '*we discover the three characters*'[68]: the word 'discover' goes back to the Elizabethans. It means the characters are there, suddenly and startlingly, before us, Faustus in his study and so forth. This is minimalism even beyond Beckett's, and it derives from Friel's insistence here that the audience must *imagine* the world Molly inhabits through language and sound. There is something Yeatsian also about this austerity, as in 'I call to the eye of the mind.'[69] In directing the play himself, Friel allowed a chair each to the performers, and a background of cornflowers. These were his only concessions to the sighted people in the theatre.

While Synge too chose blindness for theme in his *The Well of the Saints* (1905), he did not do so – as Friel did – from the point of view of the blind person. Synge is certainly part of the 'tradition' Friel invariably negotiates in his dramaturgy but strategically rewrites in order to provide a voice for modernity. Tradition becomes part of source material, as history does. Synge's treatment of the blind beggars Martin and Mary Doul, however, is rather distant from Friel's philosophical and psychological interests. Synge was preoccupied with alienation, how outsiders, tramps, playboys, analogous to artists, are ultimately expelled from the community. Blindness for Synge becomes a value, a choice, ultimately a vocation. His blind couple are cured in Act 2, lose their sight again in Act 3 and refuse to be 'cured' a second time in revolt against the 'reality' of the world that sight brings unacceptably home to them. They claim the right to be as they wish, blind outsiders. The idea of such choice is radical. It forms a less radical part of the action of *Molly Sweeney*. Nevertheless, Molly does crucially choose twice: to have the operation and to reject the seeing world later on.

In turn, an indirect source for *The Well of the Saints* was *Les Aveugles* (*The Sightless*), by Maurice Maeterlinck (1862–1949), a Belgian symbolist writer who also influenced Strindberg, Yeats and others. Lady Gregory translated his *L'Interieur* (*The Interior*) for the Abbey stage in 1907, which Synge would have known. (He was fluent in French in any event.) Maeterlinck proposed a new 'static' drama, symbolist in mood but minimalist realism in style, in an effort to highlight 'the tragical in daily life'.[70] Katharine Worth has shown how deeply Maeterlinck's little plays influenced both Yeats and Synge and rooted Irish drama in a European tradition. She calls *The Sightless* Maeterlinck's 'most uncompromising' expression of static theatre, confining actors and audience 'within almost unbearably narrow limits'.[71] It has much in common with *The Well of the Saints*: both plays can be described as 'drama of the interior'.[72] By extension, Friel's *Molly Sweeney* taps into that European legacy. This point was confirmed in April 2013 when a revival of *Molly Sweeney* in London coincided with a revival of Maeterlinck's *The Sightless* showing, as Michael Billington noted, 'ideas absorbed into the mainstream'.[73] The keynote of his drama of the 'interior', Maeterlinck said, was 'dread of the unknown that surrounds us'[74] and this is Friel's modern, existentialist theme. Tradition and modernity once again coalesce.

A Woman's World

Molly's monologues begin and end the play. There is no 'mystery' about her past comparable to Frank Hardy's omission of all mention of the stillborn baby, to which both Grace and Teddy refer and therefore reify. Molly's history is simpler, less contested. She owns it herself. And yet if we attend closely to her opening monologue about her father, another Frielian judge, we are forced to find it complex. Can it be true that by the age of five Molly had learnt from him the *names* of 'dozens of flowers and herbs and shrubs and trees'?[75] It seems a peculiar method of teaching language to a visually impaired child. She was expected to match up by touch and smell the real items with the names in her memory. The primary function of language, it has been said, is 'to make memory possible' and with it consciousness.[76] Molly offers an account of how her memory was constructed *for* her by her father. Further, she says that every evening after he got home and had had 'a few quick drinks' (denoting alcoholism?), her father carried her out to the *walled* garden. Why should she be carried rather than led by the hand? Why specify the 'walled' garden except to suggest enclosure, perhaps an Edenic concept? She calls it *his* garden, not 'our'. Is it likely her father carried her out *every* evening thus, for a lesson on botany? What, winter and summer? No. Molly is inventing from the outset. She calls it 'perform[ing] the same ritual of naming, and counting and touching and smelling' (p. 456). One thinks of the dialogue between Yolland and Owen in *Translations* when they feel godlike in inventing new words for old places: 'Welcome to Eden! [. . . .] We name a thing and – bang! it leaps into existence! [. . .] Each name a perfect equation with its roots' (*Plays 1*, p. 422). Molly remembers a childhood which is paradise and a father who is godlike. But later in the same monologue she remembers a father constantly arguing with a mentally disturbed wife. Molly remembers her mother always in her 'headscarf and wellingtons' (p. 457). How could she know those details? She remembers too her father telling her, Molly – most inappropriately – that in her blindness she was not missing much in life. Berkeley, one of Friel's as of Frank's sources on vision, distinguished between the 'pictures' on the retina of a seeing person and the 'images apprehended by the imagination alone' of an unsighted person, such that 'a man blind from his birth may perfectly imagine, understand, and comprehend them'. The mind, says Berkeley, 'is wonderfully apt to be deluded' in such matters.[77] Deluded is the word, then. Molly's contradiction between an image of a godlike father and a drunk who apparently drove her mother demented is already schizoid. We cannot take Molly's monologue as gospel truth.

Mr Rice has his own problems. Molly conflates him with her father and so his being the cause of her trauma makes it difficult to decide how far she is projecting the sins her of father onto Rice or Rice's failure back to her dead father. But Rice speaks forthrightly and may be taken as telling the truth, because so much of it tells against himself. Molly as first introduced to him 'had a full life and never felt at all deprived' (p. 459). His knowledge is, however, confined to the short time during which she was his patient and the subsequent year or less before he left Ballybeg. His facts come from the file Frank gave him. As Frank is an innocent, one may take his facts to be well based. He has a lot of faults but invention (or lying, if you will) is not one of them. Coming through Dr Rice, however, these facts carry more authority. We already know that Molly looked on herself as 'disadvantaged' rather than 'deprived' (p. 464). At first meeting, Rice was struck by her 'independence' (p. 458). Her agency is thus not in question. For his own part, Rice, a washed-up ophthalmologist with nagging memories of his glory days, sees in Molly's medical condition 'the chance of a lifetime' for him (p. 460). With Friel, 'chance' in its ambiguity is always destructive. In a later monologue Rice confesses to 'hubris' (p. 470). His personal fall is as old as that of Icarus. But he destroys Molly as well as his own future.

'I'll remember Ballybeg', Rice proclaims (p. 489). In the complex, isochronous, time pattern the play displays, use of the future tense regarding memory is unusual. Present on stage, relating his confessions of his part in the story of Molly's destruction, Rice projects forward to the very point where he stands now, on stage, a narrator from Molly's past. (The technique recalls the final monologue in *Faith Healer*.) When he shifts so emphatically into the past tense in a later monologue, Rice suggests finality in Molly's state: 'In those last few months it was hard to recognize the woman who had first come' to his house for consultation (p. 500). The phrase 'in those last few months' is used twice more within the next page. Molly's continuing presence on stage asserts the 'interior' to which Rice has no access and we, through her discourse, have.

Richard Pine queries whether *Molly Sweeney* may be read as 'a feminist fable'.[78] To explore this question, it may be useful to note the amphibian existence Molly led in blindness, at home in water, the swimming pool, or on its equivalent the dance floor. She is a kind of mermaid figure or Ondine,[79] out of her element once Frank initiates the corrective surgery which will take her out of her true realm. In folklore, the time comes when the mermaid must return to the sea, the element she has left or been 'rescued' from by the man she marries; her going back to her own world leaves a grieving husband.[80] Ibsen provided a modern take on this scenario in *The Lady from the Sea* (1888) but it remained a play about marriage. In modern times the focus is on the suffering woman, as in Heaney's poem 'Maighdean Mara'.[81] Toril Moi has pointed out that *The Lady from the Sea* is also 'about a woman driven to the edge of madness by her refusal of finitude'.[82] This would mean that Molly, like Ibsen's Ellida, the lady from the sea, fails to acknowledge the boundaries in her life, is 'unable to acknowledge the separate existence of others' and 'takes refuge in melodramatic fantasies [. . .] so as not to have to acknowledge death.'[83] The resemblance is not complete, but quite instructive in interpreting the end of *Molly Sweeney*. Toril Moi also sees *The Lady from the Sea* as leading on to *Hedda Gabler* (1890), 'where marriage and the everyday are equally empty'.[84] There is a link here too with Friel, who adapted *Hedda* for the Gate in 2008, directed by Anna Mackmin. Molly does not, like Hedda, take her own life, 'reasonable people just don't do things like that' as Friel's Judge Brack says.[85] If Molly is at all to be compared to Hedda, it must be that in marriage she too lived a life of quiet desperation.

That Molly's marriage was a mistake is obvious. Why did she enter it? There was nothing erotic about Frank Sweeney. All Molly saw – was there more? – was his global enthusiasm, and she admired his 'energy' and 'passion'; but mainly Frank was 'everything my father wasn't' (p. 477). This is a telling negative. Accordingly, Rice was Frank's rival. Everything Frank says is phallogocentric but he seems in himself to lack a phallus. Molly's frustration expresses itself in the dance she executes during the pre-op party, which resembles the kind of 'Irish wake' Gar O'Donnell hosts in *Philadelphia, Here I Come!* rendered pointless through false steps by doubtful friends. But Molly, unlike Gar, is angry at the thought of 'being used' by Frank and Rice. In defiance and 'the dread of exile', she breaks into 'a wild and furious dance' around the room, skilful in its avoiding the furniture yet 'Mad and wild and frenzied' (p. 473). In contrast to the sterility of Gar O'Donnell's world, the dance more clearly reflects the world of the Mundy sisters in *Lughnasa* and the quasi-Dionysian expression of their frustration. Molly is newly defined here, through defiance. She wants to dance, and wants the symbolism that dance signifies, but she is scheduled for a futile eye operation that will deliver her lost into an alien world. In time, Frank reaches the view that 'There seemed nothing more [he] could do' for her (p. 498). He leaves her to her fate. Just before that, Molly again defines herself as an angry woman and once more Frank stands by ineffectually. When she insists on diving off a cliff eighty feet into the sea in the dark of night, we cannot be sure she actually goes through with the idea. Perhaps it is just fantasy, Dover cliff over again. Frank construes the incident as symptomatic of 'an enormous change' of personality rather than a desire for self-expression (p. 494). Molly was unable to get him to understand how '*terrifying*' her new world was (p. 492). Frank, unlike Shakespeare's Edgar, shows no capacity to restore faith.

The play's ending is heralded by Rice's recognition that Molly was 'exiled' once she entered her mother's psychiatric hospital (p. 501). He uses the same term as Molly, implying a lost homeland. That sense of exile is a persistent image in Friel's work to denote emotional devastation. It is mainly an existential, modernist kind of psychological alienation. After all, Molly only ever wanted to *visit* the sighted world, 'this land of vision', and return 'home' like the mermaid in folklore to her 'own world' (p. 483). She fails, and is left tragically suspended between the two worlds.

Friel told the actress Catherine Byrne who played Molly in the 1994 premiere that there is hope at the end. Byrne was appalled to think so. 'I remember sitting in the middle of the rehearsal room saying, "Hope? But she dies!"'.[86] And yet in the text Molly does say that she is 'at home' at last in her 'borderline country' between fantasy and reality (p. 509). This state seems to her 'to be all right' (p. 509). Patrick Mason, who directed a revival of *Molly Sweeney* at the Gate in 2011, maintains that Molly is dead from the outset of the play: 'She is heard in the ether from another dimension'; all three characters are in their own worlds, with a need to speak, to justify; the play takes the form of a post-mortem.[87] I would not be sure about that. Mason's reply is that one is not supposed to be sure: Molly accepts irresolvable contradiction and the play ends with her query, 'And why should I question any of it any more?' (p. 509). Mason believes 'Molly is in a strange place, but that's ok too.'[88] A strange place, one may say, but one willed by her. Her final rejection of Rice and Frank (in citing his ridiculous letter) is an action to parallel Hardy's at the catastrophe of *Faith Healer*. Hers is the dominant voice at the end of *Molly Sweeney*. She is not a passive victim.

When one looks back to *Aristocrats* and *Lughnasa*, one sees that each ends in active repose, Spenser's 'eterne in mutabilitie', the triumph of art over time.[89] Such endings are not Chekhovian. They provide an alternative to history in suspending the issue of necessary change. The object is purity of form, as in Beckett's later plays such as *Rockaby* (1980), where representation of tragic feeling culminates in stillness. There is an incompletion challenging the audience to see beyond the devised repose. Yet over time, in what Jonathan Miller calls 'subsequent performances', plays themselves change, find an 'afterlife' and demand new interpretation on stage.[90] I have tried to make that point about *Translations* in Chapter 6: after the Belfast Peace Agreement, it cannot be read in the same way as when the Troubles raged. In 1994, when *Molly Sweeney* was first staged, Fintan O'Toole argued that there was 'at some level at least, an element of political metaphor at work' which is not visible nowadays.[91] He saw *Molly* as providing both a warning (against imposing fixed ways of seeing the world) and a promise (of 'the rewards that lie beyond the certainties of fixed language'). It was a time in Ireland of ceasefires and rumours of ceasefires. But when the play was given a major revival at the Dublin Gate in 2011, all this political uncertainty was over. Further, Friel no longer saw the need to direct the play himself. In handing over to Patrick Mason, he gave him as programme note a piece entitled 'Words', to which his fellow-writer Seamus Heaney added a complementary note, 'Vision'. Friel asserted: '[I]n the theatre that has engaged me, words are at the very core of it all.' Invoking the storyteller's technique – here possibly thinking of the Irish actor Éamon Kelly[92] – Friel argued that a playwright's words are 'scored' differently from poet or novelist for public utterance. The concept is musical, referring to tempo and key. The desired effect is, with the collaboration of the actors, to cast a 'public spell'. He conceded that the words are not 'fully empowered' until 'an actor liberates them and fulfils them'. Only then can the language acquire [in an echo of Synge's preface] 'its own special joy and delight' because 'what is written to be sung is now being sung'. What fascinated Friel here was the process of making private 'wisdom' available publicly to an audience. He called it 'a contrived miracle' whereby the public utterance also retains 'that private intimacy where it has its origins'.[93]

Molly Sweeney, like *Faith Healer* before it, offers the ideal stage form for this aesthetic. It is not a 'chamber piece', except perhaps in the sense of Strindberg's 'chamber plays' for his Intimate Theatre in Stockholm. It stakes the claim that in a Friel play expression itself, language, predominates. Social issues are present but *communication* of the issues is uppermost. In gifting lengthy speeches to *Molly Sweeney*, Friel is privileging her, valorising the female voice. She has her story to tell and she tells it with such eloquence, precision and passion that afterwards we fancy we have seen her swim and dance and prepare to dive off a cliff and huddle in a hospital bed feigning sleep, while all the time she is sitting quietly on a chair or standing in indeterminate space. She becomes an iconic woman lost in space but with the words to say how she got there. Finally, she realises she is a performer in a tragedy; it is for us, the audience, to register her position in full.

CHAPTER 8

'THE VODKA-AND-TONIC SOCIETY': *WONDERFUL TENNESSEE* AND *GIVE ME YOUR ANSWER, DO!*

And spare us, no less, the need
for wonder: it demands
too much suspension of belief.

– Dennis O'Driscoll, 'Spare Us',
from *Dear Life* (London: Anvil Press, 2012)[1]

Introduction

In the 1990s, *Molly Sweeney* was a Gate play Friel felt he had to do. At the same time, he wanted to do a wholly different kind of play for the Abbey, a contemporary state-of-the-nation play which probably had been long in his mind. Twenty years earlier, he had berated Irish critics for their insistence on 'relevance': 'Write of Ireland today, the critics scream. Show us the vodka-and-tonic society. Show us permissive Dublin. Forget about thatched cottages and soggy fields and emigration. We want the new Ireland.' This was not a genuine demand for 'the revelation of a new "truth" about the country' but rather a call for 'a confirmation of a false assumption'.[2] It is significant that in his 1981 version of *Three Sisters*, Andrey equates 'this endless round of vodka and cabbage-and-bacon and gossip and pretence' with 'squalor' and 'degradation' and looks to a future which will deliver a 'liberation' from it.[3] This was still Friel's own aim in writing *Wonderful Tennessee*. As Anthony Roche has pointed out, Friel had discarded his 1983 working title *Lough Derg* as too specific.[4] His urgency to speak out had to do with the vanishing sense of the sacred in Irish life and the resultant sense of loss of direction evidenced nationally. This was perhaps to look back to *Faith Healer* and the sense of mystery in that play.

Following its reasonably successful Abbey premiere in June 1993, *Wonderful Tennessee* flopped on Broadway four months later. It was an instructive failure. Frank Rich said there would be better plays that season, but 'how many of them will take us, however briefly, to that terrifying and hallowed place beyond words?'[5] Friel was probably ill-advised this time in attempting to marry a 'Broadway problem play' and a 'justification play'.[6] *Wonderful Tennessee* should have been seen off-Broadway rather than as the successor to *Dancing at Lughnasa*, to which it is merely kin.

In *Lughnasa*, Friel had drawn upon Irish pagan practices as documented by Máire Mac Neill in *The Festival of Lughnasa* (1962). For his new play, he made use of *The Last of the Name*, by Charles McGlinchey, which Friel edited for publication in 1986 from interviews between an old Donegal man and a local schoolteacher. In his introduction, Friel notes the strange 'mixed marriage of the old pagan practices with the new Christian dogmas' in McGlinchey's memory of ritual and belief.[7] Friel also highlights the 'set nights' of the Celtic calendar, which included the hybrid practices for St Brigid's Eve (31 January), such as the crosses made from rushes to invoke the saint's protection at the turning of winter into spring. These were made by the adults in every house and placed in the kitchen, above beds and also in all outhouses. 'The old people always left a rag of cloth outside on a bush that night until the morning. It had the blessing of St Brigid and was used for curses and against dangers of any kind, like the fever, or lightning, or fire, or drowning. It was called the "Bratóg Bhríde".'[8] St Brigid evolved from an ancient nature goddess.[9] This compound is vital to Friel's *Wonderful Tennessee*. In his interview with John Lahr prior to the opening of *Lughnasa* on Broadway in 1991, Friel remarked: 'I think there's a need for the pagan in life. [. . .] I don't think of it as disrupting Christianity. I think of it as disrupting civility. If too much obeisance is offered to manners, then in some way we lose or suppress the grumbling and dangerous beast that's underneath the ground.'[10] It can be claimed that *Wonderful Tennessee* takes off from this point. It deals with modern, sophisticated and secular people, who stand in need of discovering the 'dangerous beast' within the unconscious or unacknowledged within nature itself. It summons up an invisible island with a holy well, votive offerings, *bratóga*[11] and a history of piety.

This is dangerous material for contemporary urban audiences. Yet it has its place within theatre, which from earliest times and again at its rebirth in the medieval church traditionally had its presiding divinity. In the twentieth century, T. S. Eliot attempted to exploit modernism in a bid to restore a Christian society via theatre, while directors such as Peter Brook and Jerzy Grotowski worked hard to create an ascetic style of anti-commercial theatre, a Theatre of Poverty in the heart of Paris or New York. *Wonderful Tennessee* belongs to this kind of experimental theatre, to the studio, where its serious issues could be elicited from its deceptive superficiality. Then it might be seen, like Tennessee Williams's *Small Craft Warnings* (1972), as a play celebrating a sense of 'wonder' in everyday life. *Give Me Your Answer, Do!* is a play equally imbued with anxiety over contemporary spiritual values. Friel's play enacts on the one hand a backward look, a reinvestigation of tradition in its late convergence with modernity, on the other a return, although less experimentally, to *Faith Healer* and the artist's iconic role in society today. In their subdued fashion, each is radical, exploring roots/routes of personal belief in an age of obsolete roadmaps. In his way, what Friel is in pursuit of here is 'the cultural sublime'.[12]

Wonderful Tennessee and the Power of Place

In July 1970, Friel took part in a roundtable discussion by three contemporary playwrights concerning the future of Irish drama. In an awkward attempt to appease, Friel paid a compliment to Hugh Leonard, author of many commercial successes but yet to write his masterpieces, *Da* and *A Life*: 'Of the three of us sitting at this table, I think Hugh Leonard is the only one of us who is moving in the right direction. John [B.] Keane is stuck with the peasants of Kerry. Hugh Leonard is writing about the would-be sophisticates of Dublin and its surroundings, and

I am somewhere half-way between the two.'[13] Passing over the snub to Keane, author of such popular plays as *Sive* (1959), *The Field* (1965, later filmed by Jim Sheridan) and *Big Maggie* (1969), one may discern in Friel's comment on Leonard a certain self-doubt. What if Hugh Leonard (pseud. for John Keyes Byrne), for all his sophistication, were right, and the vodka-and-tonic Dublin *nouveaux riches* offered, after all, the real, the contemporary subject matter Friel had failed (in *The Mundy Scheme*, 1969) to get on the Abbey stage? After all, Leonard was to sail well beyond *The Mundy Scheme* with his satirical farce *The Patrick Pearse Motel* in 1971, where the new bourgeoisie was exposed in all its crassness. And then came *Summer* (1974).

Summer had its premiere in Olney, Maryland, but it was its Dublin Theatre Festival premiere later in 1974 that gave it real prominence. Set on a hill overlooking Dublin, it gathers three couples plus one son and one daughter for a picnic: to be precise, two picnics, for Act 2 is a reprise six years later. The play explores midlife anxieties, yearnings of love, friendship and its trials, the appeal of adultery to an antique bookseller and the wife of a friend, and love of life under the shadow of mortality (Chekhov again). Towards the end of Act 1, the adulterous wife, Jan, looks around at the beautiful setting: 'I like this spot; we ought to come back, it's unspoiled.'[14] (This is the note on which Friel's *Wonderful Tennessee* was to end.) Act 2 presents a revisitation six years later, when the place is changed utterly by housing developments all around. The characters reminisce more now. Some are more affluent than before, others less secure. Trina recalls the first picnic with nostalgia: 'All of us happy as Larry' (p. 275). But the illness of one of the party captures a different mood; depressed and broke, Jess says bleakly 'I'm going to die' (p. 283). Jan's son, now in his twenties, regards his elders dispassionately as having had their chance in life and as now 'on a train all the way to the shed' (p. 291). While they picnic lavishly, drink fine liquor and sing pop songs, the dominant mood of Leonard's six main characters is of melancholy, although his characteristic wit lightens it to the end. The point of aligning Leonard's *Summer* with *Wonderful Tennessee* is to clarify more fully than reviewers did what Friel was doing in his play. (For example, from Fintan 'Toole: 'The play, you realize, might have been called *A Day Out in the Styx*.

This is fine.')[15] Friel was not imitating Leonard; he was starting where Leonard left off in 1974. Using the same materials, he was building a different structure to describe lost souls in a different way.

In the twenty years since Leonard wrote *Summer*, Ireland had changed to an extraordinary degree. The affluence which projected Irish society into modernity in the 1960s and 1970s transformed not only the economy, but also politics and culture to a profound degree. The Catholic Church began its long journey into disgrace and loss of public confidence. A hugely stage-managed Papal visit in 1979 by John Paul II seemed at first to stem the tide of history but with the war in the North raging unabated in the 1980s and an economic recession plunging the country into stagnation and emigration patterns unseen for decades, a great depression seemed to settle over the land. To writer and former priest Michael Harding, 'In some ways, the papal visit was the funeral of Catholicism in Ireland.'[16] For other commentators, as Luke Gibbons has pointed out, 'The collapse of the social and economic policies of the 1960s and 1970s was sufficient to throw into question the whole project of modernization as it applied to a newly industrialized country such as Ireland.'[17] By the early 1990s, something like moral chaos was come again as governments fell, corruption was seen to have pervaded public life and the economy remained fragile and chronically uncertain. It was at this point that *Wonderful Tennessee* reached the Abbey stage, when Friel took it upon himself to test the slough of despond into which the Irish nation had descended. It is Friel's meditation on the pilgrim's *lack* of progress. Where Leonard would earlier project his own personal sense of mortality and midlife crisis onto the national consciousness,[18] Friel, in line with Geertz's maxim 'society's forms are culture's substance',[19] would attempt to locate and confront the malaise – individual, social and moral – which was threatening to destroy the very soul of a people. For, following Eliot, if culture is 'a way of life' and religion 'the *whole way of life* of a people, from birth to the grave' they are interdependent.[20]

To this diagnostic end, Friel gave particular attention to setting. Leonard's *Summer* is set atop Killiney Hill (or perhaps nearby Dalkey Hill) so that suburban Dublin is spread out before the eight characters as a prospect; their lives are measured against this 'strumpet city'.[21]

Friel's setting is like Leonard's – outdoors – a remote, small pier in County Donegal. In the text he gives a whole page to a detailed description. It would appear to be based on Portnoo, not far from Glenties (where *Dancing at Lughnasa* is set). The deserted stone pier resembles the *scenae frons* or scene building of a classical Greek theatre. It '*extends across the full width of the stage*' from the offstage mainland (left) to the sea (off right). It is thus surrounded by water on three sides, Friel insists, '*the auditorium, the area stage right, and the back wall*' behind the pier. The audience is imagined to be on the beach, seated as in Eugene O'Neill's theatre in Provincetown with the sea virtually under their feet. Indeed, one of the characters in *Wonderful Tennessee* in looking out at the Atlantic remarks, 'next parish Boston, folks!' (p. 356) All the trappings of a deserted fishing port are on display – bits of net, lobster pots, broken fish boxes and so on. Where in Leonard's setting a Celtic Cross adorned the hill in Act 1, to be notably removed to a museum by Act 2, in Friel there is '*A listing and rotting wooden stand, cruciform in shape, on which hangs the remnant of a life-belt.*'[22] Helen Lojek comments: 'The shape mimics that of the well-known Celtic high cross, which has a ring at the intersection of the cross's arms.'[23] This image will come into its own as the play draws to a close.

In no other play does Friel go to such lengths to set atmosphere as he does in the opening stage directions for *Wonderful Tennessee*. On this very warm day in August, there is '*silence and complete stillness*' to be destroyed by the arrival in a minibus of the six characters on their day out. Their entrance is much delayed offstage, while we hear such noises and loud voices and singing off that '*the idyllic atmosphere is completely shattered*' (p. 347). The play will end with a reversal of this arrangement before sounds of minibus and human voices '*are encompassed by the silence and complete stillness and gradually surrender to it*' (p. 445). It is as if the place itself commands this 'deserted harbour stillness' (to borrow a phrase from Heaney),[24] the pier in its stone divinity, while human presence is a form of desecration. It takes six pages of text before all the characters enter this special space in a '*clownish, parodic conga dance, heads rolling, arms flying – a hint of the maenadic*' (p. 354). One senses Friel's disapproval.

The cries we hear first off and then are repeated onstage define the major theme of the play: these people are 'lost' and in need of 'help' (p. 347). That is, all except Terry, who knows the place and has arranged the visit as a surprise. Once arrived, the others seem more lost than ever and the play concerns itself with their stories, problems, illusions and newborn hopes, culminating not exactly as *The Tempest* does with all those lost in one way or another being found 'and all of us ourselves/When no man was his own'[25] but more in that area than in Leonard's darkening sense of human decay.

What this place by the sea with a dominant pier facing front Buddha-like and forming a back-wall is, really, is a retreat. Once the minibus leaves, the driver instructed to return the following morning, the six characters are alone. The area is depopulated, and we later hear the reason for its monastic solitude. For now, the premise is that the arrivals are on their own, locked in until dawn with little else to do than take stock as they wait (in vain) to visit Frank's once-holy island. Bernard Farrell's *I Do Not Like Thee, Dr Fell* (1979) invites comparison.[26] A major Abbey success, it has as its theme the destabilising process of the Encounter Group: six characters, including the leader, allow themselves to be confined overnight in a space, a room, for the purpose of self-revelation and release from emotional and/or psychological distress. The key-holder is not due back until the following morning. This sense of enclosure is vital, because exposure is the purpose of Joe Fell, who attends solely to sabotage the proceedings from a motive of revenge and a bomb threat is his means. Although Friel has no such literal motive in *Wonderful Tennessee*, the theatricality of Farrell's play (where role-playing and unmasking are the order of the night) serves to highlight Friel's deeper purpose. His characters are in an Encounter Group without knowing it. And the group leader this time, Terry, far from being the bogus opportunist Suzy Bernstein proves to be in Farrell's play, seems himself an ill-equipped guide for the spiritual problems of his temporarily enclosed group.

Friel's group, however, is not a gathering of strangers brought together by chance but of friends among whom interrelationships suggest solidarity. Terry, the main character, married to Berna, is brother to Trish, who is married to the musician George; Angela, married to

Frank, but having an affair with Terry, is Berna's sister. Terry, supposed a rich man (but confessing later in the play to having lost all), finances his good friend Frank, who has given up his job to write a book on Time. Terry has brought them all on his birthday to see the island he has purchased, to which they are supposed to be ferried by an aged local boatman named Carlin. The mythic possibilities of this situation begin to take shape while the individual participants sing, dance and play around with motifs of 'happiness' and 'wonder' once they assess the scenery.

Most of the songs the characters sing have the word 'happy' in title or refrain and the motif is somewhat overplayed, although Angela is inclined to ironise her own celebration of happiness. It is clearly a case of false joy, if not *mauvaise foi*. One recalls Estragon's pointed question in *Waiting for Godot*: 'What do we do now, now that we are happy?'[27] All Friel wants to lay down at the outset is that his characters, like the Boy in *Godot*, don't know whether they are happy or not. We learn that Berna, Terry's wife, whom he is betraying with her sister Angela, is mentally unwell. 'She's really most content,' Terry confides to his sister, 'when she's in the nursing home' (p. 379): like Molly Sweeney perhaps. At the end of Act 1, Berna jumps into the sea off the end of the pier in an apparent attempted suicide. George, the musician, whose accordion playing is crucial to the action, is dying of cancer. Frank is unhappy in his topic: 'the book's nothing' (p. 399). That mainly leaves Angela and Terry, who are cheating on Frank and Berna, respectively. The affair is not going well. Angela is unhappy with Frank's choice of rendezvous: 'a goddamn, useless, endless, unhappy outing' (p. 423). She will change her attitude before the play ends, however.

There is also Trish, Terry's sister and George's wife, who tends to be overlooked. Trish appears to be comically slow on the uptake, incapable even of distinguishing Donegal from Sligo when told (more than once) where they have arrived. Unduly anxious, Trish is the one who at first most insists they are all 'lost'. By the end of the play, however, she has adopted the word 'wonderful' in sincere appreciation of the place. So although, having tested her shaky geography again Terry can say to 'all', 'See? Nothing changes' (p. 441), this is not quite the case. Caught up in a conventional notion of order and tidiness, which is also moral, Trish learns from the threatening conditions the place creates. As even roadies like Estragon and Vladimir find, storytelling can become mandatory to pass the time. Trish totally mishandles her narrative by revealing that she never recognised that her wedding day also marked the day when husband George turned his back on an artistic career for her sake. Nevertheless, the revelation affects the others and makes them '*withdraw into themselves*' in meditation (p. 412). The story seems to spur Berna's leap into the sea, the climax of Act 1. Further, when Trish joins in the 'makey-up' game of pitching stones aimed *not* to hit a bottle, she becomes (like Willie Diver at croquet in *Aristocrats*) its star performer, and proceeds to create a simpler ritual with the stones which mimics Terry's account of believers on the island. This ritual becomes a new ceremony in which all except Angela and George participate before leaving the stage, signifying memorial and reverence. Angela and George make their own pact about that. Thus, all unknowing, Trish, the least sophisticated of the bunch, leads several others towards self-discovery.

Plot description does little service to a play like *Wonderful Tennessee* which is about experience rather than event. Although 'wonderful' is an overused epithet, being employed forty-three times, the overuse is deliberate, overworked in order to defamiliarise, meaningless until the characters discover the wonder dulled in daily life. In Tennessee Williams's *Small Craft Warnings*, a drifter laments the loss in society of 'the capacity for being surprised'.[28] This is partly the theme here. Friel told Mel Gussow that *Wonderful Tennessee* would deal with 'the necessity for mystery' and stressed that he did not mean 'religion'.[29] As has been argued again recently, 'the language and ideology of Catholicism is a pervasive trope in all Irish writing'[30]; in Friel's work, even before *Philadelphia*, this trope is always challenged. In *Lughnasa*, it is the *interrogation* of conventional religion and the underwriting of Father Jack's ethnography which lend that play its passionate humanity. A celebration of transcendence lies at the heart of Friel's spirituality. In *Wonderful Tennessee*, there is perhaps an excessive earnestness about this, where Friel tries to reach the transcendent through exposure of blatant secularity. The character of Frank illustrates. His intellectual response to the monastic life he is studying for his book is offhand: 'Anything *to explain away* the wonderful, the mystery' (p. 397, emphasis added). Frank represents post-Enlightenment man. But after he has seen, on his own, the dolphin dancing he is transformed; the sight was both 'thrilling' and 'disturbing' (p. 421), a private experience which he struggles to make public. His narration means little to his onstage audience, who are not ready for this intrusion of the sublime. The shock awakens Frank, but to what he does not yet know. It is the kind of narrative material more commonly found in fiction (such as that of Iris Murdoch) where time for meditation and consequence is allowed. But perhaps Friel's theatre audience out front can recognise that Frank's visitation, his 'epiphany' (p. 421), calls for a response in action of the kind Frank duly delivers when he forces Terry to submit to the ritual in homage to the *genius loci*, the perceived divine presence immanent in the pier. The wonder then becomes real to all, 'a place of pilgrimage' as in Berna's strange, Heaney-like story[31] (p. 403).

The wonderful, then, becomes the genuinely marvellous, the sacred. But *how*, exactly, does this 'becoming' happen? And what meaning can it have for a modern, secular audience any more than Eliot's comparable *The Cocktail Party* had in 1949? The 'becoming' is first signalled by the line 'It is good to be here!'. Berna speaks it (p. 381) and Frank confirms (p. 400). The line is spoken by the apostle Peter on Mount Tabor, after Christ's transfiguration. The same line appears in three of the four gospels: 'Lord, it is good for us to be here: if thou wilt, let us make here three tabernacles; one for thee, and one for Moses, and one for Elias' (Mt. 17.4). Friel's point, I take it, is that there is *no* 'transfiguration' possible for his six characters. Yet what *is* open to them is to respond to the spirit of the place and learn something from its timelessness and silence. As a 'retreat', the place provides the occasion of such an experience.

Helen Lojek, however, sees the ending of *Wonderful Tennessee* as 'overwhelmingly ambivalent'.[32] Tony Corbett, for his part, argues that, 'The final epiphany of *Wonderful Tennessee* is that there are no epiphanies.'[33] Here, I would argue otherwise. Certainly, in spite of the frequent hymns sung and half-sung and played on the accordion, the sense of the sacred is strangely brutalised. René Girard has written memorably on *Violence and the Sacred* (1979), emphasising the link to ancient sacrifice. We know it too from the 'mimesis of sacrifice' which is Greek tragedy.[34] Working with this archetype means that when we talk about tradition in the Irish context, we falsify it if we omit the violence, offensive though it be. Here, Terry's story of what happened on the nearby island, *Oileán Draíochta*, sixty years earlier is crucial to the play's meaning. It is mere nostalgia to think of the place as 'Arcadia' (p. 356): a return to the deceits of *The Gentle Island* (1971). Terry's tale is of a violent murder done on the holy island in the year of the Eucharistic Congress in Dublin in 1932. A group of drunken pilgrims enacted a ritual sacrifice on a seventeen-year-old boy. The effect on the local community was devastating – as if a version of *The Lord of the Flies* had been enacted for real in their midst. The scandal went to the very heart of people and clergy, leading to the complete abandonment of the place, except for the boatman Carlin, the last link with that terrible time. And he never appears. Earlier talk in the play about the holiness of the medieval island and its monks and resident saint is altogether subverted by postcolonial history, even though Terry's story is fictional. (There *was* violence in the North at the time of the Eucharistic Congress but it was sectarian.) As in *Dancing at Lughnasa*, where the 'back hills' loom as reminder of a pagan past, in *Wonderful Tennessee* there is a schizophrenic vision of modern Ireland. Friel's entanglement of the Eucharistic Congress in his narrative, only to emphasise the darker meaning lying mythically behind the celebration of Christ's blood sacrifice, serves to transfigure the setting (scene) into '*ob*scenity.' What happened on the island is unspeakable. Yet the place itself is majestically indifferent to its history and reasserts its '*complete stillness*' when the noisy visitors leave at the end (p. 445). As Steiner remarks in *Language and Silence*, 'It is only by breaking through the walls of language that visionary observance can enter the world of total and immediate understanding.'[35] Friel had been working in that direction for some time.

That direction is mystical. Or at any rate it points towards the paradox that Yeats saw threatening his life's work at the end: 'I wanted a dance because where there are no words there is less to spoil.'[36] Beckett too looked for a 'literature of the unword [. . .] An assault against words'.[37] Yet it has to be said here that Friel's way is not always Beckett's way. Language for Friel, like life itself, is always meaningful, capable of redemption. It is difficult to imagine Friel writing the line 'fuck life'.[38] For Friel, 'life is all we have, you know'.[39] He is a man for 'rising above', to borrow a phrase from *The Home Place*. To this end, Friel generally preferred the purity of music to the imprecision of language. *Performances* (2003) was to be his most thorough statement on that question. Meantime, he continued to struggle with the 'insubstantial pageant' of theatre as a means of expressing the deeper life with symbols like the dolphin, signifying the potential freedom of the soul, and song as in some sort redemptive.

Leaving Beckett to one side, then, it is tempting to see Terry as a rundown Prospero battling with his inner Caliban ('This island's mine,' and so forth). But Terry admits he is 'only the sherpa' for the expedition (p. 356). He has no magic spells, no Ariel at his beck. Yet it is his idea, this trip, to celebrate his own birthday. It would not be true to say he engineers all that happens, and fails to happen, on stage; but he can do the banquet, for instance: he has the food hampers for all, with champagne as well as wine, gin and – yes – vodka (p. 402). Angela calls Terry 'our expert' (p. 371), or adept, a quasi-mystical term of the occult. The only occasion on which Terry asserts his authority Prospero-fashion is to Frank, '*sharply, impatiently*', concerning the boatman: 'Tell him the new owner of the island sent you for him!' (p. 377). But he shows no divine anger when Carlin does not show. He comments, rather, 'Time has no meaning for a man like that' (p. 383). It is Terry who initiates the storytelling: both of his offerings relate to the spiritual history of the island, which he does not really want his guests to reach – on this occasion. But he wants them to let its strangeness affect them individually. In that sense he is the playwright's 'surrogate', the term his wife Berna uses for her herself as love-object (p. 387).

The play ends with the performance of two quite different rituals and the second, quieter one implies catharsis. The terrible story of the blood sacrifice on the island inspires Angela (a teacher of Classics) to initiate a Dionysian counterpart on stage, with Terry as scapegoat. That moment reads as a recognition that tradition is two-faced: violent and regenerative. 'The birth of a nation,' Denis Johnston proclaimed in 1931, 'is no immaculate conception.'[40] Friel reminds us of the history of Irish modernisation (1932 being also the year when Fianna Fáil, the 'Men of Destiny', entered government under de Valera). But as Angela's re-enactment is in fun, the participants repudiate actual violence. In pre-ceasefire Ireland in 1993, this was a salutary semiotic action. The second ritual endorses tradition in its fertile, regenerative role. Taking their cue from the innocent Trish, all except Angela and George contribute a stone to create a memorial cairn without, as Richard Cave puts it, 'specific religious or Catholic connotations' but in 'a shared endeavour' to re-enact 'the patterned ritual that Terry recalled from his childhood visit to the island'.[41] Angela then extends the memorial to include George, who will be dead when they all return in a year's time. This second ritual is spontaneous and signifies reverence for the place, for tradition. It accords with the spirit of two of the songs in the play, both associated with Friel's parents. 'Oft in the Stilly Night', his father's song (to be used again in *The Home Place* more than ten years later), is played wordlessly at the opening of Scene 2, followed soon after by 'Down by the Cane-break', the play's theme song, which Terry identifies as 'Mother's Song'. George endows it '*with the tone and dignity of a hymn*' (p. 384), so that it '*sounds almost sacred*' (p. 388). He plays it twice more before the play's end; each time Berna is the first to follow George with the lyrics. It is like a blessing on her, the most troubled of the company, because it was Friel's mother's song and its promise of happiness echoes the theme of the play.[42] Thus, Terry is Friel's alter ego: the artist as gambler. When all join in with Berna, they do not mock or parody as they often do with other songs or hymns but in a '*quiet, internal personal way*' (p. 388). The others hum the melody along with George in the final rendition. A director would have to establish precisely and without embarrassment the mood evoked by this song as well as the wordless ritual of the stones. Learning to respect the dead and their aspirations is being advanced as a primary step on the journey towards self-recognition.

For Tony Corbett, *Wonderful Tennessee* is 'one of Friel's most successful investigations into contemporary Irish life'.[43] This may be extravagant. The play goes against the Irish grain in many respects, especially, as Anthony Roche has suggested, in its challenges to the 'Celtic Tiger' phase of contemporary Ireland.[44] Here, it is perhaps more prophetic of the depression to follow. It is a crisis play, then, delivered at a crucial point in Ireland's economic history, locating itself theatrically at what Patrice Pavis calls 'the crossroads of culture'.[45] It is counter-cultural. For Paul Murphy, its final 'message' is that, 'The reinvention of tradition is a vital party to modernity.'[46] Its target audience is the bourgeoisie. But with a theme as metaphysical as the loss of the sacred in modern life, *Wonderful Tennessee* may finally be seen as shaking hands with Iris Murdoch, for example, *The Sea, The Sea* (1978), after it has bidden goodbye to Hugh Leonard.

Murdoch's biographer has said 'all of her thinking' came out of the historical moment 'when God the Father departed the scene. [. . .] She wanted the idea of the holy to survive in a partly terrible world.'[47] While one could not claim *all* of Friel's thinking emanated from that moment, Conradi's summary in part applies. Looked at twenty years after its disastrous appearance on Broadway, *Wonderful Tennessee* now seems strangely inspired.

Give Me Your Answer, Do!

Genesis

This play is the sacral in wolf's clothing, an attempt by Friel to continue in a narrower focus the explorations undertaken in *Wonderful Tennessee* of the middle class, lost in what Victor Merriman terms 'neo-colonial' Ireland.[48] The problem is pathological, anomie resulting in a national loss of direction. In the new play, the focus narrows to the representative status of the artist within the family and tangentially the world beyond the domestic.

From his first notes for *Answer, Do!* Friel had the idea of a writer negotiating the sale of his papers, a commercial proposition in an increasingly commercial-minded society. Among the writer's papers is a hoard of possibly pornographic letters, which may define an 'alternative life' for the artist. Friel may here have been thinking of Joyce and the infamous 1909 letters Richard Ellmann published in 1975.[49] But soon the plot material dealt with unpublished pornographic *novels* instead. A second idea Friel had from the start was the writer's daughter, 'very shy, very silent, who appears to be seriously maimed. Who or what is she?'[50] Again, this image, as it morphed into a daughter crippled and hospitalised with some form of autism, remains problematic in the eventual play, being linked to the pornographic novels. Both have to do with the conflicting meanings of price, cost and value. There is to be a second writer, at first a dramatist but changed to a rival novelist, Garret Fitzmaurice, more successful than the protagonist (Tom Connolly). A party or picnic is to be arranged in Tom's house where the dealer/assessor has been at work reading through the archive. Friel has 'the persistent sense of a Day of Judgement – not only for the writer but for *all* the guests.'[51] This outline, to be fleshed out by the inclusion of Tom's wife Daisy and her parents, as well as with the rival writer's wife Gráinne, came to Friel within weeks. What was missing was the 'engine' or 'motor' of the play to drive the plot. At first, Friel thought he had found it in the notion of a ghostly 'Presence', a kind of Muse who has not visited for some five years, the external embodiment of the writer's soul. Friel abandoned this device in order to build up the fellow-writer who is to become the novelist's 'other' (Garret Fitzmaurice); Tom must define himself in relation to Garret's commercialism. Friel decided the daughter (Bridget) was badly brain-damaged (no stated cause) and hospitalised. The wife, Daisy, is seen as 'sluttish' and with a drinking problem. Friel then left the play for some months while *Molly Sweeney* had its New York production, resuming in January 1996. With the critical success of *Molly*, he could confidently concentrate on Tom Connolly and the question of artistic conscience.

Friel then found what for him was the engine of the play: the imminent 'verdict' to be passed on Tom's archive by the visiting dealer/buyer, eventually named David Knight. The whole play was to be about judgement and/or the balance between 'integrity' and some kind of 'recognition', monetary or personal. Thus, the shaping of the play was towards an old Frielian theme: the enemy within. The offer the dealer was perhaps to make – for the suspense in the play depends on uncertainty in this matter – was to be a form of temptation. Only one reviewer of all the four productions of *Give Me Your Answer, Do!* (the Abbey, 1997, The Hampstead 1998, The Lyric, Belfast, in 1999, and the Roundabout, New York, in 1999) picked up this Eliot-based clue, from *Murder in the Cathedral*[52]: 'The crucial resonance is with Eliot's tempters in the Cathedral, as the good Knight [punning on the dealer's name] offers Tom that which is not his to give: the benevolent view of posterity.'[53] Friel's Presence is internalised as a conscience at war with Mammon.

Friel went out on a judgemental limb himself when he chose to direct his own play about a writer fraught over such questions. His success as the director of *Molly Sweeney* may have tempted him. If so, the Abbey production, drawing poor notices, changed his mind, because afterwards he handed over to professional directors. The three other productions will be examined below. First, I want to focus briefly on the self-reflexive theme itself. Seán O'Casey's first play at the Abbey, *The Shadow of a Gunman* (1923), is a play Friel felt himself slipping into when he first teased out his ideas for *Give Me Your Answer, Do!*. O'Casey's Donal Davoren is a would-be poet and in some respects an ironic self-portrait, as was to be Thomas Kilroy's Brien in *Tea, Sex and Shakespeare* (1976).[54] In writing about writing, O'Casey was exploring identity measured against political responsibility. Post Field Day, Friel was more preoccupied with moral and philosophical issues. Although *Answer, Do!* inevitably reflects back on Friel's own situation in the 1990s as a successful writer with an archive being approached by 'the Emory man',[55] he sought in this play to transform the personal into objective terms so as to create something like a modern parable. This is an Ibsenist strategy, seen above all in *When We Dead Awaken* (1899),[56] even though the critics insisted that Friel's play was Chekhovian. *Answer Do!* is far too individualist in focus to be Chekhovian. The crux is whether the novelist Tom Connolly will sell his soul if he cashes in his manuscripts to an American university. In the play, the dealer David Knight is at times ironically referred to as God; the verdict he will reach when he assesses Tom's papers is a kind of last judgement, to be feared for its finality. Accordingly, Tom both wants and fears the outcome. Secondly, the appearance of his friend Garret Fitzmaurice, who has already sold his papers to the same buyer, works as a blatant warning. Garret is a second-rate writer, as his wife Gráinne repeatedly reminds him; the wealth his work has brought him reeks of corruption, or 'damaged goods' as the New York critic John

Simon put it.[57] Presumably, Friel intended *Answer, Do!* as a protest against acquisitiveness in all walks of life today.

Family Matters and Outcome

Friel explores the bourgeoisie with a mixture of amusement and empathy. He was determined to do this is a deceptively naturalistic style. As well as a play about the writer in society *Answer, Do!* is a play about family in which the relationships appear conventional but they are not. Unlike *Wonderful Tennessee*, the play does not feature adultery: three married couples take the stage, and although the marriages are rocky, all survive. These other characters are dream-like reflectors of the protagonist's dilemma. Loyalty is on trial. Daisy's parents, Jack and Maggie Donovan, are trapped in a misalliance: she a retired medical doctor, he a non-professional, a 'cocktail' pianist and, it emerges, a pilferer with an embarrassing history. Jack seriously embarrasses Maggie in the course of the picnic on the lawn when it is discovered he has stolen Garret's wallet. 'Look at that shabby little swindler,' is Maggie's bitter response, adding, 'That's what shaped my life. Yes,' as if still pointing at him in public.[58] Jack's resilience is one of his endearing features, however. Having caused a dreadful scene and driven Garret and Gráinne off home appalled, Jack, after a sobbing breakdown on stage, leaves and re-enters with restored insouciance: '*This is not the man who was led off by the hand a short time ago. This is the cocky, dandy, opinionated fop again*' (p. 71). Clearly, this is a pattern in his life. We get a cameo of the artist as swindler. Maggie has sacrificed health and career for his sake. She used to ask God how she could live with him: 'Give me your answer, God. But he never told me. And it's past the time for an answer now' (p. 67). The older couple function as a reverse image of Daisy and Tom.

Garret and Gráinne's relationship, a more obvious contrast to Tom and Daisy's, is satirised. The couple is framed in theatricality, '*a double-act more intuitive than rehearsed*' (p. 42). They have no children but 'gave their lives to letters instead', as Gráinne puts it (p. 45). They are, however, Bridget's godparents, although they make no attempt to visit her in hospital. Some reviewers spotted a resemblance to George and Martha in Albee's *Who's Afraid of Virginia Woolf?* (1963), and it is there: Friel's couple, witty, histrionic and negative, do fight bare-knuckled at times. But they literally lack staying power and exit when the heat is on. Nevertheless, Gráinne can *sound* subversive when she decries the 'performance' they are locked into: 'Is that any way to live?' (p. 49), posing the leading moral question. The third couple in the play is the central one: Tom Connolly and Daisy, whose marriage is under severe strain. Daisy is never seen without a glass of liquor in hand. It would have been a dry enough picnic had not the Fitzmaurices brought supplies of vodka, gin and wine. The mental illness of their daughter Bridget for ten years (she is now twenty-two) is one factor; the stress over Tom's writer's block is another, with its attendant poverty. The Connollys have changed housing with Joycean frequency and are living in an old 'manse' which – in Frielian notation – is '*now badly decayed*' (p. 16) and neglected. They undoubtedly need the money the assessor would provide should he buy Tom's papers.

Bridget, Tom and Daisy's only child, appears in two scenes in a hospital setting but never speaks. These scenes frame the play as prologue and epilogue and convey a strange atmosphere during the two visits Tom makes to Bridget, alone and speaking endlessly to her without reply. (Indeed, he invents her replies and deals with them volubly.) Bridget's mental trouble is somehow linked to Tom's writing problems: it was after her sudden illness that he wrote the two pornographic novels which David Knight eventually discovers in the house in Act 1 and which make him determined to buy the archive. When Tom enters the padded cell where Bridget is confined, he stands gazing at her rocking slowly and ceaselessly on a mattress. '*One senses quickly that this is how her life is lived*' (p. 11). Tom carries an 'abused' briefcase (p. 11), an alarming word Friel deliberately amended from his original 'battered' in his notes. It contains no more than clean clothing for Bridget; Tom will take away her soiled clothes. Daisy cannot bear to have anything to do with any of this; she never visits. There is a mystery here which the play never fully divulges. For instance, if there is a connection between Tom's pornography and Bridget's condition it remains unstated. Friel never makes 'pornography' anything more than a floating signifier.[59] This secretive attitude led some reviewers to speculate that child abuse is at the bottom of Bridget's illness. In New York, where the question arose in a post-performance discussion, it was made clear that Friel 'disavowed' paedophilia as the answer.[60] He is after something more inaccessible, the nature of suffering itself. The emphasis must remain on the awfulness of Bridget's collapse. But while talking to her, and interpolating her imagined responses, Tom shows immense empathy and joy. He is drawn in a profoundly sympathetic way to her abject state. Before he leaves the hospital, Tom is asked to authorise 'six more electric shock treatments' (p. 22). However reluctantly, he agrees. This scenario is a prelude to the anxiety and panic inhabiting the play, as Tom knows that money would enable better treatment for Bridget.

Accordingly Tom is full of trepidation over the assessment of his work, spread out in manila folders in his living room for all visitors – especially the Fitzmaurices and the audience – to notice. To have an assessor in the house is unnerving. David Knight is a strange young man, with a mental history himself, who is under pressure to buy this archive, as he has already acquired Garret Fitzmaurice's papers for his university. The Fitzmaurices are present partly out of curiosity and partly to lend support. But all of this, with the addition of Daisy's mother and her embarrassing husband Jack, makes the afternoon picnic on the lawn a very fraught one. When David says he cannot afford to lose this assignment and that he is 'depending' on Tom (p. 75), something seems terribly awry. Maggie, a retired doctor, comments: 'I don't think that young man is very well' (p. 77). Behind the Hugh-Leonard-like banter, there hangs always a miasma of undefined malaise.

Before David makes his offer, Tom's question, giving the play its title, is whether he should take it. (The Fitzmaurices have left by now.) Daisy thinks not. She makes her speech recommending rejection of whatever offer David will make without any reference to specifics. It is a soliloquy, delivered as she walks in the garden. She does not initiate a debate on the subject. She simply says, 'Oh, no, he [*sic*] mustn't sell. Of course he mustn't sell' (p. 79). Daisy's crucial speech is private, yet it contains the answer to all Tom's agonising over whether to succumb or not to the temptation. Is Daisy the enemy within or the angel of deliverance? The inference is that Tom hears her speech even though nobody comments on it: again, a piece of anti-naturalism. She says what he needs to hear: that the 'necessary uncertainty' induced by the artist's unwillingness to produce merely money-making work is at once his lot and the best human option: 'Because being alive is the postponement of verdicts, isn't it?'. Verdicts mean the end has come. And so, she concludes, echoing Beckett's *Unnamable*, 'we stagger on' (p. 80).

If Daisy seems to be Tom's 'other' at this point, his better self, it means he has now interiorised that 'ghostly Presence' Friel first envisaged as driver of the plot. But in the final scene, in which Tom talks again to Bridget in hospital, Daisy is seated alone downstage in the half-light, apparently hearing all that Tom says. What she hears after he has re-run his earlier mix of cheerful bedside chatter and fantasy, suddenly strikes panic into her soul. Tom tells Bridget that he feels he can write again, and if he were to succeed with his abandoned novel, he would come back to her and they would escape together up into the sky. He says 'just the two of us – only the two of us'. At this line, Daisy jumps to her feet '*as if she had been wakened abruptly from a sleep*', confused and anxious '*with incipient grief*'. When Tom finishes his speech to Bridget, Daisy delivers the final line of the play, '*softly, urgently*', 'Oh, Tom! – Tom! – Tom, please?' (p. 84) and, a pause ensuing, a quick blackout ends the play.

Friel told Maggie Cronin, the actress who played Daisy in the Lyric production in 1999, that the final line is ambiguous; she then felt challenged by it for her entire interpretation of the role.[61] To Kyle Donnelly, who directed the New York production later that year, Friel explicated the final line as 'Surely you couldn't do this to me?'. Both Tom's proposal to Bridget and Daisy's panic 'must be emphasised as much as is theatrically possible'. He was ashamed to admit, he told Donnelly, that Tom's proposal to Bridget is defensible while Daisy's response remains understandable. Even if this contradiction is not 'intellectually intelligible', Friel believed it 'emotionally valid'.[62] Yet Daisy's final line harks back to Pegeen's penultimate line in Synge's

Playboy: 'Oh my grief, I've lost him surely'[63] and inverts it into a different kind of heartbreak. Pegeen's 'surely' is elided and the line ends in a question mark, as in *Molly Sweeney*. The ambiguity stays. The panic remains and must be endured.

Reception

As so often during Friel's career, the Dublin critics were mainly puzzled and impatient. Most reviewers thought Friel's direction of the play a mistake and the design unhelpful. The acting spaces provided on the Abbey stage did not adequately allow for 'the private dialogues' going on simultaneously. 'The audience ear could be attuned but the eye kept getting diverted.'[64] The play itself drove reviewers, who took it as a slice of life, into oversimplification. 'What emerges,' remarked Mic Moroney in the *Independent*, 'is a cruel and depressing vision of the ageing, upper-Bohemian drinking classes.'

The reviews were more positive for the Hampstead Theatre production, directed by Robin Lefèvre in March 1998. 'This is one of Brian Friel's best, richest, toughest and most moving plays,' intoned the *Sunday Times* (5 April). Michael Coveney in the *Mail* (3 April) confessed he quite misjudged the play when he saw it in Dublin in the author's 'own messy-looking production'. The shape of the play was now 'perfect' in Lefèvre's 'positively Chekhovian' interpretation. Chekhov seems to have offered London reviewers a lifeline, and most enthused accordingly. John Gross, entitling his review 'Gin and Sorrows in Donegal' (*Sunday Telegraph*), approved the 'Chekhovian effect' of the play and averred: 'You are held, moved, intrigued and (for the most part) convinced,' although he did not say of what. Alistair Macaulay in the *Financial Times* insisted that 'being disappointed by *Give Me Your Answer, Do!* is a richer experience than being satisfied by many other plays.' Further, the play 'leaves a large and subtle impression in the mind. When it ends, you applaud as if some strange new sensation had entered your life and had then withdrawn.' That was well said.

The Lyric (Belfast) production, directed by Benjamin Twist in May 1999, was part of the national Festival in honour of Friel's seventieth birthday. Perhaps prompted by the London reviews, two notable Dublin critics took the trouble to look again at Friel's play. David Nowlan now found it 'harder and harsher and significantly more dramatic'.[65] Jocelyn Clarke, however, still found *Answer, Do!* too claustrophobic and persisted in seeing the play 'as a working through of a writer's heavily disguised assessment of his own work'. It thus 'remains essentially a dialogue between playwright and play'.[66] This assessment misses the metaphoric qualities of the play. The New York reviews, no doubt also influenced by the positive ones in London, again made Chekhov the yardstick. Unfortunately for Friel, his *Aristocrats* and version of *Uncle Vanya* played at the Lincoln Centre in summer 1999 and these Gate productions coloured the American response to *Answer, Do!* at the Gramercy off-Broadway. The *New York Post* (6 October) faulted Friel's play for not being as good as Chekhov; Ben Brantley in the *New York Times* saw it as a mere 'footnote to the work of [Friel as] a great dramatist'; Joseph Hurley in the *Irish Echo* loyally raved about cast and production, but complained of too much Chekhov in the play itself; Philip Hopkins in the *Irish Voice* referred to Friel as 'Ireland's living heir to Chekhov'; Chesley Plemmons in the *New York Times* (Sunday, 17 October) found Friel 'in Chekhovian mood', limiting 'a totally engrossing, if overly enigmatic drama with an ensemble of actors to die for'. It was left to the great John Simon in the *New York Magazine* (18 October) to forget Chekhov and look at Friel's text. He found it falling halfway between 'such sublime work' as *Translations* and 'such miscalculations' as *Wonderful Tennessee*. He caught the 'shades' of Peter Nichols's *A Day in the Death of Joe Egg*[67] (1967) – a play which had run on Broadway alongside *Philadelphia* – in Friel's Bridget and saw *Answer, Do*! as delivering 'a poisonous play end[ing] with a climactic dose of hemlock'. Presumably, Simon understood that Daisy was about to be dumped for Bridget. But, needless to say, this is not quite what Friel is saying. Patrick Mason[68] is nearer the mark: creativity is in itself destructive to relationships or to self-interest and Bridget is both victim and Muse figure.

From the production point of view, the major problem with *Answer, Do!* may be that, like *Wonderful Tennessee,* it is in Strindberg's sense a chamber play which demands an intimate stage. It deceives by its disguised subtleties. To Patrick Lonergan, both plays were written to counteract the Broadway reception of *Lughnasa* as a 'joyful play'.[69] In *Wonderful Tennessee*, the 'lost' people find a possible way out of despair. In *Answer, Do!* the despair is internalised and positively embraced. It is a given that Friel consistently dissents from contemporary materialism and its false gods. All interpretation of his plays must start there. José Lanters emphasises Friel's exploitation of the Uncertainty Principle not only in *Answer, Do!* but also in much of his work.[70] It is a salutary reminder. Theatrically, the ending of *Answer, Do!* proposes an impossibility. Equally, the final question mark radically destabilises the text. Not many audiences care for that sort of irresolution. Friel blows open the paradox of *necessary* uncertainty, if we are to be free within self-sacrifice and creativity.

CHAPTER 9
PERFORMANCES AND A GENERAL CONCLUSION

In others' works thou dost but mend the style,
And arts with thy sweet graces gracèd be;

– Shakespeare, Sonnet 78

Introduction: The Food of Love

Having addressed the question of writer's block and writer's conscience in *Give Me Your Answer, Do!*, it was appropriate that Friel should move on to consider the nature of inspiration itself. When the Director of the Gate Theatre, Michael Colgan, sent him the text of Leoš Janáček's *Intimate Letters* early in September 2002 and asked if he would be interested in writing a play on the musician's love affair in relation to the string quartet which it inspired, Friel agreed to see if there was 'a jump lead' there for him.[1] In the correspondence with Colgan which followed, Friel insisted that if the arrangement was to be a straightforward paralleling by selected passages of the *Letters* and the playing of the music, 'that process would have no interest *at all* for me'. Instead, he would hope to do two things in his play. First, to examine the 'bizarre relationship' between the seventy-four-year-old composer and the married woman (Kamila Stösslová), thirty-seven years his junior, with whom Janáček was infatuated – 'a relationship probably never consummated'. And second, 'very tentatively, very delicately' to indicate the relationship between the text of *Intimate Letters* and the Second String Quartet bearing the same title.[2] Although he was to have a few characteristic anxieties about the play when it was finished by the end of the year – its brevity, the danger inherent in having musicians on stage with lines to say, and whether the quartet should be played in part or in whole – Friel was sure of its theatricality. 'Wouldn't Simon Russell Beale be a wonderful Janáček?', he put to Colgan enthusiastically.[3] (Beale was to prove unavailable.) Also, in spite of persisting anxieties, Friel was clear about the primary function of the evening in the theatre: 'an analysis of the emotional/creative impulse that animated the Quartet'.[4] His own intimate letters to Michael Colgan (an important figure in Friel's later career at the Gate), then, reveal what the attraction of this material held for him. Like *Give Me Your Answer, Do!*, the new play would appear to have a deep, personal fascination related to artistic conscience.

The intriguing dimension about *Performances* as drama is that it is *about* the process of composition itself. Adam Phillips tells us that inspiration is quasi-religious: 'We need to be receptive to the unfamiliar; and we need to be able to wait, without certainty, for the thing we want. This, in a sense, is the faith of the believer in artistic inspiration.'[5] It certainly marks Friel's faith. 'Sitting at the desk. Leafing through notes. Hoping to find faith.'[6] The various published extracts from his working diaries give many such instances of fruitful waiting. But the play he first titled *The Real Thing*, until he recalled that Stoppard had already used that one, offered something new: a chance to study at a distance another creator whose inspiration was less divine than carnal. And if carnal then opening up mysteries. 'The version of inspiration we should trust tends to be enigmatic and disturbing to the person[s] inspired; they don't, as [T. S.] Eliot said, really understand it.'[7] Whether the exploration of Janáček's inspiration by a love affair would prove to be, in turn, inspiring for Friel and therefore disturbing, is an open artistic question.

Performances is an esoteric piece, an exquisite piece of metatheatre, 'an elusive minor masterpiece.'[8] *Performances* is one more portrait of the artist, in middle age, in love with a young married woman, an obsessed artist in a platonic relationship which fuels his musical genius, their correspondence a record of inspiration. This situation was 'bizarre' (Friel's word), although less disturbing than the father-daughter relationship in *Give Me Your Answer, Do!* Here, Friel takes up a romantic theme in a familiar scenario: foolish old man willingly debases himself with sufficient circumspection to do no harm and to come out of it with what matters most to him in the long run: a new work. Friel takes up this theme as a mature writer and therefore fully in control of his own art.[9] For the shadowy Kamila (as Janáček reified her), Friel taps into the Romantic tradition in which the womanly sublime is represented as ideal and inspirational, but seems more interested in the end product and the light in which it shows the artist.

This zone is usually entered by sophisticated artists nowadays in a complex kind of playacting. The name of the game is sublimation: 'The power of longing is more durable than the thrill of possession.'[10] Half of the thrill of Janáček's affair lay in its secrecy or disguised risk-taking. In the Loevborg-Hedda scene in Act 2 of *Hedda Gabler*, Friel showed in his version that he understood this risk-taking. There is a parallel with the Janáček-Kamila situation which forms the back story to *Performances*. Loevborg and Hedda replicate their remembered deception under Tesman's nose even as they reminisce. Loevborg says to Hedda, as they sit 'innocently' looking through the photographs of her honeymoon: 'We [he and Hedda in former times] seemed to be altogether alone in the world, *isolated in a kind of hothouse intimacy*.'[11] The italics added here draw attention to the phrase reminiscent of Janáček's title *Intimate Letters* for his string quartet inspired by the correspondence with Kamila Stösslová. There is no talk of 'hothouse intimacy' in Michael Meyer's translation of this scene, rather a probing for her confession of love.[12] Similarly, *Performances* makes the interpreter, the audience, analogous with the role of Anezka, the interviewer of Janáček. In imagining duplicity Friel makes us participants in it. When Anezka fails to understand the hothouse intimacy as she should, because the back story was a major part of her research, the audience is released into perceiving how much Janáček is withholding. As with *Answer, Do!*, the link between creativity and transgression is central. In the Gate premiere of *Performances* on 30 September 2003, directed by Patrick Mason, the Romanian actor Ion Caramitru (Janáček) showed with great finesse just how many-layered Friel's short text is.

The distancing of the love affair in *Performances*, reported via quotations from letters and assessed by the doctoral student Anezka, with whom Janáček vigorously disagrees, clears a space for the conflict between these two on stage. In turn, this central debate – to be explored below – is further rendered abstract by Friel's making clear that Janáček is long dead because the play is set in the present. *Performances* is a clever little postmodern piece ready to play tricks with audience perceptions, like *Molly Sweeney* and *Faith Healer* or the haunting last scene of *Dancing at Lughnasa*. Such moments are tipping points. Although Janáček is already dead (he died in 1928, the year he finished the string quartet *Intimate Letters*), *Performances* is set in the present and 'nothing is/But what is not'. While at one level we still have a love story, and, coupled with it the investigation of how art derives from passion, at another level we have a history play in which the dead are resurrected to participate in 'live' performance with the living: Friel using the stage again with two time schemes working simultaneously. The interviewer is real in that she shares the same world as the audience (knowing that Janáček is dead), while the musicians are both 'actual' performers and fictional characters (from Brno) who share Janáček's world as if he were alive. Janáček's lover Kamila is also dead and does not appear, although in his 2013 production Adrian Dunbar made her dimly visible upstage before the play ends.[13] Kamina's real, although spectral, presence is in Janáček's mind.

The stage presence of a musical quartet is a remarkable innovation in Friel's work, and, outside of Stoppard's *Every Good Boy Deserves Favour* (1977), which employed a whole symphony orchestra (in the Royal Festival Hall) as part of its dramaturgy, unique. Stoppard worked in the opposite direction from Friel, whose play literally 'resigns itself to music'.[14] Stoppard wrote about political dissent, identity and madness in a Russian mental asylum: the music was part of the response to terrible oppression. In Friel's play, the thesis moves towards the elevation of music as pure statement, the thing-in-itself rather than any kind of accompaniment to dialogue. The physical movement onstage of the quartet and the players' participation in the dialogue before rendering the final movement(s) of Janáček's *Intimate Letters* represent a bold concession that there is no contest: music takes and retains the honours. At the same time, there is something familiar about the manoeuvre, a revisiting of Synge. In his letters to Molly, Synge whined much as Janáček does to Kamila yet in his art Synge transcended all that, just like Janáček. Indeed, Synge began as violinist and would-be composer. Among his first attempts to write drama was an autobiographical piece declaring, 'Every life is a symphony and the translation of this sequence into music and from music again, for those who are not musicians, into literature, or painting or sculpture, is the real effort of the artist.'[15] Synge created from his relationship with Cherrie Matheson a 'hall of mirrors' in *When the Moon Has Set*, where he transformed himself into the philosopher-musician.[16] Even when Molly Allgood replaced Cherrie Matheson as Muse, Synge's allegory of love in his plays still prefigures the relationship between Janáček, Kamila and the Second String Quartet. Synge thereby mediates between Janáček and Friel, who participates in what W. J. McCormack calls the artist's 'modern daemonic', involving 'a subordinacy of self, an incompleteness doubled in ironic compensation'.[17]

Intimate Letters was to be the 'love-child' of Janáček and Kamila,[18] as clearly appears from the letter when he began the second string quartet: 'You're like a savage and that's why I love you so! [. . .]. Today I wrote that sweetest desire of mine in music. I fight with it, it triumphs. You're having a child. What fate in life would that little son have?'.[19] As with Loevborg and Thea in *Hedda Gabler*, their pure love created a new work. Janáček wrote his quartet at fever pitch in one month. He always referred to it as 'ours' and fantasised that Kamila was literally pregnant, although their love, it seems, was never consummated. Its composition brought to crisis point what had been no more an 'affair' than Shaw's correspondence with Mrs Pat Campbell, although more passionate on Janáček's part. It was becoming clear to those around him, wife, sister, niece, that this ten-year-old friendship was something far more threatening, and as they moved to intervene, Janáček decided, with his dedication of the quartet to Kamila, that his passion for her should no longer be secret. 'I won't deliver my feelings to the tender mercies of fools.'[20] He told his wife the truth and pronounced himself 'happy that there are no secrets in my life'.[21] And he began eagerly to make plans for the new life with Kamila he was not to live to enjoy. Within six months he was dead.

It's a terrific story. The love letters, later lodged in a Czech museum, remained under restricted access until 1990, when an edition was published. John Tyrrell, the translator into English in 1994, rightly calls them 'one of the most remarkable and touching collections of letters ever bequeathed by a composer to future generations'.[22] Small wonder that Friel did indeed find in them a 'jump lead' to spark his creative imagination. Art and life were to be brought into mysterious conjugation. The new play was to be minimalist, shrinking the landscape of Janáček's 1920s' world to the little measure of his workroom in Brno in the new Czech Republic. The grand passion, too naïve/romantic for the current age, is distanced as material for debate. It is as if Friel, ever the self-conscious playwright, took note of Janáček's curling lip when he wrote to Kamila: 'You're mine. [. . .] And [other] people? Their eyes are out on stalks; I've nothing but success; vigour in my compositions. Where does that fellow get it from? A riddle.' And Janáček continues, with Frielian irony: 'They burrow into it like moles in order to decipher it. I'd so love to cry out, to raise you up, display you: "Look, my dear beloved riddle of life!"'[23] Friel attempts to dramatise the riddle, leaving interested readers to be the 'moles'. He knows where inspiration is to be located and knows the door is marked 'private'. But Friel also allows Janáček to declare, 'Aren't all artists users?'[24] straight out of *Give Me Your Answer, Do!*. The story gets into his soul.

Friel deliberately cut out a great deal from the story. Kamila's husband, David Stössel, a country businessman and dealer in antiques, ever on the road, is not even the shadow of a shadow in the play. Yet it was he who saved the letters during the Nazi period (he and Kamila were Jewish), passing them on to the university in Brno before he fled to Switzerland. Kamila was already dead (from cancer, aged 43). Her father was to die in the concentration camps. Janáček's wife, Zdenka, a formidable woman, wrote an autobiography in 1935, unpublished until 1993. She accepted the relationship with Kamila until, in 1928, it suddenly leaped from harmless fantasy to imminent marriage before her eyes, and she reacted with customary fury. Again, perhaps because his focus is on the central issue of the relation between an artist's work and the circumstances of his life, Friel passes over Zdenka. He wanted to play with the material rather than make an epic of it.

In addition, Friel unobtrusively repeats the trick played in *Translations*. All characters speak English but must be thought of as speaking Czech. Everything in the play Friel decided to call *Performances* is 'translated' into modern English: even the Moravian Quartet for the actual private premiere of *Intimate Letters* at Janáček's house in May 1928, becoming in Dublin the Alba Quartet, were given lines to speak. Further, the invented character of the student who arrives to question Janáček in the play over Kamila's role in the creative process takes her name Anezka from the mistress of another Czech composer, Zdeněk Fibich (1850–1900). Pleased that Kamila was reading a book on Fibich's erotic diary in 1927, Janáček wrote to her: 'Whatever's very learned in the book, skip it. What's there that applies to us, remember it well and then tell me.' As far as he was concerned, this Anežka [*sic*], unlike Kamila, well educated, a theatre critic and translator, was merely sensual in her hold over Fibich: 'Anežka surely threw such an enormous net that he couldn't break out of it.'[25] Friel's Anezka is nothing like this: the net she tries to throw over Janáček is anything but erotic in effect. Thus, Friel skilfully interwove life, art and tradition in his adaptation of the *Letters*. If *Performances*, as has been pointed out,[26] elaborates on Yeats's poem 'The Choice', it also leaves everything strangely suspended between art and life: 'Mirror on mirror is all the show.'[27] What is represented is representation itself.

The Great Debate

There are two debates in *Performances*: language versus music and life versus art. These are obviously interrelated. The tension between language and music is an old one. There is no problem at all if music is content with the role of accompaniment. From ancient times down to the contemporary era of rock music, lyrics have fulfilled themselves through instrumental as well as vocal means. Neither is there a debate if instrumental music goes its own way, forsaking opera for example and developing its own compositional forms. The problem at the philosophical level only arises if two autonomous forms vie for supremacy.[28] What is at stake, then, is which better achieves beauty and truth in harmony: language or music. That debate is best reserved for shepherds on a hot day in Arcadia, or maybe a seminar on

George Steiner, whom Friel acknowledged in the theatre programme. In the theatre, however, as it is an art form which originated in choral music, the debate is always present in some respect. When Aristotle explored the nature of drama in *Poetics*, he prioritised plot, character, language and thought/theme over music and spectacle. The last two elements he regarded as non-essential because 'the potential of tragedy does not depend upon public performance and actors' – an amazing conclusion – and spectacle is moreover deemed irrelevant because the 'act of the mask-maker' will always provide more visual effects than can otherwise be devised.[29] While few practitioners would agree with Aristotle today, most would probably find it easy to defend the role of music as organic in the overall aesthetic of drama. Ever since Wagner's inclusion of *all* the arts within the fusion of time and space afforded by live theatre, sound-design has taken its place in drama production.

Writers like O'Casey and Brecht seemed to agree that music and drama are one, but more recently Beckett and Friel have challenged the Wagnerite assumptions. Friel seems closest to Beckett on this matter in *Performances*. In his radio plays *Words and Music* (1962) and *Cascando* (1964), Beckett, as actor Barry McGovern has shown, was concerned with 'the act of creation' itself.[30] Both plays are amusing little contests in which Beckett seems to yield the palm to music. Friel is more serious about the debate, which is a kind of mind-body dialectic: I play, therefore I am. There is no 'seems' about the primacy of music achieved at the end of *Performances* when a string quartet plays live on stage. However questionable this victory over language (or love) may be, Friel wants it so, never mind that the crusty *Observer* critic was to refer to 'this dodgy mix of play and concert' at Wiltons Music Hall.[31]

The second or main debate in *Performances* is one created by the graduate student Anezka Ungrova when she confronts Janáček with exploiting Kamila for the composition of the string quartet. In spite of the argument, the play *is* the thing. Anezka is described in Friel's text (p. 14) as '*an anxious, intense and earnest young woman*' and it shows. The Wildean critical debate will show the *un*-importance of such earnestness. Anezka's original premise, which she later abandons, is that the relationship between the quartet and the text of the love letters is central to a 'full appreciation' of the music (pp. 21–2). Reading from the *Letters* (*apparently* in manuscript, therefore photocopies), she sees a 'textbook example' of great passion serving to create a great work of art. But in pressing this commonplace, she shifts from text to the actual personhood of Kamila. In that manoeuvre, or slippage, she has created a more complex set of signifiers: text, woman, quartet. To Anezka, the text is evidence only. She fails to discriminate the faults of Janáček's epistolary style from the surety and elegance of the musical score to which she is deaf. At times, Janáček's written rhetoric is overblown but this is not something Anezka notices: it is content rather than form (style and structure) that is her concern. Moreover, as I cannot trace it in the text of *Intimate Letters*, I suspect that the letter Anezka quotes on p. 23 (like the one on p. 30) is Frielian pastiche.[32] Thus, Anezka can dismiss as 'Freudian crap' Janáček's romantic declaration (in the letter) that the quartet would be Kamila's and his joint composition, and yet find the expression of it 'deeply, deeply moving' without ever applying her response to the *music*. This lack of perception prescribes a lack of style: 'I get a little bit. . . . I just find it all so . . . ' she stammers (p. 24). She is not equipped to discuss expression. Indeed, she cannot follow Janáček when he treats her to a brief glimpse of the creative process:

> A time of frenzy. Violence even. Despair too. And then when all that ferment was about to overwhelm me – a few minutes of sudden peace – no longer – an amnesty sent from above maybe; and this fragment came to me, a little melodic tendril. Trivial, I know. (p. 24)

The Frielian eloquence of this dramatic speech, in diction, rhythm, pacing, is remarkable. With a flourish Janáček concludes: 'that's closer to the heart of it, isn't it?' almost quoting Robert Frost, but it all passes Anezka by. She is out of her depth. Perhaps Janáček recognises this as he delivers a short master-class on his own lyric, referring to 'the labyrinth of interweaving melodies' (p. 28). She misses cue after cue for her invitation to challenge the game he is playing as self-conscious artist and to rip off his mask. He is wasting his time, however, providing clues such as the distinction between raw experience and artistic transformation. Citing Wordsworth's Preface to the *Lyrical Ballads* (1802) and expecting her to understand 'emotion recollected in tranquillity' (p. 30) or referring to a production of Rostand's *Cyrano* as a means of appreciating aesthetic distance is a tutorial too far. This lady is not for learning. 'Anezka, my dear, you'd learn so much more by just listening to the music' (pp. 30–1).

As the 'my dear' suggests, there is a gender issue in this debate. When Janáček pursues his line of separating his private life from his public career, he moves closer to characterising Kamila as crude and inferior. (The argument might be extended here to Joyce's Nora.) It was in Janáček's head that Kamila was 'transformed into something immeasurably greater' (p. 34). She did not so much become the music as the reverse: the music became her. (This is very much Friel at work.) Janáček had, he claims in the play, *invented* Kamila as 'an expression of what was the very best in himself' (p. 34). The shift to the third person signifies his self-division, laid bare in vain for Anezka to recognise. Thus, Janáček minimises Kamila as a person in order to preserve his own independence. This enrages Anezka, who now drops any attempt to knit together the music and the love affair as revealed in the text of the letters: 'How dare you!' (p. 35). She objects very strongly to his 'cruel and heartless and deeply misogynistic' attitude towards Kamila (p. 36), whom she is disposed to defend as a woman. With a shrug, Janáček grandly asserts that he gave himself 'to the perfection of the work' (the quote from Yeats) in preference to concerning himself overmuch with the life. 'Crap', she says again (p. 37). He agrees. Standoff.

Tony Corbett is inclined to call this moment Anezka's 'epiphany'.[33] I wonder. It is true she changes towards Janáček and is furious with him. But surely the point is that her feminist viewpoint presents an obstacle to her accepting his attitude towards *music*? At intervals during the play, one or more of the musicians enter(s) and perform(s) briefly, lightly, playfully. Three of them are women. Janáček always responds warmly to them on a personal level, like Hamlet towards the strolling players. He is at home, literally, in their company. But Anezka shows no such warmth towards the musicians. They do not matter to her. In the end, they seem to her to gang up against her *and* Kamila as outsiders. But it is Anezka who is the 'enemy within'. When the quartet settles in to play the last two movements of *Intimate Letters*, Anezka feels unable to stay. She leaves, still insisting that Janáček is wrong to hold that 'the work's the thing' (p. 38). She fails to see that his axiom applies to herself in equal measure. She lacks the objectivity of the true critic. What she does have is defiance, which ironically links her to Janáček the artist. He had told Kamila he wrote the last movement 'charged with energy and defiance' (p. 23). Anezka does not ask 'defiance of what?' (Janáček's *Defiance*, a capriccio, was premiered on 2 March 1928.) In Friel, defiance is usually the self-assertion which defines identity. It marks the moment when Maggie begins her wild dance in *Lughnasa* and characterises Molly Sweeney in her blind dance the night before her crucial operation. Even in *Hedda Gabler*, the genius Loevborg echoes Friel: 'In the old days I spat in the face of the world with such easy defiance.'[34] It is the stance Friel approves in the artist: it was thus he saw Beckett.[35] Ruth, the second violinist in *Performances*, may therefore be taken as right when she gives as her opinion that the opening of the Second String Quartet says 'I'm my own man' (p. 19): it is Janáček asserting himself against the world, declaring his autonomy *even* in the face of Kamila's part in his creativity. A little later, when the musicians actually play the opening movement, Janáček denies that it says 'I'm my own man [. . .]. More a whistle in the dark, isn't it?' (p. 29). While in the main identifying with Janáček throughout, Friel knows Janáček is wrong here in failing to understand his own defiance.[36] Therefore, both Anezka and Janáček equally misjudge how art establishes identity. The shadow of the feminists' attack on the *Field Day Anthology* hangs over this quarrel (see Chapter 7): the ghost of Nuala O'Faoláin gets a brief walk-on role.[37] Nevertheless, when Anezka exits in anger, her quitting the space implies Janáček has acted her off the stage. And yet every Friel play needs an enemy within to bare the soul of the protagonist. *Performances*, like *Answer, Do!* or for that matter *Faith Healer*, remains open to the contrary view: the artist as villain.[38]

When the musicians start to play the final two movements of the *Intimate Letters* quartet, the stage suddenly becomes a community. Janáček, disturbed at Anezka's abrupt departure, at first tries to concentrate on the manuscript, the letters themselves, she has left behind as a final gesture of repudiation. Then, leaving the text aside, he closes his eyes in contemplation and yields to the music played live as the play ends. The ghost of Janáček himself melts into the music just as a play leaves its author to find a fuller life through players in communion with an audience. The metaphor is complete.

General Conclusion: Friel at Play

The real Janáček told Kamila that his/their string quartet would be 'inspired, a composition beyond all the usual conventions'.[39] So, too, with *Performances*, that supremely arty piece of work. Its self-reflexiveness lends it an unsettling power. Because of its brevity – it comes in at sixty-five minutes on stage – it is caviare to the general, unlikely to be a popular piece even with the thinking classes. Also, because of its requirement of a string quartet on stage, it cannot greatly attract theatre managers. In spite of that hazard, the revival of *Performances* with the Brodsky Quartet as part of Derry's City of Culture celebrations in 2013 testified to its haunting qualities. The text is therefore as capable of cueing in a general conclusion to Friel's work as *Philadelphia* is to its induction (in Chapter 2).

Performances indicates that in the twenty-first century Friel remained as interested in experimentalism as ever. Beginning with *Philadelphia* in 1964 but more obviously with *Cass McGuire* two years later, Friel served notice that while he saw his role in the modern theatre as entertainer, he could never be content with conventional realism. Even in quasi-realistic pieces he is always in various ways subversive. *The Yalta Game* (2001), based on the Chekhov short-story 'Lady with Lapdog', works in masterly fashion as a coded synopsis of Friel's play-making: 'divining other lives or investing the lives of others with an imagined life'.[40] By the end of this one-act play, Gurov is unsure which is the real life and which the imagined. And this is the space into which Friel always wishes to lead his audience. The components of Friel's experimentalism are so diverse, indeed, as to characterise him as a literal shape-changer. This diversity has several implications here.

First, there is the familiar tension between tradition and modernity. This is not quite a cliché. It refers to certain writers (I would include Heaney alongside Friel here) caught between cultural pincers, the pressure from which is at once defining and artistically enabling. There is always the supplementary question, *which* tradition? It can mean the body of established values, beliefs, history and linguistic forms within a culture, as embedded in Irish folklore and *dinnsheanchas* ('knowledge of the lore of places').[41] With Friel, the concept implies a determined loyalty towards ancestry. But, as *The Communication Cord* clearly shows, this does not mean shallow worship of the past. The criterion for Friel is always authenticity, intelligent recognition of where true value lies, feeling grounded in respect for the real. Tradition is a moral gauge of the real. Its inherent conservatism is therefore philosophically irrelevant. Friel's commitment to making the local, invented village/town of Ballybeg stand for universal experience demonstrates his fidelity to the locus central to the Gaelic short story and the metonymy of the singular. But once Friel began to write for the *New Yorker*, an awareness that modernity must be present in the short story, through point of view and style, complicated his work. This awareness is to be associated with Friel's admiration for T. S. Eliot's modernist concept of tradition and its relation to individual talent, which helped to bolster Friel's objectivity as artist. Joyce had already exemplified this necessity. Once Friel made drama his medium, Thornton Wilder's *Our Town* could be appreciated as a paradigm for combining the local and the modernist tradition(s). Friel has proved very adept at this double focus. *Philadelphia, Here I Come!* marks the first major success in this area, the dramatising of modern Irish consciousness of the cultural 'waste land'. This debased state of being, of nation, is starkly laid open in all of Friel's plays, urging a better way. Friel's endings, suddenly fusing past and present, usually summon up a new dimension offstage which is the future. 'Within his art,' said Mary McAleese, 'he confronts the great issues of Ireland, its history, religion, politics, its past, its present, and its future *on his own terms*.'[42] Not only of Ireland, it must be interpolated. Friel's terms include the transnational and the global.

Secondly, although many of Friel's most successful plays respond well to postcolonial theory, as Shaun Richards shows in his essay in the next chapter, it is noteworthy that Friel can be sceptical. The history plays, of course, cannot be read without reference to postcolonialism, and yet *The Home Place* goes against the grain in focusing on an Anglo-Irish landlord. As Csilla Bertha demonstrates in her article, also included in the next chapter, even *The Home Place* can be read as a culturally complex play, in common with much of Friel's work. Although he eschews the postcolonial debate, David Krause challenges us to keep in mind the aesthetic argument as well.

The postcolonial must also be seen in tandem with the ethical and other problems raised by globalisation. Former president Mary Robinson has raised awareness of these debates worldwide, especially in relation to central Africa. Friel does not directly intervene, but it is worth recalling that in *Molly Sweeney* the trouble-making Frank goes off to Ethiopia as to utopia ('Ethiopia is paradise', *Plays 2*, p. 507) without giving the least thought to the politics of the area. Frank's intervention, 'to set up and supervise a food convoy to Ethiopia' (p. 469), politicises foreign aid as meddling. Fools rush in. As Patrick Lonergan has pointed out, however, it is mainly in the area of international reception that the topic of globalisation arises in relation to Friel's plays.[43] Broadway has meant a lot to Friel. But in reference to the central question in *Give Me Your Answer, Do!*, it is worth noting that Friel donated his own manuscripts to Ireland's National Library rather than to any American university. Although speaking out, like Pinter, against international imperialism was never Friel's style, his heart has always been with rebels, dissidents and underdogs. In his response in 2003 to an appeal to provide a preface for a book condemning the war in Iraq, he had to wrestle with both sides in the debate. He would not be 'enlisted into the strident ranks of anti-America' because of his 'affectionate relationship with the USA' rooted in the reception granted to 'emigrant ancestors' and the 'animating and enriching' reception he himself (and his work) had experienced there for more than fifty years.[44] Also, the *language* employed by opponents of the war offended Friel: 'Their language of abuse is an abuse of language.' On the other hand, he himself found it difficult 'to express in temperate language' the prospect of being enlisted by America and her allies in support of their wrong-headed cause. So, his decision was in the end to do what he was actually doing while debating the issue: to write the preface to a book opposing the war in Iraq. 'I oppose this war with a mute [*sic*] passion, a pain of deep anxiety that cannot find coherent articulation' because there was something 'not-thought-through' about it, something 'disproportionate' and 'inimical to reason' and, above all, something 'that offends the notion of what it is to be fully human.'[45] Here, we find endorsed a credo which underpins all that Brian Friel has written.

A third force of energy in Friel's oeuvre derives from the contemporary tension between modernism and postmodernism. It is apparent in Friel's love of metatheatre. Gabriel Josipovici defines modernism as 'a response by artists to that "disenchantment of the world" to which cultural historians have long been drawing our attention'.[46] From the disgust of Gar in *Philadelphia* at the world to the angst of the Faith Healer on his treadmill or Molly in her borderline country, this disenchantment is dramatised. It would certainly describe Friel's stance, although Josipovici sees 1950 as the terminal point of modernism. Postmodernism on the other hand is defined by Paul H. Fry as 'eclectic orientation to the past' and even partially 'a return to the past, an opening up of textual possibility to traditions and historical moments of expression that modernism, with its emphasis on autonomous forms, had supposed obsolete and set aside'.[47] And here, too, Friel fits in as evidenced again by *Cass McGuire*, *Living Quarters*, *Faith Healer* and *Molly Sweeney*. It is the eclecticism that counts. Colm Tóibín has helpfully referred to 'the drama of radical instability which Friel has made his own'.[48] Like Beckett, Friel is both modernist and postmodernist, and the tension between the two styles, modes, artistic convictions, suffuses his body of drama. In this area, as noted more than once in the course of this book, Friel comes closer to Pinter also than might be expected. Each has his 'no man's land' or area of psychic geography, because, 'Instead of the avant-garde modernist's concern with opposing something monolithic [. . .] the postmodern concern is with the local and with the irreducible multiplicity of things local.'[49]

Intertextuality forms a strategy which facilitates this kind of reading. Friel assimilates his private reading into public performance in ways not many modern playwrights after Eliot bother about: Stoppard, no doubt, but not Pinter or Beckett or Shepard or (even more definitely) Mamet. Friel's cast of mind is allusive and his style accordingly understated, ironic and poetic. From *Philadelphia* on, one is alerted to the use of quotations, overt or covert, which can expand meaning: they at least contextualise it. 'Walter Mitty, Billy Liar and a few other fantasists' such as Peer Gynt, astutely observed the *Irish Times* critic in 1964, lay behind Friel's Gar O'Donnell.[50] In addition, Gar Public's use as mantra of the quotation from Edmund Burke serves as a signifier of his trauma over his dead mother, bringing history reopened like an old suitcase containing lost evidence. This manoeuvre provides the key to Friel's intertextual technique. In *Lughnasa*, Father Jack's groping to complete quotations epitomises the very *process* of intertextuality: language remembered serves to affirm or restore identity. Hugh's recitation from the *Aeneid* at the end of *Translations* is probably more difficult to construe. It is a big ask for actor and audience. In other plays, direct quotation of poems and songs works more simply to widen horizons of expectation. The opening sequence of *The Gentle Island* calls on the reader/spectator to bear in mind Goldsmith's *The Deserted Village* (1770), with its ominous vision of social collapse lying behind the death of the pastoral. In *The Freedom of the City* the text of the *Widgery Report* on Bloody Sunday is played with in a different mood. In *Translations*, again, the buried quotations from George Steiner's *After Babel* are truly modernist in function, gesturing towards the wider horizons of cultural history and linguistics. Steiner is also quoted in *Performances*, twice from *Language and Silence* (1967) and once from *Real Presences* (1989).[51] This time paraphrase minimises indebtedness; in effect, it is Steiner's *idea* of music as transcending language that Friel borrows (and acknowledged in the Gate Theatre programme). At this point, when self-consciousness concedes a borrowing, the brio of 'play' is threatened, although in *Performances* a Wildean wit still persists.[52]

This emphasis on allusiveness may lead to the mistaken inference that Friel is a purely literary playwright. To quote Lyndsey Turner, the director of the 2012 *Philadelphia* production at the Donmar Warehouse, Friel is not just a 'theatre poet' but also 'a real man of the theatre. He understands that theatre is not television and it's not film. It can do something much more immediate, much more delicate.'[53] In any case, it is no crime for a dramatist to be a good writer and to display 'aesthetic finesse, beauty, eloquence, style [. . .], the architecture of a sentence'[54] and no disgrace to be made a Fellow of the London Royal Society of Literature in 2012. Moreover, in *The Event of Literature* (2012), Terry Eagleton sees 'literature' itself as fundamentally mimetic and performative.[55] There is no bias there: Eagleton, once a playwright, wrote *St Oscar* (1989) for Field Day. In turn, Aidan O'Malley stresses: 'Field Day's political actions were intrinsically performative, in the sense that the plays brought to the fore the ways in which identities are performatively constructed.'[56] It can be noted in passing that no fewer than seven modern playwrights have won the Nobel Prize for *Literature*. So, there is no war between good writing and good theatre. Stoppard's defence is definitive when in *The Real Thing* (1982) Henry says: 'I don't think writers are sacred, but words are.' This would be Friel's view also. Abandoning the short story, that most literary of forms, he turned to theatre as the proper medium for his talents. The bridges he has built with words there are between human hearts, communities and even nations. The 'nudges'[57] he has given the world have been towards a renewal of Ireland-England relations, for which much credit is due. Whatever about poetry, drama *can* make things happen. The peace process in Northern Ireland owes a lot to the cultural and transformative power of Field Day and of Friel's imagination in the provision of thoughtful and precise language.

To single out just one other area that distinguishes Friel as very much at home in the theatre: his abiding interest in stage space. Ever since Peter Brook's groundbreaking *The Empty Space* in 1968, it has become useful to regard the dramatic event as essentially preoccupied with animating space. Friel has consistently made audiences conscious that 'space' is more than setting: action and mood are articulated *by* the space in which stories are told on stage. Helen Lojek has emphasised Friel's importance here in her study, *The Spaces of Irish Drama* (2011), in which Friel heads the list of contemporary writers including Conor McPherson, Marina Carr and Frank McGuinness who are proficient in exploiting stage space. In Chapter 8, I tried to show how in the later play *Wonderful Tennessee* Friel made the setting, a large seaside pier, come alive as a brooding spiritual presence. He designed all that in his stage directions: space is created to draw an audience into the silence emphasised at the opening and close of the play. Friel has commented: 'Silence can be both articulate and indeed eloquent; but, like language, can be riddled with ambiguities.'[58] Space can challenge language in that regard. As Chris Morash argues, 'Space is more than just part of the language of theatre; it is one of its conditions of being, as much ontological as semantic.'[59] In short, Friel is constantly aware that 'theatre constructs space that is not only structural but in which structures become signifying'.[60] For *Performances*, where a dead protagonist inhabits his work room in Moravia, the setting is '*in the style of the* [nineteen] *twenties*'[61] but the action takes place in 2003, with talk of computers and so forth. Friel's skill in creating such duality of space/time lies at the centre of his dramatic achievement. His stage designer, Joe Vaněk (working once more with director Patrick Mason), travelled to Brno to see Janáček's work room just as he had travelled Donegal viewing seaside piers in 1993 in search of Friel's idea for *Wonderful Tennessee*. He commented in a programme note for *Performances*: 'Brian Friel's play brings past into present and the white, echoing, empty rooms [of Janáček's villa] seemed the ideal visual metaphor for this dislocated world.'[62] This world then becomes animated by performers and director to create Friel's representation. Space becomes the occasion for pretence, theatre the site of resistance to certitude. Such is Friel's way. Space and place can coincide metonymically: *The Home Place* is but one, and as it happens, ironic example.

In 2013, Friel's achievements as man of the theatre were further celebrated through the Derry-Londonderry City of Culture productions of *Performances* and *Translations:* a blend of old and new, political and non-political, the metatheatrical and the naturalistic. BBC Radio 4 Extra took up the idea under the tittle 'Celebrating "the Irish Chekhov": A Brian Friel Season'.[63] Although Friel is considerably more than 'the Irish Chekhov' (whatever that is), this attention reinforces the esteem in which Friel continues to be held and indicates once again, as do the essays on his work in the chapter which follows, how central and challenging a figure he remains in the modern theatre.

CHAPTER 10
CRITICAL PERSPECTIVES

Placed Identities for Placeless Times: Brian Friel and Postcolonial Criticism

Shaun Richards

The Field Day Theatre Company, wrote W. J. McCormack, has 'set the terms for the current debate in Irish criticism.'[1] While the early years of the company may have been distinguished by the attempt, in Edna Longley's phrase, to fuse Derry and Derrida, the period from at least the mid-1980s to the present has been dominated by the influence of writers such as Frantz Fanon, Edward Said and Gayatri Spivak; the architects of colonial and postcolonial criticism. The Field Day pamphlet series of 1988, published under the general title *Nationalism, Colonialism and Literature*, included not only Said's *Yeats and Decolonisation* but also contributions from Terry Eagleton and Fredric Jameson whose reputations as critics engaged in front-line debates around colonialism and postmodernism confirmed the intellectual orbit within which Field Day intended to operate. These twin discourses of the postcolonial and the postmodern have recently been extended and, indeed, problematised, by Homi Bhabha's argument that as the experience of colonialism created a textuality which 'anticipated, *avant la lettre,* many of the problematics of signification and judgement that have become current in contemporary theory'[2] he has consequently tried 'to rename the postmodern from the position of the post-colonial'.[3] Yet this intersection is far from uncontentious, and above all for a reading of Brian Friel, whose *Translations,* the 'central text'[4] which launched Field Day in 1980, has been presented by Declan Kiberd as a work of whose postcolonial credentials Friel himself is 'well aware'.[5] The fact that over the fifteen-year period from *Translations* to *Molly Sweeney* Friel has engaged in a constant and committed interrogation of authenticity and origin rests uneasily alongside Bhabha's seemingly unnegotiable poco-pomo fusion which is predicated on 'the impossibility of claiming an origin for the Self (or Other) within a tradition of representation that conceived of identity as the satisfaction of a totalising, plenitudinous object of vision'.[6] It is this resolute denial of a 'totalising' identity which leads Simon During to assert that 'the concept postmodernity has been constructed in terms which more or less intentionally wipe out the possibility of post-colonial identity [as] post-colonialism is regarded as the need, in nations or groups which have been victims of imperialism, to achieve an identity'.[7] As Terry Eagleton pithily summarised the situation, 'essentialism is one of the most heinous crimes in the postmodernist book',[8] yet it is towards essentialism that Friel's plays of the 1990s have been drawn, albeit in often troubling and troubled ways. In pursuit of a meaningful, but not naive, authenticity, Friel has reflected and refracted contemporary theoretical concerns in the most complex and productive manner, sophisticating an analysis initiated by *Translations* and opening up areas of debate which resonate across the whole of Irish Studies.

While Robert Hogan noted that 'the most arresting character, the hedge-schoolmaster, is not the main character'[9] a significant number of critics have not only taken Hugh as *Translations*' protagonist but have also tended to read his position with regard to imminent cultural erasure as that advocated by Friel. The question as to what that position is, however, requires a more detailed analysis. In her study of the founding years of Field Day, Marilynn Richtarick advances the standard critical position in asserting that 'If any character in the play can be taken to speak for Friel, it is Hugh.'[10] However, what Richtarick takes to be 'the last word'[11] given to Hugh refers to his lines agreeing to teach English to Maire; lines taken to demonstrate that *Translations* is 'a play about living within the situation in which you find yourself, however much you may regret the circumstances that have forced such an accommodation on you'.[12] The centrality of Hugh is confirmed by Richard Pine, who argues that Hugh 'possesses, and can use, the inner strength to resolve [the] crises'.[13] Elmer Andrews has more recently acknowledged that Hugh is subject to Friel's 'subversive irony',[14] but still argues that he 'would seem to have Friel's endorsement if we are to go by [his] symbolic elevation at the end when he ascends the stairs as he speaks',[15] but takes the crucial line to be that 'confusion is not an ignoble condition'.[16] The consensual interpretation is then one which reads Friel, through Hugh, as arguing for accommodating rather than resisting cultural change; a definitively 'liberal' position which is most fully expressed in Neil Corcoran's reading of the final moments of the play: '[Hugh] recommends the persistence of the past under forms necessary to the present. . . . The cultural survival Hugh recommends is an act of subtlety, stealth and subversion, an act of reclamation in which retrospect may create the conditions of a fulfilling future.'[17] What is produced by such overreadings and selective decisions as to where the 'last words' of the play are located is a failure to acknowledge that, while Hugh does indeed fluctuate between accommodation and confusion in the face of the new world, the overall effect is of impotence rather than negative capability, torn as he is between a desolate recognition of his powerlessness in the face of the future – 'I have no idea. . . . I have no idea at all' (p. 67) – and failure adequately to recall lines evoking past glories – 'What the hell's wrong with me' (p. 68). Andrews is right to acknowledge the stage direction 'He goes towards the steps and begins to ascend' (p. 67) but what also needs to be acknowledged is the earlier direction 'He looks around the room carefully, as if he were about to leave it forever' (p. 67). While the lines delivered when Hugh is at the top of the stairs refer to his sentiment that always is 'a silly word' (p. 67) and carry the implicit suggestion that cultural flexibility rather than permanence is the desired good, this is to ignore the fact that the whole final speech from the *Aeneid* is not only delivered from the top of the stairs but is, moreover, given a particular charge by being repeated as the lights slowly fade to black by a man who has effectively abandoned the playing area to Jimmy Jack, whose mythic and historical co-ordinates are in total confusion, and Maire, who has acknowledged that she set out for somewhere but 'couldn't remember where' (p. 67). In the seventh of his 'Theses on the Philosophy of History' Walter Benjamin chastised historians who worked by means of empathy, a process through which the power of the imagination is linked to a paralysis of action. This excess of emotional identification with lost moments leads, he argues, to an all-pervading disempowering sadness and, he quotes Flaubert, 'Peu de gens devineront combien il a fallu être triste pour ressusciter Carthage.'[18] It is, of course, to Carthage that Hugh's eyes are turned as, stumbling through his fading memories of the *Aeneid,* he recites the lines recording the erasure of the promise-filled splendour of Carthage by an imperial people, 'kings of broad realms and proud in war' (p. 68). There is, then, an apparent logic to reading the play as a disempowering lament which, in Anthony Roche's phrase, 'modulates finally into a solo note of brooding desolation',[19] but this would be to produce a reading totally dependent on seeing the final scene through Hugh, so overlooking the traces of earlier moments which, like the culture and history to which they attest, still have a power to disturb apparent points of closure; in Benjamin's phrase to 'blast open the continuum of history'.[20]

One of the most telling critiques of *Translations* has been advanced by Edna Longley, whose view that it 'refurbishes an old myth'[21] is based on a reading of the play as presenting Ballybeg as 'a kind of Eden',[22] and because of the play's 'pervasive nostalgia' for a now lost Ireland it can best be understood as 'an aisling',[23] the poetic form which, in its eighteenth-century heyday, expressed 'a romantic escape from the reality of the political situation'.[24] But what needs to be more fully acknowledged is the sustaining aspect of holding to origin and authenticity in the face of their absolute erasure, whether this be through the cultural colonialism dramatised in *Translations* or in the pervasive coca-colonisation of the contemporary moment. As expressed by Stuart Hall, in the face of globalisation, it is 'positioning' which 'provides people with co-ordinates . . . [and] everybody comes from some place . . . and needs some sense of identification and belonging.'[25] It is this resolute reclamation of the name which informs the dramatic heart of *Translations* and brings into focus Friel's postcolonial opposition to a postmodernism which, as Seamus Deane observed, 'refuses the idea of naming'.[26]

The close of Act 1 sees Owen, the returnee, assert 'Owen – Roland – what the hell. It's only a name. It's the same me, isn't it? Well, isn't it?' (p. 33) and although his insistence that his 'essence' remains undiminished by the mistaken appellation is assented to by Manus, it is the intention of Act 2, which takes place only 'some days later', to undermine his certainty and so attest to what might be termed cultural essentialism. The Act opens when 'The sappers have already mapped most of the area' (p. 34), so permitting Yolland and Owen 'to take each of the Gaelic names – every hill, stream, rock, even every patch of ground which possessed its own distinctive Irish name – and Anglicise it' (p. 34). The completeness of this operation, and the denials inherent within it, are signalled by Friel's use of 'even' and 'distinctive', and it is in this context that Owen's centrality to the play becomes apparent. Early in the Act, and in what is clearly to be taken as a dawning resistance to erasure, Owen attempts to inform Yolland as to his real name, but it is only after their discussion as to the naming of Tobair Vree that he 'Explodes' with the impassioned declaration 'George! For God's sake! *My name is not Roland!*' (p. 44). The triple exclamatory force of this moment signals its intensity, and while the scene enters comic mode as they roll on the ground, drinking, laughing and extolling their power to name everything in 'perfect equation with its roots,' (p. 45) such confident assertions are revealed as hollow by comparison with Owen's determination to 'keep piety' (p. 44) with the dead, a decision which leads him to demand the right also claimed by Seamus Heaney: 'To be at home/In my own place and dwell within/ Its proper name – '[27] The completeness of Owen's conversion, which sees him opening Act 3 with the statement 'I think we should go back to the original [name]' (p. 54), could be taken as regressive from the standpoint of a postmodernism which rejects as naive nostalgia any 'paradisaic representation of a lost "organic" society',[28] but such ideas are parodied through Yolland and, as Friel noted at the time of the play's composition, the environment of Ballybeg must suggest from the outset 'a dying climate – no longer quickened by its past'[29]; the bleak opening set peopled by characters who are variously dumb, lame and alcoholic, confirming the realisation of this intention. While there is then no return to Eden in Owen's action, it is still, as asserted by Manus in his Act 1 defence of Doalty's acts of sabotage, a 'gesture', 'Just to indicate . . . a presence' (p. 18). As Seamus Heaney noted in his review of the first production, Owen 'cannot quite manage to see himself',[30] and while this is true of his life as 'Roland', it overlooks his final Act assertion 'I know where I live' (p. 66) which, by implication, is in the 'proper name'. This return to the source is, moreover, one of the central concepts of postcolonial criticism.

As outlined by Frantz Fanon, colonialism 'turns to the past of the oppressed people, and distorts, disfigures and destroys it'.[31] The resurrection of a past national culture, therefore, 'does not only rehabilitate that nation and serve as a justification for the hope of a future national culture. In the sphere of psycho-affective equilibrium it is responsible for an important change in the native.'[32] Although it may be '[R]epressed, persecuted, humiliated, betrayed', it is in the source culture that, as Amilcar Cabral argues, will be found the preservation of identity and the point of resistance, and in terms directly relating to *Translations*, he asserts that the return to the source effects the denial 'of the culture of the dominant power over that of the dominated people'.[33] While perceiving the potentiality for regression inherent in such a move, Fanon is equally clear that writers 'ought to use the past with the intention of opening the future'.[34] What needs to be interrogated in the light of the above is the extent to which Hugh's advocacy of assimilation into the names of the 'new home' is dramatised as opening up a future which offers anything more than the condition of 'mimic men' which, far from 'disclosing the ambivalence of colonial discourse' as Bhabha asserts,[35] 'disrupts its authority' and merely ensures second citizenship.

George Steiner's assertion that in some epochs 'a civilisation is imprisoned in a linguistic contour which no longer matches . . . the changing landscape of fact'[36] enters the play through Hugh, but it is the more dramatically powerful counter position of Owen that demands attention, namely that 'the very differences which have always been read as symptoms of inadequacy are capable of being re-read as indications and figurations of values radically opposed to those of the dominant culture'.[37] Hugh's confusion of resigned acceptance and elegiac, but passive, resistance holds the play's fading final minutes, but the counter movement of Owen's return to his roots is given the celebratory counterforce; a creative tension which unites Friel with other postcolonial writers concerned to resist a dominant strain in postmodernist thought 'that would privilege identity as constructed, hybrid, fragmented, conjunctural'.[38] Indeed, it is the 'undue haste in deconstructing essentialist notions of identity'[39] which informs the post-*Translations* drama of the 1990s as Friel warily negotiates his way back from Hugh's 'confused' doctrine of assimilation with its inadequate appreciation of the 'risks inherent in uncritical adulations of "hybridity" as an empowering strategy'[40] to a more sophisticated comprehension of the need to be called by the proper name. For what may follow on from making a new home in the 'changing landscape of fact' is not necessarily 'material progress of the kind hoped for, but cultural confusion and a diminished sense of enterprise'.[41] It is this 'cultural confusion' which is summarised by Kate's realisation in *Dancing at Lughnasa* that 'hair cracks are appearing everywhere; that control is slipping away; that the whole thing is so fragile it can't be held together much longer. It's all about to collapse'.[42]

While readings of *Dancing at Lughnasa* as offering 'consoling, nostalgic, unified images of Irishness'[43] are understandable, the reality is paradoxically both more disturbing and potentially sustaining than this interpretation suggests. The mellowing effect of the narrator Michael's memory on the dramatisation of his childhood summer of 1936 cannot override the economic and emotional poverty which is experienced by his mother and aunts. Their courage and humour are less remnants of some now-lost post-independence idyll than forms of resistance to de Valera's Free State based on residual cultural formations which 'still seem to have significance because they represent areas of human experience, aspiration and achievement which the dominant culture neglects, undervalues, opposes, represses, or even cannot recognise'.[44] Raymond Williams identifies this 'reaching back' with the 'default of a particular phase of the dominant culture',[45] a comment which has a particular resonance in *Dancing at Lughnasa* where the ceaseless projection into the changing landscape of fact brings with it the loss of income as a delayed industrial revolution destroys the cottage-industry economy of the sisters, and the emigration of Rose and Agnes leads, not to a blissful state of hybrid harmony, but to drink, destitution and death. The response to these conditions is to dance; an act whose value is contained in Father Jack's description of the ritual dances of Ryanga: 'You lose all sense of time . . . !' (p. 48).

The process of colonisation, as Yolland recognised in *Translations*, has brought an end to 'Ancient time' (p. 40) and, by implication, its cultural values and practices. But Irish decolonisation has only reinforced the repression of a truly indigenous culture whose 'pagan practices', says Kate, 'are no concern of ours – none whatever!' (p. 17). The fact that Kate is a national schoolteacher in the Free State, the enforcer of the process in which, as Bridget expressed it in *Translations*, 'You'll be taught to speak English and every subject will be taught through English' (p. 22), only underlines the extent of Friel's revision of Hugh's lines of cultural accommodation, as Ireland's adoption of colonial structures oppresses its own residual cultural forms and values. Their continuing presence is made manifest in the constant yearning to dance, with even the conformist Kate succumbing to an impulse which while 'out of character [is] at the same time ominous of some deep and true emotion' (p. 22). As Helen Gilbert has argued, dance in drama 'offers a site of resistance to hegemonic discourses through its representation of the body on stage as a moving subject'.[46] This disruption of repression and reclaiming of the body is at the heart of the scene and is signalled as such in the stage directions: they do, however, require further consideration, for while 'there is a sense of order being consciously subverted' there is also a mood 'of near hysteria being induced' (p. 22). This is emotion as eruption rather than ritual, and while the originary moment of the Lughnasa dance to whose passions the sisters are drawn has parallels with the ceremony in Ryanga evoked by Father Jack, the point is clearly made that there 'it grows naturally into a secular celebration; so that almost imperceptibly the religious ceremony ends and the community celebration takes over' (p. 48). Once the connective tissue between the sacred and the profane is ruptured, there can be no innocent return to the source. In this context of loss, time as history and process is perceived as the threat which severs the link to authentic identity, while to dance is to attempt to gain access to what is lost. The impossibility of the venture is embodied in Father Jack who has erased the co-ordinates of both identity and language, caught as he is between past and present, a signal of the destructive consequences of returning to a past which a culture has lost the power to accommodate; the point being highlighted by the injuries sustained by the Sweeney boy during the corruption of ritual sacrifices carried out in the back hills. But neither, as evidenced in the enforced decline of all the sisters, is there any recompense in the pressing world of the modern.

As suggested above, the significant past to which the drama is oriented is not specifically the childhood evoked in Michael's memories and, in the first production, by Joe Vanek's mellow set of natural plenitude; rather it is the pagan past which, while yearned for subliminally, cannot be re-entered this side of mental equilibrium. What Friel is then dramatising is the simultaneous need and practical impossibility of literally returning to the source, while also suggesting in the most powerful of dramatic ways that it is that source which has a sustaining potential far in excess of anything offered by contemporary culture. The conclusion of the play sees Michael articulating the longing to penetrate language and 'be in touch with some otherness' (p. 71), but that 'otherness', exiled to the back hills of 1930s' Donegal in *Dancing at Lughnasa*, is even more painfully absent from the 'lost' Ireland of the contemporary moment. It is this double sense of emotional need and practical impossibility which drives Friel's drama as it interrogates the feasibility of holding to 'the proper name' with an increasing sense of the truth inherent in Fredric Jameson's assertion that 'the memory of precapitalist societies may become a vital element [in] the invention of the future'.[47]

From the standpoint of postmodernism, however, such a turn to memory as a creative contributor to a future based on origin and authenticity is a disabling fantasy. David Harvey goes so far as to claim that 'place-bound nostalgias' inhibit the process of 'Becoming' in that they are predicated on what Heidegger refers to as 'the land of Motionless Childhood'.[48] This ideal of memory and history as meaningful and sustaining is a constant across much postmodern thought. The idea that 'ethnic identity and difference are socially produced in the here and now, not archaeologically salvaged from the disappearing past',[49] is rendered with such absolutism that it allows no space for the recognition that without a sense of origin the coordinates for a meaningful and self-determined future are absent, individuals and nations becoming simply the flotsam to be taken in the direction of the strongest current. While the postmodern perception is that '[I]n a world that is increasingly characterized by exile, migration and Diaspora, with all the consequences of unsettling and hybridisation, there can be no place for such absolutism of the pure and authentic',[50] those actually experiencing the powerlessness of the periphery contest that 'Home . . . is . . . that which we cannot not want.'[51] Postmodernism is then a threat to the postcolonial subject because, as defined by Seamus Deane, '[it] supplants the search for a legitimate mode of nomination and origin, [which] is surely to pass from one kind of colonising experience into another'.[52] This perception is widely shared within the postcolonial world. As noted by Ashis Nandy, 'When the religious reformers of 19th-century India spoke of protecting cultures, it seemed an obscurantist ploy. Today, when the juggernaut of modernity threatens every non-Western culture, the slogan no longer seems a revivalist conspiracy. It has become a plea for minimum cultural plurality in an increasingly uniformised world.'[53] Moreover, as viewed by Aijaz Ahmad, it is postmodernism's 'debunking of all myths of origin, totalising narratives, determinate and collective historical agents' which has led to the stripping away of 'the historical reality of the sedimentations which do in fact give particular collectivities of people real civilisational identities'.[54] While such critics are aware that this desire for origin can 'elicit a nostalgia for a past golden age that never was', there is also a far more sophisticated awareness in evidence than that suggested in any simple return to the source: '[a] problematic which recognises the desire for safety and the construction of an identity while it problematises that construction'.[55] It is this 'critical traditionalism',[56] in Nandy's telling phrase, which Friel addresses in *Wonderful Tennessee.*

The play opens as three couples move west from their cosmopolitan existences into the 'Bloody Indian territory'[57] of Donegal. In bidding 'Bye, civilisation' (p. 6) the couples are seeking, at various levels of consciousness, for access to a sustaining source which, in an echo of Yolland in *Translations,* is of 'Another world altogether' (p. 10). The difference, however, is that these Irish couples, as the sisters of *Dancing at Lughnasa*, are alienated from their own cultural inheritance, attempting a return to the island of Oilean Draiochta, or island of

Otherness or mystery, in order 'To be in touch again' (p. 20). The island, however, is never reached by the characters as Friel underlines the position advanced by *Dancing at Lughnasa* that the desire to return to 'Arcadia' (p. 8) can at best be accommodated, never achieved.

As the characters 'all . . . gaze out at the island, each with his/her thoughts' (p. 17), the nature of the desire is made explicit; the island being 'Wonderful', a 'destination of wonder', 'The wonderful – the sacred – the mysterious' (pp. 17–18). But as they look out, it is Trish who speaks the crucial lines 'Dammit, I've lost it again. You're sure it's not a mirage?' (p. 18). The voyage is an explicit attempt to regain a lost childhood as the island, 'remembered, however vaguely', is to be purchased by Terry 'In memory of my father, maybe' (p. 27). In the past the father visited the island as an expression of religious faith, but 'People stopped believing, didn't they? Nobody does that sort of thing nowadays' (p. 20). Yet what informs the play is the premise that the desire 'to remember again' (p. 20) remains constant in lives which, while superficially having all the trappings of modern, material success, are riven by failures of finance, health and sanity.

The visit to the island is nominally to celebrate Terry's birthday. Focus is on Frank, who is working on a magnum opus, *The Measurement of Time and its Effect on European Civilisation*, in which both the act of analysis and that analysed locates him, and his 'lost' friends, within a system predicated on the pursuit of a progress which eradicates that sense, noted by Yolland, of 'experience being of a totally different order' (p. 40). As Massey has argued, 'With Time are allied History, Progress, Civilisation, Science, Politics and Reason, portentous things with gravitas and capital letters. With space, on the other hand, are aligned the other poles of these concepts: stasis, ("simple") reproduction, nostalgia, emotion, aesthetics, the body.'[58] It is this desire for the space of 'home' and 'Ancient time', a desire shared, and suppressed, by the sisters of *Lughnasa* until it explodes in the dance, which drives the characters of *Wonderful Tennessee:* 'he's taking us home!' (p. 25) is the cry which greets Terry's intention of buying the island. Yet there is a decisive advance on the analysis proferred by the earlier play in the understanding of ritual; the means by which 'Ancient time' is opened to the future.

The almost fatal exposure to unaccommodated ritual which scarred the Sweeney boy in *Dancing at Lughnasa* has its specific echo in *Wonderful Tennessee*, and notably also from the 1930s, in the story of Sean O'Boyle, dismembered in a drink-fuelled ritual killing which led, effectively, to the destruction of the community. Ritual has its place in *Wonderful Tennessee* too. But in the mock-dionysiac disrobing of Terry, just as in the votive offering enacted in the play's conclusion as the characters enact the ceremonial prayers recalled by Terry from his childhood, it is not ritual as blind replaying of the past for 'If the past were to be exactly repeated in detail, it would smother the present.'[59] Friel's characters have accommodated the past in a way analogous to Angela's game of 'how close can you get without touching it' (p. 55) which opens Act 2, a game played by pitching lobster-pot weights at an empty bottle placed close to the lifebelt stand which becomes the focus of the votive offering. The comment on first finding the weights is 'Amazing. Another world altogether' (p. 10) and it is this comment, along with the stage direction, 'When the game ends there is a small mound of stones' (p. 54), which encapsulates Friel's position. The 'Simple domestic instincts' (p. 71), the vestiges of residual cultural practices, lead the characters to perform a contemporary version of the ancient prayer rounds, and stimulate a harmonious conclusion in which the play's opening line 'Help! We're lost!' (p. 1) is replaced by voices singing 'loudly, joyously, happily' (p. 78). The fact that the celebration of *Wonderful Tennessee* was followed by the desolation of *Molly Sweeney* is testimony to Friel's gnawing anxiety on issues of origin and authenticity as this deceptively private drama enlarges understanding of his position with regard to the most public and national of debates.

Through surgery, Molly is to be 'translated' into a world of sight, a disruption explicitly equated with the spatial and cultural displacements of the earlier plays: 'suddenly I knew why I was so desolate. It was the dread of exile, of being sent away. It was the desolation of homesickness.'[60] As Molly records this moment of fear 'a strange thing happened', one which echoes across all those earlier moments in which elements of residual culture breakthrough in a disturbing, but also sustaining, manner as Molly involuntarily starts to dance: 'Mad and wild and frenzied. But so adroit, so efficient. No timidity, no hesitations, no falterings . . . with complete assurance, with absolute confidence' (pp. 31–2). The effect of the operation is to project her from a world in which she is at ease into the visual equivalent of the linguistic displacement of *Translations* in which everything is raw, new and unnamed: 'a very foreign world, too. And disturbing; even alarming' (p. 50). In the aftermath of the ultimately unsuccessful operation, Molly inhabits what she terms a 'borderline country' and, in the most significant of qualifications, changes the declaration 'I'm at home there' for the more guarded 'Well . . . at ease there' (p. 67). The lines from the surgeon Mr Rice resonate across Friel's plays of the 1990s and back to *Translations* itself, all works which engage with the sense that it is history, ritual, 'home' which provide psychological stability for all subjects, not only the postcolonial, in the postmodern world of flux and fissure: 'She wasn't in her old blind world – she was exiled from that. And the sighted world, which she had never found hospitable, wasn't available to her anymore' (p. 59).

While *Molly Sweeney*, in common with *Faith Healer*, is a play of voices and memories rather than action, there is one event referred to which summarises Friel's most recent expression of his fundamental commitment to 'the proper name'; namely the story of the relocation of the badgers. The 'saving' of the badgers involves their relocation to a new home, but once released from captivity 'they went wild' and in a 'mad panic' which reverses Molly's wild but graceful dance in her blindness, they rush 'straight back to the old sett at the edge of the water – the one we'd destroyed with all our digging' (pp. 60–1). Declan Kiberd may be correct to assert that Friel 'is no nostalgic revivalist, no exponent of the dreamy backward look',[61] but it is equally clear that there is a powerful sentimental connection to 'the homology between a culture, a people, or a nation and its particular terrain'.[62] It is the implications of this position which remain to be addressed.

In the postmodern moment, as argued by Homi Bhabha, 'the transmission of *cultures of survival* does not occur in the ordered *musée imaginaire* of national cultures with their claims to the authentic "past" and a "living present"',[63] rather the time for 'organic notions of cultural value'[64] has been replaced by the flow and flux of transnational hybridity. Aijaz Ahmad, however, contests this 'vacuous . . . notion of cultural hybridity',[65] asserting that this 'stripping of all cultures of their historicity and density . . . subordinates cultures, consumers and critics alike to a form of untethering and moral loneliness that wallows in the depthlessness and whimsicality of postmodernism – the cultural logic of Late Capitalism.'[66] The idea that such depthlessness can be progressively, rather than regressively countered by a sense of origin and authenticity is a fundamental problem with Ahmad's anti-postmodern position; indeed, as he recognises, 'pure identity politics'[67] can produce protofascisms. But, as Benita Parry asks, 'Does revisiting the repositories of memory and cultural survivals in the cause of post-colonial refashioning have a fixed retrograde valency?' The question is unambiguously answered: 'Such censure is surely dependent on who is doing the remembering and why.'[68] Indeed, as argued by Ien Ang, it is the stress on authenticity and origin which 'provides a counterpoint to the most facile forms of postmodernist nomadology',[69] and across Friel's drama, from the flirtation with hybridity in *Translations* to the residual essentialism of *Molly Sweeney*, 'the driving imperative is to salvage centred, bounded and coherent identities – placed identities for placeless times.'[70]

The Failed Words of Brian Friel

David Krause

Words alone are certain good.

– W. B. Yeats's 'The Happy Shepherd' (1889)[1]

But I've gotta use words when I talk to you,

– T. S. Eliot's 'Sweeney Agonistes' (1930)[2]

Dancing as if language no longer existed because words were no longer necessary. . . .

– Brian Friel's *Dancing at Lughnasa* (1990)[3]

I want to begin by talking about words and how they are necessary on the page in order to succeed on the stage. In the summer of 1994, Redmond O'Hanlon, a lecturer at University College, Dublin, joined the chorus of Irish critics who had attacked the Abbey Theatre's recent revival of *The Doctor's Dilemma* as an illustration of how the excessively 'wordy' Bernard Shaw might be more of a bore than a genius in the theatre. 'Words, words, words,' Dr O'Hanlon was reported as saying in the *Irish Times* of 20 July 1994 when asked why Shaw's supposedly dated plays have remained a valid subject for academic study if not for stage production: 'Traditionally,' he said, 'academics find it very hard to deal with a text as a performance text. They prefer to approach it as a literary text and therefore Shaw has plenty for them. They are terrified of the notion that a play text is a very incomplete thing, and that it's just a scenario for a performance. Most academics can't deal with that. They prefer words that can stand up on their own, far away from the stage.'

These simplistic comments in favour of the stage raise the misleading notion that drama and theatre are opposing forces, which ignores the obvious fact that mutually dependent upon each other. It is not my aim, however, to defend the often prolix Shaw here – although I believe I could make a strong case for two of his best plays, *Pygmalion* and *St Joan,* both of them succeeding brilliantly on the page as well as the stage, mainly owing to the two remarkable young heroines in those plays whose sharp and memorable words cleverly and comically expose the folly of the supposedly superior men in their lives. That spirited victory for women is another matter of considerable significance, although it should be apparent that, contrary to Dr O'Hanlon's remarks, the actresses who perform the lively roles of Eliza and Joan are able to distinguish themselves on the stage because Shaw had initially distinguished himself with eloquent words on the page. Rather than 'just a scenario for a performance', what we encounter on the stage will be 'just a performance' unless the words of the text are as distinctive and inevitable as the notes in a Mozart sonata – or as close to that ideal as one can expect. It is safe to say that the words or notes contain the infinite possibilities of a fine performance.

At the same time that the Abbey Theatre was performing *The Doctor's Dilemma,* the Gate Theatre across the city produced Brian Friel's new play, *Molly Sweeney* on 9 August 1994.[4] While there is no direct connection between these two quite different plays, there are some page-and-stage correspondences that indicate why the actress cast as Friel's young heroine might be limited by a 'wordy' misconception of her character. If Friel's Molly Sweeney, with her static and one-dimensional monologues, cannot compare to Shaw's fluid and fully rounded Eliza and Joan – or, in a broader and probably unfair comparison, to Joyce's Molly Bloom in her sensuous flow of uninhibited monologues – Friel's failure can be traced back to the pages of his text. And, in another aspect of his ambitious failure, Friel's decision to be the director of his play means that he was responsible for the stage as well as the page.

I intend here to examine Friel's most recent three plays, *Molly Sweeney* (1994), *Wonderful Tennessee* (1993) and *Dancing at Lughnasa* (1990), because I suspect that a series of similar dramatic intentions reveal a pattern of recurring problems with the language in these works. They are all memory plays based upon recollections of possibly 'wonderful' or miraculous experiences in the past which are deflated or destroyed by the harsh realities of the present. This denial of expectations leads to somewhat predictable and stock resolutions for the characters who are all victims of circumstances beyond their control. These people look back with nostalgia, not anger, and for their mood of hope and resignation Friel gives them soft and self-pitying words that tend to sentimentalise the impossible, yet curiously redemptive, quest for those elusive moments.

In several of his more successful plays, such as *Faith Healer* (1979) and *Translations* (1980), Friel's troubled characters lash out and refuse to seek that nostalgic comfort in defeat which we find in his recent work. There are a number of problems of inconsistent characterisation and vague motivation in the three latest plays, but the main failure lies in Friel's inability to create a vital and resilient language, a spoken idiom of rich and sharp words – what Synge called 'richness' and 'reality' in his preface to *The Playboy of the Western World* (1907)[5] – words that do not deflate or discredit the unfulfilled aspirations of the characters.

Perhaps I should add, as a rejoinder to Dr O'Hanlon's superficial remarks about page and stage, that I saw all three plays on the stage first, before I was able to confirm my disappointment by locating the source of the failures in the published texts – with the exception of *Molly Sweeney*, which was not available in print when the following comments were written.

I

Molly Sweeney

Beautifully wrought and exquisitely written . . . Go see.

– *Irish Times*

Superb . . . it is a must.

– *Irish Press*

I urge you to see this challenging, absorbing drama.

– *Irish Independent*

In spite of the glowing Irish reviews, Brian Friel has once again promised more than he has performed with his new play, *Molly Sweeney*. The heading for David Nowlan's embarrassingly adjectival review in the *Irish Times* (10 August 1994) reads 'Friel's Simple Premise Yields Rich Drama'; and although what we observe on the stage of the Gate Theatre presents an all too 'simple premise' about a blind woman whose sight is miraculously and ironically restored by difficult surgery, the three characters involved in the story struggle with a potentially 'rich drama' that is not fully realised. The theatrical execution is unfortunately too static and perhaps as simple as the premise.

It is a 'story' more than a drama because Friel made the crucial decision to *narrate* rather than *dramatize* his premise and its unfolding; he allowed his three characters to offer a series of separate, if sometimes overlapping, monologues about their failed lives. They never talk to each other; they narrate or emote their hopes and fears to the voyeuristic audience. Even in the more deeply probing and more sinister *Faith Healer*, where Friel had also employed this somewhat static three-character monologue form, the conflicting voices create the suspense of powerful but limited speeches as in a radio play.

Most of Molly's monologues or set-speeches are based upon a total recall of her childhood after she had lost her sight as a baby. Somewhat too readily and vividly she remembers all the simple pleasures of her early years with her father, and we learn that her sightless world was redeemed by her insight into the world of nature, of the flowers she loves and with which her father associates her. Molly's blindness has therefore become an idyllic state of freedom from the sighted world. This is indeed a simple and common enough premise. Along the way she mentions her mother, who suffered from such severe depression she had to be kept in an asylum (p. 15); and this pregnant detail prepares us for the not-so-surprising shock at the end. When Molly's sight is restored, if indeed her vision does fully return, she is unable to cope with the harsh reality of the sighted world that appears as a nightmarish half-world. She is therefore, like her mother, confined to a hospital-asylum.

There is an apparent parallel here to Synge's *The Well of the Saints* (1905) where the blind Douls, whose sight was miraculously restored, fight back and opt for their original state of blindness rather than endure the insensitivities and cruelties of the sighted world.[6] Unlike the aggressive Douls, however, who are rounded characters with tainted as well as attractive traits, Molly remains a one-dimensional figure transfixed, trapped by her situation. Friel, as director as well as playwright, did not give Catherine Byrne, the actress who plays Molly on one level of crisp articulation and beaming smiles virtually throughout her performance, an opportunity to develop direct, or subtle, contrasts between her state of grace in blindness and the shock of terror or despair in her new state of sightedness.

Who was at fault here? Friel the playwright? Friel the director? Or Ms. Byrne the actress? In a short essay in the Gate Theatre programme, 'In Search of Miracles', Richard Pine, who is identified as having written a book on Friel's drama, comments on what presumably should be Molly's two conflicting attitudes: 'the brief light of childhood and that of her last autism . . . her dance of anger and despair.' It is precisely that disturbing contrast between the compensatory light of childhood and the sudden dance of despair that is missing from this performance of the play. Only once, for a fleeting moment near the end, does Byrne's Molly seem to assume a brief countenance of depression, or a vague hint of what might be autism, after which she promptly returns to her crisp speech, becoming her smiling and unaware self again.

Only Mr Rice, the uneasy ophthalmologist who constantly surveys his failures as an inadequate surgeon and subsequently a betrayed husband (and now hiding out in the little hospital in Ballybeg – Friel's mythic village) is given an opportunity to examine and judge himself. The urbane and veteran actor T. P. McKenna plays him with the profound anguish of a world-weary Chekhovian doctor. His past defeats set up an illusory sense of victory after he operates on Molly and restores her sight – only for him to discover that she cannot cope with reality, any more than he can now in his mock-heroic state. McKenna's tormented and stumbling Mr Rice – unfortunately constricted to monologues by Friel's radio-play form – is potentially the most complex and most interesting character in the play, yet he is only given a tangential function in relation to Molly's unresolved fate.

This leaves the third voice, Molly's husband Frank, played with farcical enthusiasm by the inventive Mark Lambert, whose lively character is not allowed to develop, to become aware of his failures and try to cope with them – or most important of all, to come to terms with Molly's fate. This lack of awareness and sensitivity could be read as one of two darker aspects of the play, but it can also be seen as a failure of authorial imagination. Friel makes Frank a colourful eccentric, somewhat like the fanciful Casimir in an earlier play, *Aristocrats* (1979), except that Frank is drawn in one fixed dimension as a man in search of special projects that inevitably collapse. One of his early comic passions, trying to raise Iranian goats in Ireland for their rare cheese, fails. Frank then becomes involved in a series of equally absurd plans, until he meets and marries Molly, whose restored sight becomes his central passion in the play, a passion destined to be defeated.

Why then did Friel send Frank off on a new project in Abyssinia (now Ethiopia) at the end of the play, without a word from him about Molly and her tragic condition, completely ignoring his intense love for her? Why did Frank, who was so eloquent about his Iranian goats (pp. 18–20), so enlightened about his library reading on the sensation and perception theories of Locke and Berkeley (p. 21), theories that might carry hints about Molly's disturbed condition – why did this passionate and probing Frank leave for Africa without a word about the shattered Molly? Why didn't her fate deserve as much concern as those absurd goats?

While it might be possible to say that there are some 'beautiful', 'challenging' and 'absorbing' theatrical tableaux in this ambitious and disturbing play, it must be conceded that Friel's continuing quest for nostalgic and elusive miracles (in his last three works, *Molly, Tennessee* and *Lughnasa*) remains a courageous but static and failed artistic endeavour. Here, the tragicomic premise is simple but the complex character of Molly Sweeney is stillborn.

II

Wonderful Tennessee

The drama is made serious – in the French sense of the word – not by the degree in which it is taken up with problems that are serious in themselves, but by the degree in which it gives the nourishment, not very easy to define, on which our imaginations live. We should not go to the theatre as we go to a chemist's, or a dram-shop, but as we go to a dinner, where the food we need is taken with pleasure and excitement. . . . The drama, like the symphony, does not teach or prove anything.

– J. M. Synge, preface to *The Tinker's Wedding: A Comedy in Two Acts* (1907)[7]

A play that is obviously and often obtrusively concerned with the problem of purgation and salvation rituals, *Wonderful Tennessee* is a transparent parable about six characters in search of an illusive and presumably holy island, 'Oileán Draiócht̓a. . . . Island of Otherness,' we are told, 'Island of Mystery. . . . The wonderful - the sacred.'[8] The three married couples are outsiders rather than the usual natives of Friel's mythical village in Donegal, for they have arrived on Ballybeg pier after a four-hour ride in a minibus, presumably from Dublin, where Terry, the host and guide of the adventure, is in business as a 'turf accountant' or bookie (p. 12). Now they are waiting for the local ferryman to bring them out to the fabled island off the coast for their pilgrimage, and while they wait they sing songs and tell stories. During this time, Friel gives them an opportunity to drop a more or less constant catalogue of weighty Greek, Celtic and Catholic symbolic references related to their spiritual quest.

Unlike Synge's desired non-didactic drama, Friel's play, while it may not prove anything, certainly aims to teach the characters, and possibly the audience, that a journey to a holy place, even if unfulfilled, is, by its very intention, good for the soul. This spiritual therapy is confirmed by many incidents, particularly at the start when we learn that the Ballybeg ferryman is appropriately named Carlin, suggesting a connection to Charon, the ferryman of Greek mythology who conducts the souls of the dead across the river Styx to the redemptive Underworld. No need to belabor the link between those who wait for an invisible Carlin and for an invisible Godot.

Thereafter, a number of classical allusions remind us that Friel has created something of an echo-chamber of Greek rites of sacrifice and redemption throughout the play. Angela, who we hear 'teaches Classics' (p. 21), seldom allows us to forget this fact with her repeated invocations of orgiastic celebrations in honour of Dionysus and the strange blood-sacrifice rituals of the Eleusinian Mysteries. The ubiquitous Angela could safely be called the blatant maenad of the play. For example, she praises the cancer-stricken George for his grand accordion music by kissing him, placing a seaweed wreath on his head and saying, 'You should be wearing a toga and playing a lyre and gorging yourself with black grapes. . . . There! Dionysus!' (pp. 10–11). When she leads the group in a wild song and dance version of 'I Want to be Happy,' Friel adds in the stage directions that they perform *'a clownish, parodic conga dance, heads rolling, arms flying – a hint of the maenadic'* (p. 6) – those frenzied maenadic creatures who celebrate the orgiastic and sacrificial cult of Dionysus.

When the pilgrims are not singing and dancing while they wait for Carlin, they tell stories and we hear a number of significant tales about sacrifice and redemption, tales that draw connections between Greek, Celtic and Catholic miracles. As the host of the group, Terry conveniently narrates the background of the mysterious 'Island of Otherness,' which curiously enough he bought with the last of his bookie funds. He explains how at the tender age of seven he once made a pilgrimage to the island with his father who, according to Terry's sister Trish, 'believed in nothing' (p. 21). Friel's six pilgrims might be trying to find something to believe in, although this spiritual message is telegraphed too often. One of Friel's problems, as a playwright, may be that he is more concerned with his parable than his people, who are each identified by a set of fixed traits in their one-dimensional roles.

Then there is the problem Friel creates by allowing the various symbolic stories to sound as if they were all conceived by an extraordinarily knowledgeable playwright, rather than by the supposedly ordinary characters. As storytellers, these people suddenly become very learned in ways that betray Friel's scrupulous method of research. This ventriloquism can readily be illustrated. For example, if Terry's story about the 'spectral, floating island' sounds too erudite and lyrical for a Dublin bookie, he implies he memorised some of it '[f]rom a pamphlet . . . [his] father had' (p. 18), but then he goes on to recall exactly what happened when he was seven and spent a purgatorial night on the island with his unbelieving father:

> We fasted from the night before, I remember. And for the night you were on the island you were given only bread and water. [. . .] There were three beds – you know, mounds of stone – and every time you went round a bed you said certain prayers and then picked up a stone from the bottom of the mound and placed it on the top. [. . .] And I remember a holy well, and my father filling a bottle with holy water and stuffing the neck with grass [. . .]. And there were crutches and walking sticks hanging on the bush; and bits of cloth [. . .] a handkerchief, a piece of a shawl—bleached and turning green from exposure. Votive offerings – isn't that the English word? And there's the ruins of a Middle Age church dedicated to Saint Conall. (*To* Frank) Isn't that the period you're writing your book about? (pp. 19–20, intervening dialogue omitted)

Terry's carefully chosen words here make him sound like a Friel pamphlet. He goes on to say that the pilgrims of that time brought poitín to the island and took part in 'drunken orgies', which predictably inspires Angela to cry out with a salute, 'Saint Dionysus' (p. 20). Gradually, the Greek rituals assume Catholic affinities and Friel strains to make the symbolism fit the stories. Did the pilgrims go to a sacred place to celebrate Dionysus or to seek a cure? Perhaps they go to bear witness to a holy shrine, 'to attest', as Bema says, to its sacredness (p. 20), which is what they do at the end when, as good Catholics, they ignore Dionysus and enact the ritual of votive offering mentioned in Terry's story.

There are other storytellers whose tales fit together to support the playwright's preconceived plan for an overlapping of sacred symbols. As Terry indicated in mentioning the medieval church dedicated to St Conall, Frank is presumably writing a book about the same saint and the period in which the invention of the clock allowed monks to be regimented by timed prayers with miraculous results. Although those early clocks were primitive, Frank admits, he launches into the following rhapsody:

> [. . .] crude time-pieces; sophisticated egg-timers. But with these new instruments you could break the twenty-four hours into exact sections. And once you could do that, once you could waken your monks up at *fixed* hours two or three times a night, suddenly [. . .]. Think about it. At the stroke of midnight – at 2.00 a.m. – at 4.00 a.m. – at 6.00 a.m. – you chase your monks out of their warm beds. Into a freezing chapel. Fasting. Deprived of sleep. Repeating the same chant over and over again. And because they're hungry and disoriented and giddy for want of sleep [. . .] of course they hallucinate – see apparitions – whatever [. . .]. Whatever it is we desire but can't express. What is beyond language. The inexpressible. The ineffable. (pp. 40–1)

If this clever explanation of hallucinations – in a play that contains little humour and less irony – provides a deflation as well as a defence of miracles, it is another example of the playwright's superimposed wise words, because Frank is so often a frivolous and teasing twit throughout the play that it is difficult to believe he could be capable of writing a profound book on any subject. Friel also allows the mundane Frank to adopt the unlikely persona of a hallucinating monk when he suddenly thinks he sees the spectral island rising out of the mist. A symbolic dolphin dances for him, and he declares he has had his 'Ballybeg epiphany' (p. 60). Frank is out of character here, and it is Friel who has had the 'ineffable' experience. This epiphanic ritual strikes again on a more Catholic than Greek motif when the distressed, but suddenly anointed, Bema tells the extraordinary story of the miracle of the 'Holy House of Loreto' – how 'in the year 1294 [. . .] a small, white-washed house' flew from Nazareth to Loreto:

> That small, whitewashed house rose straight up into the air, right away up into the sky. It hung there for a few seconds as if it were a bird finding its bearings. Then it floated – flew – over the Mediterranean Sea [. . .] until it came to [. . .] a small town

> called Loreto in the centre of Italy. Then it began to descend, slowly down and down and down [. . .]. And there it sits to this day. And it is known as the Holy House of Loreto – a place of pilgrimage, revered and attested to by hundreds of thousands of pilgrims every year. (pp. 44–5)

Loreto is not a Greek shrine. Nevertheless, in a final and not particularly successful attempt to connect classical and Catholic rituals, Friel chooses Terry to tell one more story, a dark tale about the symbolic killing of a young Irish boy who was torn to pieces many years ago on the holy 'Island of Otherness' by a band of wild revellers full of 'wine [. . .] music and [. . .] dancing' (p. 63). The House of Loreto has been overwhelmed by this bloodletting allusion to the *Bacchae* of Euripides. Terry's sister Trish is shocked by the sacrificial story; she calls it 'hateful' and the island 'evil' (p. 64). Angela, however, appropriately and accurately associates it with the Eleusinian Mysteries of the life-restoring harvest in which the seasons have to change and there must be a death before there can be a rebirth (p. 72). But is it possible for the Catholic Trish to be reconciled to the Eleusinian Angela?

At this point, therefore, and probably much sooner, one has to wonder if Friel's dualistic parable is entirely valid – if the uninhibited savagery of the Dionysian rituals is compatible with the ascetic and pietistic rituals of Irish Catholicism. Can those frenzied maenads who gorge on the juice of black grapes join hands with the devout worshippers of holy water and Holy Loreto? Friel's answer in favour of a tempered non-Greek resolution comes at the conclusion when the six pilgrims, acting as if they had been rehearsed in Terry's story about his childhood visit to the island, place their symbolic stones on a mound by the rotting life-belt stand, which is described as 'cruciform in shape' ([vii]). Then they place pieces of their clothing on the makeshift cross as votive offerings and they depart, singing happily.

The recurring outbursts of song – folk ballads, popular songs, hymns – are meant to maintain the joyful and reverent mood of the play with their significant titles and words about the 'happy' and 'wonderful' spirit of the pilgrims – that title word 'wonderful', for example, is repeated forty-five times in a text of seventy-eight pages.

The main song, 'Down by the Cane-Brake,' tells the story about lovers 'high and dry on the O-hi-o' who dream about taking their boat – a ferryboat? –'back to Tennessee' (p. 33) – their ideal island? If the songs provide background music for the play, the characters unfortunately become background figures for the parable; as a result, Friel's symbolic pilgrimage dominates the characters, who happen to have troubled personal problems that are submerged.

In what might be called an undeveloped subtext, the people's play, Terry's wife Bema is in the midst of a breakdown and feeling suicidal because she is unable to bear children; as an apparently bankrupt bookie, the lavish living Terry is having an unlikely, as well as guiltless, affair with the erudite Angela, so busy proclaiming her classical allusions she has no qualms about betraying her sick sister Bema; as the aspiring writer, Frank plays inane tricks on everyone but remains madly in love with his unfaithful wife Angela; George, who cheerfully plays the accordion while stoically dying of throat cancer, is the husband of Trish, Terry's sister, who may be forgetful and silly at times but remains faithful.

All we know about these characters lies submerged below their general attitudes, and Friel never gives them an opportunity to confront each other or themselves in their suspended situations. Although often influenced by the tragicomedies of Chekhov, Friel must have decided to minimise or suppress the typically Chekhovian conflicts of his three couples in order to pursue his parable. It is also possible that such dramatic confrontations could not be developed because the fixed form and single setting of the play place all six characters on the pier practically all the time, ruling out any alternating or overlapping *agons* or conflicts when two or three people might break off from the group and clash, ineptly but directly.

In a parallel and constricting way, Friel here creates something like the static effect that goes with the monologues in *Molly Sweeney*, where the characters are locked into their isolated narrative voices. The playwright continues to suffer from the limitations of a chosen form, which here remains close to a radio play. The hortatory and superimposed words of the pilgrims are a problem, as were the dreamy and sentimental words of Molly. Finally, Friel must have felt committed to the demands of an overbearing didactic impulse.

III

Dancing at Lughnasa

This matter, I think, is of importance, for in countries where the imagination of the people, and the language they use, is rich and living, it is possible for a writer to be rich and copious in his words, and at the same time to give the reality which is the root of all poetry, in a comprehensive and natural form.

– J. M. Synge's Preface to *The Playboy of the Western World* (1907)[9]

It should not come as a surprise that a play might be both theatrically effective and artistically disappointing at the same time. This is not an uncommon contradiction in the theatre, where the visual imagery sometimes dominates the verbal imagery. Synge insisted that language in the theatre should have a literary as well as a theatrical context, that the words should be 'rich and copious', and based upon 'the reality which is the root of all poetry'. In *Dancing at Lughnasa* Friel has created a world of genuine characters, deeply rooted in reality, but his words, the language of his people, far from being rich or copious, lack the essential and fulsome poetry and rhythm of dramatic speech. He has written a play that is more attractive for the eye than the ear.

After seeing a very popular production of *Dancing at Lughnasa* and then reading the published text, I suspect that audience approval and positive reviews do not automatically mean high artistic achievement. The play has been acclaimed in Dublin, London and New York; the casts have performed with distinction, and with comparable contributions by directors and set designers; but Friel seems to have been reluctant to probe below the attractive surface of his predictable and comforting reality in order to release the rich poetry of drama. He has constructed a memory play that recreates the aura of an idyllic past, an indulgence in nostalgia that calls for a sentimental tone and flattened language that do not lead to a very complex or profound experience. Webster's Dictionary provides an appropriate definition of nostalgia: 'a wistful or excessively sentimental sometimes morbid yearning for return to or of some past period or irrecoverable condition'.[10]

Friel's narrator remembers a wistful, often comic and sometimes morbid tale about the frustrated but animated five Mundy sisters in the little town of Ballybeg and their attempts to escape from their uneventful and uncertain daily lives. Michael, the narrator, now a young man, relives what he calls a 'nostalgic' time back in 1936 when he was a boy of seven, particularly two days of that period that '[fascinate]' him so much he says he perceives them as 'dream music [. . .] so alluring and so mesmeric that the afternoon is bewitched, maybe haunted, by it [. . .] everybody seems to be floating on those sweet sounds' (p. 71).

Part of the problem of the play might be that those alluring visual sounds, often dance sounds, become so sweet and mesmeric that we are meant to float along with Michael's sentimental reverie as the only way to ease the inevitable hardships of life. The dream reaches a high point when his five frustrated aunts, reacting impulsively to the sudden music that blares out of their eccentric radio set, the 'Marconi', break into a frenzy of uninhibited dancing, as their tribute to the festival of Lughnasa, the Celtic god of August whose pagan ritual commemorates the annual harvest (pp. 21–2). That wild dance, which exhilarates the audience as well as the aunts, becomes the central and perhaps too easily earned symbol of the play, although it is theatrically an exciting visual and rhythmic symbol of Friel's theme of repression and sublimation. It is a memorable moment, and while it is enough to sustain Michael's haunted nostalgia, it cannot entirely encourage us to overlook the morbid or hard moments that run through the play, the collapse of the family and the tragic death of two aunts. It is a commonplace emblem of romantic poetry, often parodied for its oversimplified sentimentality, that love conquers all, *amor vincit omnia.* Are we now to take comfort from the Lughnasa emblem that dance conquers all, *saltatio vincit omnia*? Perhaps not, happy lovers and dancers might reply, but it feels so good. Feeling is all?

Another character who apparently believes that dance conquers all is Gerry Evans, the errant and ne'er-do-well father of Michael by the unwed and impressionable mother Chris. Gerry, however, is so unreliable and unbelievable, he leaves behind too many false hopes and disenchanted dancing aunts. Then in something like a quixotic afterthought, he decides to go off to fight for the Loyalists in Spain – much to the distress of the Catholic loyalist Kate – but this lone reference to the world of strife outside Ballybeg in the 1930s is too marginal to be developed in any significant way. Furthermore, many mature people in the audience, unlike the innocent characters on the stage, know something about the implications of the Spanish Civil War. Perhaps the well-meaning but irresponsible Gerry is a dangling and shallow character who undermines the sublimation motif by turning the vital ritual of dancing into a frivolous caper.

The most interesting, and the only intriguing and complex, character in the play is Father Jack, the dying and distracted uncle who, after returning from twenty-five years as a Missionary priest in a leper colony in Africa, has, ironically, exchanged his Catholic faith for an acceptance of the Ugandan faith. In his vivid if sometimes broken memory, we hear him embracing the powerful African ritual of the harvest, which is curiously close to the pagan ritual of Lughnasa. Here, Friel's implications are enormously resonant. He seems to have a unique gift for creating such eccentrically and independently eloquent characters as Father Jack; for example, there is also that fantasising and frolicking jester, Casimir O'Donnell, in *Aristocrats*.

Except for Father Jack, and in a much less impressive way Michael, who is so sentimentally garrulous in his celebration of nostalgia, none of the characters, particularly the crucial aunts, are eloquent, let alone copious with words.[11] Seamus Deane in his glowing introduction to Friel's *Selected Plays* (1984) correctly reminds us that 'Brilliance in the theatre has, for Irish dramatists, been linguistic.' Speaking of some of the six plays in this volume, Deane says these are 'fiercely *spoken* plays,' and then adds: 'Language, in a variety of modes and presented in a number of recorded ways, dominates to the exclusion of almost everything else.'[12]

Is it not strange to note, therefore, that in *Dancing at Lughnasa*, which has been called one of Friel's most successful plays, almost everything else seems to dominate, especially dancing, to the exclusion of language – aside from the ironic eloquence of Father Jack – with no sign of a variety of modes or 'recorded ways', whatever they might be? To be blunt, the five aunts seldom if ever resort to richly or 'fiercely *spoken*' words; no striking or memorable phrases leap out at us; no words I wanted to take pleasure in or remember when I saw the play and later read the text. If Friel decided to write this play in a flattened style, using commonplace words because his Ballybeg people in reality lived commonplace lives, he failed to allow for the distinction between life and art. It should be obvious that the artist does much more than hold up a mirror or tape recorder to catch life, which cannot be reduced to literally accurate words or pictures. Synge and O'Casey in drama, Wordsworth and Whitman in poetry, among many others in both fields, have vividly illustrated how the oral tradition, the *spoken* language, can provide abundant sources of rich and poetic words, and a wide range of idiomatic imagery.

An examination of some representative passages in Friel's play indicates that the characters seldom speak in vivid, rhythmic or figurative language. Michael's comments do not rise above gushes of nostalgia that are intended to pass for 'poetical' memory, and there are no signs of genuinely colourful or striking talk by the aunts, who are denied introspective or complex thoughts of any length or depth. Kate has only one relatively long but plain speech about how the family is 'collaps[ing]' (pp. 35–6). Maggie drifts into an unremarkable and rambling speech about a dance contest (p. 20). Rose explains in a matter-of-fact way how she went to meet a young man (p. 59). They never search beneath their skins and on the whole tend to talk in brief and banal monosyllables. For example, this is how they react to the arrival of the philandering Gerry:

Kate How dare Mr Evans show his face here.

Maggie He wants to see his son, doesn't he?

Kate There's no welcome for that creature here.

Rose Who hid my Sunday shoes?

Maggie We'll have to give him his tea.

Kate I don't see why we should.

Maggie And there's nothing in the house. (p. 24)

Ordinary life is often full of small talk, but dramatic language on stage should be heightened to sound extraordinary in its seemingly ordinary manner. In another example, after Gerry dances with Agnes in Act 2, their dialogue limps along in the following staccato manner:

Gerry You're a great dancer, Aggie.

Agnes No, I'm not.

Gerry You're a superb dancer.

Agnes No, I'm not.

Gerry You should be a professional dancer.

Agnes Too late for that.

Gerry You could teach dancing in Ballybeg.

Agnes That's all they need.

Gerry Maybe it is! (p. 65)

Attempts by the aunts to reach for colourful imagery are limited to three trite similes and two trite metaphors in Act 1. Chris says her hair looks 'like a whinbush' (pp. 5, 27); Rose mentions someone whose 'trousers caught fire and he went up like a torch' (p. 16); Maggie says one young fellow was '[b]ald as an egg' (p. 19). Maggie calls the judges at a dance contest 'blind drunk' (p. 20); Gerry wants to be believed by saying 'Cross the old ticker' (p. 28). In Act 2, there are two bland figures of speech: Maggie says of herself, 'this chicken is weak with hunger' (p. 57); and again it is Maggie who says Gerry and Father Jack in their fancy hats are '[s]trutting about like a pair of peacocks!' (p. 69).

Chicken and peacocks, that's all. And Friel's peacock image is innocuous, in contrast, for example, to O'Casey's sharply ironic exposure of a cheerfully vain and comically deceitful 'paycock'. An even more significant aspect of this contrast involves the way O'Casey – like Synge, Behan and Beckett – takes a tragicomic double view of a character, giving him or her, a 'Captain' Jack Boyle in *Juno and the Paycock* or a Bessie Burgess in *The Plough and the Stars,* contradictory or multiple traits: attractive and culpable, cowardly and wise, arrogant and courageous. And with shrewd variations, all these Irish dramatists share this dual and ironic approach to character with Chekhov, for it is also an outstanding technique in his dark comedies. Although Friel says he has a special affinity for Chekhov, little Chekhovian influence can be found in *Dancing at Lughnasa,* where his five aunts are such straight and non-ironic characters, it would not be appropriate to suggest a parallel between the Five Sisters and Chekhov's *Three Sisters,* a play which Friel has actually translated. The Friel sisters, each in their own transparent and limited ways, are locked into such rigid and one-dimensional portraits that they are as predictable as they are superficially attractive. Only Father Jack reflects some uneasy and credible dualism as he struggles to cope with his convoluted and tragicomic acceptance of the wild African rituals, in contrast to his vanishing clerical Catholicism. On this point, Friel's complex characterisation of Father Jack's African and Christian impulses is vastly more successful than the similar attempts to reconcile contradictory rituals in *Wonderful Tennessee.* Furthermore, in the New York production, Father Jack was played so movingly and imaginatively by the very sensitive Donal Donnelly, with such a mixed air of mysterious sadness and bumbling bravado, that many palpable Chekhovian as well as Irish strokes of tragicomedy were clearly evident.

In an overall final view of the play, however, perhaps an embarrassing parallel to Thornton Wilder is more appropriate than a flattering comparison to Chekhov. Wilder's *Our Town* is also a sentimental memory play that celebrates the simple good things of life through the use of a nostalgic narrator who glorifies everyday events in Grover's Corners, as Michael remembers and celebrates the simple good times in Ballybeg. Wilder's Emily helps the Stage Manager by remembering things like 'Mama's sunflowers. And food and coffee. And new-ironed dresses and hot baths . . . and sleeping and waking up.'[13] Friel's Michael looks back and remembers as the aunts act out their simple pleasures, singing songs and laughing, picking and eating bilberries, washing their hair, applauding when the 'Marconi' performs and, above all, letting go with the sheer joy of dancing. To be sure, there are sad deaths too in Grover's Corners, as there is the pathetic death of the two aunts from Ballybeg; but life goes on in both towns, thanks to the glowing and sentimental memory of the Stage Manager and Michael. In both plays, it is thc memory of the ordinary happy times that endures. It is the memory of dancing not death that overwhelms Michael as he delivers his mesmerised curtain speech:

> But there is one memory of that Lughnasa time that visits me most often. [. . .] When I remember it, I think of it as dancing. Dancing with eyes half closed because to open them would break the spell. Dancing as if language had surrendered to movement [. . .] this wordless ceremony. [. . .] Dancing as if language no longer existed because words were no longer necessary. . . . (*Slowly bring up the music. Slowly bring down the lights.*) (p. 71)

Dancing conquers all? Why do I resist this sweet spell, this half-shut-eyed vision, this oversimplification of life and Lughnasa, life anywhere, in which a nostalgic memory of dancing makes words unnecessary, as the music rises and the lights fade? Why do I prefer my own memory of Synge who insisted that words on the stage must be 'rich and copious'; why do I prefer my own memory of Yeats who from the beginning in one of his earliest poems assured us that 'Words alone are certain good'?

Memory, Art, *Lieux de Mémoire* in Brian Friel's *The Home Place*[1]

Csilla Bertha

Brian Friel frames the action in *The Home Place* (2005) by performances of a distant choir singing Thomas Moore's famous 'Oft in the Stilly Night', reset in three-part harmony and conducted by a drunken schoolmaster, heard in Ballybeg Lodge in the opening and closing scene. Utilising the song, he brings to the surface interiorised communal and hidden personal memories, emotions, desires. I am going to discuss in this chapter how memory, evoked by an artwork, in this case a haunting song, operates within another artwork, here a play. Building on the theories of *lieux de mémoire* by the influential French philosopher and historian, Pierre Nora, I will analyse how this song that preserves collective memories sets into motion further personal memories, responses and even action. Through remembering and embracing those memories, one of the play's protagonists finds her way back from the liminality of her position to the centre of her life, her identity, and moves towards emotional, spiritual homecoming. Remembrance is an existential relation to the past and to the self; memory is essential to both individual and communal identity. Sites of memory located in art may point to the possibility of liberation from colonial suppression, as it happens in the play's action and through that metaphorically to liberation from defacing globalisation – the reality at the time of Friel's writing the play. At the same time, Friel's play makes audiences aware of the impossibility of going back to any pure, authentic source culture as Moore's poems and songs themselves grew out of both Irish and English traditions. Yet despite all the irony Moore's songs and the play's choir director are imbued in, Moore's oeuvre does hold a mirror up to the Irish caught between those traditions. The poet in writing those poems, the choir director in keeping them alive and his daughter in listening to and absorbing them, all exercise not only the 'duty to remember' but – at least the

Irish protagonists – also the 'duty to forget' (Paul Riceour) in stepping beyond personal wounds and moving towards forgiveness. This ethical aspect of memory, combined with the magical power of internalised cultural memory and the sacred conveyed by art, all converge in the 'tremendous mystery' (Hedwig Schwall) of the final moments of *The Home Place*.

Art as Site of Memory

Sites of memory have always been crucially important in the life of a community, but their role has been acknowledged and theorised only in the last few decades due, in great part, to Pierre Nora, who reinstalled memory into its significant position in relation to history. He famously observed that those sites 'where memory crystallizes and secretes itself' are created and revered when memory itself is fading, and they are needed just 'because there are no longer *milieux de mémoire*, real environments of memory'.[2] Thus, the sites of memory are positioned between memory and history, spontaneous and deliberate, individual and officially communal remembering. Almost anything can become a *lieu de mémoire*; archives, museums, anniversaries, memorials, celebrations, objects, events, symbols, concepts and so forth depending on the significance attached to them and on the 'will to remember' (p. 19). Within the broad scale of *lieux de mémoire* Nora, however, does not pay much attention to the arts. But clearly works of art, although taking a unique position, can easily become active sites of memory – as so many works of Irish literature illustrate. An artwork itself, while deliberately preserving some memory, may generate further spontaneously emerging memories and thus affect the thinking or behaviour of the viewers/listeners.

Brian Friel's *The Home Place*, written in the heyday of the Celtic Tiger, defiantly evokes that kind of personalised collective memory in the protagonist that is fast receding or disappearing in the reality of the time and dramatises its transforming, home-bringing effect. Similarly to Joyce's device of an unexpectedly heard song bringing back overwhelming memories in 'The Dead', the sound of a Thomas

Moore song performed by a school choir affects so strongly one of the protagonists that the memories that well up from deep in her unconscious will lead her to make decisions that run contrary to her disposition, social and material interests. Kevin Whelan analyses Joyce's short story in the context of some historical events, particularly the horrors of the Famine that lived on so strongly in collective memory that it was for long impossible to speak about them. He claims that only sublimating them into art seemed possible, and Irish modernists did exactly that, 'espoused the importance of representation as a process which rescues presence and fullness from depletion and shrivelling. . . . The artist restores the aura in the aesthetic realm which had been stopped by the brute contingencies of politics.'[3] In 'The Dead', the folksong 'The Lass of Aughrim' reawakens Gretta's memory of the young Galway man Michael Furey who died for love of her in his youth and who 'becomes the symbol of a rich, passionate life which has vanished'. The song 'summons the deep, oral, Irish-language, Jacobite, Gaelic past of the west of Ireland' which sharply contrasts with Gabriel's 'shallow bourgeois present, typecast as a provincial journalist' (p. 103).

Moore's songs, similarly, are a significant part of Irish cultural memory as he filled the Irish melodies with his romantic poetry, so that they became crucial in Irish romantic cultural nationalism. Luke Gibbons points out the huge power of Moore's songs after the defeat of the 1798 rebellion by the United Irishmen, for whom 'Gaelic culture was a living presence, a force to be reckoned with. . . . The subaltern culture of the dispossessed was imbued not just with romantic pathos but with radical sentiment.'[4] Moore is considered the voice of the nation and his songs were 'especially necessary' for his people 'at the time he sang them' (42), as Clement O'Donnell, the musician and conductor of the choir in *The Home Place* explains. The political and historical allusions and the lamentation for lost beauty and richness proved consoling.

As opposed to them, memories of the past preserved in history – that is official historiography, history-making – are always deeply politicised and, as common experience has it, offer the story of the victors. Or, in the words of the well-known traditional singer Frank Harte: 'Those in power write the history, those who suffer write the songs.'[5] The story of the victims usually recedes into oral history as long as oral culture exists, and into collective memory as long as communal memory exists. Friel's responses to this dichotomy include, perhaps most famously, his *Making History* (1988), which features Hugh O'Neill and his chronicler, Cardinal Lombard, the latter dramatised in the process of creating a version of history that he believes will suit his nation's needs. In that situation the general truth, however, is somewhat twisted (as so often with Friel) because here the written version of what happened is produced by one of the victims, who nevertheless victimises the (person of the) loser even more than the historical events do (by depriving him from the memory of the strong support of his loving wife Mabel). Living memory – that of O'Neill, the subject of history – is superseded by written history, in this case serving the purpose of the self-appreciation and emotional survival of the Irish.

Friel himself created a changing, moving, living site of memory in his fictitious Ballybeg which he filled in play after play with fragments of Irish life, history, consciousness to offer different aspects of the past evoked or rejected, forgotten or resurrected. Within or related to Ballybeg, Friel also invented images, characters and dramatic events that became part of collective memory and turned works of art, predominantly music within his plays, into *lieux de mémoire*. This process then self-reflexively investigates the function of art as a site of memory. Deploying one form of art within another, such as play-within-the-play or painting, sculpture, music within a play, enables authors such as Friel to represent the possible effects of the evocation of half-lost or repressed memories in art.

In *Philadelphia, Here I Come!* (1964), *Aristocrats* (1979), *Dancing at Lughnasa* (1990), *Wonderful Tennessee* (1993), *Performances* (2003) and other plays songs, hymns, piano pieces or, in the last one, a string quartet, carry significance not only because of their aesthetic value but also because of the personal, collective, cultural memories they convey, which communicate between history and memory. In *Aristocrats,* Friel presents his perhaps most extended example of the intricacies of the ways memory-places work as the Chopin pieces and various parts of the Ballybeg Big House bring to the surface real and imaginary memories. Casimir's stories arise from listening to his sister playing the piano or tumbling into pieces of furniture that, in his mixture of memory and imagination, have the imprints of past greatness, involving artists and writers. All these function as necessary buttresses to his fragile sense of identity and self-worth. It is as if Friel were to dramatise Nora's axiomatic separation of memory and history: 'Memory attaches itself to sites, whereas history attaches itself to events' (p. 22) in his contrastive presentation of Casimir's (artistic) creative memory and Tom Hoffnung the American historian's recordings of his wild stories, and then challenging their truth-value with his fact-hunting investigation.

Cultural Memory in *The Home Place*

In *The Home Place*, Thomas Moore's songs act as catalysts of change. Like many other Friel plays before, this one also connects the past with the present and individual fate with the communal. Unlike in earlier plays, however, here the decaying, doomed community is that of the Anglo-Irish Ascendancy, the landed aristocracy, who, at the time of the play's present (the late nineteenth century, the beginning of the Land Wars and of the Cultural Renaissance) do not seem to understand why the natives object to their insensitive colonial practices. The excesses of such behaviour, exemplified in the stereotypical coloniser Richard Gore's anthropometric measurements, are dramatised as unambiguously destructive and disgusting. Yet the good-intentioned local landlord Christopher Gore, too, whose family after having lived in that same place for centuries is still referred to by the locals as the 'lodgers', although personally not responsible for the colonial situation, becomes defeated by it. Both in terms of practical realities (he must obey the Irish rebels and chase away his cousin because of his racist manoeuvres) and in personal, emotional terms (Margaret, the Irish 'chatelaine' of the Lodge, rejects his passionate offers of marriage).

Memories of the past are evoked verbally, in direct rememberings, through the stage imagery (both physical and fictional), and, most prominently, through song and music. The downfall of the Gore family and their class is foreshadowed by the falcon and the trees in the estate. The falcon circling around the house, appearing at the beginning and then reappearing at the end of the play – with the play structurally recreating that circling movement – immediately taps into Irish cultural memory embedded in literature. As Yeats's falcon in 'The Second Coming' heralds the possibility of a new dispensation by 'turning and turning in a widening gyre' that indicates that 'the centre cannot hold', so in *The Home Place* the old era is coming to its end. The tree imagery in more concrete terms parallels and reconfirms the story of the downfall of the Big-House inhabitants' world. The foreign trees, planted by the Anglo-Irish grandfather Gore, are overgrown by local trees and can be saved only at the price of cutting out many of the latter. The planted specimens need extra protection because they are not well acclimatised to their new place, and one of them is 'still hankering after Kenya' whence it came. The tree symbolism gains further significance in the light of the strong Irish tradition of reverence for trees, many of which were endowed with magic power.[6] Among the sacred trees in old Irish literature and folklore, some are related to the origins of a tribe and are 'regarded as a symbol of that sept's nobility and endurance', causing 'misfortunes' to befall people who interfere with them or cut them out.[7] Even though Friel does not identify the native trees on the Gore estate with specific sacred or magic powers, the danger of the local trees being felled in order to preserve the foreign ones speaks about colonial practices as well as the danger the colonisers bring upon themselves by those practices. The image of the two landlords – father and son – accidentally splashing themselves with the whitewash used for marking the trees to be culled and the verbal transfer of the term 'doomed' from the trees to the humans again predicts changes.

The most powerful form of cultural memory in the play occurs when Margaret's father, the drunken Clement O'Donnell, directs his children's choir who sing Thomas Moore's song 'Oft in the Stilly Night' at the beginning and the end of the play. Cultural memory proves an effective force of resistance, both as deliberate recollection and as involuntary, spontaneous and therefore irresistible evocation. Ian Assmann, partly relying on Maurice Halbwachs' differentiation between 'memory' and 'tradition', defines cultural memory as differing from biographical or fundamental memory in the sense that whereas the latter is based on personal remembering and lasts only through three or four generations, cultural memory is more related to tradition, events, places, relations, fixed points in the past that are preserved deliberately by the group of people for whose identity such memory is important.[8] Cultural memory and identity are deeply interrelated; neither personal nor cultural identity can exist without healthy remembering. As Assmann stresses, it is existentially important for a community to preserve parts of the past that otherwise would fade and be in danger of disappearing. Instead of repeated reconstructions of history, this preservation can be done through transforming communicative remembering into tradition, into commemoration (pp. 64–5) or through religion, in which the *lieux de mémoire* are placed inside, in the emotional, spiritual life (p. 209). Art can also operate in a similar fashion, transforming and preserving interiorised cultural memory.

In *The Home Place*, this nature of memory appears to create the divide between the Irish natives and the English 'lodgers'. The latter share biographical memories which, significantly, go back only three or four generations. They have only personal memories of the home place in Kent, which strengthen their nostalgic longing and feeling of loss but do not provide any sustaining force nor any practical possibility of return when reality in Ireland proves untenable for Christopher. This memory of Kent turns out to be only a dreamworld which lingers in the helpless mind without a therapeutic force: 'I can't tell you how beautiful the home place is at this time of year. And how tranquil. And how – replete. . . . A golden and beneficent land. Days without blemish.'[9]

The 'natives', however, can be guided back to their own culture with the help of cultural memory. The memories the Irish Margaret and her father share are *both* personal and communal, both involuntary and deliberate, carrying historical meaning. Margaret grew up with Moore's songs, singing, sharing them with others, being the 'prime chorister' (p. 23) of her father's chorus, which then became part of her being, her identity. Cultural memory is deeply embedded even in her 'biographical' remembering and this personalised, internalised cultural memory will lead her not only spiritually but also physically back home, to her own culture and tradition. Art as an active site of memory, may then be located not only between memory and history but also between, and so combining, the two kinds of memory that Aristotle so neatly distinguished as *mnēmē* and *anamnēsis* which became in Latin *memoria* and *reminiscentia*, the former a 'simple presence in the mind' while the latter meaning 'recollection', *ars memoriae*, the art of memory, memory as deliberate action. Or, as Paul Ricoeur, further elaborates on the distinctions, 'simple evocation' versus an 'effort to recall'.[10]

Memory and the arts, and memory and history have been, after all, in close, organic, we can say familial relation since the Greeks: Mnemosyne, the embodiment of memory, is the mother of all the nine muses, including not only those of the arts but also Clio, that of history. And if 'memory is Mnemosyne, The Ur-Art, the mother of the Muses, then we are entitled to wonder whether She doesn't need (and has a right to expect) the support of the goddesses who are her children'.[11] To continue the metaphor, the muses of the arts carrying the genes of Memory in themselves, by their very existence and nature help the survival of memory, especially collective and cultural memory. Clio of History (and especially what she became: history-making), taking a more artificial course, would respond more to external (ideological, political, rational) needs. The muses of the arts and by extension the arts themselves – descendents of Mnemosyne/Memory and sisters of Clio/History – by uniting spontaneous memory and deliberate recollection, may bridge the gap between memory and history like and as *lieux de mémoire*.

Yet both Moore's songs and their advocate, Clement O'Donnell in *The Home Place*, are enwrapped in multiple ironies. George O'Brien rightly points out that Moore's friendship with, and acceptance by, English poets problematises his status as the representative of Irish culture as it gives him also 'two homes, that of Irish song and that of English literary fashion'.[12] In another aspect, although Moore 'himself believed . . . that he was saving a dying art form – and the cultural identity which it embodied – and giving it a new life, . . . the process of translation involved the extinction of the material *qua* folksong and its metamorphosis into a ballad culture which largely emasculated its raw energy in favour of a more domesticated charm.'[13] As is the nature of *lieux de mémoire*, here also, while evoking the memory of past events, they reflect on the discontinuity between past and present; while they attempt to bridge this distance, they also retain an awareness of the distance: 'Our relation to the past is now formed in a subtle play between its intractability and its disappearance, a question of a representation – in the original sense of the word – radically different from the old ideal of resurrecting the past' (Nora, p. 17). In its capacity of transforming and embodying memories, art tends to join the 'representation' and the 'resurrection' of the past within the present, so when the past recedes into history, art is still able to make it contemporaneous with the present and thus help the dialogue between past and future to continue.

In *The Home Place*, the drunken schoolmaster Clement O'Donnell – a literary descendant of *Translations*'s Hugh O'Donnell – is well aware of the irony of the situation and of his own position in it when he associates himself with the poet who is 'a romantic man and given to easy sentiment, as I am myself. . . . But he has our true measure. . . . He divines us accurately. He reproduces features of our history and our character' (p. 42). Clement himself, who set Moore's songs into three-part harmony which his school choir sings to 'the envy of every school in the kingdom' (p. 36), is simultaneously both a serious and a deeply ironic 'true measure' of his nation. Confirming the colonial stereotype of the drunken but charming, artistic Irishman of irrational talent, applying the very word 'divining' to Moore, and by extension to himself, Clement becomes related to that early Friel diviner in the short story of that title who, alone among all the much better equipped people, using only his twig, is able to find the missing body under water. This latter-day diviner, a faulty, inadequate embodiment of the artist archetype, similarly to his water-divining predecessor arriving with a 'reek of whiskey off him', still has greater power than the coloniser Richard with his pseudo-scientific method of measuring people. External measuring can only serve external interests, whereas being the internal 'measure' of a people – the sounding board of their feelings, grievances and desires – may have a long-lasting emotional hold on them.

If Moore cannot become the 'true measure' of the Irish in an originary sense, his oeuvre does hold up a mirror to them, exactly through the reality of the forced Union (1801), after which Moore's *Irish Melodies* were born. And if his songs were composed in the in-between or rather, dual literary/artistic tradition, so was the whole culture caught between those traditions. No return to the authentic Gaelic-Irish culture was allowed in any earlier Friel play either, only glimpses or memories of it hinted at alternative worlds and value systems. Here, the 'true measure' of Irish culture being itself somewhat of a mixture indicates a further step away from the possibility of returning to the source or, rather, that the source itself is already a result of the duality. Yet within this duality the viewpoint is still that of the 'native' culture, the feelings accompanying lost freedom and past beauty. In the famous 'Oft in the Stilly Night' that Clement's choir repeatedly sings, the images of all the friends 'I've seen around me fall/Like leaves in wintery weather' and 'the banquet hall deserted' evoke the deprivations due to the lost rebellion and it is only 'fond mem'ry' and 'sad mem'ry' that brings back the joys of the past.

The evocation of 'The smiles, the tears,/Of childhood years,/The words of love then spoken' in Moore's song speaks to Margaret in more than one way. It reinforces her remembrance of some of her long-repressed memories of her own happy childhood in the village with friends that she lost by going to live in the Big House. And more directly, music brings back her own experience of singing those songs in her father's chorus. Because cultural memory often is 'counter-factual' and works as 'counter-history',[14] by evoking events that are in contrast to the 'facts' of present reality, they can also inspire resistance to the present social/political situation. The music thus destabilises Margaret's acceptance of her liminal position as an esteemed servant to the landlord's family with the prospect of even entering that family but always remaining inferior by birth. It lifts her out of the daily routine of that world and the alien culture surrounding her and helps her to join the other Irish characters in gravitating homewards. She starts out in strictest denial of her situation while, somewhat reminiscent of Owen in *Translations*', she seems happy enough to serve the Anglo-Irish landlords; playing superior to Sally, the native servant, never answering her questions about her relation to her home; sharply refusing to communicate with her cousin, Con, and even more sharply rebuking her father. She is the 'proper little English woman' (p. 61) in her manners, elegant and aloof, admired by all the English gentlemen, and mocked by Sally: 'You'd do anything to be one of the toffs, Maggie, wouldn't you?' (p. 17) Margaret obviously admires and mimics the ruling class – mimicry being a common feature of the colonised – and 'exemplifies [one] facet of the peasant subalternity, that which denies its own identity'.[15] Her position is beginning to be weakened by the 'wondrous' music that in the opening scene keeps her 'enraptured' and 'mesmerised', but then, as soon as the singing is over, she becomes 'freed' (pp. 11–12). Later, under the influence of disturbing events, she recalls childhood memories of playing with other children in the village and even becomes ironical with Christopher when referring back to Richard's measurements – the first time she voices any criticism of colonial practices. These steps in her involuntary and, later, more conscious journey homeward, culminate in the play's closing scene when the opening image is repeated of Margaret listening to her father's choir enraptured, as again she is 'absorbed in the music and in her own memories' (p. 73). Moore's songs, embedded in her childhood memories, no matter how ironic their coincidence with the 'true measure' of the Irish may be, evoke both personal and collective cultural memories as Moore 'obsessively revisits' his 'familiar ground of vanished possibilities and the betrayed present'.[16]

The 'betrayed present' of Ireland at the time of the writing of the play – the early years of the twenty-first century – is the globalising world of the Celtic Tiger economic boom. By that time, the experience of British colonisation became only a memory and can be deployed as a warning against globalisation, against giving up and losing one's own cultural treasures, however mixed they may be, like Moore's songs. The Tiger period, like British colonisation, would end – and the prophecy of the play was soon fulfilled in reality – and returning to one's own culture, reclaiming what is still available of it could prove sustaining. That realisation does not come from outside, nor with violent politics – Margaret rejects Con's and the other local people's rebellion – but may touch the Irish through the emotional force of art, music, songs, and literature.

The Mystery of Art as a Guide to Homecoming

The play closes with Margaret's ambiguous but prophetic-sounding words: 'Just listen [to the music]. Because in a short time Father will come up here for me' (p. 75). Instead of choosing to marry either father or son of the Anglo-Irish family, she presumably will return to the home where she is bound by personal and cultural memories.[17] The '*desiderium nostrorum*' experienced and named by Hugh O'Donnell in *Translations* captures her in Moore's songs. Unlike Owen, who (in all probability) joins the armed rebels at the end of *Translations*, Margaret yields to the captivating force of the music over her soul. This moment arises rather unexpectedly, and remains, in Hedwig Schwall's term, 'unpsychologised'[18] – although not unprepared for as we see Margaret in the opening moments of the play listening mesmerised to the same song. In the closing scene, her total absorption in the music appears as if stepping out of ordinary reality, calling attention to the hidden, unacknowledged but still extant power of tradition. Or, as Schwall insightfully interprets it, 'Margaret's restitution has something of the "*tremendum mysterium*" which belongs to the heart of a community' (p. 71). Schwall arrives at this statement after a detailed, brilliant analysis of the play's characters in terms of Jan Patočka's categorisation of political attitudes as also appears in Derrida's commentaries on the development of responsibility in the Platonic and Christian traditions. The three types or stages of responsibility in Patočka and Derrida are the 'orgiastic or demonic type: the irresponsibility of the symbiotic figure' whose characteristics Schwall finds in the 'possessive' figures of *The Home Place*, primarily the stereotypical coloniser Richard Gore but also in a different way in the rebellious colonised Con. The second, the Platonic type, with relative responsibility and a split inside between the demonic mystery and reason, she identifies with Christopher Gore in his in-between position, with the gap in him between theoretical and practical conscience and his basic failure to bridge the distance between the two sides (Anglo-Irish landlords and native tenants and servants) he is hoping to link. The third type and the third step in the history of politics and responsibility is the Christian 'absolute responsibility' (Christian being used in a broad sense because in Derrida's discussion it includes Abraham's acceptance of his having to sacrifice Isaac, which analysis is, of course, based on Kierkegaard's famous analysis of Abraham's sacrifice). Schwall finds Clement's position in several ways related to Abraham's archetypal sacrificial act because Clement also gave up his first-born to the Anglo-Irish landlord to become his chatelaine and waits for her return. Schwall's suggestion that the sacrifice was brought for his need of alcohol (evidently, the correspondence between spirits and the spiritual is age-old) might be the one strained point of this almost-too-neat scheme. She emphasises Clement's Christian generosity, self-denial and big-heartedness to the community, which originates somewhere beyond himself, wondering whether his 'abyssal secret' may be his needing the drink to help 'the others to transcend their misery' (p. 70). This would come down to sacrificing his daughter *for* the community, for which point I see little evidence in the play.[19] Schwall's arguing that Margaret's uncharacteristic rudeness with her father could be better understood on the basis of this 'secret' sounds convincing, however. And Margaret herself is the other figure of this type who experiences the 'mystery that makes us tremble' and 'incarnates the mysteries of this heterogeneous community' (p. 71). At the end, both Margaret and Clement 'fit into what passes and remains, a voice for a nation that is split into at least two nations, each of which have "homes" that house split families and subjects that are split' (p. 71).

This 'tremendum mysterium' is brought forth by the song and music whose momentum changes the whole register of the play as basic realism becomes abandoned and the play moves into a more symbolic realm. Or we could also call it a utopian realm in the sense that cultural memory enables the utopian instinct to speculate on what could have happened if history took a different turn when the past was open to other directions.[20] If the events Moore's song invokes ended differently – if Irish independence were achieved at the end of the eighteenth century instead of the subsequently forced Union with England, the whole situation in the present of the play would be different, perhaps without the rift between Anglo-Irish and English and Irish, Big House and village, inhuman treatment of locals by intruding coloniser Richards and violent threats from native Cons, and the place would offer more homeliness for everybody concerned. All that is speculation whose truthfulness is never to be proved in history. Yet in the play Margaret's last words point towards such a (utopian) homecoming.[21]

The 'duty to remember', as Paul Ricoeur asserts in one of his many meditations on the nature of memory and its ethics, includes 'to keep alive the memory of suffering over against the general tendency of history to celebrate the victors. . . . We need . . . a kind of parallel history of, let us say, victimisation, which would counter the history of success and victory.' This duty 'consists not only in having a deep concern for the past, but in transmitting the meaning of past events to the next generation . . . it is an imperative directed towards the future.'[22] He also speaks about the duty to forget (the violations, the wounds) in order to finally arrive at forgiving. Thomas Moore's writing his poems and setting them to the Irish melodies to keep the memory of the suffering of the defeated alive, then Clement's setting this music into harmony and teaching his children's choir to sing those songs are all exercises in the duty to remember – and to make people remember, to remind. Under its influence then Margaret involuntarily, spontaneously moves closer to identify with the 'victims', her own people, and as the next step, to forgetting her personal wounds inflicted by her father and so, through this combination of remembering and forgetting, reaches forgiveness. She becomes liberated from her anger and although rejects marriage to Christopher, she remains compassionate towards him. Considering Nora's claim that '[m]emory installs remembrance within the sacred' as opposed to history which is 'always prosaic' (p. 9), this ethical aspect of memory and the recognition of cultural memory's magic power can sit comfortably with Schwall's placing the play in a (broadly speaking) spiritual and religious context with the ethical dimension of 'absolute responsibility'. Whether we approach the interpretation of those final moments of *The Home Place* from the direction of memory, art or religion, because they all are related in some way to the sacred, we arrive at the tremendous mystery.

Carrying feelings attached to memories and memories attached to feelings, music contributes to building or rebuilding identity – both individual and communal. Moore's songs, as art in general, may affect different layers of the human psyche and often several of them simultaneously. These songs are admired even by the arch-coloniser Richard who is touched by their haunting beauty but naturally they do not evoke in him the 'affection' of the 'simple evocation' of memory that they produce in some of those inside the culture. Sally, on the other hand, is not enchanted by them but hears them matter-of-factly, as part of life. She still belongs to the community and lives within the *milieu de mémoire* so such evocations of memory are not necessary for strengthening her identity. Margaret absorbs their full effect, including the music, the magic power of the words, the historical-cultural references. The songs function as *lieux de mémoire* for her who was separated from and then by choice separated herself from her community, does not live in the natural milieu of those cultural memories and her exilic, liminal position problematised her identity.

'Art-knowing' as different from the 'now-dominant rational/analytical/statistical ways of knowing', Don Gifford asserts, is 'compounded of the intuitive, the affective, the mythopoeic aspects of human experience, with the proviso that those aspects of our experience, the abilities to intuit, to feel, to mythopoeticize can be schooled, trained, coordinated toward their own ways of getting things right'.[23] Representing art within art, presenting its ways of working, can be one of the ways of this schooling in a non-rational manner. As another Friel play, *Performances* declares, music remains superior to words because it reaches into 'that amorphous world of feeling' and speaks 'the language of feeling itself; a unique vocabulary of sound created by feeling itself'[24] and so influences people's behaviour and actions. In *The Home Place*, music 'speaking' feelings, combined with images and words which themselves have become part of cultural memory, brought in through intertextuality, such as Yeats's falcon, Friel's own created site of memory (Ballybeg) and images, concepts from and references to his earlier works, multiplies overlapping layers of memory. Art and the artist, as in several other Friel plays, still share some traces of the shamanic-druidic sort of being in touch with the spiritual, in accordance with Denis Donoghue's insistence on the necessity of the mystery of the arts 'as the very condition they appear at all'[25]: '[e]ven in a world mostly secular, the arts can make a space for our intuition of mystery' (p. 129).

Internalised cultural memory stimulates the necessary move of the Irish in *The Home Place* from liminality back to the centre of their own world; a move towards a cultural, emotional, spiritual home. While today, unlike in the play's time, it is no longer the colonial world that has to be fought against, it is just as necessary to reawaken the need for finding one's own place in the face of 'impermanence and anonymity'[26] that *Philadelphia, Here I Come!* had warned against as early as 1964. In the twenty-first century, the danger for the Irish of facelessness arises in their own home place, in the Ireland of the Celtic Tiger and post-Tiger years. As *The Home Place* suggests, one way of circumventing this danger leads through the non-linear processes of remembering, through the *lieux de mémoire* communicated through and embedded in the mystery of art. Despite the multiple splits in the individuals, the homes and the nation, there is still a possibility to experience homecoming, renewing the power of belonging in ways that point beyond rational, pragmatic considerations. In that, in contemporary times, as always, art can and does give guidance. Donoghue's emphasis, partly building on Gilles Deleuze's and Roberto Mangabeira Unger's notions of how the extraordinary, which is associated with the experiences of religion, the sacred, art and love, bear 'upon the procedures of daily life' and is 'the starting point for the critique and transformation of social life' (pp. 28–9), once again, helps to reconcile Schwall's religious-philosophical-ethical approach to *The Home Place* with my insistence on the significance of collective memory and of art as a site of memory in identity-building and homecoming, because both interpretations arrive at the mystery whether 'tremendous' or just the presence of the extraordinary within the ordinary.

NOTES

Chapter 1: Situating Friel

1. Quotation by kind permission of Thomas Kilroy and Gallery Press: Loughcrew, Co. Meath.
2. Brian Friel, *Essays, Diaries, Interviews: 1964–1999*, ed. Christopher Murray, London: Faber, 1999, pp.18–19. Cf. W. B. Yeats, 'Emotion of Multitude', *Essays and Introductions*, London: Macmillan, 1961, pp.215–16.
3. Here see Richard Rankin Russell, 'Brian Friel's Short Fiction: Place, Community, and Modernity', *Irish University Review*, Vol. 42, No. 2 (2012), pp.298–326.
4. Brian Friel, *A Month in the Country: After Turgenev*, Loughcrew: Gallery Press, 1992, p.98. See Christopher Murray, '"If the mask fits, wear it, I say": Dissension and Identity in the Plays of Brian Friel', *Hungarian Journal of English and American Studies*, Vol. 15, No. 2 (2009), pp.331–45. Hugh Kenner's early book on Eliot carried the subtitle, *Invisible Poet*, London: W.H. Allen, 1960.
5. Brian Friel, 'The Theatre of Hope and Despair', in *Essays, Diaries, Interviews*, pp.15–24 (p.19).
6. Oscar Wilde, *Letters*, ed. Rupert Hart-Davis, New York: Harcourt, Brace & World, 1962, p.466: 'I was a man who stood in symbolic relations to the art and culture of my age.'
7. Friel, *Diaries, Essays, Interviews*, p.19.
8. T. S. Eliot, 'Tradition and the Individual Talent', *The Sacred Wood: Essays on Poetry and Criticism*, London: Methuen, 1960, pp.47–59 (p.49).
9. *Kalendarium: Maynooth College Calendar for 1948–49*, Dublin: Browne and Nolan, 1948, p.90.
10. Brian Friel to Christopher Murray, 15 June 2011.
11. Joe Frawley, cited in Liam Maher (ed.), *I Remember Neil Kevin (1903–1953): An Assessment of his Life and of his Writing*, Roscrea: J.F. Walsh, 1990, p.212.
12. Peter Connolly, cited in Liam Maher (ed.), *I Remember Neil Kevin*, p.216.
13. Neil Kevin, 'The Fault of Cheapness', *Irish Ecclesiastical Record* (1939), 349, cited in Liam Maher (ed.), *I Remember Neil Kevin*, p.120.
14. Neil Kevin, *No Applause in Church*, Dublin: Clonmore & Reynolds, 1947, p.25.
15. Brian Friel, *Plays Two*, London: Faber, 1999, p.398.
16. George O'Brien, '"Meet Brian Friel": The *Irish Press* Columns', *Irish University Review*, special issue: Brian Friel, ed. Anthony Roche, Vol. 29 (1999), pp.30–41 (pp.30–1).
17. The *Irish Press* was founded by Éamon de Valera in 1931 as the voice of his republican party, Fianna Fáil, which came into power in 1932 and dominated Irish politics in the Free State and the Republic. See entry by Eddie Holt in *The Encyclopaedia of Ireland*, ed. Brian Lalor, Dublin: Gill & Macmillan, 2003, p.552.

18. Oscar Wilde, *The Importance of Being Earnest*, in *Complete Works*, ed. Vyvyan Holland. London and Glasgow: Collins, 1966, p.371.
19. Neil Kevin, 'On Being Sincere', *No Applause in Church*, pp.40–8 (p.42).
20. George O'Brien, op. cit., pp.36, 38.
21. Neil Kevin, *No Applause in Church*, p.48.
22. Brian Friel, 'Words', programme note, *Molly Sweeney*, Gate Theatre (Dublin), 28 June 2011. This note was first published as no.1 of 'Seven Notes for a Festival Programme' in 1999. See Brian Friel, *Essays, Diaries, Interviews*, pp.173–4.
23. Denis Donoghue, *On Eloquence*, New Haven and London: Yale University Press, 2008, pp.2, 169.
24. Patrick Kavanagh, 'The Parish and the Universe', *Collected Pruse*, London: McGibbon and Kee, 1967, pp.281–3 (p.282).
25. The award was presented by *Cumann Thír Chonaill* at the Burlington Hotel, Dublin, on 5 March 2011.
26. Brian Friel, 'Self-Portrait', *Essays, Diaries, Interviews*, p.41.
27. Anthony Roche, *Brian Friel: Theatre and Politics*, Basingstoke: Palgrave Macmillan, 2011, p.5.
28. Brian Friel, untitled tribute, *Enter Certain Players: Edwards-MacLiammoir and the Gate 1928–1978*, ed. Peter Luke, Dublin: Dolmen Press, 1978, p.21.
29. Christopher Murray, 'Brian Friel, Tyrone Guthrie and Thornton Wilder', *Irish Theatre International*, Vol. 2, No. 1 (August 2009), pp.16–27. See also Patrick O'Donnell, 'The Irish Roots of the Guthrie Theatre', PhD Dissertation, School of English, Drama and Film, University College Dublin, 2010.
30. Friel, *Essays, Diaries, Interviews*, p.22.
31. Jochen Schulte-Sasse, Foreword, Peter Szondi, *Theory of the Modern Drama*, ed. and trans. Michael Hays, Cambridge: Polity Press, 1987, pp.vii–xvi (p.ix).
32. Peter Szondi, 'Friedrich Schlegel and Romantic Irony', cited by Jochen Schulte-Sasse, Foreword, *Theory of the Modern Drama*, p.x.
33. Samuel Beckett, 'Recent Irish Poetry [1934]', *Disjecta: Miscellaneous Writings and a Dramatic Fragment*, ed. Ruby Cohn, London: Calder, 1983, pp.70–6 (p.70).
34. Edward Said, 'Yeats and Decolonization' in Seamus Deane (ed.), *Nationalism, Colonialism, and Literature*, Minneapolis: University of Minnesota Press, 1990, pp.69–95 (p.74).
35. Shaun Richards, 'Irish Studies and the Adequacy of Theory: The Case of Brian Friel', *Yearbook of English Studies*, Vol. 35 (2005), pp.264–78 (pp.272, 276).
36. Ulf Dantanus, 'Revolution and Revelation: Brian Friel and the Postcolonial Subject' in John Strachan and Alison O'Malley-Younger (eds), *Essays on Modern Irish Literature*, Houghton-le-Spring, Tyne & Wear: University of Sunderland Press, 2007, pp.77–91 (p.80).
37. Lionel Pilkington, *Theatre and the State in Twentieth-Century Ireland: Cultivating the People*, London and New York: Routledge, 2001; Patrick Lonergan, *Theatre and Globalization: Irish Drama in the Celtic Tiger Era*, Basingstoke: Palgrave Macmillan, 2009; Victor Merriman, '*Because we are poor*': *Irish Theatre in the 1990s*, Dublin: Carysfort Press, 2011.
38. David Grant, *The Stagecraft of Brian Friel*, London: Greenwich Exchange, 2004.

39. Cited by D. E. S. Maxwell, *Brian Friel*, Lewisburg: Bucknell University Press, 1973, p.109.
40. Éamonn Jordan, 'The Meta-Theatricalization of Memory in Brian Friel's *Dancing at Lughnasa*' in Edric Caldicott and Anne Fuchs (eds), *Cultural Memory: Essays on European Literature and History*, Oxford and Bern: Peter Lang, 2003, pp.129–45 (p.145).
41. Brian Friel in interview with Ciaran Carty in 1980, *Essays, Diaries, Interviews*, pp.82–3.

Chapter 2: Coming of Age: *Philadelphia, Here I Come!*

1. Peter James Harris, *From Stage to Page: Critical Reception of Irish Plays in the London Theatre, 1925–1996*, Bern and Oxford: Peter Lang, 2011, p.160.
2. Bernard Shaw, 'The Problem Play – A Symposium' in E. J. West (ed.), *Shaw on Theatre*, New York: Hill and Wang, 1959, p.63.
3. Lyndsey Turner to Christopher Murray, 30 October 2012, quoted by permission.
4. Samuel Beckett, *Play* [1963], in *The Complete Dramatic Works*, London: Faber, 1990, p.313.
5. See Ulf Dantanus, *Brian Friel: A Study*, London, Faber, 1988, pp.55–70. The most comprehensive study of the early plays is by Anthony Roche, *Brian Friel: Theatre and Politics*, Basingstoke: Palgrave Macmillan, 2011, pp.8–31.
6. Sam Hanna Bell, *The Theatre in Ulster*, Dublin: Gill and Macmillan, 1972, p.71.
7. Ibid., pp.60–7.
8. See Lionel Pilkington, 'Theatre and Cultural Politics in Northern Ireland: The *Over the Bridge* Controversy, 1959', *Eire-Ireland*, Vol. XXX, No. 4 (1996), pp.76–93.
9. Anthony Roche, op. cit., p.24.
10. See James McGlone, *Ria Mooney: The Life and Times of the Artistic Director of the Abbey Theatre, 1948–1963*, Jefferson, NC: McFarland, 2002, pp.196–8.
11. Brian Friel, address at Queen's University, 20 February 2009, when the Brian Friel Theatre was opened in his honour. The director Sir Tyrone Guthrie had also been chancellor of the university, hence Friel's allusion on this occasion. As early as 1964, he had acknowledged Guthrie's influence, in 'The Giant of Monaghan', *Holiday* (May 1964).
12. Brian Friel, 'Self-Portrait' in Christopher Murray (ed.), *Brian Friel: Essays, Diaries, Interviews 1964–1999*, London: Faber, 1999, p.42. Hereafter this source is referred to in the texts as *Essays*.
13. M. J. Molloy, *The Wood of the Whispering: A Comedy in Three Acts* [1961], in *Selected Plays of M. J. Molloy*, ed. Robert O'Driscoll, Gerrards Cross: Colin Smythe, 1998, p.111.
14. See Tom Garvin, *Preventing the Future: Why Was Ireland So Poor for so Long?*, Dublin: Gill & Macmillan, 2005.
15. See Sister Marie Huber Kealy, *Kerry Playwright: Sense of Place in the Plays of John B. Keane*, Selinsgrove: Susquehanna University Press and London: Associated University Press, 1993, pp.111–24.

16. Paul Delaney (ed.), *Brian Friel in Conversation*, Ann Arbor: University of Michigan Press, 2000, p.40.
17. Tom Murphy, *Plays: 4*, London: Methuen Drama, 1997, p.162.
18. Nationalist, Irish-language enthusiast and manager of the Abbey after Yeats's death. See Peter Kavanagh, *The Story of the Abbey Theatre,* New York: Devin-Adair, 1950, reprinted Orono, ME: National Poetry Foundation/University of Maine, 1984; Hugh Hunt, *The Abbey: Ireland's National Theatre 1904–1979*, Dublin: Gill and Macmillan, 1979; Robert Welch, *The Abbey Theatre 1899–1999: Form and Pressure*, Oxford: Oxford University Press, 1999.
19. Ernest Blythe, 'Preface' to John Murphy, *The Country Boy: A Play in Three Acts*, Dublin: Progress House, 1960, n.p.
20. John Murphy, *The Country Boy*, p.17. All subsequent quotations are hereafter referenced by page numbers in the text.
21. Ernest Blythe, *The Abbey Theatre*, Dublin: Abbey Theatre, *c.*1965, n.p. This, pamphlet was meant as a defence of Abbey policy under his management.
22. The Abbey Archives show that Blythe was too modest: the figure was 101 for 1959. *The Country Boy* was revived in 1960 for a further 30 performances and again in 1965 (when Friel's *Philadelphia* was revived at the Gate) for 48 performances. Meantime, the Group successfully revived *The Country Boy* in July 1959 for 7 weeks and again in February 1960. I am grateful to Scott Boltwood for this latter information.
23. Brian Friel to Christopher Murray, 24 August 2012.
24. Shakespeare, *The Winter's Tale*, 4.1.26.
25. T. S. Eliot, 'Hamlet and His Problems', in *The Sacred Wood: Essays on Poetry and Criticism'* [1920], reprinted London: Methuen, 1960, pp.95–103 (p.100).
26. Brian Friel, *Philadelphia, Here I Come!,* in Brian Friel: *Plays One*, London: Faber, 1996, p.98. All subsequent quotations from *Philadelphia* are from this edition, to which page numbers refer.
27. See Brian Friel, 'Self-Portrait', in *Essays*, p.39.
28. Tyrone Guthrie, in Paul Delaney, *op. cit.*, p.41.
29. *Hamlet* and *Three Sisters* were the two productions Guthrie directed. Friel has said that he also saw Molière's *The Miser*, directed by Douglas Campbell, in rehearsal. See Delaney, p.37.
30. Brian Friel, 'The Returned Yank', *Irish Press*, 10 August 1963, p.8. There is nothing in this piece about Minneapolis or playwriting. Likewise, the ten pieces published under the heading 'American Diary' between 20 April and 29 June lack any information on theatre. See also George O'Brien, '"Meet Brian Friel": The *Irish Press* Columns', *Irish University Review*, Vol. 29 (1999), pp.30–41, and Scott Boltwood, *Brian Friel, Ireland, and the North*, Cambridge: Cambridge University Press, 2007, pp.10–38.
31. Brian Friel, 'An Observer in Minneapolis', in Delaney, p.37. The reference to curtain-lines may hark back to Ria Mooney, to whom Friel had to admit he didn't know what she, then directing his *The Enemy Within*, meant by the term. See Christopher Murray, 'Brian Friel, Tyrone Guthrie and Thornton Wilder', *Irish Theatre International*, Vol. 2, No. 1 (August 2009), pp.16–27 (p.17).
32. Tyrone Guthrie, 'Theatre as Ritual', *In Various Directions*, London: Michael Joseph, 1965, p.39.

33. Brian Friel to Ulf Dantanus, undated, cited in *Brian Friel: A Study*, p.87.
34. W. B. Yeats, 'The Theatre', in *Essays and Introductions*, London and New York: Macmillan, 1961, p.170.
35. For example, Yeats's *Words upon the Window-pane* (1930). *Purgatory* (1938) and the posthumously staged *The Death of Cuchulain*. See also Christopher Murray, 'Friel's "Emblems of Adversity" and the Yeatsian Example' in Alan J. Peacock (ed.), *The Achievement of Brian Friel*, Gerrards Cross: Colin Smythe, 1993, pp.69–90.
36. Henri Bergson, 'From *Laughter*, trans. Fred Rothwell, in *Comedy, Meaning and Form*, ed. Robert W. Corrigan, San Francisco: Chandler, 1965, pp.471–7 (p.474).
37. Deirdre Bryan and Maureen Murphy, entry on Patrick Joseph Peyton, *Dictionary of Irish Biography*, eds. James McGuire and James Quinn, Cambridge: Cambridge University Press/Royal Irish Academy (Dublin), 2009, vol. 8, pp.88–9.
38. Thomas Kilroy, 'The Early Plays' in Anthony Roche (ed.), *The Cambridge Companion to Brian Friel*, Cambridge: Cambridge University Press, 2006, p.11.
39. Arthur Miller, 'Introduction to the *Collected Plays*' in Robert A. Martin (ed.), *The Theater Essays of Arthur Miller*, New York: Viking Press, 1978, p.135.
40. Lyndsey Turner to Christopher Murray, 30 October 2012, quoted by permission.
41. John Gassner, *Form and Idea in Modern Theatre*, New York: Holt Rinehart, 1956, p.135. For a photograph of Mielziner's set for *Salesman*, see J. L. Styan, *Modern Drama in Theory and Practice*, 1, *Realism and Naturalism*, Cambridge: Cambridge University Press, 1983, p.142.
42. Éamonn Kelly, *The Journeyman*, Dublin: Marino Books, 1998, p.83.
43. Adam Phillips, *Missing Out: In Praise of the Unlived Life*, London: Hamish Hamilton, 2012, p.134.
44. Brian Friel, *Plays Two*, London: Faber, 1996, p.30.
45. Christopher Murray, 'Palimpsest: Two Languages as One in *Translations*', in Donald E. Morse, Csilla Bertha, and Mária Kurdi (eds), *Brian Friel's Dramatic Artistry*, Dublin: Carysfort Press, 2006, pp.93–108.
46. William Shakespeare, *Hamlet*, 3.3.41–2.

Chapter 3: Formation of an Aesthetic

1. Friel Archive, National Library of Ireland, MS 37,052/2.
2. Thomas Wolfe, *You Can't Go Home Again*, New York: Harper & Row, 1940, p.56.
3. Thomas Kilroy, 'The Early Plays' in Anthony Roche (ed.), *The Cambridge Companion to Brian Friel*, p.12.
4. Éamonn Kelly, *The Journeyman*, Dublin: Marino Books, 1998, p.121.
5. Friel in interview with Fintan O'Toole, in *Essays, Diaries, Interviews*, ed. Christopher Murray, p.107.
6. Mary Corcoran, 'The Process of Migration and the Reinvention of Self: The Experience of Returning Irish Emigrants', *Éire-Ireland*, Vol. 37, No. 1–2 (2002), pp.175–91 (p.178). The following quotations are from this source, to which page numbers in parenthesis refer.

7. D. E. S. Maxwell, *Brian Friel*, p.78. See also Richard Pine, *The Diviner: The Art of Brian Friel*, pp.97–119; and John Boyd, 'Soundings' in Paul Delaney (ed.), *Brian Friel in Conversation*, pp.91–2.
8. Brian Friel, *The Loves of Cass McGuire*, London: Faber, 1967, p.20. All subsequent quotations refer to this edition.
9. Julie Kavanagh, 'Friel at Last' in Delaney (ed.), *Friel in Conversation*, p.219.
10. Brian Moore, *The Lonely Passion of Judith Hearne*, London: Granada, 1979, p.187.
11. Anthony Roche, *Brian Friel: Theatre and Politics*, p.71, emphasis added.
12. *The Portable Jung*, ed. Joseph Campbell, Harmondsworth: Penguin, 1976, p.123.
13. Samuel Beckett, *Murphy* [1938], London: Picador, 1973, p.64.
14. Friel to Hilton Edwards, 7 April 1965, Friel Archive, National Library of Ireland, MS 37,052/1.
15. Friel Archive, National Library of Ireland, MS 37,052/2, underlining in original.
16. Ibid., doubly underlined.
17. Anne Righter, *Shakespeare and the Idea of a Play*, Harmondsworth: Penguin, 1967, pp.59–147. See also G. Wilson Knight, 'Shakespeare Interpretation', *The Wheel of Fire*, London: Methuen 1949, pp.1–16. Knight emphasised the need to see each of Shakespeare's plays 'as an expanded metaphor' (p.15).
18. Anthony Roche, *Brian Friel: Theatre and Politics*, p.49. See also Maria Szasz, *Brian Friel and America*, Dublin: Glasnevin Publishing, 2013, pp.178–86.
19. See John P. Harrington, *The Irish Play on the New York Stage 1874–1966*, Lexington: University Press of Kentucky, 1997, p.154, and Maria Szasz, *Brian Friel and America*, pp.171–7.
20. Brian Friel in interview with Desmond Rushe, *Essays, Diaries, Interviews*, ed. Murray, p.31.
21. Nevertheless, they are to be found. See Christopher Murray, 'Friel and O'Casey Juxtaposed', *Irish University Review: Special Issue Brian Friel*, ed. Anthony Roche, Vol. 29 (1999), pp.16–29.
22. John P. Harrington, op. cit., p.156.
23. Brian Friel, 'The Theatre of Hope and Despair', in *Essays, Diaries, Interviews*, p.19.
24. John P. Harrington, op. cit., p.164.
25. Cited by Margaret MacCurtain, 'Siobhan McKenna (1922–86)' in James McGuire and James Quin (eds), *Dictionary of Irish Biography*, 9 vols, Cambridge and Dublin: Cambridge University Press and the Royal Irish Academy, 2009, 6, pp.37–9 (p.39).
26. Micheál Ó hAodha, *Siobhán: A Memoir of an Actress*, Dingle, Co. Kerry: Brandon, 1994, p.107.
27. Harry White, *Music and the Irish Literary Imagination*, Oxford: Oxford University Press, 2008, p.206. See also Harry White, 'Brian Friel and the Condition of Music', *Irish University Review*, Vol. 29 (1999), pp.6–15; and Patrick Burke, '"Both Heard and Imagined": Music as Structuring Principle in the Plays of Brian Friel' in Donald E. Morse, Csilla Bertha and István Pálffy (eds), *A Small Nation's Contribution to the World: Essays on Anglo-Irish Literature and Language*, Gerrards Cross: Colin Smythe, 1993, pp.43–52.
28. J. M. Synge, 'Autobiography', in *Collected Works*, 4 vols, Gerrards Cross: Colin Smythe, 1982, p.2 (*Prose*), ed. Alan Price, pp.3–15 (p.3).

29. Bernard Shaw, 'The Play of Ideas' in E. J. West (ed.), *Shaw on Theatre*, New York: Hill and Wang, 1959, p.294.
30. Friel in interview with Desmond Rushe, *Essays, Diaries, Interviews*, p.33.
31. Further details are supplied by Patrick Burke, '"Both Heard and Imagined": Music as Structuring Principle in the Plays of Brian Friel', op. cit., pp.51–2.
32. Harry White, however, is disturbed by the contradiction, calling rhapsody and concerto 'mutually exclusive forms' in 'Brian Friel and the Condition of Music', *Irish University Review*, op. cit., p.10.
33. See Mark Fitzgerald, 'Ireland's Queen and Her Art's Magic Power', programme note, *Tristan und Isolde*, Wide Open Opera, Dublin Theatre Festival, September–October 2012. James Joyce exploited this local origin in *Finnegans Wake* (1939).
34. J. Cuthbert Hadden, *The Operas of Wagner: Their Plots, Music and History*, London: Jack, 1910, p.103.
35. Micheál Ó hAodha, *Siobhán*, op. cit., p.107.
36. See also F. C. McGrath, *Brian Friel's (Post)Colonial Drama: Language, Illusion, and Politics*, Syracuse: Syracuse University Press, 1999, pp.81–2.
37. Brian Friel, 'Self-Portrait', in *Essays, Diaries, Interviews*, p.39.
38. Augustine, *Confessions*, Book X, chapter 8, trans. William Watts, Loeb edition, 2 vols, Cambridge, MA: Harvard University Press, 1912, pp.2, 119. In 'Self-Portrait' (*Essays*, p.39) Friel speaks of memory as 'the storehouse of the mind' which is an echo of Augustine's definition in chapter VIII of Book X: *lata praetoria memoriae, ubi sunt thesauri innumerabilium imaginum* ('the spacious palaces . . . where the treasures of innumerable images are stored'). In 2013 the Victoria & Albert Museum titled an exhibition 'The Palace of Memory'.
39. Ibid., chapter XXIII, p.139, italics added.
40. Augustine, *De Trinitate*, XII, 1.2, PL 42, col. 999, cited and trans. by Kathleen Donohue, 'Saint Augustine's *De Quantitate Animae*: A Study', M.Litt. dissertation, School of Classics, University College Dublin, 2005, p.59, emphasis added.
41. Brian Friel, 'Memories and Vagaries', *Irish Times*, 29 March 1960, p.8, italics added.
42. Paul Ricoeur, *Memory, History, Forgetting*, trans. Kathleen Blamey and David Pallauer, Chicago: University of Chicago Press, 2006, p.55.
43. Friel, 'Memories and Vagaries', op. cit., italics added.
44. Brian Friel, 'Among the Ruins', *Selected Short Stories*, Dublin: Gallery Press, 1979, p.106.
45. This is commonplace in Irish cultural history, where neo-Platonism lies everywhere. Denis Donoghue is one of the best expounders of its force in Yeats, for example, in *We Irish: Essays on Irish Literature and Society*, Berkeley: University of California Press, 1986. See also Richard Kearney, *Transitions: Narratives in Modern Irish Culture*, Dublin: Wolfhound, 1988. At the humbler level of Irish drama, see Paul Vincent Carroll, *Shadow and Substance: A Play in Four Acts*, London: Macmillan, 1938.
46. Denis Donoghue, *The Arts Without Mystery*, London: British Broadcasting Company, 1983.
47. Brian Friel, undated note, Friel Archive, National Library of Ireland, MS 37,052/2, underlining in original, double-underlining for 'then'.
48. Ibid. The following quotations are from the same manuscript.

49. Patrick Burke, 'Artists and Users in the Later Plays of Ibsen and Friel' in Ros Dixon and Irina Ruppoo Malone (eds), *Ibsen and Chekhov on the Irish Stage*, Dublin: Carysfort Press, 2012, p.73.
50. Brian Friel, untitled programme note for *The Loves of Cass McGuire*, Abbey Theatre, 10 April 1967, copy in Friel Archive, National Library of Ireland, MS 37,053/2.
51. For the full history of the struggle of the players in Elizabethan England, see E. K. Chambers, *The Elizabethan Stage*, 4 vols, Oxford: Clarendon, 1923, 1, pp.236–307. For the 1572 Act, see vol. 4, pp.269–71.
52. Brian Friel, *Crystal and Fox: A Play in Six Episodes*, London: Faber, 1970, p.57. All quotations from the play are from this edition, referred to by page numbers in the text.
53. Ciara O'Farrell, *Louis D'Alton and the Abbey Theatre*, Dublin: Four Courts, 2004, pp.32–62.
54. See Anthony Roche, 'Pinter and Ireland' in Peter Raby (ed.), *The Cambridge Companion to Harold Pinter*, Cambridge: Cambridge University Press, 2001, pp.175–91. See also Harold Pinter, 'Mac', in *Plays Three*, London: Faber, 1991.
55. Brian Friel, note dated 4 December 1967, Friel Archive, National Library of Ireland, MS 37,060/1.
56. Friel, note, dated 20 November 1967, Friel Archive, National Library of Ireland, MS 37,060/1.
57. Alan Ayckbourn, *The Crafty Art of Playmaking*, London: Faber, 2002, pp.4, 80.
58. See, for example, John Orr, *Tragicomedy and Contemporary Culture: Play and Performance from Beckett to Shepard*, Basingstoke: Palgrave Macmillan, 1991.
59. *Brian Friel in Conversation*, ed. Paul Delaney, p.63.
60. Friel note, dated 15 January 1967, Friel Archive, National Library of Ireland, MS 37,060/2, underlining in original.
61. Friel note, typed, dated 10 November 1967, Friel Archive, National Library of Ireland, MS 37, 060/1, underlining in original.
62. Richard Pine, *The Diviner*, op. cit., p.108.
63. Terry Eagleton, *On Evil*, New Haven and London: Yale University Press, 2010, p.76.
64. Eugene O'Neill, *Long Day's Journey into Night*, New Haven and London: Yale University Press, 1956, p.153. For the Abbey premiere of the play in 1959 see Edward L. Shaughnessy, *Eugene O'Neill and Ireland: The Critical Reception*, Westport, CT: Greenwood Press, 1988.
65. Friel note, dated 4 December 1967, Friel Archive, National Library of Ireland, MS 37,060/1.

Chapter 4: Speaking Out: *The Freedom of the City* and *Volunteers*

1. London: Bloomsbury, 2012. Quotation by kind permission of Howard Jacobson and Bloomsbury Publishing Ltd.
2. John Willett (ed.), *Brecht on Theatre: The Development of an Aesthetic*, New York: Hill and Wang, 1964, p.44.
3. Bertolt Brecht, 'A Short Organum for the Theatre' in John Willett (ed.), *Brecht on Theatre*, p.201.

4. Douglas Murray, *Bloody Sunday: Truth, Lies and the Saville Inquiry*, London: Biteback Publishing, 2012, p.2.
5. Brian Friel, *Essays, Diaries, Interviews*, ed. Christopher Murray, p.110.
6. Ibid.
7. F. C. McGrath, *Brian Friel's (Post)Colonial Drama: Language, Illusion, and Politics*, Syracuse: Syracuse University Press, 1999, p.96.
8. *Daily Telegraph* review, 28 February 1973. For a full account of the London production of *The Freedom of the City*, see Peter James Harris, *From Stage to Page: Critical Reception of Irish Plays in the London Theatre, 1925–1996*, Bern and Oxford: Peter Lang, 2011, pp.171–200. For the American reception, see Maria Szasz, *Brian Friel and America*, op. cit., pp.193–202.
9. Ulf Dantanus, *Brian Friel: A Study*, London: Faber, 1988, p.139.
10. For the online publication of the Saville Report see http://webarchive.nationalarchives.gov.uk/report-bloody-sunday-inquiry.org. This is dated 17/10/2010. Accessed 26 November 2012.
11. See Douglas Murray, *Bloody Sunday: Truth, Lies and the Saville Inquiry*, pp.302–5 (p.304).
12. See Friel's 1982 interview with Fintan O'Toole, in *Essays, Diaries, Interviews*, p.110.
13. T. S. Eliot, 'Tradition and the Individual Talent' in *The Sacred Wood: Essays on Poetry and Criticism*, London: Methuen, 1960, pp.47–59 (p.54).
14. Brian Friel in interview with Eavan Boland (1973), in *Essays, Diaries, Interviews*, p.58.
15. Richard Pine, *The Diviner: The Art of Brian Friel*, Dublin: University College Dublin Press, 1999, p.134.
16. *Bloody Sunday, 1972: Lord Widgery's Report of Events in Londonderry, on 30 January 1972*, London: Stationery Office, 2001. All subsequent quotations are from this edition.
17. Brian Friel, *The Freedom of the City*, in *Plays 1*, London: Faber, 1996, p.168. This is the text, a reissue of that in *Selected Plays*, 1986, used throughout this chapter and will be referred to hereafter as *Plays 1*.
18. Yet see Widgery *Report*, pp.21–2, claiming, 'There is not a shred of evidence' to support the 'suggestions' that 1 PARA had been brought to Derry 'either to flush out any IRA gunmen in the Bogside and destroy them' or as 'a punitive force [. . .] to give the residents a rough handling and discourage them from making or supporting further attacks on the troops'. The Saville Inquiry was to show that there was, indeed, such a plan in the mind of General Ford.
19. *Eyewitness Bloody Sunday*, ed. Don Mullan, Dublin: Wolfhound, 1997, p.96 and see also p.72.
20. See Edward Daly, *Mister, Are You a Priest? Jottings by Bishop Edward Daly*, Dublin: Four Courts, 2000, pp.187–200. Later on, Daly praised the Saville Inquiry but was still angry with Widgery's *Report*: 'He had all the evidence to make the right decision.' See interview with Patsy McGarry, '"Bloody Sunday changed my life in every way" says former Bishop of Derry', *Irish Times*, 20 March 2007.
21. Anthony Roche, *Brian Friel: Theatre and Politics*, Basingstoke: Palgrave Macmillan, 2011, pp.105–29.
22. *Dr Johnson on Shakespeare*, ed. W. K. Wimsatt, Harmondsworth: Penguin, 1969, 'Preface', pp.69–71.

23. Peter Brook, *The Empty Space*, New York: Discus/Atheneum, 1969, p.71.
24. Ibid., p.72.
25. Stephen Watt, 'Friel and the Northern Ireland "Troubles" Play' in Anthony Roche (ed.), *The Cambridge Companion to Brian Friel*, p.36.
26. T. S. Eliot, 'Gerontion', *The Complete Poems and Plays*, London: Faber, 2004, p.38.
27. Pine, *The Diviner: The Art of Brian Friel*, p.134.
28. Colin Wilson, *The Outsider*, London: Pan Books, 1963, p.14.
29. Éamonn McCann, *War and an Irish Town: New and Updated Edition*, London: Pluto Press, 1980, p.57. See Widgery *Report*, p.20. The British ambassador to Ireland also deliberately used the term 'hooligans' to identify those who burned down the embassy in Dublin after Bloody Sunday. See Diarmaid Ferriter, *Ambiguous Republic: Ireland in the 1970s*, London: Profile Books, 2012, p.129.
30. Brian Friel, 'An Observer in Minneapolis' in Paul Delaney (ed.), *Brian Friel in Conversation*, p.39.
31. Hugh Hunt, *The Abbey: Ireland's National Theatre 1904–1979*, Dublin: Gill and Macmillan, 1979, pp.183–4.
32. *Brendan Behan's Borstal Boy*, adapted for the stage by Frank McMahon, Dublin: Four Masters, 1971. The play was to have a long life on the Dublin stage, with Niall Toibin playing the older Behan.
33. See Tomás Mac Anna, *Fallaing Aonghusa: Saol Amharclainne* [A Theatrical Life], Dublin: Clócomhar, 2000, pp.238–40.
34. Hugh Hunt, *The Abbey*, p.211.
35. It might be said that in pursuit of theatricality, Morrison's production of *The Freedom of the City* deviated from realism. I recall an Elizabethan-style inn-yard setting into which was flown the Mayor's parlour with a stained-glass backdrop, and a quasi-Shakespearean fluid use of space.
36. John Devitt, in conversation with Nicholas Grene and Chris Morash, *Shifting Scenes: Irish Theatre-Going, 1955–1985*, Dublin: Carysfort Press, 2008, p.88.
37. Friel, 'The Theatre of Hope and Despair', *Essays, Diaries, Interviews*, p.22, emphasis added.
38. Eric Bentley, *The Theatre of Commitment and Other Essays on Drama in Our Society*, New York: Atheneum, 1967, p.200. The following quotations are from this source.
39. Theodor Adorno, 'Commitment', trans. Francis McDonagh, in *Aesthetics and Politics*, ed. Ronald Taylor, London: Verso, 1980, pp.177–95 (p.190).
40. See Christa Velten-Mrowka, '"Am I a con man?": Brian Friel's idea of the self-reflective artist, viewed in the light of Adorno's Aesthetic Theory' in Patrick Lonergan and Riana O'Dwyer (eds), *Echoes Down the Corridor*, Dublin: Carysfort Press, 2007, pp.95–106.
41. E. B. [Eric Bentley], 'Bertolt Brecht' in John Gassner and Edward Quinn (eds), *The Reader's Encyclopedia of World Drama*, London: Methuen, 1970, pp.78–85 (p.84).
42. Fachtna O'Kelly, *Irish Press*, 28–29 March 1975, in Brian Friel, *Essays, Diaries, Interviews*, pp.61–2.
43. F. C. McGrath, *Brian Friel's (Post)Colonial Drama*, p.125.

44. Anthony Roche, *Brian Friel, Theatre and Politics*, pp.93–104.
45. Richard Pine, *The Diviner: The Art of Brian Friel*, p.143.
46. Michael Billington, *State of the Nation: British Theatre Since 1945*, London: Faber, 2007, p.152.
47. Friel Archive, National Library of Ireland, MS 37,069/1, note dated 3 September 1973.
48. Diarmaid Ferriter, *Ambiguous Republic*, op. cit., p.138.
49. Ibid., p.216.
50. For the text, see Brian Friel, *Crystal and Fox and The Mundy Scheme*, New York: Farrar, Straus and Giroux, 1970. Rejected by the Abbey Theatre, *The Mundy Scheme* premiered at the Olympia Theatre, Dublin, on 10 June 1969, directed by Donal Donnelly. It opened at the Royale Theatre, New York, on 11 December 1969 and closed after ten previews and two performances. See Maria Szasz, *Brian Friel and America,* pp.190–3.
51. Patrick F. Wallace, 'A Re-Appraisal of the Archaeological Significance of Wood Quay' in John Bradley (ed.), *Viking Dublin Exposed: The Wood Quay Saga*, Dublin: O'Brien Press, 1984, pp.112–43 (p.114).
52. Howard Clarke, 'The Historian and Wood Quay' in John Bradley (ed.), *Viking Dublin Exposed*, pp.144–53 (p.152).
53. Angret Simms, 'A Key Place for Dublin Past and Present,' in John Bradley (ed.), *Viking Dublin Exposed*, pp.154–63 (p.154).
54. Richard English, *Irish Freedom: The History of Nationalism in Ireland*, Basingstoke: Macmillan, 2006, pp.80–1.
55. Ibid., pp.248–52.
56. Brian Friel, *Volunteers*, London: Faber, 1979, p.44. All subsequent quotations are from this edition, to which page numbers refer.
57. Samuel Beckett, *The Complete Dramatic Works*, pp.117–18.
58. Howard Jacobson, 'What if Joseph K. Did It?' in *Whatever It Is I Don't Like It*, London: Bloomsbury, 2011, pp.277–8. Quoted by permission of Mr Jacobson and the publisher.
59. Ulf Dantanus, *Brian Friel: A Study*, p.153.
60. Seamus Heaney, 'Digging Deeper: Brian Friel's *Volunteers*', reprinted in *Preoccupations: Selected Prose 1968–1978*, London: Faber, 1980, pp.214–16. My quotations refer to this edition of Heaney's review.
61. Dennis O'Driscoll, *Stepping Stones: Interviews with Seamus Heaney*, London: Faber, 2008, p.179.
62. For an excellent comparative essay, see Ruth Neil, 'Digging into History: A Reading of Brian Friel's *Volunteers* and Seamus Heaney's "Viking Dublin: Trial Pieces"', *Irish University Review*, Vol. 16 (1986), pp.35–47.
63. O'Driscoll, *Stepping Stones*, p.179.
64. W. B. Yeats, 'Anima Hominis', *Mythologies*, London: Macmillan, 1959, p.331.
65. 'They know that Hamlet and Lear are gay/Gaiety transfiguring all that dread' from 'Lapis Lazuli'; 'for we/Traffic in mockery' from 'Nineteen Hundred and Nineteen'. See W. B. Yeats, *Collected Poems*, London: Macmillan, 1950, pp.236, 338.
66. Seamus Heaney, *Preoccupations*, p.215, emphasis added.

67. Seamus Heaney contributed a programme note, 'Volunteers', Friel Archive, National Library of Ireland, MS 37,070/8. See also Anthony Roche, *Brian Friel: Theatre and Politics,* pp.103–4.
68. Patrick Burke, 'Friel and Performance History' in Anthony Roche (ed.), *Cambridge Companion to Brian Friel*, p.125.

Chapter 5: *Living Quarters* and *Faith Healer*

1. London: Fourth Estate, 2011, p.13. Reprinted by permission of HarperCollins Publishers Ltd.
2. Seamus Deane, 'The Writer and the Troubles', *Threshold*, Vol. 25 (summer 1974), pp.13–17.
3. Ibid., p.15.
4. Seamus Deane, 'After Derry, 30 January 1972', *Gradual Wars*, Shannon: Irish University Press, p.16.
5. Deane, 'The Writer and the Troubles', p.15.
6. Brian Friel, *Volunteers*, London: Faber, 1979, p.58.
7. Brian Friel, *Give Me Your Answer, Do!*, Loughcrew: Gallery Press, 1997, p.79.
8. Michael Billington, *State of the Nation: British Theatre since 1945*, London: Faber, 2007, p.367.
9. See Albert de Giacomo, *T.C. Murray, Dramatist: Voice of Rural Ireland*, Syracuse: Syracuse University Press, 2003; and Robert Hogan, 'The Brave Timidity of T.C. Murray', *Irish University Review*, Vol. 26 (1996), pp.155–62.
10. Travis Bogard, *Contour in Time: The Plays of Eugene O'Neill*, Oxford: Oxford University Press, 1972, pp.119–23; and Edward L. Shaughnessy, *Eugene O'Neill in Ireland: The Critical Reception*, Westport, CT: Greenwood Press, 1988, pp.35–6.
11. Michael Lloyd, 'Brian Friel's Greek Tragedy: Narrative, Drama, and Fate in *Living Quarters*', *Irish University Review*, Vol. 30, No. 2 (2000), pp.244–53 (p.250).
12. Brian Friel, 'Self-Portrait', *Essays, Diaries, Interviews*, ed. Christopher Murray, London: Faber, 1999, p.39.
13. Susan Basnett-McGuire, *Luigi Pirandello*, Basingstoke: Macmillan, 1983, p.117.
14. Seamus Deane, *Celtic Revivals*, London: Faber, 1985, p.166.
15. Anthony Roche, *Brian Friel: Theatre and Politics*, pp.122–5.
16. Brian Friel, *Plays 1*, London: Faber, 1996, p.175. Subsequent quotations are from this edition, referred to by page numbers in parentheses.
17. Christopher Murray, 'Pirandello and Brian Friel: Some Affinities' in John C. Barnes and Stefano Milioto (eds), *Le due trilogie Pirandelliane*, Palermo: Palumbo, 1992, pp.207–15 (p.214).
18. Brian Friel Papers, National Library of Ireland, MS 37,072/1, notes dated December 1975–January 1976.
19. Brigitte Le Juez, *Beckett before Beckett*, trans. Ros Schwartz, London: Souvenir Press, 2007, pp.56–69.
20. Richard Pine, *The Diviner: The Art of Brian Friel*, p.157.
21. Sophocles, *Ajax*, in *Electra and Other Plays*, trans. E. F. Watling, Harmondsworth: Penguin, 1953.

22. Albert Camus, 'There is but one truly philosophical problem and that is suicide' in *The Myth of Sisyphus*, trans. Justin O'Brien, Harmondsworth: Penguin, 1955, p.11. See Christopher Murray, 'The Representation of Suicide in Modern Irish Drama: Part One, 1900–1950' in Chloé Avril and Ronald Paul (eds), *At Home in the World: Essays and Poems in Honour of Britta Olinder*, Gothenburg: University of Gothenburg Press, 2008, pp.173–87.
23. Al Alvarez, *The Savage God: A Study of Suicide*, London: Bloomsbury, 2002, p.146.
24. Brian Friel, *Essays, Diaries, Interviews*, p.24. See also p.181, n.12.
25. Albert Camus, *The Rebel: An Essay on Man in Revolt*, trans. Anthony Bower, New York: Vintage Books, 1956, p.13.
26. Ibid., emphasis added.
27. Ibid., p.16.
28. Ibid., p.17.
29. Ibid., p.19.
30. Ibid., p.22, emphasis added.
31. Brian Friel, 'The Theatre of Hope and Despair', *Essays, Diaries, Interviews*, p.19.
32. *Irish Times*, 17 June 1989, cited Bridget Hourican, *Dictionary of Irish Biography*, Cambridge: Cambridge University Press and Royal Irish Academy, 2009, 5, p.692.
33. See also Terence Brown, '"Have we a context?": Transition, Self and Society in the Theatre of Brian Friel' in Alan J. Peacock (ed.), *The Achievement of Brian Friel*, pp.190–201 (p.192).
34. Joe Dowling, 'Staging Friel' in Alan J. Peacock (ed.), *The Achievement of Brian Friel*, pp.178–89 (p.188).
35. Augusto Boal, *Theatre of the Oppressed*, trans. Charles and Maria-Odilia Leal McBride, London: Pluto, 1979.
36. See Garry Wills, *Witches and Jesuits: Shakespeare's **Macbeth***, New York and Oxford: Oxford University Press, 1995.
37. Unsigned note, *The Bergman Collection: The Magician*, Tartan DVD, 1994. I am indebted to the late John Devitt for bringing this film to my attention.
38. Ibid.
39. Geoffrey Macnab, *Ingmar Bergman: The Life and Films of the Last Great European Director*, London: I.B. Tauris, 2009, p.106.
40. Consider John Donne, 'And new philosophy calls all in doubt', *An Anatomy of the World* (1611) line 205, referring to the scientific discoveries of Copernicus and Galileo. Likewise, in the 1590s, Michel de Montaigne's essays, such as 'On Experience', emphasised that to philosophise is to doubt, an idea dramatised in *Hamlet*.
41. W. B. Yeats, *Essays and Introductions*, London: Macmillan, 1961, p.523.
42. *The Poetics of Aristotle*, trans. Stephen Halliwell, London: Duckworth, 1987, p.37, emphasis added.
43. Maria Szasz, *Brian Friel and America*, Dublin: Glasnevin Publishing, 2013, p.205.
44. Brian Friel, '*Faith Healer* Comes to New York', *Princeton University Library Chronicle*, Vol. LXVIII, No. 1 & 2 (autumn 2006–winter 2007), pp.516–18.
45. Walter Kerr, '*Faith Healer*: A Play That Risks All', *New York Sunday Times*, 15 April 1979, pp.9–10.
46. David Barnett, 'Staging the Indeterminate: Brian Friel's *Faith Healer* as a Postdramatic Theatre-Text', *Irish University Review*, Vol. 36 (2006), pp.374–88.

47. T. S. Eliot, 'The Possibility of a Poetic Drama', *The Sacred Wood*, London: Methuen, 1960, pp.60–70 (p.68).
48. T. S. Eliot, 'The Three Voices of Poetry', *On Poetry and Poets*, London: Faber, 1957, pp.89–102 (p.100). See also Denis Donoghue, *The Third Voice: Modern British and American Verse Drama*, Princeton: Princeton University Press, 1959.
49. Katharine J. Worth, 'Precursor and Model' in Arnold P. Hinchcliffe (ed.), *T.S. Eliot: Plays, A Casebook*, Basingstoke: Macmillan, 1985, pp.60–70 (pp.60, 62).
50. Marvin Carlson, 'Theater and Dialogism' in Janelle G. Reinelt and Joseph R. Roach (eds), *Critical Theory and Performance*, Ann Arbor: University of Michigan Press, 1992, pp.313–23 (pp.314, 317).
51. Brian Friel, *Faith Healer*, in *Plays 1*, London: Faber, 1996, p.376. Subsequent quotations are from this edition, to which page numbers in parentheses refer.
52. Ibsen, in encouraging a fellow-writer to stand up against calumny, remarked: 'Aristocracy of spirit is the only weapon against this kind of thing. Appear indifferent.' Michael Meyer, *Ibsen: A Biography*, Harmondsworth: Pelican Books, 1974, p.374 and see also p.572.
53. Thomas Kilroy, 'Theatrical Text and Literary Text' in Alan J. Peacock (ed.), *The Achievement of Brian Friel*, pp.91–102 (p.102).
54. Brian Friel, *Essays, Diaries, Interviews*, p.111.
55. Samuel Beckett, *Disjecta: Miscellaneous Writings and a Dramatic Fragment*, ed. Ruby Cohn, London: Calder, 1983, p.145.
56. Samuel Beckett, *Proust and Three Dialogues with Georges Duthuit*, London: Calder, 1965, p.67.
57. R. D. Laing, *Self and Others*, 2nd edn, Harmondsworth: Penguin, 1971, p.32, italics in original.
58. R. D. Laing, Preface, *The Divided Self*, second edition, Harmondsworth: Penguin, 1965, p.11.
59. T. S. Eliot, 'Little Gidding', *The Complete Poems and Plays*, London: Faber, 2004, p.197.
60. Eliot, 'The Dry Salvages', *Complete Poems and Plays*, p.190.
61. Robert Tracy, 'Brian Friel's Rituals of Memory', *Irish University Review*, Vol. 37 (2007), pp.395–412 (p.396).
62. Nicholas Grene, 'Five Ways of Looking at *Faith Healer*' in Anthony Roche (ed.), *The Cambridge Companion to Brian Friel*, pp.53–65 (p.53).
63. Denis Donoghue, *The Arts Without Mystery*, London: British Broadcasting Co., 1983, p.12.
64. Frank Kermode, *The Genesis of Secrecy*, Cambridge: Harvard University Press, 1979, p.xi.
65. Ibid., p.126. Of course, in the Roman Catholic Church, up to recent times, private interpretation of the bible was not allowed. In that context, *Faith Healer* is protestant, counter-cultural.
66. *Brian Friel in Conversation*, ed. Paul Delaney, Ann Arbor: University of Michigan Press, 2000, p.125.
67. See Maria Szasz, *Brian Friel and America*, pp.204–6.
68. Joe Dowling, 'Staging Friel' in Alan J. Peacock (ed.), *The Achievement of Brian Friel*, pp.178–89 (p.180).
69. Ibid., p.188.
70. Information from Joe Dowling, 4 February 2013.

71. Sebastian Barry, 'Dying to Mourn: on Donal McCann', *Irish Times*, 17 November 2001, *Magazine*, p.82.
72. In December 2012, Joe Dowling guest-directed *The Dead* at the Abbey in a dramatisation by Frank McGuinness. Earlier that year, he played Frank Hardy at the Guthrie in Minneapolis. The two stories have a certain amount in common.
73. *Donal McCann Remembered*, eds. Pat Laffan and Faith O'Grady, Dublin: New Island, 2000, p.188.
74. Ibid., p.29, emphasis added.
75. Ibid., in interview with Gerry Stembridge, pp.165–94 (p.190).
76. Eugene O'Neill, *Long Day's Journey into Night*, New Haven and London: Yale University Press, 1956, p.152.
77. *W.B. Yeats and T. Sturge Moore: Their Correspondence 1901–1937*, ed. Ursula Bridge, London: Routledge & Kegan Paul, 1953, p.156.
78. Philip Larkin, 'Church Going' in *Poems: Selected and with an Introduction by Martin Amis,* London: Faber, 2011, pp.6–8.

Chapter 6: A Kind of Trilogy: *Making History*, *Translations* and *The Home Place*

1. See Aidan Breen, entry for Colum Cille (Columba), *Dictionary of Irish Biography*, Cambridge: Cambridge University Press and Royal Irish Academy, 2009, vol. 2, pp.706–8.
2. 'Colm Cille's Exile', trans. James Carney, in *The Penguin Book of Irish Poetry*, ed. Patrick Crotty, London and New York: Penguin Books, 2010, pp.34–6 (p.35).
3. Brian Friel in interview with Peter Lennon, *Essays, Diaries, Interviews*, p.2.
4. Robert Bolt, Preface, *A Man for All Seasons*, London: Heineman, 1960, p.xii.
5. Michael Billington, *State of the Nation: British Theatre since 1945*, London: Faber, 2007, p.145.
6. See Marilynn J. Richtarik, *Acting Between the Lines: The Field Day Theatre Company and Irish Cultural Politics 1980–84*, Oxford: Clarendon Press, 1994; and Aidan O'Malley, *Field Day and the Translation of Irish Identities: Performing Contradictions*, Basingstoke: Palgrave Macmillan, 2011.
7. Hiram Morgan, entry on Hugh O'Neill, *Dictionary of Irish Biography*, Vol. 7, pp.764–72 (p.765).
8. Brian Friel, programme note for Field Day production of *Making History*, Guild Hall, Derry, September 1988, in *Essays, Diaries Interviews*, p.135.
9. Brian Friel, 'Making a Reply to the Criticisms of *Translations* by J. H. Andrews', in *Essays, Diaries, Interviews*, p.119.
10. Thomas Kilroy, *The O'Neill*, Loughcrew: Gallery Press, 1995, p.8.
11. Hiram Morgan, 'Hugh O'Neill', op. cit., p.768.
12. Thomas Kilroy, 'A Generation of Playwrights', op. cit., p.136. See also 'Thomas Kilroy in conversation with Gerald Dawe', *Krino13: Theatre and Ireland*, Dublin: Anna Livia Press, n.d [c.1990], pp.1–8 (p.2).

13. Tadhg Ó hAnracháin, 'Peter Lombard', *Dictionary of Irish Biography*, Vol. 5, pp.552–6 (p.554).
14. Sean O'Faolain, *The Great O'Neill: A Biography of Hugh O'Neill Earl of Tyrone, 1550–1616*, Cork: Mercier Press, 1970, p.276.
15. Brian Friel, *Making History*, in *Plays 2*, London: Faber, 1999, p.257. All subsequent quotations from the play refer to this edition, designated by page numbers in parentheses.
16. I have in mind here specifically Hayden White, 'The Historical Text as Literary Artifact' in his *Tropics of Discourse: Essays in Cultural Criticism* [1978], paperback edn. Baltimore and London: Johns Hopkins University Press, 1985, pp.81–100.
17. O'Faolain, *The Great O'Neill*, p.277.
18. Brian Friel, *Translations*, in *Plays 1*, London: Faber, 1996, p.446.
19. Edmund Spenser, *A View of the Present State of Ireland* [written 1596, published 1633], in *The Field Day Anthology of Irish Literature*, ed. Seamus Deane et al., London: Faber, and Derry: Field Day, 1991, vol. 1, p.189. See also *Spenser in Ireland: The Faerie Queene 1596-1996*, a special issue of *Irish University Review*, ed. Anne Fogarty, Vol. 26, No. 2 (1996).
20. See *Dictionary of Irish Biography*, 7, 769. Charles Blount, Lord Mountjoy (1563–1606), triumphantly finished the Nine Years' War in Ireland in which Essex had signally failed. It was Mountjoy who defeated the Irish under O'Neill at Kinsale in 1601 and forced the withdrawal of the Spanish; in 1603, he made O'Neill submit to Queen Elizabeth's authority, after which he became Lord Lieutenant of Ireland. See also *The Oxford Companion to Irish History*, ed. S. J. Connolly, Oxford: Oxford University Press, 1998, pp.371–2.
21. *Dictionary of Irish Biography*, 7, 769.
22. The scene is indebted to O'Faoláin's wonderful, novelist's account as he ended his biography, 'Idly his fingers touch the Archbishop's manuscript', etc., *The Great O'Neill*, pp.280–1. Friel is both playing with O'Faoláin's text and 'making' his own.
23. Mrs Malaprop in Richard Brinsley Sheridan's *The Rivals* (1775), in *The Dramatic Works of R.B. Sheridan*, World's Classics edition, Oxford: Oxford University Press, 1906, Act 4, Scene 2, p.66.
24. Brian Friel, *Essays, Diaries, Interviews*, p.75.
25. Kevin Whelan, 'Between: The Politics of Culture in Friel's *Translations*', *Field Day Review*, Vol. 6 (2010), pp.7–27 (p.8).
26. Brian Friel, *Making History*, *Plays 2*, p.335.
27. Brian Friel, *Translations*, in *Plays 1*, London: Faber, 1996, pp.394–5. All subsequent quotations from *Translations* refer to this edition by page numbers in parentheses.
28. 'The set itself suggests the instability not just of this small town [Ballybeg] but of the island as a whole.' Helen Heusner Lojek, 'Mapping the Territory: Brian Friel's *Translations* (1980)', *The Spaces of Irish Drama: Stage and Place in Contemporary Plays*, New York: Palgrave Macmillan, 2011, pp.15–36 (p.17).
29. Brian Friel, *The Communication Cord*, London: Faber, 1983, p.11.
30. Brian Friel, *Essays, Diaries, Interviews*, p.52.
31. Ibid., p.54.
32. Lionel Trilling, *Sincerity and Authenticity*, London: Oxford University Press, 1972.
33. Edward Said, *Culture and Imperialism*, London: Vintage, 1994, p.273.

34. Helen Lojek, 'Brian Friel's Plays and George Steiner's Linguistics: Translating the Irish', *Contemporary Literature*, Vol. 35, No. 1 (spring 1994), pp.83–99 (p.90).
35. Ciarán Deane, 'Brian Friel's *Translations*: The Origins of a Cultural Experiment', *Field Day Review*, Vol. 5 (2009), pp.7–47 (p.17).
36. Ibid., p.18.
37. Lady Gregory, *Our Irish Theatre* [1913], Gerrards Cross: Colin Smythe, 1972, p.20.
38. Cited by Ciarán Deane, op. cit., p.9.
39. Brian Friel in interview with Matt Wolf, in Paul Delaney (ed.), *Brian Friel in Conversation*, Ann Arbor: University of Michigan Press, 2000, p.200.
40. W. B. Yeats, 'Samhain: 1904', in *Explorations*, New York; Collier, 1973, p.157.
41. Cited by Ciarán Deane, op. cit., p.12.
42. Brian Friel, in interview with Paddy Agnew (1980), in *Essays, Diaries, Interviews*, pp.85–6.
43. Cited by Ciarán Deane, op. cit., p.33.
44. 'What was enacted on stage was a scene of transformation; what the play accomplished was also an act of translation. [. . .] Modern Irish theatre begins here,' with the performance of *Cathleen Ní Houlihan*. Robert Welch, *The Abbey Theatre 1899-1999*, Oxford: Oxford University Press, 1999, p.16.
45. Chris Morash, *A History of Irish Theatre 1601-2000*, Cambridge: Cambridge University Press, 2002, pp.233–41 (p.240).
46. Stephen Gwynn, *Irish Literature and Drama in the English Language: A Short History*, London: Thomas Nelson, 1936, p.160.
47. Seamus Deane, *Strange Country: Modernity and Nationhood in Irish Writing since 1790*, Oxford: Clarendon, 1997, p.70.
48. George Steiner, *After Babel: Aspects of Language and Translation*, New York and London, Oxford: Oxford University Press, 1975, p.47.
49. Charles McGlinchey, *The Last of the Name*, ed. with introduction by Brian Friel, Belfast: Blackstaff Press, 1986, p.7.
50. Garry Hynes's production of *Translations* initiated at the McCarter Theatre in Princeton in October 2006 and later opened at the Manhattan Theater Club in New York. At Princeton, Hynes spoke in advance with the artistic director of the McCarter about the play. See 'Speaking of *Translations*: A Conversation with Garry Hynes and Emily Mann', *Princeton University Library Chronicle*, Vol. LXVIII (autumn 2006–winter 2007), pp.519–25. In a question-and-answer session after the first performance, a pressing question was what becomes of Yolland at the end of the play. See also Anthony Roche, *Brian Friel: Theatre and Politics*, pp.131–2.
51. Seamus Heaney, *North*, Faber: 1975, pp.37–8.
52. Colm Tóibín, *New Ways to Kill Your Mother: Writers and Their Families*, London and New York: Penguin Group, 2012, p.3.
53. Brian Friel, 'Preface: Where We Live' in Michael Herity (ed.), *Ordnance Survey Letters: Donegal [...] 1835*, Dublin: Four Masters, 2000, pp.vii–ix.
54. Ibid., p.ix.
55. J. M. Synge, *The Playboy of the Western Word*, in *Collected Works*, op. cit., vol. 3, *Plays*, ed. Ann Saddlemyer, *Book 1*, p.161.
56. Aidan O'Malley, *Field Day and the Translation of Irish Identities*, op. cit., p.20.
57. Nicholas Grene, *The Politics of Irish Drama*, pp.41–2.

58. Brian Friel in interview with Matt Wolf, in Paul Delaney (ed.), *Brian Friel in Conversation*, p.200.
59. Kevin Whelan, 'Between: The Politics of Culture in Friel's *Translations*', op. cit., p.8.
60. After the opening of the 2013 production of *Translations*, directed by Adrian Dunbar at the Millennium Forum in Derry, Brian Friel wondered what the actor Des McAleer was thinking as he said the final speech. To my mind, McAleer succeeded in creating the new Hugh, capable of bearing the burden of tradition and yet convinced that change has its good qualities too.
61. Harry White, *Music and the Irish Literary Imagination*, Oxford: Oxford University Press, 2008, p.225.
62. Brian Friel to Christopher Murray, 4 April 2012.
63. See Conor Cruise O'Brien, *Writers and Politics: Essays and Criticism*, Harmondsworth: Penguin, 1976, p.14.
64. Dennis O'Driscoll, *Stepping Stones: Interviews with Seamus Heaney*, p.415.
65. Brian Friel, *Plays 2*, p.283.
66. William Shakespeare, *Julius Caesar*, 4.3.18–19.
67. W. B. Yeats, *Explorations*, London: Macmillan, 1962, p.347, n.1, emphasis added.
68. The old idea of an extra province in Ireland was made current again in the important journal *The Crane Bag* (1977–81), eds. Mark Patrick Hederman and Richard Kearney. In their opening editorial, the editors put forward the fifth province as a place 'marked by the absence of any particular political and geographical delineation, something more like a dis-position', *Crane Bag*, Vol. 1, No. 1 (spring 1977), p.4. The Field Day pamphlets were to grow out of this 'disposition', Seamus Deane being on the board of both *Crane Bag* and Field Day.
69. Brian Friel, *The Home Place*, Loughcrew: Gallery Press, 2005, p.11. All subsequent quotations are from this edition, referred to by page numbers in parentheses.
70. Austin Clarke, 'The Planter's Daughter', *Poems 1917-1938*, Dublin: Dolmen Press; Oxford: Oxford University Press, 1974, p.173. First published in 1929, Clarke's poem has been much anthologised.
71. Terence Brown, *Ireland: a Social and Cultural History 1922-2002*, London: Harper Perennial, 2004, p.99.
72. Ibid., p.415.
73. See David Hammond, *A Centenary Selection of Moore's Melodies*, with an introduction by Seamus Heaney, Skerries, Co. Dublin: Gilbert Dalton, 1979, p.61.
74. Thomas Moore, prefatory letter to the third edition of the *Melodies*, cited by Ronan Kelly, *Bard of Erin: The Life of Thomas Moore*, London: Penguin Books, 2009, p.160.
75. Brian Friel, 'Seven Notes for a Festival Programme, 4: Music', in *Essays, Diaries, Interviews*, p.176.
76. Harry White, *Music and the Irish Literary Imagination*, p.224.
77. Susannah Clapp, review of *The Home Place* at the Comedy Theatre, London, following its premiere at the Dublin Gate, in the *Observer*, 29 May 2005, 'Review', p.10.
78. Seamus Deane, *The Field Day Anthology of Irish Writing*, op. cit., I, p.1053.
79. Ibid., p.1056. Deane writes of Moore's skill in 'transformation of one culture into the idiom of another'.
80. Leigh Hunt, in *Byron and his Contemporaries*, cited by David Hammond, op. cit., p.12.

81. Declan Kiberd, 'Synge's *Tristes Tropiques*: *The Aran Islands*', in *Irish Classics*, London: Granta, 2000, pp.420–39 (p.438).
82. Stephen Jay Gould, *The Mismeasure of Man*, New York: Norton, 1981; revised and expanded edition London and New York: Penguin Group, 1997. In his text of *The Home Place*, Friel appends an extract from A. C. Haddon, 'Studies in Irish Craniology: The Aran Islands, Co. Galway', a paper read before the Royal Irish Academy 12 December 1892. This was the main source for Richard Gore's character.
83. J. M. Synge, *Collected Works*, op. cit., II (*Prose*), p.162.
84. Ibid., p.149.
85. Terence Brown, 'Music: The Cultural Issue', *The Literature of Ireland: Criticism and Culture*, Cambridge: Cambridge University Press, 2010, p.42, emphasis added. Brown is here commenting on a passage in Synge's *Aran Islands* (*CW*, 2, 99–100).
86. George O'Brien, 'The Late Plays' in Anthony Roche (ed.), *The Cambridge Companion to Brian Friel*, p.97.
87. John Hewitt, 'The Colony' in Alan Warner (ed.), *The Selected John Hewitt*, Belfast: Blackstaff Press, 1981, p.24.
88. Brian Friel, *Uncle Vanya: A Version of the Play by Anton Chekhov*, Loughcrew: Gallery Press, 1998, pp.85–6. In February 2012, a new production, directed by Mick Gordon for the Lyric Theatre, Belfast, forcibly brought home to me the connection with *The Home Place*, which Gordon also directed in Belfast in February 2009.
89. Csilla Bertha, 'Art as a *lieu de mémoire* in Brian Friel's *The Home Place*' in Ríonach uí Ógáin et al. (eds), *Sean, Nua agus Síoraíocht: Féilscríbhinn in Ómós do Dháithí Ó hÓgáin* [Festschrift], Dublin: Coiscéim, 2012, pp.52–64 (p.55). A revised version is included in Chapter 10 of the present book.
90. Brian Friel, *Plays 1*, p.90. On the preceding page, Gar Private interprets the music as a plea for 'pity'.
91. Clifford Geertz, After the Revolution: The Fate of Nationalism in the New States', *The Interpretation of Cultures*, New York: Basic Books, 1973, p.238.

Chapter 7: *Aristocrats, Dancing at Lughnasa* and *Molly Sweeney*

1. Harmondworth: Penguin, 1964, p.154. Quotation by kind permission of the Society of Authors, on behalf of the Bernard Shaw Estate.
2. London: Routledge, 2010, p.76. Quotation by kind permission of Dr Gerardine Meaney and Routledge Press.
3. Zsuzsa Csikai, 'A Complex Relationship: Chekhov's Plays and Irish Author-Translators' in Marianna Gula, Mária Kurdi and István D. Rácz (eds), *The Binding Strength of Irish Studies: Festschrift in Honour of Csilla Bertha and Donald E. Morse*, Debrecen: Debrecen University Press, 2011, pp.227–36 (p.235). See also Robert Tracy, 'The Russian Connection: Friel and Chekhov', *Irish University Review*, Vol. 29 (1999), pp.64–77; Richard Pine, 'Friel's Irish Russia' in Anthony Roche (ed.), *Cambridge Companion to Brian Friel*, Cambridge: Cambridge University Press, 2006, pp.104–16; and Ros Dixon and Irina Ruppo Malone (eds), *Ibsen and Chekhov on the Irish Stage*, Dublin: Carysfort Press, 2012.

4. 'It's a work of love.' Brian Friel, in interview with Elgie Gillespie (1981), *Essays, Diaries, Interviews*, p.99.
5. Brian Friel, *Three Sisters: A Translation of the Play by Anton Chekhov*, Loughcrew: Gallery Press, 2008. The subtitle on the cover reads '*after Chekhov*' in contrast to the 1981 cover stating '*A translation*'.
6. Brian Friel, *A Month in the Country: After Turgenev*, Loughcrew: Gallery Press, 1992, Preface, p.7, emphasis added.
7. Ibid., a note on Ivan Turgenev (1818–83), pp.9–11 (p.10).
8. Brian Friel, *Plays One*, London: Faber, 1996, p.304. All subsequent quotations from *Aristocrats* are from this edition, to which page numbers will refer in parentheses.
9. Brian Friel, *Selected Stories*, p.60.
10. Patrick Burke, 'Friel and Performance History', *Cambridge Companion to Brian Friel*, p.124.
11. In his preface, Bernard Shaw referred to *The Cherry Orchard* as the cultural context for *Heartbreak House* and subtitled his comedy *A Fantasia in the Russian Manner on English Themes*.
12. Brian Friel, 'The Diviner', *Selected Stories*, pp.17–26.
13. Bernard Shaw, *Heartbreak House*, Harmondsworth: Penguin, 1964, p.129.
14. *The Book of Judith*, in *The New English Bible with the Apocrypha*, Oxford: Oxford University Press, 1970.
15. Seamus Deane, 'The Name of the Game' in Alan J. Peacock (ed.), *The Achievement of Brian Friel*, Gerrards Cross: Colin Smythe, 1993, pp.111–12.
16. Brian Friel, *Dancing at Lughnasa*, in *Plays Two*, London: Faber, 1999, p.48. Subsequent quotations are from this edition, to which page numbers will refer parenthetically.
17. Thomas Kilroy, 'Friendship', *Irish University Review: Special Issue – Brian Friel*, ed. Anthony Roche, Vol. 29, No. 1 (1999), p.88.
18. For an excellent development of this point, see Éamonn Jordan, 'The Meta-Theatricalization of Memory in Brian Friel's *Dancing at Lughnasa*' in Edric Caldicott and Anne Fuchs (eds), *Cultural Memory: Essays on European Literature and History*, Oxford and Bern: Peter Lang, 2003, pp.129–45.
19. Many modern Irish plays are, in effect, dream plays. See Gunnar Fridén, *National Theatre and the Twentieth-Century Irish Play*, Gothenburg: University of Gothenburg, 2010, pp.166–82.
20. Brian Friel, interview with Paddy Agnew, *Essays, Diaries, Interviews*, p.84.
21. Tony Coult, *About Friel: The Playwright and the Work*, London: Faber, 2003, p.109.
22. Catriona Clutterbuck, '*Lughnasa* After *Easter*: Treatments of Narrative Imperialism in Friel and Devlin', *Irish University Review*, ed. Anthony Roche, Vol. 29, No. 1 (1999), pp.101–18 (p.112).
23. Tony Coult, *About Friel*, op. cit., p.199.
24. Ibid., p.195.
25. Ibid., p.196.
26. David Krause, 'The Failed Words of Brian Friel', *Modern Drama*, Vol. 40 (1997), pp.359–73, included in Chapter 10 of this book.
27. The phrase is from William Wordsworth's 'Ode: Intimations of Immortality from Recollections of Early Childhood', lines 67–8: 'Shades of the prison-house begin to close/Upon the growing Boy.'

28. George Steiner, 'Absolute Tragedy', *No Passion Spent: Essays 1978–1995*, New Haven and London: Yale University Press, 1996, pp.129–41 (p.129).
29. Helen Lojek, '*Dancing at Lughnasa* and the Unfinished Revolution', *The Cambridge Companion to Brian Friel*, pp.78–90 (p.82).
30. Ronald Dworkin, 'What is a Good Life?', *New York Review of Books*, 10 February 2011, pp.41–3 (p.41).
31. Ibid., p.42.
32. John Osborne, *Look Back in Anger: A Play in Three Acts*, London: Faber, 1960, p.84.
33. Brian Friel, *Essays, Diaries, Interviews*, p.146.
34. Ibid., p.148.
35. Victor Merriman, *'Because we are poor': Irish Theatre in the 1990s*, Dublin: Carysfort Press, 2011, p.189.
36. Patrick Lonergan, *Theatre and Globalization: Irish Drama in the Celtic Tiger Era*, Basingstoke: Palgrave Macmillan, 2009, pp.43–54.
37. Éamonn Jordan, *Dissident Dramaturgies: Contemporary Irish Theatre*, Dublin: Irish Academic Press, 2010, p.53.
38. Claudia W. Harris, 'The Engendered Space: Performing Friel's Women from Cass McGuire to Molly Sweeney' in William Kerwin (ed.), *Brian Friel: A Casebook*, New York and London: Garland, 1997, pp.43–75 (p.54).
39. Anna McMullan, 'Performativity, Unruly Bodies and Gender in Brian Friel's Drama', *Cambridge Companion to Brian Friel*, pp.142–53 (p.142). See also her '"In touch with some otherness": Gender, Authority and the Body in *Dancing at Lughnasa*', *Irish University Review*, Vol. 29 (1999), pp.90–100.
40. Lionel Pilkington, 'Getting a Feel for Friel', *Irish Times*, 3 February 2007, 'Weekend', p.10.
41. Here, see Roger Scruton, *The Uses of Pessimism and the Danger of False Hope*, London: Atlantic Books, 2010, pp.153–65.
42. Joan Fitzpatrick Dean, *Ireland into Film: Dancing at Lughnasa*, Cork: Cork University Press/The Film Institute of Ireland, 2003.
43. *Brian Friel in Conversation*, ed. Paul Delaney, p.214.
44. Joan Fitzpatrick Dean, op. cit., pp.51–2.
45. Bernadette Sweeney, *Performing the Body in Irish Theatre*, Basingstoke: Palgrave Macmillan, 2008, p.121.
46. Thomas Kilroy, 'Friendship', op. cit., p.88.
47. Mary Robinson deliberately used the phrase *mná na hÉireann* in her inaugural speech as the first woman to be president of Ireland, in December 1990, and pronounced: 'as a woman, I want women who have felt themselves outside history to be written back into history'. See Richard Aldous (ed.), *Great Irish Speeches*, London: Quercus, n.d. [c.2008], pp.169–70.
48. Anthony Roche, *Brian Friel: Theatre and Politics*, p.169.
49. Samuel Beckett, *Happy Days*, in *Complete Dramatic Works*, London: Faber, 1990, p.156.
50. Oliver Sacks, *An Anthropologist on Mars*, London: Picador, 1995, pp.102–44. The story was first published in the *New Yorker* 10 May 1993.
51. Christopher Murray, '*Molly Sweeney* and its Sources: A Postmodern Case History', *Etudes Irlandaises*, Vol. 23, No. 2 (autumn 1998), pp.81–98; reprinted in Brian Friel's

Dramatic Artistry, eds. Donald E. Morse, Csilla Bertha and Mária Kurdi, Brian Friel's *Dramatic Artistry*, Dublin: Carysfort Press, 2006, pp.229–49.

52. Gerry Moriarty, 'Playwright Brian Friel Quits Field Day' in Paul Delaney (ed.), *Brian Friel in Conversation*, pp.236–7 (p.237).
53. Anthony Roche, *Brian Friel: Theatre and Politics*, p.192.
54. Anna McMullan, 'Performativity, Unruly Bodies and Gender in Brian Friel's Drama', *Cambridge Companion to Brian Friel*, p.145.
55. Claudia W. Harris, op. cit., p.64.
56. Simone de Beauvoir, *The Second Sex* (1953), in Anthony Easthope and Kate McGowan (eds), *A Critical and Cultural Theory Reader*, second edition, Maidenhead: Open University, 2004, p.54.
57. Nuala O'Faoláin, 'The Voice that Field Day Didn't Record', *Irish Times*, 11 November 1991, p.14.
58. *The Field Day Anthology of Irish Writing: Irish Women's Writing and Traditions*, Volume IV and Volume V, eds. Angela Bourke et al., Cork: Cork University Press in association with Field Day, 2002. I acknowledge here Seamus Deane's clarification of these events to me, 28 February 2013.
59. Lauren Onkey, 'The Woman as Nation in Brian Friel's *Translations*', in Kerwin (ed.), *Brian Friel: A Casebook*, op. cit., pp.159–74 (p.162).
60. Karen M. Moloney, 'Molly Astray: Revisioning Ireland in Brian Friel's *Molly Sweeney*', *Twentieth Century Literature*, Vol. 46, No. 3 (autumn 2000), pp.285–310 (p.294).
61. Tony Coult, *About Friel*, p.157.
62. Anthony Roche, *Brian Friel: Theatre and Politics*, p.192.
63. Karen M. Moloney, op. cit., p.303.
64. Brian Friel, in interview with Ciaran Carty in 1980, *Essays, Diaries, Interviews*, pp.82–3.
65. See the diary entries for December 1993, in *Essays Diaries, Interviews*, pp.159–62.
66. Brian Moore, *I Am Mary Dunne*, Harmondsworth: Penguin, 1973, p.9. Friel admired Moore's courage in writing this book. See Colm Tóibín, *New Ways to Kill Your Mother: Writers and Their Families*, London: Viking, 2012, p.150.
67. John Berger, *Ways of Seeing*, London and Harmondsworth: BBC/Penguin, 1972, p.7.
68. Brian Friel, *Molly Sweeney*, in *Plays Two*, p.455. All subsequent quotations from *Molly Sweeney* refer to this edition.
69. W. B. Yeats, *At the Hawk's Well*, in *Collected Plays*, London and New York: Macmillan, 1953, p.136. This opening line is spoken by the narrator, who is also First Musician. Beckett's Winnie borrows it in *Happy Days*, in *The Complete Dramatic Works*, London: Faber, 1990, p.164.
70. Maurice Maeterlinck, *The Treasure of the Humble*, trans. Alfred Sutro, London: George Allen, 1892, pp.97–119.
71. Katharine Worth, *The Irish Drama of Europe from Yeats to Beckett*, London: Athlone Press, 1978, p.81.
72. Ibid., p.128.
73. Michael Billington, 'The Blind/The Intruder – Review', *The Guardian*, 8 April 2013.
74. Maeterlinck, cited by Katharine Worth, *The Irish Drama of Europe*, p.77.
75. Brian Friel, *Molly Sweeney*, in *PlaysTwo*, London: Faber, 1999, p.455. All subsequent quotations from *Molly* refer to this edition.

76. Don Gifford, *Zones of Re-membering: Time, Memory, and (un)Consciousness*, ed. Donald E. Morse, Amsterdam: Rodopi, 2011, p.66.
77. George Berkeley, *Works on Vision*, ed. Colin Murray Turbayne, New York: Bobbs-Merrill, 1963, pp.142–3. The quotations are from 'The Theory of Vision' (1732).
78. Richard Pine, *The Diviner: The Art of Brian Friel*, p.296.
79. Jean Giraudoux's play on this theme, *Ondine*, directed by Louis Jouvet, was staged in Paris in 1939; Leslie Caron played the mermaid in an English translation at the Aldwych in 1961. However, there is *Ondine* the movie, 2009, directed by Neil Jordan and best forgotten.
80. Maureen Murphy, 'Siren or Victim: The Mermaid in Irish Legend and Poetry', in Donald E. Morse and Csilla Bertha (eds), *More Real than Reality: The Fantastic in Irish Literature and the Arts*, Westport, CT: Greenwood Press, 1991, pp.29–39.
81. Seamus Heaney, *Wintering Out*, London: Faber, 1972, pp.56–7. Nuala Ní Dhomnaill also has a poem entitled 'An Mhaighdean Mara' [The Sea-Woman], in *Selected Poems*, Dublin: Raven Arts, 1988.
82. Toril Moi, *Henrik Ibsen and the Birth of Modernism: Art, Theater, Philosophy*, Oxford: Oxford University Press, 2006, p.306.
83. Ibid.
84. Ibid., p.318.
85. Brian Friel, *Hedda Gabler: After Ibsen*, Loughcrew: Gallery Press, 2008, p.103.
86. Tony Coult, *About Friel: The Playwright and the Work*, p.156.
87. Patrick Mason, in interview with Christopher Murray, Dublin, 9 August 2012.
88. Ibid.
89. Edmund Spenser, *The Faerie Queene*, Book 3, Canto 6, line 419. The passage describes Adonis as the perfect image of the creative artist.
90. Jonathan Miller, *Subsequent Performances*, New York: Viking Penguin, 1986.
91. Fintan O'Toole, 'The End of the World', programme note, *Molly Sweeney*, Gate production at the Almeida Theatre, 27 October 1994. O'Toole's note replaced that by Richard Pine, 'In Search of Miracles', in the original programme, Gate, 9 August 1994.
92. Éamonn Kelly, the actor who played the first S. B. O'Donnell in *Philadelphia, Here I Come!* and appeared in other Friel plays, was also a noted raconteur in the traditional Irish style and had much success with his one-man shows, for example, *In My Father's Time* (1975), directed by Michael Colgan. See Kelly, *The Journeyman*, Dublin: Marino Books, 1998, pp.152–4.
93. Brian Friel 'Words', programme note, *Molly Sweeney*, Gate Theatre, 28 June 2011. 'Words' was part of 'Seven Notes for a Festival Programme' (1999) and is included in *Essays, Diaries, Interviews*, pp.173–4.

Chapter 8: *Wonderful Tennessee* and *Give Me Your Answer, Do!*

1. Quotation by kind permission of Anvil Press Poetry.
2. Brian Friel, 'Plays Peasant and Unpeasant' in Christopher Murray (ed.), *Essays, Diaries, Interviews*, p.53.

3. Brian Friel, Anton Chekhov's *Three Sisters: A Translation*, Dublin: Gallery Books, 1981, p.104.
4. Anthony Roche, *Brian Friel: Theatre and Politics*, London: Palgrave Macmillan, 2011, p.187. Lough Derg is a medieval Christian penitential site in Co. Donegal, also known as St Patrick's Purgatory.
5. Frank Rich, 'Futile Wait for a Ferry to a Mythical Island', *New York Times*, 25 October 1993, cited by Maria Szasz, *Brian Friel and America*, Dublin: Glasnevin Publishing, 2013, p.227.
6. Márton Mesterházi, 'A Practitioner's View on *Wonderful Tennessee*', *Hungarian Journal of English and American Studies*, ed. Csilla Bertha, Vol. 2, No. 2 (1996), pp.143–53. Mesterházi was Script Editor in Drama/Literature at Hungarian Radio, Budapest, from 1964 to about 2005 and oversaw the broadcast of many Irish plays.
7. Brian Friel (ed.), *The Last of the Name [by] Charles McGlinchey*, Belfast: Blackstaff Press, 1986, p.3.
8. Ibid., pp.138–9. See also Robert Welch, *Kicking the Black Mamba: Life, Alcohol and Death*, London: Darton, Longman and Todd, 2012, p.146.
9. Séamus Ó Catháin, *The Festival of Brigit: Celtic Goddess and Holy Woman*, Blackrock, Co. Dublin: DBA Publications, 1995.
10. *Brian Friel in Conversation*, ed. Paul Delaney, Ann Arbor: University of Michigan Press, 2000, p.214.
11. Brian Friel, *Wonderful Tennessee*, in *Plays 2*, London: Faber, 1999, p.371. Subsequent quotations from this play are from this edition, to which page numbers in parentheses refer.
12. Sanford Budick, *The Western Tradition: Terms and Paradigms of the Cultural Sublime*, New Haven and London: Yale University Press, 2000. In the theatre, however, the sublime functions as catharsis.
13. Brian Friel, *Essays, Diaries, Interviews*, p.35. The discussion, chaired by Fergus Linehan, was first published in the *Irish Times*, 12 July 1970.
14. Hugh Leonard, *Summer*, revised edition [1988], *Selected Plays of Hugh Leonard*, ed. S. F. Gallagher, Gerrards Cross: Colin Smythe; Washington, DC: Catholic University of America Press, 1992, p.267. All quotations are from this edition, to which page numbers refer.
15. Fintan O'Toole, '*Wonderful Tennessee*, by Brian Friel', *Irish Times*, 10 July 1993, reprinted in *Critical Moments: Fintan O'Toole on Modern Irish Theatre*, eds. Julia Furay and Redmond O'Hanlon, Dublin: Carysfort Press, 2003, pp.112–15 (p.113).
16. Michael Harding, *Staring at Lakes: A Memoir of Love, Melancholy and Magical Thinking*, Dublin: Hachette Books, 2013, p.97.
17. Luke Gibbons, 'The Myth of Modernization in Modern Ireland', *Transformations in Irish Culture*, Cork: Cork University Press/Field Day, 1996, p.84.
18. 'One day in 1973 I knew that I was going to die.' Hugh Leonard, describing the origins of *Summer*, op. cit., Introduction, p.5.
19. Clifford Geertz, 'Thick Description: Toward an Interpretive Theory of Culture', *The Interpretation of Cultures: Selected Essays*, New York: Basic Books, 2000, p.28.
20. T. S. Eliot, *Notes Towards the Definition of Culture*, London; Faber, 1962, p.31, italics in original.

21. Denis Johnston, *The Old Lady Says 'No!'* [1929], *The Dramatic Works of Denis Johnston*, Volume 1, Gerrards Cross: Colin Smythe, 1977, p.74. The strumpet city is Dublin. The phrase provided the title of James Plunkett's 1969 historical novel, which Hugh Leonard successfully adapted to RTE television.
22. Brian Friel, 'Set' for *Wonderful Tennessee, Plays Two*, no pagination [344].
23. Helen Heusner Lojek, *The Spaces of Irish Drama: Stage and Place in Contemporary Plays*, New York and Basingstoke, 2011, p.142, n.45. See also Helen Lojek, 'Space in *Wonderful Tennessee*', *Irish Theatre International*, ed. Paul Murphy, Vol. 2, No. 1 (August 2009), pp.48–61.
24. Seamus Heaney, 'Settings xxiv', *Seeing Things*, London: Faber, 1991, p.80.
25. William Shakespeare, *The Tempest*, 5.1.212–13, ed. Stephen Orgel, Oxford: Oxford University Press, 1994, p.199.
26. Bernard Farrell, *I Do Not Like Thee, Doctor Fell*, Dublin: Co-Op Books, 1979.
27. Samuel Beckett, *The Complete Dramatic Works*, London: Faber, 1990, p.56.
28. Tennessee Williams, *Small Craft Warnings*, Act 1, in *Period of Adjustment* and other plays, Harmondsworth: Penguin, 1982, p.214.
29. Brian Friel, *Essays, Diaries, Interviews*, p.148. The traditional Irish religious sense is now moribund. See Dennis O'Driscoll's final collection, *Dear Life*, London: Anvil Press Poetry, 2012.
30. Eamon Maher and Eugene O'Brien (eds), *Breaking the Mould: Literary Representations of Irish Catholicism*, Bern and Oxford: Peter Lang, 2011, Introduction, p.7.
31. Seamus Heaney, 'Lightenings viii', *Seeing Things*, p.62. This poem on 'the marvellous' as the inversion of the laws of nature strikes a note of awe quite similar to what Friel is after.
32. Helen Lojek, 'Space in *Wonderful Tennessee*', op. cit., p.57.
33. Tony Corbett, 'Effing the Ineffable: Brian Friel's *Wonderful Tennessee* and the Interrogation of Transcendence' in Eamon Maher and Eugene O'Brien (eds), *Breaking the Mould*, op. cit., pp.213–31 (p.231).
34. Northrop Frye, 'Archetypal Criticism: Theory of Myths', *Anatomy of Criticism: Four Essays*, New York: Atheneum, 1966, p.214.
35. George Steiner, *Language and Silence: Essays 1958–1966*, Harmondsworth: Penguin, 1969, p.31.
36. W. B. Yeats, the Old Man's prologue, *The Death of Cuchulain* [1939, first staged 1945], *Collected Plays*, London: Macmillan, 1953, p.439.
37. Samuel Beckett, 'German Letter of 1937' in Ruby Cohn (ed.), *Disjecta: Miscellaneous Writings and a Dramatic Fragment*, London: Calder, 1983, pp.51–4, and trans. Martin Esslin, pp.170–3 (p.173).
38. Samuel Beckett, *Rockaby*, in *The Complete Dramatic Works*, p.442.
39. Brian Friel in interview with Desmond Rushe (1970), in *Essays, Diaries, Interviews*, p.31.
40. Denis Johnston, *The Moon in the Yellow River*, op. cit., Vol. 2, p.152. *The Moon* premiered at the Abbey on 27 April 1931.
41. Richard Allen Cave, 'Questing for Ritual and Ceremony in a Godforsaken World: *Dancing at Lughnasa* and *Wonderful Tennessee*' in Donald E. Morse, Csilla Bertha and

Mária Kurdi (eds), *Brian Friel's Dramatic Artistry*, Dublin: Carysfort Press, 2006, pp.181–204 (p.201).

42. Brian Friel, 'Seven Notes for a Festival Programme', 4, 'Music', in *Essays, Diaries, Interviews*, pp.176–7.
43. Tony Corbett, *Brian Friel: Decoding the Language of the Tribe*, revised and updated, Dublin: Liffey Press, 2008, p.107.
44. Anthony Roche, *Brian Friel: Theatre and Politics*, pp.183–91.
45. Patrice Pavis, *Theatre at the Crossroads of Culture*, trans. Loren Kruger, London and New York: Routledge, 1992.
46. Paul Murphy, 'Brian Friel's *Wonderful Tennessee*, or What was Lost in *Translations*' in Melissa Sihra and Paul Murphy (eds), *The Dreaming Body: Contemporary Irish Theatre*, Gerrards Cross: Colin Smythe, 2009, pp.137–50 (p.149).
47. Peter J. Conradi, *Iris: The Life of Irish Murdoch*, New York: Norton, 2002, pp.587–8.
48. Victor Merriman, *'Because we are poor': Irish Theatre in the* 1990s, Dublin: Carysfort Press, 2011, Introduction, pp.1–15.
49. *Selected Letters of James Joyce*, ed. Richard Ellmann, London: Faber, 1975.
50. Brian Friel Papers, National Library of Ireland, MS 37,134/1, note dated 12 June 1995.
51. Brian Friel Papers, MS 37,134/1, note dated 16 June 1995, emphasis in original.
52. By Eliot-based, I refer back to Chapters 1 and 3 where I locate Eliot as a shaper of Friel's aesthetic.
53. Luke Clancy, 'A question of literary value', *The Times*, 21 March 1997.
54. Although Friel mentions Donal Davoren in his notes (Friel Papers, NLI, 16 June 1995), he never refers to Thomas Kilroy's *Tea and Sex and Shakespeare*, which features a writer similarly struggling with writer's block. Kilroy's text, however, was not published until 1998, Loughcrew: Gallery Press.
55. A phrase used in a letter from Brian Friel to Richard Pine, 2 January 1997, Friel Papers, National Library of Ireland, MS 37,136/2, titled 'Abbey Theatre 1997'. The reference is to the interest shown by Emory University in acquiring the papers of contemporary Irish writers, including Friel. Here, see Richard Pine, *The Diviner: The Art of Brian Friel*, p.305.
56. Patrick Burke, 'Artists and Users in the Later Plays of Ibsen and Friel' in Ros Dixon and Irina Ruppo Malone (eds), *Ibsen and Chekhov on the Irish Stage*, Dublin: Carysfort Press, 2012, pp.61–74.
57. John Simon, 'Damaged Goods', *New York Magazine*, 18 October 1999, p.57. Brian Friel Papers, NLI, MS 37,136/9. I draw upon these papers for London and New York reviews. *Damaged Goods* was the English title of Eugène Brieux's sensational play in 1902.
58. Brian Friel, *Give Me Your Answer, Do!*, Loughcrew: Gallery Press, 1997, p.67. Subsequent quotations are from this edition, to which page numbers in parentheses refer.
59. See also Christa Velten-Mrowka, '"Be Faithful to the Routine Gestures": Old Themes in Fermentation in Brian Friel's *Give Me Your Answer, Do!*', *Nordic Irish Studies*, Vol. 5 (2006), pp.157–64.
60. Marjorie Gunner, 'On & Off Broadway', *Italian Tribune*, 21 October 1999.
61. Maggie Cronin to Brian Friel, 1 August 1999, Friel Papers, NLI, MS 37,136/6.

62. Brian Friel to Kyle Donnelly, 21 August 1999, Friel papers, MS 37,136/7.
63. J. M. Synge, *The Playboy of the Western World*, *Collected Works*, Vol. 4, *Plays 2*, p.173.
64. David Nowlan, 'The ear attuned but eye diverted', *Irish Times*, 17 March 1997.
65. David Nowlan, 'Give Me Your Answer, Do!', *Irish Times*, 21 April 1999.
66. Jocelyn Clarke, 'No questions asked', *Sunday Tribune*, 25 April 1999, 'Review', p.7.
67. Peter Nichols, a writer Friel respects, described naturalism as 'a purgative reform that became an inflexible genre', and preferred experimentalism. See Michael Billington, *State of the Nation: British Theatre since 1945*, London: Faber, 2007, p.190. *A Day in the Death of Joe Egg*, London: Faber, 1967, is an obvious source for the play Friel chose not to write.
68. Patrick Mason in interview with Christopher Murray, Dublin, 9 August 2012.
69. Patrick Lonergan, '"Dancing on a One-Way Street": Irish Reactions to *Dancing at Lughnasa*' in John P. Harrington (ed.), *Irish Theater in America: Essays on Irish Theatrical Diaspora*, Syracuse: Syracuse University Press, 2009, pp.147–62 (p.158).
70. José Lanters, 'Brian Friel's Uncertainty Principle', *Irish University Review*, Vol. 29 (1999), pp.162–75.

Chapter 9: *Performances* and a General Conclusion

1. Brian Friel Papers, National Library of Ireland, MS 49,255/1. Colgan had similarly invited Friel to write a version of *Uncle Vanya* (1998).
2. Ibid., Friel to Colgan 8 October 2002, italics in original.
3. Ibid., Friel to Colgan, 8 December 2002.
4. Ibid., Friel to Colgan, 28 January 2003.
5. Adam Phillips, 'Divine Inspiration', *The Observer*, 12 March 2006, *Review*, p.4.
6. Brian Friel, 'Extracts from a Sporadic Diary: *Give Me Your Answer, Do!* (1995–96)', *Essays, Diaries Interviews,* p.170. This is a typical stance taken when Friel was beginning a play.
7. Adam Phillips, op. cit., p.4.
8. Tony Corbett, *Brian Friel: Decoding the Language of the Tribe*, revised edition, Dublin: Liffey Press, 2008, p.158.
9. I have in mind here Eliot's emphasis on 'maturity' as distinguishing 'the universal classic'. See T. S. Eliot, 'What is a Classic?' in *On Poetry and Poets*, London, Faber: pp.53–71 (p.55).
10. Friel Papers, NLI, MS 49,253/3, Notes, 12.
11. Brian Friel, *Hedda Gabler: After Ibsen*, Loughcrew: Gallery Press, 2008, p.57, italics added. Friel's *Hedda* premiered at the Gate in 2008, with a new production at the Old Vic in 2012, both directed by Anna Mackmin.
12. Henrik Ibsen, *Hedda Gabler*, trans. Michael Meyer, London: Hart-Davis, 1962, p.66.
13. *Performances* was presented by Millennium Forum Productions in the Great Hall, Magee College, Derry, 14–23 February 2013, with Allan Corduner as Janáček and Masha Dakie as Anezka, and The Brodsky Quartet.

14. Harry White, *Music and the Irish Literary Imagination*, Oxford: Oxford University Press, 2008, p.222.
15. J. M. Synge, *When the Moon Has Set*, *Collected Works*, Vol. 3, *Plays Book I*, ed. Ann Saddlemyer, Gerrards Cross: Colin Smythe, 1982, p.174.
16. W. J. McCormack, *Fool of the Family: A Life of J.M. Synge*, London: Weidenfeld & Nicolson, 2000, p.181.
17. Ibid., p.191.
18. Richard Pine, 'The Real Thing?', programme note for *Performances*, world premiere, Gate Theatre, 30 September 2003, directed by Patrick Mason.
19. *Intimate Letters: Leoš Janáček to Kamila Stösslová*, ed. and trans. John Tyrrell, London: Faber, 1994, p.200. Subsequent quotations refer to this edition.
20. Ibid., p.210.
21. Ibid., p.217.
22. Ibid., Preface, p.xvi.
23. Ibid., p.227.
24. Brian Friel, *Performances*, Loughcrew: Gallery Press, 2003, p.25. All subsequent quotations are from this edition, to which page numbers in parentheses refer. *Performances* was also published by Faber (London), 2005, where the pagination is different.
25. *Intimate Letters*, pp.161–2.
26. Anthony Roche, *Brian Friel: Theatre and Politics*, Basingstoke: Palgrave Macmillan, 2011, p.206.
27. W. B. Yeats, 'The Statues', *Collected Poems*, London: Macmillan, 1950, p.375. 'The Choice' is on p.278. Friel paraphrases the latter in *Performances*, p.37.
28. See Susanne Langer, *Feeling and Form*, London: Routledge and Kegan Paul, 1953.
29. Stephen Halliwell, *The Poetics of Aristotle: Translation and Commentary*, London: Duckworth; Chapel Hill: University of North Carolina Press, 1987, p.39.
30. Barry McGovern, 'Beckett and the Radio Voice' in Christopher Murray (ed.), *Samuel Beckett: 100 Years*, Dublin: New Island, 2006, p.139.
31. Susannah, Clapp, 'Man about the house', *Observer*, 16 July 2006, 'Review', p.19.
32. The letter Anezka cites in *Performances*, p.30, relating to a performance of *Cyrano de Bergerac*, is a condensed rephrasing of Janáček's magnificent letter to Kamila, 15 April 1928, *Intimate Letters*, pp.252–3.
33. Tony Corbett, *Brian Friel: Decoding the Language of the Tribe*, p.158.
34. Brian Friel, *Hedda Gabler: After Ibsen*, p.81.
35. *Brian Friel in Conversation*, ed. Paul Delaney, Ann Arbor: University of Michigan Press, 2000, p.71.
36. There may be an allusion here to Tom Murphy, *A Whistle in the Dark*, in *Plays: 4*, London: Methuen Drama, 1997, p.86, where Michael kills his brother in mistaken defiance.
37. As pointed out in Chapter 7, the writer Nuala O'Faolain's strong attack on the *Field Day Anthology* in the *Irish Times*, 11 November 1991, initiated a general feminist attack which angered Friel. I argue there that he made *Molly Sweeney* something of a riposte to the feminists. Here, I am suggesting that the memory of the attacks still lingered in 2003.

38. The play Patrick Burke prefers to align with *Performances*, however, is Ibsen's *When We Dead Awaken*. He sees *Performances*, rightly, I believe, as 'posing challenges virtually unique in modern theatre'. See Patrick Burke, 'Artists and Users in the Later Plays of Ibsen and Friel' in Ros Dixon and Irina Ruppo Malone (eds), *Ibsen and Chekhov on the Irish Stage*, Dublin: Carysfort Press, 2012, pp.61–74 (p.69).
39. *Intimate Letters*, op. cit., p.281.
40. Brian Friel, *The Yalta Game: After Chekhov*, Loughcrew: Gallery Press, 2001, p.12.
41. Declan Kiberd, *Inventing Ireland*, London: Cape, 1995, p.107.
42. 'Remarks by President Mary McAleese at the conferring of the Aosdána Torc on Mr Brian Friel', 22 February 2006, emphasis added. Copy courtesy the Arts Council of Ireland.
43. Patrick Lonergan, *Theatre and Globalization: Irish Drama in the Celtic Tiger Era*, Basingstoke: Palgrave Macmillan, 2009.
44. This point is also well made by Maria Szasz in *Brian Friel and America*, Dublin: Glasnevin Publishing, 2013, pp.244–50.
45. Brian Friel, 'Preface' in Conor Kostick and Katherine Moore (eds), *Irish Writers Against War*, Dublin: O'Brien Press, 2003, p.7.
46. Gabriel Josipovici, *What Ever Happened to Modernism?*, New Haven and London: Yale University Press, 2010, p.11.
47. Paul H. Fry, *Theory of Literature*, New Haven and London: Yale University Press, 2012, p.195.
48. Colm Tóibín, 'Brian Friel's Restless Imagination', programme note for *Philadelphia, Here I Come!*, Donmar Warehouse, 26 July 2012.
49. Austin Quigley, 'Pinter, Politics and Postmodernism' in Peter Raby (ed.), *The Cambridge Companion to Harold Pinter*, Cambridge: Cambridge University Press, pp.7–27 (p.13).
50. 'K' [Seamus Kelly], 'Brian Friel's Sadly Comic Story', *Irish Times*, 29 September 1964, p.6.
51. See George Steiner, *Real Presences*, London: Faber, 1989, p.196, and *Language and Silence*, London: Pelican Books, 1969, p.64, and cf. Brian Friel, *Performances*, pp.28, 31.
52. As I have argued in Chapter 1, Friel's interest in style was cultivated at Maynooth College. For the Wildean influence on *Faith Healer*, see Graham Price, 'An Accurate Description of What Has Never Occurred: Brian Friel's *Faith Healer* and Wildean Intertextuality', *Irish University Review*, Vol. 41 (2011), pp.93–111.
53. Lyndsey Turner to Christopher Murray, 30 October 2012. Quoted by kind permission.
54. Denis Donoghue, *On Eloquence*, London and New Haven: Yale University Press, 2008, p.13.
55. Terry Eagleton, *The Event of Literature*, New Haven and London: Yale University Press, 2012, p.30. He adds: 'This is one reason why Bertolt Brecht saw theatrical performance as our natural condition.'
56. Aidan O'Malley, *Field Day and the Translation of Irish Identities; Performing Contradictions*, Basingstoke: Palgrave Macmillan, 2011, p.20.
57. Tom Stoppard, *The Real Thing*, revised edition, London: Faber, 1983, p.54.

58. Brian Friel to Christopher Murray regarding the pier and silence in *Wonderful Tennessee*, 24 February 1994.
59. Chris Morash, 'Making Space: Towards a Spatial Theory of Irish Theatre' in Nicholas Grene and Patrick Lonergan (eds), *Irish Drama: Local and Global Perspectives*, Dublin: Carysfort Press, 2012, pp.7–21 (p.7). See also Shaun Richards and Chris Morash, *Mapping Irish Theatre: Theories of Space and Place*, Cambridge: Cambridge University Press, 2013.
60. Anna Ubersfield, *Reading Theatre* (1999), cited by Chris Morash, 'Making Space', op. cit., p.10.
61. Brian Friel, *Performances*, op. cit., p.11.
62. Joe Vanek, 'Vaněk & Janáček', programme note, *Performances*, Gate Theatre, 30 September 2003.
63. The Millennium Productions of Friel's plays for the Derry's City of Culture 2013 festivities began on 14 February with *Performances* and continued on 13 March with *Translations*. The BBC Radio 4 productions began with Friel's version of Ibsen's *Hedda Gabler* and *Faith Healer*, both broadcast on 9 March 2013.

Chapter 10: Critical Perspectives

Placed Identities for Placeless Times: Brian Friel and Postcolonial Criticism

1. W. J. McCormack, *The Battle of the Books*, Gigginstown: Lilliput, 1986, p.55.
2. Homi Bhabha, 'The Postcolonial and the Postmodern', *The Location of Culture*, London: Routledge, 1994, p.173.
3. Ibid., p.175.
4. Seamus Deane, quoted in John Gray, 'Field Day Five Years On', *The Linenhall Review*, Vol. 2, No. 2, (1985), p.8.
5. Declan Kiberd, *Inventing Ireland*, London: Jonathan Cape, 1995, p.624.
6. Homi Bhabha, 'Interrogating Identity', *The Location of Culture*, p.46.
7. Simon During, 'Postmodernism or Post-colonialism Today' in Thomas Docherty (ed.), *Postmodernism: A Reader*, Hemel Hempstead: Harvester Wheatsheaf, 1993, p.449. As During argues, 'The post-colonial desire is the desire of decolonized communities for an identity', p.458.
8. Terry Eagleton, *The Illusions of Postmodernism*, Oxford: Basil Blackwell, 1996, p.97.
9. Robert Hogan, *Since O'Casey and Other Essays*, Gerrards Cross: Colin Smythe, 1983, p.131.
10. Marilynn J. Richtarick, *Acting Between the Lines: The Field Day Theatre Company and Irish Cultural Politics 1980–1984*, Oxford: Clarendon Press, 1994, p.33.
11. Ibid., p.32.
12. Ibid.
13. Richard Pine, *Brian Friel and Ireland's Drama*, London: Routledge, 1990, p.176.
14. Elmer Andrews, *The Art of Brian Friel*, London: Macmillan, 1995, p.178.
15. Ibid.

16. Brian Friel, *Translations*, London: Faber, 1981, p.67. All subsequent quotations are from this edition and will be entered directly in the text.
17. Neil Corcoran, 'The Penalties of Retrospect: Continuities in Brian Friel' in Alan Peacock (ed.), *The Achievement of Brian Friel*, Gerrards Cross: Colin Smyth, 1993, p.27.
18. Walter Benjamin, 'Theses on the Philosophy of History', *Illuminations*, London: Fontana, 1973, p.248. ('Few will be able to guess how sad one had to be in order to resuscitate Carthage.')
19. Anthony Roche, *Contemporary Irish Drama: From Beckett to McGuinness*, Dublin: Gill and Macmillan, 1994, p.255.
20. Benjamin, p.254.
21. Edna Longley, *Poetry in the Wars*, Newcastle upon Tyne: Bloodaxe Books, 1986, p.191.
22. Ibid.
23. Edna Longley, *The Living Stream: Literature & Revisionism in Ireland*, Newcastle upon Tyne: Bloodaxe Books, 1994, p.159.
24. Alan Harrison, 'Literature in Irish 1600–1800' in Seamus Deane (ed.), *The Field Day Anthology of Irish Writing* Vol. II, Deny: Field Day Publications, 1991, p.276.
25. Stuart Hall, 'The Meaning of New Times' in David Morley and Kuan-Hsing Chen (eds), *Stuart Hall: Critical Dialogues in Cultural Studies*, London: Routledge, 1996, p.237.
26. Seamus Deane, 'Introduction', Terry Eagleton, Fredric Jameson, Edward W. Said, *Nationalism, Colonialism and Literature*, Minnesota: University of Minnesota Press, 1990, p.19.
27. Seamus Heaney, 'An Open Letter', *Ireland's Field Day*, London: Hutchinson, 1985, p.26.
28. Jean-François Lyotard, *The Postmodern Condition: A Report on Knowledge*, Manchester: Manchester University Press, 1986, p.15.
29. Brian Friel, 'Extracts from a Sporadic Diary', quoted by Sean Connolly, 'Translating\ History: Brian Friel and the Irish Past', in Peacock (ed.), p.155.
30. Seamus Heaney, 'Review of *Translations*' in John P. Harrington (ed.), *Modern Irish Drama*, New York: W. W. Norton, 1991, p.558.
31. Frantz Fanon, 'On National Culture', *The Wretched of the Earth*, London: MacGibbon and Kee, 1965, p.170.
32. Ibid.
33. Amilcar Cabral, 'Identity and Dignity in the Context of the National Liberation Struggle' in Africa Information Service, *Return to the Source: Selected Speeches by Amilcar Cabral*, New York and London: Monthly Review Press, 1973, p.63.
34. Fanon, p.187.
35. Homi Bhabha, 'Of Mimicry and Man: The Ambivalence of Colonial Discourse', *The Location of Culture*, p.88. For Simon During, 'For the post-colonial to speak or write in the imperial tongue is to call forth a problem of identity.' *Postmodernism*, p.458.
36. George Steiner, *After Babel: Aspects of Language and Translation*, Oxford: Oxford University Press, 1975, p.21.
37. Abdul Jan Mohamed and David Lloyd, 'Introduction: Toward a Theory of Minority Discourse', *Cultural Critique*, Vol. 6 (Spring 1987), p.10.
38. Smadar Lavie and Ted Swedenburg, 'Introduction: Displacement, Diaspora, And Geographies of Identity' in Smadar Lavie and Ted Swedenburg (eds), *Displacement,*

Diaspora, and Geographies of Identity, Durham and London: Duke University Press, 1996, p.17.

39. Luke Gibbons, *Transformations in Irish Culture*, Cork: Cork University Press, 1996, p.176.
40. Ibid.
41. Declan Kiberd, *Inventing Ireland*, London: Jonathan Cape, 1995, p.652.
42. Brian Friel, *Dancing at Lughnasa*, London: Faber, 1990, p.35. All subsequent quotations are from this edition and will be entered directly in the text.
43. Roche, p.106.
44. Raymond Williams, *Marxism and Literature*, Oxford: Oxford University Press, 1977, pp.123–4.
45. Ibid., p.123.
46. Helen Gilbert, 'Dance, Movement and Resistance Politics' in Lavie and Swedenburg (eds), *Displacement, Diaspora and Geographies of Identity*, p.345.
47. Fredric Jameson, 'Reflections on the Brecht-Lukacs Debate', *The Ideologies of Theory*, Essays *1971–1986, Volume 2: The Syntax of History*, London: Routledge, 1988, p.145.
48. David Harvey, *The Condition of Postmodernity*, Oxford: Basil Blackwell, 1989, p.218.
49. Michael Peter Smith, 'Postmodernism, Urban Ethnography, and the New Social Space of Ethnic Identity', *Theory and Society*, Vol. 21, No. 4 (August 1992), p.513.
50. David Morley and Kevin Roberts, 'No Place Like Heimat' in Erica Carter, James Donald and Judith Squires (eds), *Space and Place: Theories of Identity and Location*, London: Lawrence and Wishart, 1993, p.27.
51. Dorinne Kondo, 'The Narrative Production of "Home", Community, and Political Identity in Asian American Theatre' in *Displacement, Diaspora and Geographies of Identity*, p.97.
52. Seamus Deane, 'Introduction', p.19.
53. Ashis Nandy, 'Cultural Frames for Social Transformation: A Credo', *Alternatives*, Vol. XII, No. 1 (January 1987), p.114.
54. Aijaz Ahmad, *In Theory, Classes, Nations, Literature*, London: Verso, 1992, pp.39 and 11.
55. Kondo, p.97.
56. Nandy, p.116. There is a clear link between this concept and what Gayatri Spivak has referred to as 'the strategic use of a positivist essentialism'. See 'Subaltern Studies: Deconstructing Historiography', in *In Other Worlds: Essays in Cultural Politics.* London: Routledge, 1988, p.205. Seamus Deane has brought these ideas into an Irish context with his acknowledgement of 'the need that people have to construct an historical identity [and] the viability of essentialist arguments as political strategies'. See Dympna Callaghan, 'An Interview with Seamus Deane', *Social Text*, Vol. 38 (1994), p.40.
57. Brian Friel, *Wonderful Tennessee*, London: Faber, 1993, p.8. All subsequent quotations are from this edition and will be entered directly in the text.
58. Doreen Massey, 'Politics and Space/Time' in Michael Keith and Steve Pile (ed.), *Place and the Politics of Identity*, London: Routledge, 1993, p.148. See also Genevieve Lloyd, *The Man of Reason: 'Male and Female' in Western Philosophy*, London: Routledge, 1993.
59. Kiberd, p.689.

60. Brian Friel, *Molly Sweeney*, London: Faber, 1994, p.31. All subsequent quotations are from this edition and will be entered directly in the text.
61. Kiberd, p.616.
62. Lavie and Swedenburg, 'Introduction', p.1.
63. Bhabha, 'The Postcolonial and the Postmodern', p.172.
64. Ibid., p.175.
65. Ibid.
66. Aijaz Ahmad, 'The Politics of Literary Postcoloniality', *Race and Class*, Vol. 36, No. 3 (January–March 1995), p.17.
67. Ibid., pp.16–17.
68. Benita Parry, 'Resistance Theory/Theorising Resistance or Two Cheers for Nativism' in Francis Barber, Peter Hulme and Margaret Iversen (eds), *Colonial Discourse/ Postcolonial Theory*, Manchester: Manchester University Press, 1994, p.174.
69. Ien Ang, 'On Not Speaking Chinese: Postmodern Ethnicity and the Politics of Diaspora', *New Formations*, Vol. 24 (Winter 1994), p.18.
70. Kevin Robins, 'Tradition and Translations: Natural Culture in its Global Contexts' in John Comer and Sylvia Harvey (eds), *Enterprise and Heritage: Crosscurrents of National Culture*, London: Routledge, 1991, p.41.

The Failed Words of Brian Friel

1. W. B. Yeats, 'The Song of the Happy Shepherd' in Richard J. Finneran (ed.), *The Poems*, rev. edn, vol. I of *The Collected Works of W.B. Yeats*, New York: Macmillan, 1989, p.7.
2. T. S. Eliot, *Sweeney Agonistes: Fragments of an Aristophanic Melodrama*, London: Faber, 1932, p.29.
3. Brian Friel, *Dancing at Lughnasa*, London: Faber, 1990, p.71. Subsequent references appear parenthetically in the text.
4. Brian Friel, *Molly Sweeney*, London: Penguin, 1994, p.9. Subsequent references appear parenthetically in the text.
5. J. M. Synge, preface to *The Playboy of the Western World: A Comedy in Three Acts*, in Ann Saddlemyer (ed.), *The Playboy of the Western World and Other Plays*, Oxford: Oxford Drama Library, 1995, p.96.
6. See J. M. Synge, *The Well of the Saints: A Play in Three Acts*, in Ann Saddlemyer, op. cit., pp.51–94.
7. J. M. Synge, preface to *The Tinker's Wedding: A Comedy in Two Acts*, in Ann Saddlmeyer ... op cit., p.28.
8. Brian Friel, *Wonderful Tennessee*, London: Samuel French, 1993, pp.17–18. Subsequent references appear parenthetically in the text.
9. J. M. Synge, preface to *The Playboy of the Western World*, in Ann Saddlemyer ... p.95.
10. *Webster's Ninth New Collegiate Dictionary*, s.v. 'nostalgia'.
11. Seamus Deane, introduction to *Selected Plays*, by Brian Friel, London: Faber, 1984, p.12.
12. Ibid., p.19.
13. Thornton Wilder. *Our Town: A Play in Three Acts*, New York: Coward-McCann, 1938, p.124.

Memory, Art, Lieux de Mémoire *in Brian Friel's* The Home Place

1. This is a revised and expanded version of the essay, 'Art as a *lieu de mémoire* in Brian Friel's *The Home Place*', published in a *Festschrift* in honour of the Irish folklorist Dáithí Ó hÓgáin' in Ríonach uí Ógáin, William Nolan and Éamonn Ó hÓgáin (eds), *Sean, Nua agus Síoraíocht. Féilscríbhinn in ómós do Dháithí Ó hÓgáin*, Dublin: Coiscéim, 2011, here published by kind permission of the editors.
2. Pierre Nora, 'Between Memory and History. Les Lieux de Mémoire', *Representations*, Vol. 26 (Spring 1989), p.7. Further references to this essay will be given in the text.
3. Kevin Whelan, 'Between Filiation and Affiliation. The Politics of Postcolonial Memory' in Clare Carroll and Patricia King (eds), *Ireland and Postcolonial Theory*, Cork: Cork University Press, 2003, p.102.
4. Luke Gibbons, 'Towards a Postcolonial Enlightenment. The United Irishmen, Cultural Diversity and the Public Sphere' in Clare Carroll and Patricia King (eds), *Ireland and Postcolonial Theory*, Cork: Cork University Press, 2003, p.91.
5. Quoted by Honor O'Connor, 'Carrying the Songs: The Poetry of Moya Cannon' in *The Binding Strength of Irish Studies*, Debrecen: Debrecen University Press, 2011, p.199.
6. 'The ancient Celts may have worshipped trees, . . . and certain trees are mentioned persistently in Celtic tradition. . . . Many letters in the ogham alphabet of early Ireland are named for trees.' James MacKillop, *Dictionary of Celtic Mythology*, Oxford and New York: Oxford University Press, 1998, p.364.
7. Dáithí Ó hÓgáin mentions among the many beliefs surrounding trees those concerning great trees 'growing at the inauguration centre of a sept . . . regarded as a symbol of that sept's nobility and endurance' and the fact that 'it was considered a disastrous defeat if a rival group cut down the tribal tree.' . . . 'The belief long survived that a very old and notable tree, termed a bile, was in some way sacred, and accounts in both literature and folklore tell of misfortune befalling people who interfere with such a bile or cut it down.' *The Lore of Ireland*, Cork: Collins, 2006, p.196.
8. Ian Assmann, *A kulturális emlékezet*, Budapest: Atlantisz, 1992, pp.52–3. All the quotations from this book are my translations from the Hungarian.
9. Brian Friel, *The Home Place*, Loughcrew: Gallery, 2005, p.62. Further references to this play will be given in the text.
10. Paul Ricoeur, *Memory, History, Forgetting*, trans. Kathleen Blamey and David Pellauer. Chicago and London: The University of Chicago Press, 2004, pp.15–20 *passim*, Further references to this book will be given in the text.
11. Don Gifford, *Zones of Re-membering. Time, Memory, and (un)Consciousness*, ed. Donald E. Morse, Amsterdam-New York: Rodopi, 2011, p.100.
12. George O'Brien, 'The Late Plays' in Anthony Roche (ed.), *The Cambridge Companion to Brian Friel*, Cambridge: Cambridge University Press, 2006, p.99.
13. Richard Pine, 'A Guest of Cultural Politics: The Twentieth-Century Musical Legacy of Thomas Moore', *Hungarian Journal of English and American Studies*, Vol. 8, No. 1 (Spring 2002), p.102.
14. Edric Caldicott and Anne Fuchs, 'Introduction' in Edric Caldicott and Anne Fuchs (eds), *Cultural Memory. Essays in European Literature and History*, Bern: Peter Lang, 2003, p.22.

15. Scott Boltwood. *Brian Friel, Ireland, and the North*, Cambridge: Cambridge University Press, 2007, p.211.
16. Kevin Whelan, op. cit., p.93.
17. Boltwood, surprisingly, does not seem to take into consideration the ending and does not speak about her change when he states that 'Margaret ends the play in a position that is materially better [than Chris in *Dancing at Lughnasa*], but less promising nonetheless.' Op. cit., p.212.
18. Hedwig Schwall, 'A Poor Forked Anima(l), or, The Hills Are Alive with the Sound of Moore', *The European Messenger*, Vol. 14, No. 1 (2005), p.71. Further references to this essay will be given in the text.
19. Although Schwall does not mention it, in the Friel oeuvre outside this play there are precedents, the most powerful being Frank Hardy in *Faith Healer* who clearly sacrifices himself and his nearest and dearest for serving his 'gift' and with that, those who need healing. For being able to work, he also needs increasing amounts of alcohol.
20. Kevin Whelan, op. cit., p.93.
21. The utopian, anti-essentialist aspects of 'home' and 'homeland' in *The Home Place* are discussed in detail in Alison O'Malley-Younger, 'There's No "Race" Like Home: Race, Place and Nation in Brian Friel's *The Home Place*', *Nordic Irish Studies*, Vol. 5 (2006), pp.165–79.
22. Paul Ricoeur, 'Memory and Forgetting' in Richard Kearney and Mark Dooley (eds), *Questioning Ethics*, London: Routledge, 1999, pp.10–11.
23. Don Gifford, op. cit., p.102.
24. Brian Friel, *Performances*, Loughcrew: Gallery, 2003, p.31.
25. Denis Donoghue, *The Arts Without Mystery*, London: The British Broadcasting Company, 1983, p.11.
26. *Philadelphia, Here I Come!*, in *Selected Plays*, London and New York: Faber, 1984, p.52.

SELECTED BIBLIOGRAPHY

Brian Friel

Plays

Plays One: Philadelphia, Here I Come!, The Freedom of the City, Living Quarters, Aristocrats, Faith Healer, Translations. London: Faber, 1996. This text is a reprint of the *Selected Plays of Brian Friel*. London: Faber, 1986.

Plays Two: Dancing at Lughnasa, Fathers and Sons, Making History, Wonderful Tennessee, Molly Sweeney. London: Faber, 1999.

Plays Three: Three Sisters, A Month in the Country, Uncle Vanya, The Yalta Game, The Bear, Afterplay, Performances, The Home Place, Hedda Gabler. London: Faber, 2014.

Other Friel plays in chronological order; dates in parentheses refer to first production:

The Enemy Within (1962), Newark, DE: Proscenium Press, 1975; Loughcrew: Gallery Press, 1979.

The Loves of Cass McGuire (1966), New York: Noonday Press, 1966; London: Faber, 1967; Loughcrew: Gallery Press, 1984.

Lovers (*Winners/Losers*, 1967), New York: Farrar Straus, 1968; London: Faber, 1968; Loughcrew: Gallery Press, 1984.

Crystal and Fox (1968), London: Faber, 1970; Loughcrew: Gallery Press, 1984.

The Mundy Scheme (1969), New York: Samuel French, 1970.

The Gentle Island (1971), London: Davis-Poynter, 1973; Loughcrew: Gallery Press, 1993.

Volunteers (1975), London: Faber, 1979; Loughcrew: Gallery Press, 1989.

American Welcome (1980), in *The Best Short Plays of 1981*, ed. Stanley Richards. Radnor, PA: Chilton Books, 1981.

Anton Chekhov's Three Sisters: A Translation (1981), Dublin: Gallery Books, 1981; revised as *Three Sisters: A Translation of the Play by Anton Chekhov* (2008), Loughcrew: Gallery Press, 2008.

The Communication Cord (1982), London: Faber, 1983.

Making History (1988), London: Faber, 1989.

The London Vertigo (1992), Loughcrew: Gallery Press, 1990.

A Month in the Country: After Turgenev (1992), Loughcrew: Gallery Press, 1992.

Give Me Your Answer, Do! (1997), Loughcrew: Gallery Press, 1997; New York: Plume/Penguin, 2000.

Uncle Vanya: A Version of the Play by Anton Chekhov (1998), Loughcrew: Gallery Press, 1998.

The Yalta Game: After Chekhov (2001), Loughcrew: Gallery Press, 2001.

Three Plays After: The Yalta Game, The Bear, and Afterplay (2002), Loughcrew: Gallery Press, 2002.

Performances (2003), Loughcrew: Gallery Press, 2003; London: Faber, 2005.

The Home Place (2005), Loughcrew: Gallery Press, 2005.
Hedda Gabler: after Ibsen (2008), Loughcrew: Gallery Press, 2008.

Short Stories

The Saucer of Larks. New York: Doubleday; London: Victor Gollancz, 1962.
The Gold in the Sea. New York: Doubleday; London: Victor Gollancz, 1962.
Selected Stories: with an introduction by Seamus Deane. Dublin: Gallery Press, 1979.

Non-Fiction

[Untitled tribute to the founders of the Gate Theatre, Dublin], *Enter Certain Players: Edwards-Mac Liammoir and the Gate 1928-1978*, ed. Peter Luke. Dublin: Dolmen Press, 1978, pp.21–2.
(Ed. with introduction), *The Last of the Name: Charles McGlinchey*. Belfast: Blackstaff Press, 1986.
Essays, Diaries, Interviews: 1964-1999, ed. Christopher Murray. London: Faber, 1999.
Brian Friel in Conversation, ed. Paul Delaney. Ann Arbor: University of Michigan Press, 2000.
'Preface: Where We Live', *Ordnance Survey Letters: Donegal* [1835], ed. Michael Herity, Dublin: Four Masters Press, 2000, pp.vii–ix.
'Preface', *Irish Writers Against War*, eds. Conor Kostick and Katherine Moore, Dublin: O'Brien Press, 2003, p.7.

Archival

The Brian Friel Papers, National Library of Ireland, MSS 37,041-37,806. See Collection List No. 73, compiled by Helen Hewson, dated 2003.
The Brian Friel Papers (Additional), National Library of Ireland, MSS 42,091-42,093 and 49,209-49,350. See Collection List No. 180, compiled by Fergus Brady et al., dated 2011.
The Field Day Papers, MS 46,873, MS L 168-171, and MSS 42,038-42,039. See Collection List No.148, compiled by Emma Saunders, dated 2010.

Bibliography

George O'Brien, *Brian Friel: A Reference Guide 1962-1992*. New York: G. K. Hall/Simon & Schuster Macmillan, 1995.
Irish University Review, 'IASIL Bibliography Bulletin', published annually in the autumn issue, from Vol. 2, No. 1 (1972) to present.

Further Reading

Readers and scholars are directed in the first place to the endnotes to the ten chapters in this book, especially for articles on Friel's work, the details of which are not replicated here.

(a) Books on Friel

Andrews, Elmer, *The Art of Brian Friel: Neither Reality Nor Dreams*. London: St Martin's Press, 1995.

Boltwood, Scott, *Brian Friel, Ireland, and the North*. Cambridge: Cambridge University Press, 2007.

Corbett, Tony, *Brian Friel: Decoding the Language of the Tribe*. Revised, Dublin: Liffey Press, 2008.

Coult, Tony, *About Friel: The Playwright and the Work*. London: Faber, 2003.

Dantanus, Ulf, *Brian Friel: A Study*. London: Faber, 1988.

Grant, David, *Student Guide to the Stagecraft of Brian Friel*. London: Greenwich Exchange, 2004.

Higgins, Geraldine, *Brian Friel*. Tavistock, Devon: Northcote House/British Council, 2011.

Jones, Nesta, *Brian Friel*. Faber Critical Guides Series. London: Faber, 2000.

McGrath, F. C., *BrianFriel's (Post) Colonial Drama: Language, Illusion, and Politics*. Syracuse: Syracuse University Press, 1999.

Maxwell, D. E. S., *Brian Friel*. Lewisburg: Bucknell University Press, 1973.

O'Brien, George, *Brian Friel*. Boston: Twayne, 1990.

Pelletier, Martine, *Le Théâtre de Brian Friel: Histoires et histoires*. Villeneuve d'Ascq: Septentrion Universtity Presses, 1997.

Pine, Richard, *The Diviner: The Art of Brian Friel*. Dublin: University College Dublin Press, 1999.

Roche, Anthony, *Brian Friel: Theatre and Politics*. Basingstoke: Palgrave Macmillan, 2011.

Russell, Richard Rankin, *Modernity, Community, and Place in Brian Friel's Drama*. Syracuse: Syracuse University Press, 2013.

Szasz, Maria, *Brian Friel and America*. Dublin: Glasnevin Publishing, 2013.

(b) Collections of essays

Irish University Review, Special issue: Brian Friel, ed. Anthony Roche, Vol. 29, No. 1 (1999).

The Cambridge Companion to Brian Friel, ed. Anthony Roche. Cambridge: Cambridge University Press, 2006.

Harp, Richard and Robert C. Evans (eds), *A Companion to Brian Friel*. West Cornwall, CT: Locust Hill Press, 2002.

Kerwin, William (ed.), *Brian Friel: A Casebook*. New York and London: Garland, 1997.

Morse, Donald E., Csilla Bertha, and Mária Kurdi (eds), *Brian Friel's Dramatic Artistry: 'The Work Has Value'*. Dublin: Carysfort Press, 2006.

Murphy, Paul (ed.), *Irish Theatre International*, Vol. 2, No. 1 (August 2009), special issue on Brian Friel.

Peacock, Alan (ed.), *The Achievement of Brian Friel*. Gerrards Cross: Colin Smythe, 1993.

(c) Other

Anderman, Gunilla (ed.), *Voices in Translation: Bridging Cultural Divides*. Clevedon: Multilingual Matters, 2007.

Billington, Michael, *State of the Nation: British Theatre since 1945*. London: Faber, 2007.

Brandt, George W. (ed.), *Modern Theories of Drama: A Selection of Writings on Drama and Theatre 1850-1990*. Oxford: Clarendon, 1998.

Brown, Terence, *Ireland: A Social and Cultural History 1922-2002*. Revised, London: Harper Perennial, 2004.

Caldicott, Edric and Anne Fuchs (eds), *Cultural Memory: Essays in European Literature and History*. Bern: Peter Lang, 2003.

Cave, Richard Allen, *New British Drama in Performance on the London Stage: 1970 to 1985*. Gerrards Cross: Colin Smythe, 1987.

Cave, Richard and Ben Levitas (eds), *Irish Theatre in England: Irish Theatrical Diaspora Series: 2*. Dublin: Carysfort Press, 2007.

Dean, Joan Fitzpatrick, *Ireland into Film: Dancing at Lughnasa*. Cork: Cork University Press/Film Institute of Ireland, 2003.

Deane, Seamus, *Celtic Revivals: Essays in Modern Irish Literature 1880-1980*. London: Faber, 1985.

Deane, Seamus and Ciarán Deane (eds), *The Field Day Review*. Dublin: Field Day Publications, in association with the University of Notre Dame, 2005 to present.

Deane, Seamus, et al. (eds), *The Field Day Anthology of Irish Writing*, 3 vols. Derry: Field Day Publications, 1991.

Dixon, Ros and Irina Ruppo Malone (eds), *Ibsen and Chekhov on the Irish Stage*. Dublin: Carysfort Press, 2012.

Dubost, Thierry (ed.), *Drama Reinvented: Theatre Adaptations in Ireland (1970–2007)*. Brussels: Peter Lang, 2012.

Duncan, Dawn, *Postcolonial Theory in Irish Drama from 1800 to 2000*. Lewister, New York, and Lampeter, Wales: Edwin Mellen Press, 2004.

Eagleton, Terry, *On Evil*. New Haven and London: Yale University Press, 2010.

Ferriter, Diarmaid, *Ambiguous Republic: Ireland in the 1970s*. London: Profile Books, 2012.

Fitzpatrick, Lisa (ed.), *Performing Feminisms in Contemporary Ireland*. Dublin: Carysfort Press, 2013.

Fitz-Simon, Christopher (ed.), *Players and Painted Stage: Aspects of the Twentieth Century Theatre in Ireland*. Dublin: New Island, 2004.

Fridén, Gunnar, *National Theatre and the 20th Century Irish Dream Play*. Gothenburg: University of Gothenburg, 2010.

Gassner, John and Ralph G. Allen, *Theatre and Drama in the Making*, 2 vols. Boston: Houghton Mifflin, 1964.

Gifford, Don, *Zones of Re-membering: Time, Memory, and (un)Consciousness*, ed. Donald E. Morse. Amsterdam: Rodopi, 2011.

Goodman, Lizbeth and Jane de Gay (eds), *The Routledge Reader in Politics and Performance*. London and New York: Routledge, 2000.

Grene, Nicholas, *The Politics of Irish Drama: Plays in Context from Boucicault to Friel*. Cambridge: Cambridge University Press, 1999.

Grene, Nicholas and Patrick Lonergan (eds), *Irish Drama: Local and Global Perspectives*. Dublin: Carysfort Press, 2012.

Guthrie, Tyrone, *In Various Directions*. London: Michael Joseph, 1965.

Harrington, John P. (ed.), *Irish Theater in America: Essays on Irish Theatrical Diaspora*. Syracuse: Syracuse University Press, 2009.

Harris, Peter James, *From Stage to Page: Critical Reception of Irish Plays in the London Theatre, 1925-1996*. Bern and Oxford: Peter Lang, 2011.

Herron, Tom and John Lynch, *After Bloody Sunday: Ethics, Representation, Justice*. Cork: Cork University Press, 2007.

Jordan, Éamonn, *Dissident Dramaturgies: Contemporary Irish Theatre*. Dublin: Irish Academic Press, 2010.

Josipovici, Gabriel, *What Ever Happened to Modernism?* New Haven and London: Yale University Press, 2010.

Kiberd, Declan, *Inventing Ireland*. London: Jonathan Cape, 1995.

Kosok, Heiz, *Plays and Playwrights from Ireland in International Perspective*. Trier: WVT, 1995.

Kurdi, Mária, *Representations of Gender and Female Subjectivity in Contemporary Irish Drama by Women*. Lampeter: Edwin Mellen Press, 2010.

Laffan, Pat and Faith O'Grady (eds), *Donal McCann Remembered: A Tribute*. Dublin: New Island Press, 2000.

Lojek, Helen, *The Spaces of Irish Drama: Stage and Place in Contemporary Plays*. New York: Palgrave Macmillan, 2011.

Lonergan, Patrick, *Theatre and Globalization: Irish Drama in the Celtic Tiger Era*. Basingstoke: Palgrave Macmillan, 2009.

Lonergan, Patrick and Riana O'Dwyer (eds), *Echoes Down the Corridor*. Dublin: Carysfort Press, 2007.

Luckhurst, Mary (ed.), *A Companion to Modern British and Irish Drama 1880-2005*. Oxford: Blackwell, 2006.

Mackintosh, Iain (ed.), *The Guthrie Thrust Stage: A Living Legacy*. London: Association of British Theatre Technicians, 2011.

Maher, Eamon and Eugene O'Brien (eds), *Breaking the Mould: Literary Representations of Irish Catholicism*. Bern and Oxford: Peter Lang, 2011.

Malcolm, Janet, *Reading Chekhov: A Critical Journey*. London: Granta, 2012.

Meaney, Gerardine, *Gender, Ireland and Cultural Change*. New York and London: Routledge, 2010.

Merriman, Victor, *'Because we are poor': Irish Theatre in the 1990s*. Dublin: Carysfort Press, 2011.

Moi, Toril, *Henrik Ibsen and the Birth of Modernism: Art, Theatre, Philosophy*. Oxford: Oxford University Press, 2006.

Morash, Chris, *A History of Irish Theatre 1601-2000*. Cambridge: Cambridge University Press, 2002.

Morash, Chris and Shaun Richards, *Mapping Irish Theatre: Theories of Space and Place*. Cambridge: Cambridge University Press, 2013.

Murray, Douglas, *Bloody Sunday: Truth, Lies and the Saville Inquiry*. London: Biteback Publishing, 2012.

Nagler, A. M., *A Source Book in Theatrical History*. New York: Dover, 1959.

O'Driscoll, Dennis, *Stepping Stones: Interviews with Seamus Heaney*. London: Faber, 2008.

O'Malley, Aidan, *Field Day and the Translation of Irish Identities: Performing Contradictions*. Basingstoke: Palgrave Macmillan, 2011.

O'Toole, Fintan, *Critical Moments: Fintan O'Toole on Modern Irish Theatre*, eds. Julia Furay and Redmond O'Hanlon. Dublin: Carysfort Press, 2003.

Phillips, Adam, *Missing Out: In Praise of the Unlived Life*. London: Hamish Hamilton/ Penguin, 2012.

Pilkington, Lionel, *Theatre and the State in Twentieth-Century Ireland: Cultivating the People*. London and New York: Routledge, 2001.

Pilný, Ondřej, *Irony and Identity in Modern Irish Drama*. Prague: Litteraria Pragensia, 2006.

Pine, Emily, *The Politics of Irish Memory: Performing Remembrance in Contemporary Irish Culture*. Basingstoke: Palgrave Macmillan, 2011.

Richards, Shaun (ed.), *The Cambridge Companion to Twentieth-Century Irish Drama*. Cambridge: Cambridge University Press, 2004.

Richtarik, Marilynn J., *Acting Between the Lines: The Field Day Theatre Company and Irish Cultural Politics 1980-1984*. Oxford: Clarendon Press, 1994.

Ricoeur, Paul, *Memory, History, Forgetting*, trans. Kathleen Blamey and David Pellauer. Chicago and London: University of Chicago Press, 2004.

Roche, Anthony, *Contemporary Irish Drama*, 2nd edn. Basingstoke: Palgrave Macmillan, 2009.

Sihra, Melissa and Paul Murphy (eds), *The Dreaming Body: Contemporary Irish Theatre*. Gerrards Cross: Colin Smythe, 2009.

Steiner, George, *After Babel: Aspects of Language and Translation*. New York and London: Oxford University Press, 1975.

Strachan, John and Alison O'Malley-Younger (eds), *Essays on Modern Irish Literature*. Sunderland: Sunderland University Press, 2007.

Styan, J. L., *Modern Drama in Theory and Practice*, 3 vols. Cambridge: Cambridge University Press, 1983.

Sweeney, Bernadette, *Performing the Body in Irish Theatre*. Basingstoke: Palgrave Macmillan, 2008.

Tóibín, Colm, *New Ways to Kill Your Mother: Writers and Their Families*. London and New York: Penguin Group, 2012.

Trench, Rhona (ed.), *Staging Thought: Essays on Irish Theatre, Scholarship and Practice*. Bern and Oxford: Peter Lang, 2012.

Urban, Eva, *Community Politics and the Peace Process in Contemporary Northern Irish Drama*. Bern and Oxford: Peter Lang, 2011.

Watt, Stephen, Eileen Morgan, and Shakir Mustafa (eds), *A Century of Irish Drama: Widening the Stage*. Bloomington: Indiana University Press, 2000.

Welch, Robert, *The Abbey Theatre 1899-1999: Form and Pressure*. Oxford: Oxford University Press, 1999.

White, Harry, *Music and the Irish Literary Imagination*. Oxford: Oxford University Press, 2008.

Worth, Katharine, *The Irish Drama of Europe from Yeats to Beckett*. London: Athlone Press, 1978.

NOTES ON CONTRIBUTORS

Csilla Bertha teaches at the University of Debrecen, Hungary. She is a member of the advisory board of *Irish University Review*, the editorial board of the *Hungarian Journal of English and American Studies*, and a founding member of *CISLE*. She is the author of *Yeats the Playwright*, the first book on Yeats's drama to be published in Hungary (Budapest, 1988), and has co-authored and co-edited volumes of essays on Irish literature and culture, including *More Real Than Reality* (Westport, CT: Greenwood Press, 1991), *The Celebration of the Fantastic* (Westport, CT: Greenwood Press, 1992), *A Small Nation's Contribution to the World* (Debrecen, 1993), *Worlds Visible and Invisible* (Debrecen, 1994) and *Brian Friel's Dramatic Artistry* (Dublin: Carysfort Press, 2006). She has also edited Hungarian poetry in translation and with Donald E. Morse has translated a volume of Transylvanian-Hungarian plays into English under the title *Silenced Voices* (Dublin: Carysfort Press, 2008).

David Krause is best known for his critical biography *Sean O'Casey: The Man and His Work* (New York: Macmillan, 1960, revised 1975) and his four-volume edition of the *Letters of Sean O'Casey* (1975–92). He is also author of the critical study *The Profane Book of Irish Comedy* (Ithaca and London: Cornell University Press, 1982) and many articles and reviews. He was Professor of English at Brown University for many years and died in 2011.

Shaun Richards is Professorial Research Fellow at St Mary's University College, London, United Kingdom. The co-author with David Cairns of the seminal *Writing Ireland: Colonialism, Nationalism and Culture* (Manchester University Press, 1988) and editor of *The Cambridge Companion to Twentieth-Century Irish Drama* (Cambridge University Press, 2004), he has published on Irish theatre and drama in a range of major journals and edited collections. His most recent project, co-authored with Chris Morash, is *Mapping Irish Theatre: Theories of Space and Place* (Cambridge University Press, 2013).

INDEX

Bold page references denote where Friel's plays are discussed in detail